TEIKYO WESTMAR UNIV. LIBR
P9-CRS-910

Teachers, Computers, and Curriculum

Teachers, Computers, and Curriculum

Microcomputers in the Classroom

PAUL G. GEISERT
Computer Carousel

MYNGA K. FUTRELL
California State University, Sacramento

91-1975

ALLYN AND BACON
Boston London Sydney Toronto

Copyright © 1990 by Allyn and Bacon
A Division of Simon & Schuster, Inc.
160 Gould Street
Needham Heights, MA 02194

All rights reserved. No part of the material protected by this copyright notice may be reproduced or utilized in any form or by any means, electronic or mechanical, including photocopying, recording, or by any information storage and retrieval system, without the written permission of the copyright owner.

Trademark information appears on pp. 339–340.

Series Editor: Sean W. Wakely
Series Editorial Assistant: Carolyn O'Sullivan
Editorial-Production Service: Editing, Design & Production, Inc.
Cover Administrator: Linda K. Dickinson
Cover Designer: Dick Hannus
Manufacturing Buyer: Tamara Johnson
Indexer: Paul Geisert

Library of Congress Cataloging-in-Publication Data

Geisert, Paul G.
Teachers, computers, and curriculum : microcomputers in the classroom / by Paul G. Geisert and Mynga K. Futrell.
p. cm.
Includes bibliographical references.
ISBN 0-205-12293-0
1. Computer-assisted instruction. 2. Microcomputers—Study and teaching. 3. Education—Data processing. 4. Computer managed instruction. I. Futrell, Mynga K. II. Title.
LB1028.5.G42 1989
371.3'34—dc20 89-36232
CIP

Printed in the United States of America
10 9 8 7 6 5 4 3 2 95 94 93 92 91

Photo Credits:
pp. 14, 110, 168, 174, 199, 211, 233, 294 © by Stuart Spates.
pp. 42, 313 by Robert Harbison.
pp. 82, 144 by Mike Penney.

Brief Contents

Brief Contents

Contents

Preface

We have written *Teachers, Computers, and Curriculum* to help teachers gain the knowledge and skills they need to use microcomputers effectively in the classroom. The book is as much a text on teaching as one about computers. Our focus throughout is on teachers and the decisions they make concerning classroom computer use. We maintain that the computer is simply a tool, albeit a powerful one, and that a teacher can become proficient in the professional use of that tool and can make sensible and valuable decisions concerning when and how the microcomputer is integrated into teaching activities and student learning experiences.

If you are to use a computer appropriately in the classroom—enhancing your teaching and your students' learning—then you must make sound instructional decisions concerning microcomputer use and implement those decisions within your classroom setting. The content and organization of *Teachers, Computers, and Curriculum* reflect a greater emphasis on development of proficiencies in classroom implementation and curricular integration than is customary in books on computers for educators.

Organization of the Text

Although a textbook in format, this book is organized to guide your learning of content and to facilitate your access to hands-on experiences with computers.

At the beginning of each chapter are objectives identifying what you should gain from your reading and study. A checklist at each chapter's end will help you evaluate your learning. In chapter introductions, we provide broad questions to focus your study and to get you moving down the same cognitive pathways we are taking.

The content of *Teachers, Computers, and Curriculum* is not specific to one type of computer. The text presents concepts generic to using computers in the classroom, rather than ideas related to Apple, IBM, Commodore, or other brands of computers.

Each chapter has an activity section to provide hands-on computer or computer-related activities illustrative of the content of the chapter. (Activities in the first chapter differ because it is primarily an introduction.) We encourage you to do as many of the activities as you can, but we do not assume you will be able to carry out all of them independently. Many of the activities are to be used by an instructor in a learning lab to provide concrete experiences that complement the chapter's concepts.

In most chapters, we list selected computer programs you may wish to examine. These software suggestions were derived from various review processes and, in some cases, from the personal experiences of the authors. We also include readings and references for each chapter. A glossary of terms is presented at the end of the book.

Supplemental Materials

An *Instructor's Manual* accompanies *Teachers, Computers, and Curriculum* and facilitates the use of this text in a course of study. The Focus sections of the manual orient the instructor to the major chapter concepts and are helpful for syllabus planning. The Maps of key chapter ideas are handy tools for instructors to use when preparing classroom presentations. These graphic outlines can also be employed directly with students as advance organizers, topics of class discussion, or chapter reviews.

The *Instructor's Manual* includes a number of other features to assist an instructor. For example, there are reproducible transparencies for overhead projection in classroom presentations and additional activity suggestions for selected portions of the text. The manual also provides model student responses to the review checklists in every chapter, along with a bank of objective test items for measuring student achievement of chapter learning goals.

Instructors: Information on obtaining classroom courseware to complement *Teachers, Computers, and Curriculum* is available from your local Allyn and Bacon representative.

A Message to the Reader

Whether you are currently preparing for teaching, are new to the profession, or are an experienced professional, you can expect to be asked by a parent, administrator, or prospective employer, "Are you using computers in your classroom?" It is common today for a teacher to be encouraged to use computers in teaching and to address the curricular issues presented by microcomputers in today's world. The arrival of this new and powerful technology has made classroom computer use a matter for all teachers to consider, regardless of the level or subject matter they teach.

"Do you use computers?" is a reasonable question to ask any teacher. After all, more and more of the world's information is processed electronically. Information, the currency of teaching and learning, is changing its form, and it is fair to expect educators to respond in some fashion. But the real challenge for the classroom teacher is less one of simply using computers than of making them useful in the instructional endeavor.

A teacher's success in using electronic technology rests, in part, on professional skill in microcomputer use. It also depends on making wise decisions about using a computer to enhance instruction. Computer use necessitates asking in situation after situation, "Is there some aspect of my teaching that can be done better with a computer?" The answers will vary with time, circumstance, and curriculum.

We hope that you look forward to learning about microcomputers and their use in teaching. We want you to conclude your study of this book with a feeling of confidence in your abilities as a computer-using teacher and with a sense of enthusiasm. Microcomputers, when understood and used properly, can contribute in many ways to your students' learning. We have sought to reduce your fears about computers and provide a realistic and experimental perspective on classroom microcomputer use.

Microcomputers offer exciting approaches to teaching that were not even dreamed of twenty years ago, but the extent to which the educational potential of microcomputer technology will be realized remains to be seen. Some teachers will use microcomputers to revolutionize their classrooms. Perhaps you will be one of them.

Acknowledgments

We would like to extend our thanks to the following reviewers of the manuscript for their time and invaluable suggestions: Les Blackwell, Western Washington University; William Merrill, Central Michigan University; Albert Nous, University of Pittsburgh; Janet Parker, University of Louisville; and David Salisbury, Florida State University.

We would also like to thank the following professionals for providing assistance in the preparation and production of the text: Linda Ennis, Linda Daly, Annette Joseph, and Rebecca Stefoff.

Our final acknowledgment goes to Sean Wakely, our editor, for his contributions and encouragement.

1

Using Computers in Teaching

A Professional Goal

OBJECTIVES

- State a rationale for acquiring computer-using proficiencies.
- List and define major areas of knowledge and skills associated with being a computer-using teacher.
- Identify a variety of different teacher uses of microcomputers in the school setting.
- Describe computer literacy in educational contexts and identify problematic aspects in the application of the term.
- Distinguish computer use for the general purpose of instructing and guiding students from computer specialization.
- Name and contrast two computer-focused content domains that may be found in a school's instructional program.
- Characterize the difficulty of operating a microcomputer with a user-friendly program.
- Characterize (with an analogy) the *level* of the computer literacy understanding actually needed by computer-using teachers.
- Describe some benefits to be gained from using computer terminology and engaging in hands-on computer learning.

INTRODUCTION

Here you are beginning Chapter 1. Just how will you be different by the end of Chapter 12? If you cannot now produce handouts or work sheets using a microcomputer and its printer, or if you are not able to decide where a computer should be located, which students should use it, and how their computer use will be managed, then these proficiencies will be targets for you to work toward as you study this text. If, when you finish the book, you *can* demonstrate all these capabilities, you will indeed have changed. What changes are in store for you?

You can predict some of the big changes by comparing yourself as you are now with this description of the proficiencies we hope you will have when you get to the end of this book.

Self-Check of Computer-Use Competencies

[ ] You will be able to operate a microcomputer with commercial programs and feel comfortable using different brands of machines and handling and storing computer programs.

[ ] You will be able to use a microcomputer in a variety of circumstances with an assortment of programs and know the limitations of the computer in performing certain kinds of tasks.

[ ] You will be able to use computer-assisted instruction and computer-managed instruction and identify appropriate situations in which to employ these strategies.

[ ] You will be able to identify and acquire software that not only matches your classroom and curricular needs, but is effective as well.

[ ] You will be competent in the care and utilization of microcomputers. You will be able to identify and name the fundamental parts of microcomputers, and describe what it takes to keep them operating, and what to consider when selecting a new one.

[ ] You will be knowledgeable about some simple aspects of the inner workings of microcomputers and the history behind their development, and you will have ideas about what microcomputers may be like in the future.

[ ] You will be able to decide whether or not to learn more about computing, incuding whether you should develop any programming skills.

[ ] You will be able to create computer-centered learning tasks, and to step back and become a learning manager while the computer does the teaching.

[ ] You will be able to use microcomputers in your classroom to support and enhance your curriculum, to select programs that are best for you and your students, and to manage computer time effectively and equitably.

[ ] You will have some insight into the role of computers and computing within a school's curriculum and be able to contribute in constructive ways to decision making about computer use in your school.

Whatever your starting competencies may be, the checklist above should prove useful to you, since we have listed there proficiencies we think every computer-using teacher should possess. You can think of the listing as a "target" picture of yourself, one you will be working toward as you study this book.

You can probably achieve most of the knowledge goals in this text through reading and study. The affective goals, too, are quite likely to be achieved this way. But, to gain skills in microcomputer use, you'll have to do more than read. You must interact with microcomputers. So, at the end of each chapter of this book you will find activities, the large majority of which consist of hands-on experiences with microcomputers. In order to become proficient in computer use, you should perform as many of these activities as you can. For most readers, this book will be part of a course being taught by an instructor who can provide or lead you to appropriate activity resources. If this is not true in your situation, we urge you to locate resources on your own and do as many activities as you can.

Goals

- How is this text organized?
- Why should teachers become computer users?
- How does a computer relate to a school's curriculum?

GETTING MICROCOMPUTERS AND TEACHERS TOGETHER

If a microcomputer doesn't make life easier or more rewarding for a teacher, then it makes little sense to spend time and effort in learning how to use one. The fact is, however, that more and more teachers are making room for computers in their classrooms. The Office of Technology Assessment (1988) reports that virtually all U.S. public schools have at least one computer, and the acquisition of computers by schools is continuing. Teachers have recognized what the devices have to offer.

Power

What is it that moves teachers to employ microcomputers? They have found that computers help them become more efficient in performing everyday tasks. More important, they have discovered how, by using a computer, they can do a better job of teaching. These teachers have learned just how powerful microcomputers are, and how this power can be put to their own professional purposes.

A microcomputer can do things in a classroom a teacher simply cannot do. For example, can you remember exactly what problems every member of the class got right and wrong on his or her practice exercises two days ago, and present new problems that exactly match his or her skills? A microcomputer can do this, and much more. Of course we recognize that a teacher can do many things better than a computer can, and that's why a teacher and a microcomputer can make such a great teaching team.

Subsequent chapters will focus on microcomputers' particular strengths as teachers' aids and, we hope, begin to build a sound case for certain educational uses of computers. We would expect that as you are exposed to and have experiences with computers, you will become impressed by the various computational, graphic, vocal, linguistic, or manipulative powers that you observe. For such a small machine, a microcomputer has a lot of talents.

Microcomputer power must be tempered by reality, however. Not everything a computer can do can be employed by a computer-using teacher in a typical classroom with a normal amount of planning. The fact that a microcomputer can do some fancy task that a human would never be able to do is of little use to a teacher if the right programs are not available for the teacher's specific needs, or for the needs of the students, or for the context within which teacher and students must function.

It is important, too, that we not present microcomputers with unbridled enthusiasm or paint them as educational panaceas, so we will spend some portion of this book acquainting you not only with their power, but also with important limitations and problem aspects of microcomputer use. One thing is clear, however. A teacher who uses a computer can gain a tremendous number of additional talents to employ, and this is certainly an important reason why so many teachers are becoming computer-users (Hunter, 1984). It is also why it will be worth your time and effort to learn how to use computers to enhance your own teaching and other aspects of your professional role.

Ease

Whereas in the past using a computer meant that one had to write a computer program to make it work, this is no longer true. Today's microcomputers have become very "user-friendly." This is due partly to changes in computers and partly to improvements in software. Operating a classroom microcomputer today is easy primarily because software publishers have produced lots of ready-to-use computer programs for classroom application.

Many worthwhile computer products are designed specifically for people who do not like to write their own programs, or who do not know (or wish to know) how. This advance has all but eliminated the need for a teacher to learn to write programs in order to use computers to help out in the classroom.

Compared with the maintenance needs of other classroom machines, microcomputers rate extremely well when it comes to upkeep. The computer we are using to write this book has operated with absolutely no repairs since the day it was purchased over six years ago.

MICROCOMPUTERS AND SCHOOLS – A CHANGING PICTURE

Although the discussion thus far has concentrated on individual teachers getting interested in microcomputers for their own instructional programs, we would be remiss if we did not direct your attention to the impact that microcomputers are having on schools in general, and on the teaching role in particular. As you think about your career as a teacher, you will want to consider the fact that microcomputer use within education is burgeoning, and computing proficiencies are increasingly being expected of members of the teaching profession.

The 1980s saw a tremendous surge in microcomputer-related activity within every component of the national educational scene. In the early 1980s elementary and secondary schools in the United States had acquired just over 300,000 microcomputers. The number tripled in just one year and has been on the rise ever since (Office of Technology Assessment, 1988). The decade dramatically enhanced the microcomputer availability picture, particularly within the nation's elementary schools (see Figure 1.1). The 1980s also saw vast numbers of school districts reconsidering their K–12 curriculum in terms of students' learning experiences with computers, and almost every state established either high school graduation requirements or guidelines for students' computer-related learning.

Computer-Focused School Curricula

Looking at the K–12 educational spectrum, we have identified two major computer-related curricular strands. Although these two strands overlap to some extent, our intent here is to contrast these two curriculum categories.

Computer Science

The oldest type of curriculum connected with computers is *computer science*. When computers gained sufficient importance in society, colleges and universities began to develop programs of instruction to train computer professionals.

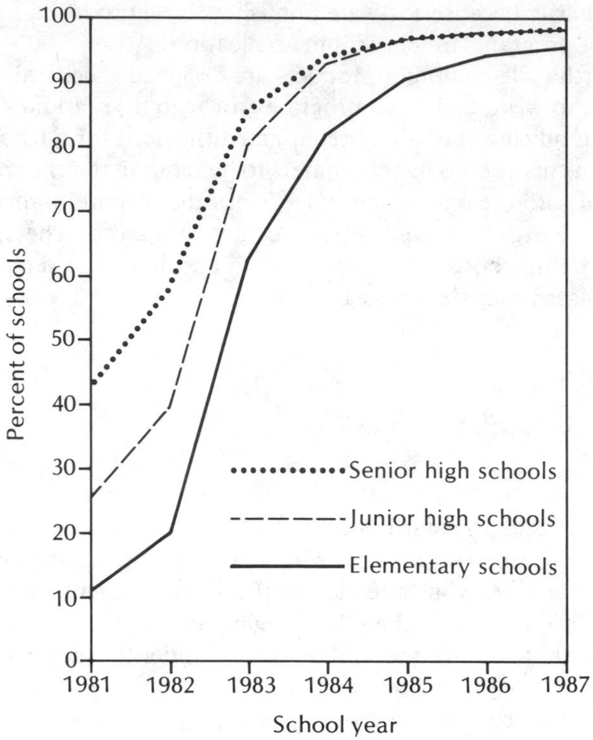

FIGURE 1.1 How many schools have computers?

Eventually departments of computer science were established on large numbers of college campuses. In time, some high schools began generating courses designed to help their students prepare to enter such programs. Computer science courses at the secondary level are no longer a rarity, and some large school systems have quite an array of courses for students to take.

What is high school computer science all about? It is probably best thought of as an introduction to the concepts taught in college computer science departments. The role of computer science in high school is to train students in computing concepts, computer programming, and computer operations. The reason for offering such instruction in the school is so that some fraction of the students will be adequately prepared to go on to college and to further studies in computer science, or perhaps into some computer-related vocational field.

Whereas in the past courses in computer science at the secondary level were taught usually by teachers in physical science, mathematics, or vocational education, recent years have seen several states instituting credential requirements for teaching computer science subject matter. Whether a secondary computer science curriculum consists of a complex sequence of courses (rare, particularly in smaller school systems) or of just one or two courses in a programming language (more typical), its overall orientation will be toward providing students with some subset of computing knowledge from the discipline of computer science.

Since microcomputing technology has gained in prominence, many schools have expanded their computer science offerings. This is certainly a worthy endeavor, given that we need many trained professionals in computer operations, but it is important not to extend computer science beyond its domain. It is all too easy for educators, as they seek to prepare all students for a world in which computers play so large a role, to confuse courses and concepts needed for computer science specialization with the computer-related instruction that all students should receive.

Computer Literacy

Computer literate is a term applied to any of the various populations of persons who know quite a bit about computers, but are not, and do not intend to become, computer professionals. Computer competent and computer proficient are terms sometimes used in such characterizations, but literate is the word most often encountered in the literature.

Although definitions of *computer literacy* vary both with the group of interest and with the definer, they tend to include the following goal areas:

1. knowledge of the history of computing,
2. understanding of how computers work and how they can be programmed,
3. awareness of the use of the computer to aid learning and solve problems,
4. insight into business and industrial applications of computers, and
5. awareness of the present and possible future effects of computer technology on society (Geisert and Futrell, 1984).

For any group to which it is applied, be it high school graduates or elementary students, senior citizens or college-educated citizens, veterinarians or librarians, teachers or administrators, "computer literate" generally connotes a level of understanding about computers *and* of skill in their use. Later in this chapter we will use this term with respect to teachers, but for now let's look at how schools have been confronting the question, "How can we prepare our students for lives that, to an increasing extent, will be intertwined with and affected by computers?"

This past decade has seen educators endeavoring to define the computer-related knowledge and skills that their students should have, and developing programs of instruction to achieve the goals they define. Several states have mandated specific competencies or courses for high school graduates, and a number of others have drawn up K–12 guidelines for local district action. Consequently, teachers, administrators, and curriculum coordinators in these states have been directing a great deal of effort toward the design and implementation of computer literacy programs for students.

There remains a lack of consensus about just how much computer-related knowledge students really need. While it is clear that our society is undergoing an information technology revolution brought on by advances in computing technology, no one knows exactly how far microcomputers will go in changing our lifestyles. Just what do students need to know to be adequately prepared for living, working, and interacting with microcomputers? How aware do they need to be about computers' capabilities? How informed on issues deriving from and related to computers should they be? How much experience with computers do they need?

Some proponents of computer literacy programs claim that any real understanding of computers necessitates study of computer programming, and they advocate that all students be taught some computer language. Other educators argue that this is just a holdover from computer science, and that such instruction is not only unnecessary, but, in many cases, undesirable in that it may produce an aversion to computers with some students. These latter educators see no reason whatsoever for students to learn to program when so many useful and user-friendly programs are now available.

It has been argued by some that most aspects of computer literacy can be taught using only a textbook without the presence of a microcomputer at all. Certain topics, such as the use of computers in banking, stores, tax records, and so forth, do not require student access to a "real live" microcomputer. But most schools that have developed computer literacy curricula in elementary and secondary schools have planned hands-on experiences to learn *about* computers for their students. There are educators who recommend postponing instruction that treats computers as subject matter to the secondary level, preferring to let elementary children acquire simple hands-on experience *with* computers as they learn regular curricula.

As microcomputers continue to proliferate in society and as citizens increasingly deal with the influence of computers in their everyday lives, we can probably expect to foresee continued growth in parental and public anticipation of computer-related experiences for youngsters.

Changing Expectations for Teachers

With so much activity focused on schools acquiring computers and having students learn about and with them, it appears that the public's expectations for teachers' computer-related knowledge and skills has also increased. Teachers have been and are continuing to be affected.

This change is evidenced in part by the actions taken by many state departments of instruction to reconsider teacher certification requirements and to guide school districts in planning for teacher in-service training (Texas State, 1982). At the local levels, there have been extensive in-service training endeavors. At the university level, schools of education are attending increasingly to the computing knowledge and skills of their graduates.

The major thrust within the educational profession has been one of promoting microcomputer use by teachers and ensuring that schools are staffed by teachers able to use microcomputers whenever it is appropriate to do so in their instructional programs.

MICROCOMPUTERS FROM A TEACHER'S PERSPECTIVE

With such changes well underway, there is an impetus for prospective teachers to obtain microcomputer experiences during their undergraduate education and for practicing teachers to develop proficiencies in microcomputer use. Certainly, becoming a computer-using teacher is a sound professional move. But it seems reasonable to wonder just what proficiencies are really needed. This topic has been a matter of some debate.

Proficiency Level Expectations for Teachers

Numerous writers and educators have spoken on the concept of computer education for teachers and on the merits of various efforts to produce "computer literate" teachers (Anderson, 1983; East, 1983; Rogers et al., 1984). Goals and competencies have been proposed by various individuals and organizations. Still, there remains a lack of consensus and a great deal of confusion about what teachers need to learn.

Part of the problem in defining computer skills and knowledge for teachers arises from the fact that educators are integrating microcomputers into instructional programs in at least two different ways: (1) as *tools* for teaching subject matter, and (2) *as* subject matter. For example, in one part of a school some classroom computers may be serving a teacher who uses them to deliver instruction (drill and practice), to manage instruction (diagnostic testing), as measuring instruments for science experiments, and for producing home reports or handouts. Simultaneously, in another part of the school, identical microcomputers might be the content of another teacher's computer science or computer literacy instruction, with students learning to program them, or finding out what the insides are like, or testing the electronic circuits.

To this latter teacher, computers and/or computing are the ends of instruction, and the teacher has to possess the knowledge *about* the technology that goes with the specific computer-focused curriculum being taught. The first teacher, however, might teach any subject or level and needs only the skills and knowledge to be able to use the computer effectively in teaching the curriculum, whether it be middle school art, American history, or second grade arithmetic (see Table 1.1).

TABLE 1.1 Some Ways a Teacher Can Use the Computer

Program Type	*Teacher Has the Ability to:*
Word processor	—type documents in an extremely flexible manner, saving, retrieving, modifying, and printing them with great ease.
Spreadsheet	—manipulate words and numbers, such as in creating a very flexible gradebook.
Test generator	—type, store, and modify various types of tests, and to print out complete tests (including alternative forms).
Diagnostic testing program	—give student a brief test on a computer, and use the computer's diagnosis of what the student does or does not know in a given subject (a good example is mathematics).
Copy program	—make additional copies of computer programs for classroom use (when permitted by the publisher).
Database program	—organize, store, modify, and retrieve information of almost any type.
Text analyzer	—check the reading level of a given text by typing some portion(s) into the computer and getting a sophisticated statement of the level at which the text was written.
Puzzle generator	—create puzzles from lesson words.
Authoring system	—create his or her own computer lessons.
Electronic blackboard	—display for a whole class the material presented on the screen of a single microcomputer.
Appointment book	—create an electronic calendar/appointment book for scheduling class and school events.

These two different uses of microcomputers in schools—as *tools* in the hands of teachers to teach their classes and curricula, or as *subject matter* of computer-related curricula, often have not been differentiated adequately when efforts were made to decide what teachers should know. Keep the distinction in mind as you study this book, however, because your goal will be to acquire the computer-related skills and knowledge for microcomputer use, not for subject matter specialization in computers.

Computer-Use Proficiencies for Teaching

It is important for you to recognize that a wide range of needs for computer-related skills and knowledge exist within the teaching profession. The specific proficiencies that are the major focus of this book, however, are those that a teacher of any subject at any level, from preschool to postdoctoral, will need. Our target is what we have referred to already as the *"computer-using teacher."* Let's describe our idea of such a teacher.

A computer-using teacher is one who makes use of computers to help students learn. This may happen in a very direct manner (by having the computer doing some teaching, for example, or by using a computer to manage students' learning), or indirectly (such as using a microcomputer and word processing program to prepare tests and work sheets for the next day's activities).

Any teacher can become a computer-using teacher (although perhaps not a very sophisticated computer-using teacher) in a matter of minutes by being taught a few simple procedures that will put a microcomputer into action with students or for the teacher.

Since the goals of a computer-using teacher are not to teach about computers, or to teach a computer-related curriculum, the computer itself is more of a teaching partner than an object of study. Computers play a role in instruction similar to that of other media such as overhead projectors, textbooks, work sheets, or films. The computer is important to the degree that it contributes to the teaching and learning process. For the computer-using teacher, the microcomputer is a means for reaching ongoing instructional goals.

In one sense it might be simpler to teach about computers than to employ them to teach. A computer-using teacher must be able to integrate a computer into an existing curriculum—judging when it will do a task well and matching the computer's capabilities with the instructional program for which the teacher is responsible.

Curriculum as a Framework for Computer Use

When you, as a computer-using teacher, use microcomputers as means for reaching ongoing curricular goals, you are taking part in a third area of computer-related activity in schools. The instructional goals of computer-using teachers are in art, science, mathematics, language arts, social studies, or other disciplines, not in computers.

Figure 1.2 summarizes the three major domains of school computer use. In each domain the teachers make use of one or more microcomputers to reach specific curricular goals and objectives.

In Figure 1.2 at the locations where the three major domains overlap, events that represent interactions of the two adjacent domains take place. Look at Figure 1.3 to see examples of some overlap activities.

Your own teaching interests will be determined by the particular curriculum that you teach, and your task will be to employ the microcomputer effectively to reach your curriculum goals. How should you proceed?

Matching Your Proficiencies and Needs

Using microcomputers in your teaching means, in our view, bringing the computer into your world, and not the reverse. Perhaps you haven't noticed it yet, but this chapter has been sticking to the topic of teachers and teaching thus far.

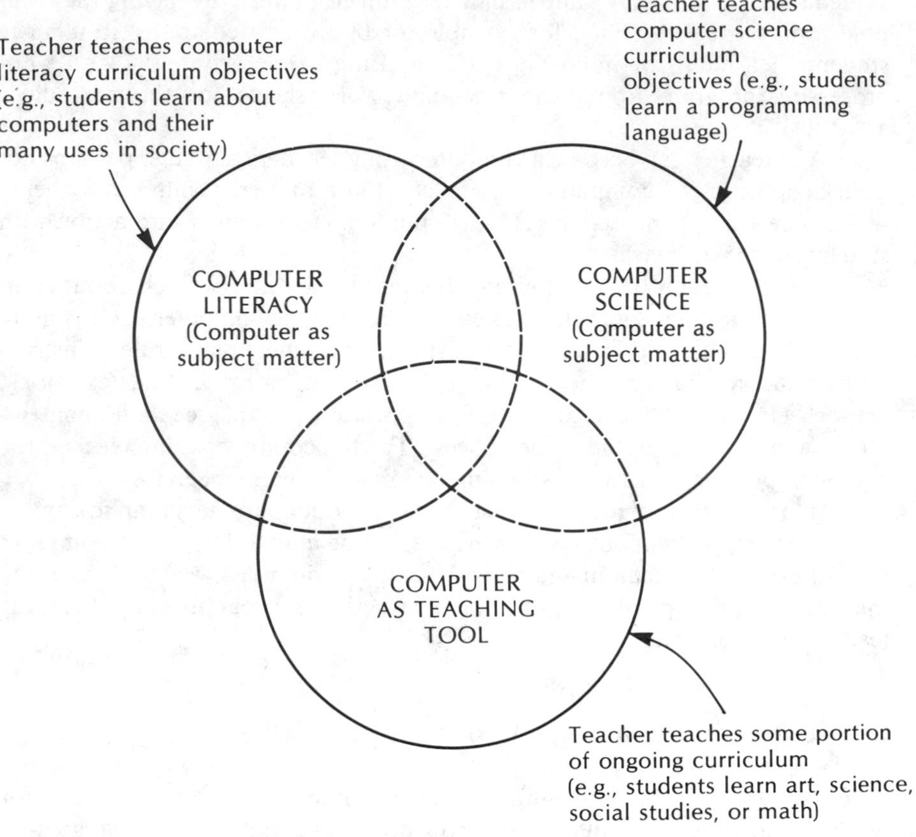

FIGURE 1.2 Three Domains of School Computer Use

We've purposefully avoided bombarding you with all the parts and pieces of microcomputers, and we have done so primarily because we wish to convey the importance of viewing microcomputers from the perspective of your own professional role. We hope you will continue in that vein as we move on to focus on the microcomputer as a machine.

Whatever your current situation, a basic familiarity with how microcomputers work is a must if you are to build the realistic perception of microcomputers that a computer-using teacher needs to have. The next chapter is "A Teacher's Computer Primer," and it is intended to provide just such a conceptual grounding. In it, we've tried not to skip computer concepts that would be important to full understanding of the programming and hardware chapters that come later on in the book.

It is possible, of course, that you have accumulated a considerable amount of experience with computers already. Or, perhaps you aren't "into" computers yet. We are hoping that, as you proceed on through this book, you will recognize our inability to judge which reader you are and freely weigh the relevance of the information presented, setting your study priorities accord-

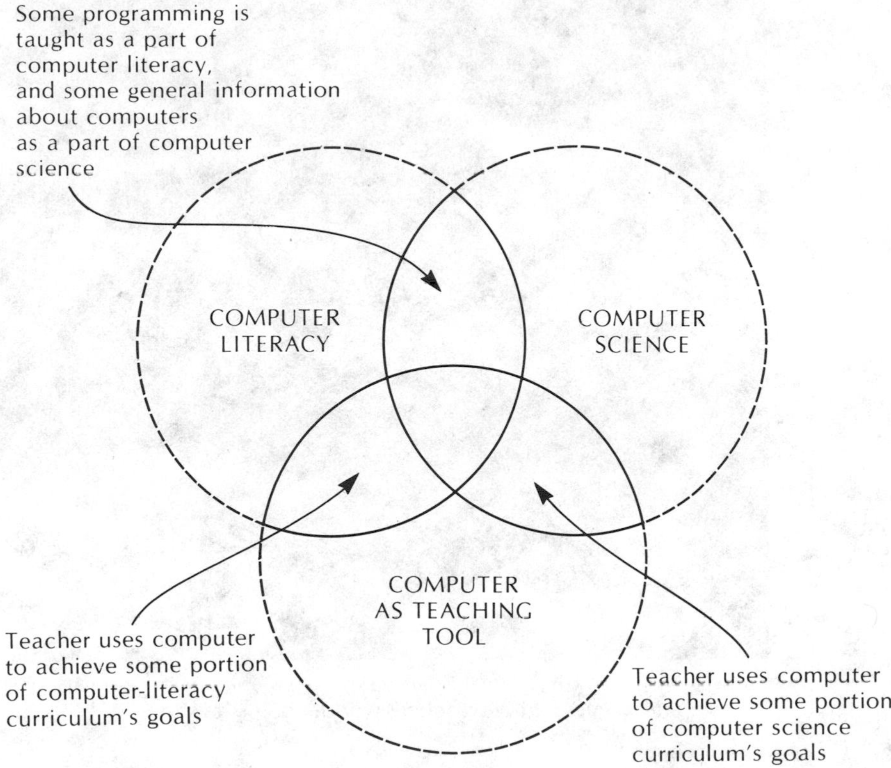

FIGURE 1.3 Regions of Overlap of the Three Domains of Computer Activity

ingly. We fully expect that portions of content will be old hat to some readers, but brand new to others. There's another difference to be expected, too.

It is a fact that some teachers are hesitant about using computers so, for a while, we'll be emphasizing the approachability of microcomputers at the same time we discuss how they work and how they can be used in teaching. We would ask your forbearance if you need no such emphasis and encourage you to just skip lightly through any sections that appear to be intended for those readers who would put themselves more on the hesitant (or even reluctant) side. The following section has just such an intent.

EASING INTO COMPUTERS

Teachers who express reservations about using computers tend to have various reasons behind their discomfort or distaste, some based on preconceived notions and others on past experiences. In this section we will attempt to dispel some common myths and set forth a frame of mind that may be helpful.

The computer comes into the teacher's world, not the reverse.

Learning How to Operate a Microcomputer

Myth One: Operating a computer is hard. Truth: Putting a microcomputer to work seems to get easier every day. It certainly does not have to involve programming. When computers first appeared in classrooms, teachers who used computers tended to be those who enjoyed (or at least didn't mind) the challenge of communicating with a computer in its language. Today, the computer skills to be learned before operating a computer are few. In fact, learning to operate the computer itself is so simple that a teacher who can handle a photocopy machine will have already conquered an equivalent challenge. Usually, the learning involved is comparable to what a first-time operator of a phonograph would face.

The following is a description of a teacher reviewing a new math drill. What this teacher does to operate the computer is quite typical. The actual computer operating procedure is italicized below.

Scenario on Operating a Microcomputer

A teacher has obtained a computer program from a book publisher. It consists of a flat, rectangular disk unit in a paper envelope, and a written booklet of instructions (called program documentation). Here are the steps.

1. *The teacher removes the disk from its envelope, carefully inserts the disk into a slot in the computer, and turns the computer on.* The computer whirs for a few seconds, and a menu of choices comes on the screen.

2. *The teacher reviews the menu choices* (acting like a student) *and touches a key on the computer keyboard to make a selection.* Soon an addition problem is presented on the screen, and the teacher is asked to solve it.

3. After figuring out the answer, *the teacher types* the numbers for the sum. The computer determines if the answer is correct or not and puts an appropriate comment on the screen. It then presents another problem to the teacher.

4. After a number of problem iterations, in which *the teacher's necessary actions are directed by sentences on the computer's screen*, the computer analyzes the teacher's progress (recall that the teacher is acting as a student) and decides that the practice needed has been accomplished. The computer informs the teacher that the drill is completed.

5. The computer then puts on the screen a summary statement of the type of problems attempted, the teacher's success rate, and what should be studied next. *The teacher removes the disk from the computer and turns it off.*

The type of teacher actions described in the scenario exemplifies a significant proportion of teachers' microcomputer operation today. As you can tell from the teacher's actions, the microcomputer itself is a simple machine to operate. Once it has been set up and made ready for operation, there is literally nothing for a user to do, other than to provide it a program (see Figure 1.4) and respond by pushing various keys.

Being able to operate a computer is one thing; understanding how a computer operates is another.

Learning How a Microcomputer Operates

Myth Two: You simply can't understand how a computer really works. Truth: You can to the level you *need* to know. Let's use a familiar analogy to point out various levels of understanding a user might need. We will use the car user, instead of the computer-user.

Knowledge Levels and Cars

You can be a rider and not even own or drive a car. As a rider, you need not know how to name mechanical parts of a car, how to evaluate a car to discriminate a good one from a bad one, or how to service or get someone to service a car. However, we would expect a proficient passenger to know how to get in

FIGURE 1.4 Inserting a Program Disk

and out of the car, how to buckle up, and certain social courtesies (such as sharing gas expenses).

As a driver, you would have passed a driver's licensing exam. You would be able to answer questions about road signs and laws, and pass a road test. A driver need not pay much attention to what is under the hood, how a transmission works, or even how to buy a car, however. It is safe to say that, overall, most drivers will know more than most riders about cars and car operation.

As a car hobbyist, you would read manuals and books and talk about the topic and be capable, perhaps even sophisticated, in some aspects of cars. You might be expert in dismantling and reassembling engines, in changing oil and lubricating the chassis, in repairing the upholstery, or in body work.

Were you a professional, who is paid for services, we could expect you to be trained and certified or to have gained sufficient experience and competence to receive pay for your skills in some aspect of driving or working on cars.

Knowledge Levels and Computers

As you may be able to guess, this book's focus is on practical everyday expectations for the kind of knowledge about computers one needs at the "riding and driving" levels. There will be some knowledge expected of "what is under the hood" and how to do "maintenance checks" at these levels of acquaintance with microcomputers.

Though such learning is beyond the scope of this book, you may become a hobbyist later and go well beyond the proficiencies required for general operation. In so doing, you will be following your instincts and your interests to acquire additional knowledge and greater skill. Should you reach an expert level in classroom microcomputing, you'll be akin to the individual who spends lots of time "under the hood."

Talking across Levels

In the world of computers, there is an abundance of hobbyist-level individuals although, due to changes that have taken place, their proportion among the riders and drivers is dwindling. When computers were first used in schools, a significant fraction of the teachers using them had to engage in activities more like what a computer enthusiast (sometimes called a "buff" or a "hacker") would engage in today, and they learned a lot in doing so.

Countless teachers became computer users after being introduced to the machine by a fellow teacher. In the early 80s it was quite common for more experienced computer users to share what they had learned with those who had not yet fallen in love with the machine and, in doing so, they added to the ranks of computer users. The process of spreading the word did not always succeed, however.

It seems that experienced computer users sometimes tend to present what they know in a way that can intimidate newcomers to computing. Computer buffs are notorious for their seeming inability to speak in plain language; they tend to speak what is sometimes jokingly referred to as "computerese." Many a computer novice has been turned off by being on the receiving end of too much unnecessary computer terminology fired too fast in succession with too few familiar words interspersed. Though there is less of a problem of communicating across levels than there used to be, you may encounter experienced computer users who have difficulty talking at a rider/driver level. As they share their computer expertise with colleagues, they tend to say more that is nice to know than necessary.

If you are fairly new to computers, one real advantage of the next chapter is that, after studying it, you will be better able to talk computers with others. The chapter introduces many of the terms that are the *lingua franca* of computer users at all levels. When you accomplish its learning goals, you'll have acquired the largest portion of the basic knowledge about microcomputer operation needed at the rider level, and quite a chunk of what a driver needs to know. You'll also perhaps be better at deciphering any computerese speakers you encounter.

Some Advantages of "Hands-On" Learning

"Hands-on" is certainly the best way for you to begin to get really comfortable with computers. The machines tend to seem less mysterious and intimidating as they become more familiar, more ordinary.

Hands-on has other advantages, too. By actually trying out activities on computers, you tend to maximize your ability to apply what you learn about them through reading. Were you to leave the driving to others as you study the book, you would gain limited, albeit useful, knowledge about microcomputers and their use in teaching. But practicing some driving skills at the same time will certainly pay off for you. We can assure you that comfort, knowledge, and skills increase most rapidly with hands-on experience.

Variety in experience is useful, too. If you can get hands-on experience in various situations—on different machines and with different types of tasks—you'll become a better driver. The main payoff will be later. Like an automobile driver, you will begin to sense the real advantages of getting places you want to go on your own. You'll be less dependent on other people as you spend more time at the keyboard. And, we trust that as you become more familiar with machines through reading and activities, you will feel more and more positively toward their potential as classroom aides for teachers such as yourself.

If you haven't yet had any hands-on experiences with a microcomputer, then we encourage you to start right away by doing the activities identified as being for novice users that you will find at the end of Chapter 2.

SUMMARY AND REVIEW CHECKLIST

One important aim of this chapter was to have you understand the scope and purpose of this book and to present the book's general conception of computer-using teachers as individuals who have learned to use computers in their professional roles. We have stressed the computer's ease of operation, its power, and its growing importance in education, both as a tool for teaching and learning, and as curricular subject matter. We hope we have done so in such a way that you will feel positively toward the idea of acquiring the knowledge and skills required to be an effective computer-using teacher.

You can use the checklist of Chapter 1 objectives below to determine if you have or have not yet mastered the specific instructional intent of this chapter. In addition to serving as a basis for self-evaluation of your knowledge of chapter material, the statements can guide you in planning further study.

Checklist

[ ] I can state reasons why a teacher should acquire computer-using proficiencies.

[ ] I can list and define several areas of knowledge and skills associated with being a computer-using teacher.

[ ] I know a variety of ways that teachers use microcomputers in the school setting.

[ ] I can state in general terms what computer literacy means and explain why stricter definition is not advisable.

[ ] I can identify some differences between using a computer for the general purpose of instructing and guiding students and using it to teach computer concepts.

[ ] I can name and contrast two computer-focused content domains that may be found in a school's instructional program.

[ ] I can describe the level of difficulty of operating a microcomputer with a user-friendly program.

[ ] I can make an argument that there are actually various levels of understanding needed by computer-using teachers, but I can characterize a general range.

[ ] I can state some benefits to be gained from using computer terminology and engaging in hands-on computer learning.

SUGGESTED ACTIVITIES

1. Begin a scheduled reading program, reading microcomputer-related articles that would be of interest to a computer-using teacher. Professionally, the best way to keep abreast of new developments in the use of microcomputers in the classroom is through reading in current journals.
   a. Identify articles in periodicals that feature classroom applications of microcomputers. There are articles written for teachers at all levels. Here are some journals to get your investigation started:
      Electronic Learning
      Classroom Computer Learning
      The Computing Teacher
      Educational Technology
      Electronic Education
   b. "Search backwards" from the current date to identify articles on the topic of microcomputers in journals whose focus is toward teaching, not microcomputers. Many general education or teaching journals have been featuring articles on microcomputers and teaching. For example, such articles can be found in the areas of mathematics, language, science, art, and social studies. The journals of professional

organizations, such as the National Science Teachers Association, the National Council of Teachers of Mathematics, and the Council on Exceptional Children also feature articles.

2. Analyze articles that you locate and read. Determine the extent to which they deal with the following terms or concepts from this chapter:
   teacher computer use
   computer science goals
   student computer use
   computer literacy goals

3. Explore the topic of "microcomputers and teachers" using the selected publications that are listed in the *Readings* and the *References* sections that follow. Reading such publications will provide you with a number of points of view toward the topic. Many state departments of education have published information pertinent to a computer-using teacher, and new ones are being produced continuously. Check your library for such materials and note differences in their focus: computer science, computer literacy, computer-using, or some combination thereof. At the same time you may want to check state certification requirements for these areas. In the future you may wish to seek certification for your own computer-using competencies.

4. Use one or more of the software items described in the following *Worth a Look: Software* section.

WORTH A LOOK: SOFTWARE

User-Friendly Programs: Computer Use

Comparison Kitchen. DLM Teaching Resources; Apple II family and IBM/MS-DOS computers. A program to teach primary children to discriminate and conceptualize sizes and amounts as they play Cookie Hunt, Bake Shop, and other activity games. A useful first encounter with computer-based learning.

The Print Shop. Broderbund; Apple II family, Atari, Commodore, IBM/MS-DOS, Macintosh computers. For all ages, this easy-to-use (simply choose one item per screen) program produces signs, banners, cards, and so forth. A great way to get started using computers.

User-Friendly Programs: Computer Literacy

For Teachers Only. D.C. Heath/Collamore; Apple II family computers. This is an introductory program for teachers who are inexperienced in using a microcomputer.

The Friendly Computer. MECC; Apple II family, IBM/MS-DOS, and Commodore computers. This has five programs to introduce preschool to third grade students to the major parts of the computer, the keyboard, and their use.

Micro Discovery. Science Research Associates; Apple II family computers. An introductory program to introduce students in intermediate grades through junior high to the basics of microcomputing.

Computer Discovery: A Computer Literacy Program. Science Research Associates; Apple II family, TRS-80, and IBM/MS-DOS computers. A computer literacy program for beginners in junior or senior high or college. Topics covered include computer history, hardware and software, simple programming, and the computer's role in society.

READINGS

Becker, H. "School Uses of Microcomputers: Not a Fad, but. . . ." *Educational Technology*, March, 1984: 33–34.

Bitter, G., and Camuse, R. *Using a Microcomputer in the Classroom.* Reston, VA: Reston Publishing Company, Inc., 1984.

Caissey, G. *Microcomputers and the Classroom Teacher.* Bloomington, IN: Phi Delta Kappa Educational Foundation, 1987.

Coburn, P. et al. *Computers in Education.* Reading, MA: Addison-Wesley, 1985.

Flake, J. et al. *Fundamentals of Computer Education.* Belmont, CA: Wadsworth Publishing, 1985.

Gray, P., and Tafel, J. *Computers Plus: A Program to Develop Computer Literacy Among Educators.* Portland, OR: Northwest Regional Educational Laboratory, 1984.

Hoffmeister, A. *Microcomputer Applications in the Classroom.* New York: CBS Publishing, 1983.

Kurshan, B. *Computer Literacy: Is It for Everyone?* Paper presented at the World Congress on Education and Technology, June, 1986 (ERIC Document #290429).

Moursund, D. "Individual Computer Literacy Education Plan: A Powerful Idea." *The Computing Teacher*, 1983, 11(4), 3–4.

Office of Educational Research and Improvement. *Teacher Preparation in the Use of Computers.* Washington, DC: Office of Educational Research and Improvement, 1986.

Office of Educational Research and Improvement. *Teachers' Views on Computer Use in Elementary and Secondary Schools.* Washington, DC: Center for Statistics, 1986.

Northwest Regional Educational Laboratory. *Technological Literacy Skills Everybody Should Learn.* Portland, OR: NREL, National Institute of Education, 1984.

Pantiel, M., and Patterson, B. *Kids, Teachers, and Computers.* Englewood Cliffs, NJ: Prentice-Hall, 1984.

Papert, S. *Mindstorms: Children, Computers and Powerful Ideas.* New York: Basic Books, 1980.

Pea, R. D., and Sheingold, K. *Mirrors of Minds: Patterns of Experience in Educational Computing.* Norwood, NJ: Ablex Publishing, 1987.

Sutphin, D. "Educating Teachers on Instructional Applications of Microcomputers." *Technological Horizons in Education* 14(6): 54–58 (February 1987).

Taylor, R., ed. *The Computer in the School: Tutor, Tool, Tutee.* New York: Teachers College Press, 1980.

Toffee, S. J., ed. *Computers in Education.* Guilford, CT: The Dushkin Publishing Group, 1986.

Woodrow, J. E. J. "Educators' Attitudes and Predispositions towards Computers." *Journal of Computers in Mathematics and Science Teaching* 6(3): 27–37 (Spring 1987).

REFERENCES

Anderson, C. A. "Computer Literacy: Changes for Teacher Education." *Journal of Teacher Education*, 34(5): 6–9 (September/October 1983).

East, J. P. *Topics: Computer Education for Colleges of Education.* New York: ACM, 1983.

Geisert, P., and Futrell, M. "Computer Literacy for Teachers." *ERIC Digest*, Syracuse, NY: ERIC Clearinghouse on Information Resources, 1984.

Hunter, B. *My Students Use Computers.* Reston, VA: Reston Publishing Company, 1984.

Office of Technology Assessment. *Power On! New Tools for Teaching and Learning.* Washington, DC: U.S. Government Printing Office, 1988.

Rogers, J. B., Moursund, D. G., and Engel, G. L. "Preparing Precollege Teachers for the Computer Age." *Communications of the ACM.* March 1984: 195–200.

Texas State, Office of the Deputy Commissioner for Professional Development and Support. *Essential Computer Competencies for Educators.* Austin, TX: Texas Education Agency, 1982.

2

A Teacher's Computer Primer

OBJECTIVES

- Name the essential components of all microcomputers and state the function of a microcomputer's major operating parts.
- Identify variations in microcomputer components and the relevance of these variations, if any, to users.
- Describe the functions of the most common peripheral devices on school computers.
- Identify by sight typical computer peripherals and name their important parts.
- Distinguish between hardware and software.
- Describe some ways that software programs influence microcomputer actions and use.
- Describe the importance of a disk operating system to computer operation.
- Portray basic requisites of caring for microcomputer hardware and software.

INTRODUCTION

According to the *New World Dictionary*, the term "primer" denotes "a textbook giving the first principles of any subject." This chapter is a type of primer, since its content encompasses most of the basics on which a teacher can build a thorough understanding of contemporary microcomputers. The chapter learning goals clearly reflect some first principles of computers that are relevant to computer-using teachers.

Goals

- What are computers?
- How are they made?
- How do they work?
- What does it take to work them?

If you already know and understand computer architecture and operation, this chapter can serve as a self-check for you, or perhaps it will be useful as a refresher. It is written, however, with some concern not to overwhelm new computer users. The nitty-gritty of computer architecture and operation, presented too quickly, can be somewhat intimidating, and we have tried to avoid creating that condition.

CONCEPTUALIZING CLASSROOM COMPUTERS

Computers come in a variety of brands, styles, and sizes. There are computers that sit in laps and fit in briefcases. They travel from home to school and back again, go to the library, and can even be used while flying around the world in an airplane. There are computers large and small that don't go anywhere at all. Some computers sprout wires in all directions and seem to be connected to everything around them. Other computers have no wires in sight and don't even plug in. With all this diversity of forms and components, how is a teacher to get a conceptual grip on a microcomputer?

A couple of concepts will prove useful to you as you set about this task. Here is perhaps the most important one: *all microcomputers are basically alike.*

Some Similarities among Microcomputers

How is it that a good auto mechanic can take in and fix just about any make or model car? The mechanic does not need to be trained to fix each of the hundreds of kinds of cars that could drive into his or her garage, because, basically, all cars are alike. They have almost all the same parts arranged in just about the same ways. If one knows how to overhaul a distributor on one car, the probability is high that one could do it for 99% of the other cars on the road. The key to learning how to fix all cars is to learn the general pattern of the form and function of the parts of a car.

The importance of pattern holds true for microcomputers as well as for cars, washing machines, lawnmowers, and photocopy machines. And as far as operating these various machines goes, the similarities are even greater. After you learn to drive a Ford, learning to handle another type of car presents little challenge. If you can identify and work with the parts for one microcomputer, it is easy to spot and use the same parts on other microcomputers. Where microcomputers are concerned, the number of parts the average teacher deals with is very small.

Look at the microcomputer pictured in Figure 2.1. It is analogous to your basic Chevrolet sedan, standard transmission, no radio, no extra power, and certainly no whitewalls.

Essentially all microcomputers have their keyboard and screen, and a "computing part" shielded by a case. The arrangement of these items may vary, and, commonly, a number of other items will be attached to the basic configuration. Still, the basic elements are apparent.

With some experience with different microcomputer models, one finds

FIGURE 2.1 The No-Frills Microcomputer

the commonalities between machines even more apparent. To frequent users, the basic functional components of any new microcomputer to which they are introduced will be as obvious as the main components of any model of car would be to the holder of a driver's license.

As is true with automobile drivers, microcomputer users can also count on there being an appropriate arrangement of parts shielded from view to allow the machine to function. Across brands of computers, there will be similarities in the inherent operational patterning of components "under the hood," no matter the diversity in outward appearance.

How Microcomputers Function Alike

Thinking of an automobile as a transportation machine helps one to better understand its underlying structure. Similarly, thinking of a microcomputer as an information handling machine will help you to understand it.

The business of any computer is in manipulating information, making decisions using information, storing information, and doing many of the things that humans do with information. Its reason for being is information handling.

To function, a microcomputer needs a method of taking information in, processing the information, and sending information out. A computer's information flow is illustrated in Figure 2.2. The figure shows: the moving of information into a computer—*input*; information handling inside the computer; and the moving of information out of the computer—*output*.

The manipulation of information inside the computer is generally termed *information processing* or *data processing*, and it is conducted by a device called a *microprocessor.* When processing information, the microprocessor is using internal information storage devices called *memory.* One can liken memory to a huge number of storage boxes (mailboxes) and picture the microprocessor sorting the information (mail), and storing it or retrieving it as appropriate.

In Figure 2.2 the flow of information in a microcomputer is represented

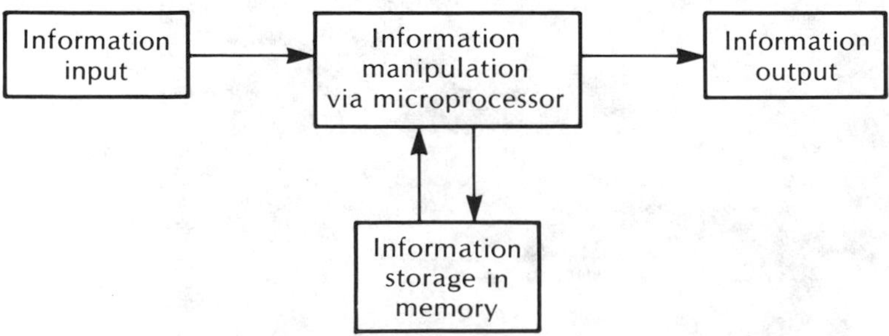

FIGURE 2.2 Basic Computer Operations

by the arrows. The actual pathways and controls for the information flow are built into the electronic components inside the machine, the microprocessor and the memory. Also *input devices* and *output devices* are part of the picture. The basic configuration in the figure applies to all microcomputer systems.

Hardware and Software

Because all computers function essentially the same way, a common vocabulary for describing and explaining the devices and how they handle information has evolved. Let's look for a moment at some of the most useful computer lingo.

The microprocessor and memory, like the keyboard, screen, and all of the other metal and plastic components of a computer are known as its *hardware*. Computer hardware can be thought of as the physical equipment in a computer system, and, for any given microcomputer, will include all the devices and components housed in or connected to the computer. The computer's microprocessor, however, is the central element in the system no matter what its physical location amidst the other hardware. The microprocessor is as crucial to a microcomputer's information handling as is the engine of a car to its locomotion capability.

As an electronic device, a microprocessor consists of arrangements of things such as wires and electronic switches especially designed to receive and transfer electrical signals. The manner by which the processor manipulates the signals it receives, the actual routing of the signals through the circuits, is under the control of the computer's programs.

We have used the term *program* several times already without defining it or explaining what it is that a program does. A computer's program controls how information is received into the computer, how it is handled inside the computer, and how it is sent back outside of the computer. We think it better to postpone dealing with the mechanics of this control process—how a program actually directs electronic signals through circuits and makes something worthwhile happen—for a while. For now, you can simply think of the program as a series of internal instructions directing microprocessor activity and begin to focus on distinguishing different types of programs.

A set of resident computer programs, governing the microcomputer's basic nature, is always inside the machine. These foundation programs are not, as a rule, changed, added to, or subtracted from. They can be thought of as the microcomputer's genetics. The resident programs are automatically activated each time the computer is turned on and they remain intact when it is turned off.

Additional computer programs can be placed into a microcomputer from outside by the computer user, using the keyboard or a computer disk. These are transitory programs, which operate for periods of time. This type of program is commonly called *software*. Software is used to activate and to add capabilities to a microcomputer's repertoire of actions. Software augments the computer's inherent capabilities. Computer software programs are activated by a user, and they cease to function when the computer is turned off.

An example of a resident computer program is the set of instructions governing the flow of information into a microcomputer from its keyboard. These resident commands and controls ensure that when a key is depressed the microprocessor is sent a message that the event has happened. Another example of a resident program is the internal instructions that enable the computer to print characters (letters, numbers, punctuation symbols) on the screen of the computer.

A math drill and practice program is an example of a software program that would be entered into the microcomputer from outside. That set of instructions to the computer augments its existing capabilities to enable the computer to show math problems on the screen, to draw graphics, to accept student answers, to evaluate those answers by comparing student answers to correct answers, and to provide appropriate feedback about the correctness of the answers. Software of an instructional type is often called *courseware*. This term is used to describe a category of software that enables a microcomputer to act in some ways like a teacher or to perform tasks that directly facilitate instruction in teaching and learning settings.

Table 2.1 summarizes the important terms presented in this section, and provides a description of each.

TABLE 2.1 Terms Relating to Microcomputer Operation

Item	*General Function*
Hardware	The physical equipment in a computer system
Input device	Means for moving information from outside the computer to the microprocessor
Microprocessor	An electronic logic device that can process information and make decisions
Memory	Internal storage devices that store information and instructions for the microprocessor to use
Output device	Means for moving information from the microprocessor to outside the computer
Computer program	Instructions on how a microprocessor is to move and manage information
Resident program	A computer program that is in the computer, ready to run or running
Software	A computer program that is input to the microprocessor and memory
Courseware	Computer software that has instructional application

OPERATING COMPONENTS FOR CLASSROOM MICROCOMPUTERS

A microcomputer user interacts with the machine by providing information to the computer for it to manipulate and by receiving the results of the computer's information handling processes. Since this is the case, let's look further at the input and output facets of computer operation.

We have made two arbitrary categories of input and output devices: those that are quite common in classrooms and those that are especially convenient in some situations, or that are required for specialized uses. In this chapter we will deal mostly with the primary components, those that seem to be widely used as means for input and output to a classroom microcomputer. Some alternate input and output devices will be shown, but we want to keep you focused on the typical components, so we'll postpone dealing with devices that have less widespread application until later chapters when we can deal with them in instructional contexts.

Getting Information *into* a Microcomputer

When you turn on a no-frills microcomputer, it already possesses a good deal of information, stored as instructions in the machine's built-in memory. But even with this information, all it does is sit there and blink, or display some words like "XYZ Company, Model #6." The blinking symbol, usually a short line or arrow on the screen, is called a *cursor*, and is the standard signal that the computer is waiting for further data or instructions from you. This information needs to be entered into the machine from the outside using an input device.

Keyboard

The most widely recognized microcomputer input device is the *keyboard*. Computer keyboards typically are patterned like their predecessors, typewriter keyboards, and have a QWERTY set of keys. QWERTY refers to the top line of letters on the left side of the keyboard.

Computer keyboards may differ in their overall size. The standard is about the same area as a standard typewriter keyboard, but some are considerably smaller, with keys spaced closer together. Keyboards differ greatly in the number of keys and their positions in respect to the user. Four important keys on just about every contemporary computer's keyboard are the *arrow keys*, which are used to move the cursor position up, down, left, and right. A scan of various computer brands in search of the location of these keys will provide clues to keyboard variability. Look also for the presence of special key sets, such as a number *keypad* for quick numerical entry, and for special *function keys*, generally marked F1, F2, and so on. These features naturally affect the size of a computer's keyboard (see Figure 2.3).

Other variations include the size and shape of keys, the amount of pressure it takes to depress a key, whether there are actual keys or simply a flat, imprinted membrane, and whether a key makes a "click" or not when pushed.

Variations in computer keyboards can be quite important. For example, special keyboards are available for special populations of users, such as persons who have motor disabilities that prohibit standard typewriter-styled input. Colorful keyboards designed for use with preschoolers feature oversized keys and modified functions that little fingers with poor motor coordination can handle.

Keyboards may be built into the computer's case, connected to it by a flexible cable, or completely detached, sending their information via infrared signals through the air (like a remote TV controller).

Keyboard variability factors may help determine how suitable a keyboard is for a specific purpose. Clearly, a second grade student has different keyboard needs than a professional secretary.

Mouse

A *mouse* is an input device found on certain computer models. The mouse serves a function that is similar to the arrow keys on a standard keyboard; that is, it allows one to make rapid movements of a cursor from one place on the screen to another. In programs that make use of the mouse, the cursor will often be pictured as an arrow (or other special mark). By moving the mouse on the table surface adjacent to the computer (or on a special "mouse pad" that facilitates this action), the user moves the arrow from place to place on the screen in order to make specific program choices. With programs that use graphics, such as drawing programs, the mouse is an indispensable input device since it allows one to make curved lines, sweeping movements, and detailed motions.

Disk Drives

A keyboard or mouse serves a user as the primary input method for sending information directly to a computer. When one wants to put stored information into a computer, the usual method is by means of a *disk drive* and computer *diskette.* A disk drive is a device that has the capability to decode information it locates on a computer diskette and to send that information to the microprocessor for manipulation. A disk drive handles a specific type of diskette, usually a 5¼-inch version or a 3½-inch make in a hard plastic case.

Computer diskettes are called by many names, and it remains to be seen which of the various terms will prove most popular. Besides computer diskettes, one hears of disks, mini-disks, floppy disks, floppy diskettes, or just plain floppies. Whatever you may choose to call them, diskettes in their protective covers can be seen in multiplying numbers wherever microcomputers are found.

A diskette is a convenient storage medium for microcomputer information. Its information, saved as magnetic spots on the diskette's surface, can be accessed by the drive head in the disk drive unit. When a microcomputer user

A IBM keyboard

B Apple IIe keyboard

C Apple Macintosh keyboard

D IBM portable keyboard

FIGURE 2.3 Various Computer Keyboards

inserts the diskette into the disk drive device, the diskette is rapidly rotated by the drive and the drive head reads (copies) the information off the disk (leaving the original information still on the diskette). The accessed information is then transferred from the disk drive to the microprocessor (it is sent down a set of wires from the disk drive to the microprocessor). The microprocessor then uses the information to control what appears on the screen and other actions.

Getting Information *from* a Microcomputer

The output devices with the most widespread classroom use are the screen, the disk drive, and the printer.

Screen

Microcomputer output can appear in the form of characters or graphics on the TV-like display screen. The screen may be a television screen controlled by the microprocessor or it may be a computer *monitor*. Monitors are specifically designed to produce images based on computer output. Both TVs and monitors use cathode ray tubes (CRTs) to produce the images, but other forms of display screens may be used with smaller, portable microcomputers. Screens vary in size from a four-inch diagonal through forty inches. The images may be in black and white, in a single color such as amber or green on a black background (monochrome), or in full color (refer to Figure 2.4).

Televisions are often used with microcomputers because of their availability and the fact that they can be utilized for both TV reception and computer use. Due to its basic electronic design, however, a TV screen cannot provide the clarity and resolution that a computer monitor can.

A computer monitor, although it costs no more than a TV of the same size, generally provides much sharper pictures than the TV. Resolution factors become very important to the user who spends much time in front of a screen. In the classroom, it is often imperative that written text and numbers be easily read by a class. In these cases a monitor should be employed rather than a TV.

For the purposes of using a computer with an entire class, a computer *projection panel* can be used. This monitor is flat, thin, and transparent. It is placed on a overhead projector and its image is projected onto a screen just like a transparency. It is large enough and bright enough to be seen by the entire class. Teachers use this setup as an "electronic blackboard."

Disk Drive

Output of information via a disk drive works exactly in reverse of the input procedure. The microcomputer sends information to the disk drive's recording head and the information is transferred to the diskette. The information can thereby be stored (practically indefinitely) until it is needed as input. Without some means of storage, the information contained in the computer's *volatile*

A Apple IIe

B Macintosh full-page display monitor

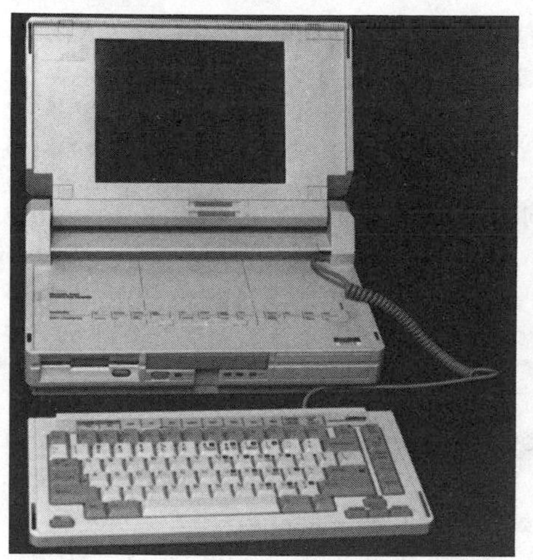

C Portable liquid-crystal computer

D Macintosh

E IBM screen

FIGURE 2.4 Various Computer Screens

memory would be lost should the computer be turned off. Disk storage is also needed for computer-generated output as it becomes too voluminous to be contained in the computer's own internal memory.

In response to the demands for greater storage space, manufacturers created the *hard (or fixed) disk*, which is a considerable improvement over floppy disk technology. They developed a diskette that was less flexible (firmer or harder). By spinning this disk at higher speeds, enormous amounts of information could be stored on a smaller surface area. The reduction in size enables the hard disk to be placed inside the computer, often located on a simple card that can be plugged into a slot in the computer.

The typical hard disk stores ten to sixty times the information of the floppy diskette (that is one million to fifty million pieces of information). The trade-off that needed to be made to perfect the hard disk was that it must remain in its sealed container. Therefore a hard disk cannot be swapped back and forth between machines and users as the floppy version can. The diskette remains the versatile method of getting stored information into and out of the computer. The hard disk is the diskette counterpart that remains inside the computer storing large amounts of program information.

Printer

An extremely important device is the *printer.* School printers come in two main varieties—dot matrix printers and laser printers (refer to Figure 2.5).

The *dot matrix printer* uses a print head that has a number of wires or "pins" that can be made to strike against a ribbon and create an impression as the print head moves across the surface of the paper. By having the computer vary the number and timing of the striking of the pins, the printer can cause any character, number, or segment of a graphic to be printed. In other words, the dot matrix printer receives electronic information from the computer and translates it into patterns of pin strikes.

Dot matrix printers vary in price depending on their speed of printing, the variation in paper widths they will accommodate, the character sets they can print (for example, some include foreign language character sets, bold and italic typeface sets, and so on), and the number of pins in the print head (more wires means clearer print).

The printer often makes use of a *tractor feed* to guide paper (which has holes along the edges) through the printer. With this device paper is continuously fed into the printer from a box containing a supply of the familiar fanfold style computer paper. This arrangement is both inexpensive and handy to use in the classroom. Some printers have special arrangements that allow them to accommodate various types of paper and feed individual sheets of paper into the printer. Other printers have internal memory units to which a microcomputer can send print information, and then leave the printer to do its job while the computer goes on to a new task.

The *laser printer* is a form of printer that might be found more often at a

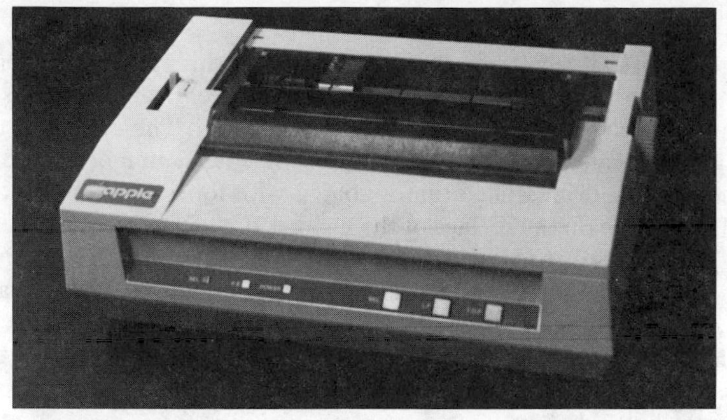

A Apple dot matrix printer

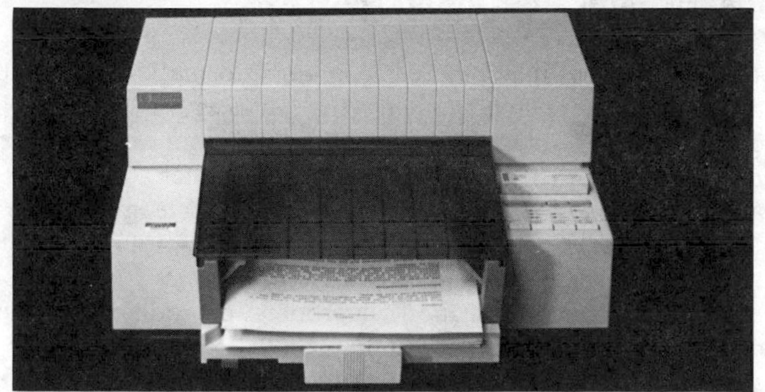

B IBM DeskJet printer

C Apple letter-quality printer

FIGURE 2.5 Typical Computer Printers

school or district level than in a classroom. In this type of printer, the computer controls a beam of laser light, which is swept rapidly across a printing drum that is covered with a light sensitive material. The computer uses the laser light to create an electrostatic pattern of letters, numbers, and characters on the printing drum. The drum is coated with toner (ink) and rotated on paper. The pattern on the surface of the drum is transferred to the paper.

The merits of the laser printer lie in its ability to print clear characters of many shapes and sizes, and its ability to print high resolution graphics (pictures, charts, graphs). Of course this capability comes at a higher price than the dot matrix printer. In schools, the laser printer is likely to be used in a central office for important publications, or in drafting classes to produce computer-aided designs.

Secondary Input and Output Devices

Various other devices may be used to input information into and/or receive information from a microcomputer. These devices are either less commonly seen or have more specific applications than the input and output devices discussed thus far. For example, special *probes* and other attachments for receiving data from environmental sensors have considerable importance for science instruction. An *inkjet printer* can output data in the form of colorful graphs or charts. Another type of printer, the *daisywheel printer*, is used as an output device in some business education classrooms to produce letter-quality print much like that of an electric typewriter.

Schools often have a *mark sensing device* that reads printed information from a special test-taking card that the student marks with a #2 pencil. This input device senses the student's marks and inputs them into a computer for scoring and record-keeping. Some school systems have a *scanner*. This input device reads printed pages and sends the text on the page to the computer.

A *modem* receives and sends information over telephone lines. Another device, which also uses telephone transmission, is the *facsimile machine* (fax). Fax permits quick and easy transfer of a printed page from one location to another.

Figure 2.6 shows our basic microcomputer somewhat souped up with several of the many available options. These options are generally not standard equipment on classroom microcomputers and are commonly termed *computer peripherals*, a category of add-ons to the basic microcomputer. Peripherals are the kinds of items that tend to confuse a computer novice who is seeking to identify a computer amidst an assortment of boxes and wires, as you will note when attempting to locate the three basic computer components among the various frills in the figure.

Tables 2.2 and 2.3 provide a review of the major computer input and output components presented, along with a brief summary of the roles played by some of the accessory devices pictured in Figure 2.6.

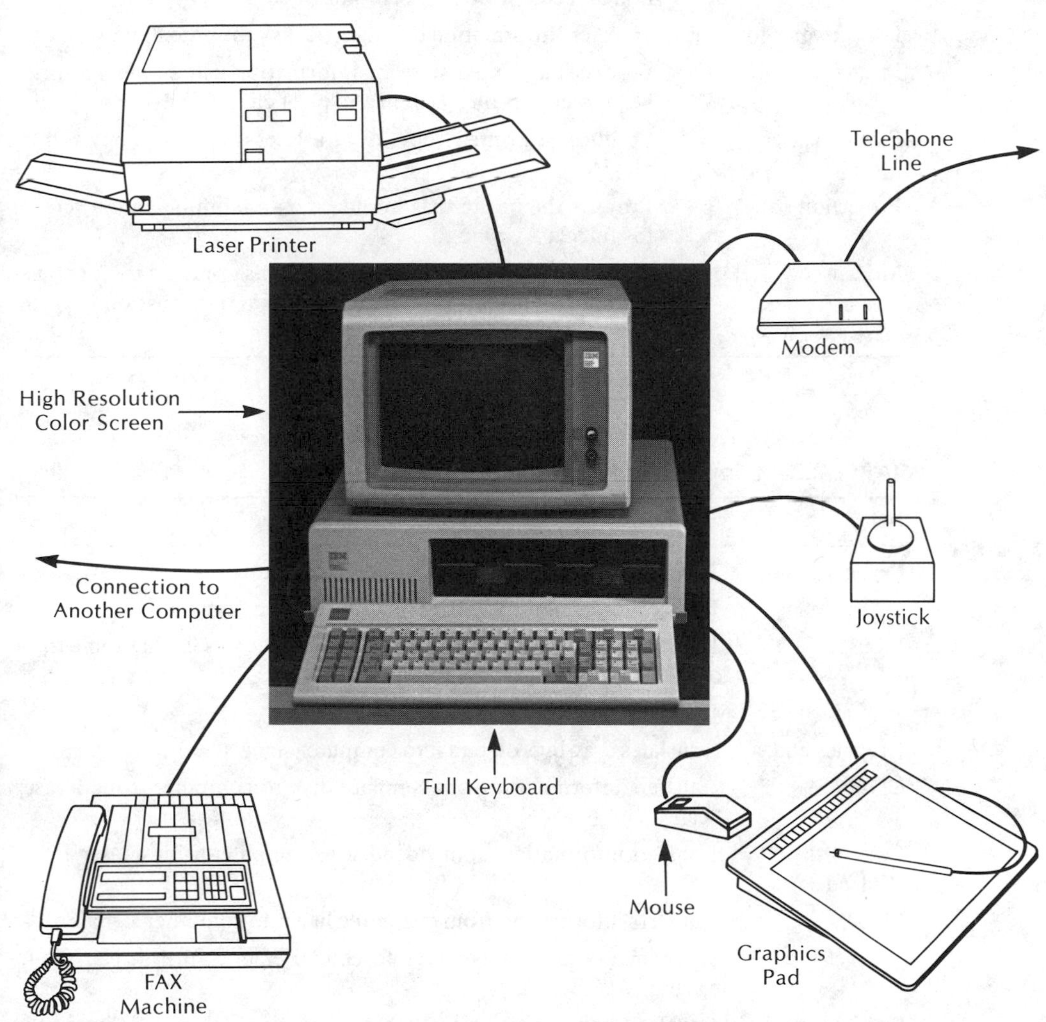

FIGURE 2.6 A Hot-Rod Computer

TABLE 2.2 Common Computer Output Devices

Item	*General Function*
Screen—TV	Produces information for viewing while computer is in use
Screen—monitor	Functions the same as the TV screen, but with higher resolution and clarity (in monochrome or color)
Disk drive	Transfers information to magnetic disk for potential use later
Printer—dot matrix	Produces a printed sheet of information using pins in a print head to impact on a ribbon and print characters
Printer—laser	Produces a printed copy using a laser and photocopy principles
Projection panel	Projects the image that would be on a monitor onto a screen, for full class viewing
Modem	Translates computer signals into signals appropriate for transmission via telephone wire or decodes a transmission into signals a computer can use

TABLE 2.3 Some Microcomputer Input Devices

Item	*General Function*
Keyboard	Transfers information typed by user to computer
Disk drive	Transfers information from magnetic disk to computer
Mouse	Translates its own movement into computer signals having some form of meaning
Joystick	Translates movement into a computer signal
Graphics pad	Translates drawings on pad into computer signals
CD-ROM	Transfers information from compact disk to computer using a laser beam
Laser-disk (Videodisc)	Transfers information from videodisc to computer using a laser
Modem	Transfers information from telephone line into computer signals
Scanner	Scans images and sends image to computer in a form it can use in programs
Specialized screen	Translates light emitted from light pen or the touch of a finger on the screen into computer signals

COMPONENTS INSIDE THE COMPUTER

We have examined how information gets into and out of computers. What happens inside? Although there are a number of other components inside a microcomputer, the two major conceptual parts to focus on are the microprocessor and memory.

The Microprocessor

The microprocessor is the electronic component that manipulates information. A *logical device*, it makes the computer's fundamental decisions. For example, the ability to add, subtract, multiply, divide, compare numbers and words, and store and retrieve information from disk storage resides in the microprocessor. The microprocessor is able to process millions of pieces of information each second, which is one of the factors that makes it so capable when it comes to doing jobs that require lots of repetitive calculations or text manipulations.

Microprocessors vary, and microcomputer enthusiasts are often heard to mutter things like "Z-80" and "8088" and "Intel 80386," which are the names of microprocessors. For the typical teacher there is little difference between the various microprocessors—for, although one may be faster or more efficient than another, the difference will not be enough at first for the average person to recognize or care about.

The microprocessor is indeed the center of all microcomputer activity. It takes in, processes, and distributes outward all the information passing through the computer, and it handles the internal transportation and use of information the computer already has within it.

Memory

If a microprocessor did not have the capability of calling on some sort of internal memory, it would be extremely limited in its processing capabilities. Therefore, a microprocessor is not restricted to manipulating only the information put into the computer from some external source. It can also call upon two types of internal computer memory, one whose content is permanently fixed (the *R*ead *O*nly *M*emory, or *ROM*), and one that can be changed by the computer user or the microprocessor (the *R*andom *A*ccess *M*emory, or *RAM*).

Both types of internal memory consist of a large number of *electronic cells* that can store coded information. We will postpone describing or contrasting the role of these two forms of memory in the computer's information handling process until Chapter 10. For now, you need only recognize that RAM and ROM are both places (like mailboxes) for computer information. Any information you enter into the computer yourself will be temporarily placed in RAM boxes, whereas the bank of ROM boxes is reserved for information that governs computer functioning. Should the electricity go off, the content of RAM is irretrievably lost, but ROM content will remain and keep the computer in readiness for operation just as soon as the power comes back on.

At this point, you need not go beyond the components of microcomputer operation presented in Figure 2.7 to be adequately informed of the basics of microcomputer function.

DRIVING A MICROCOMPUTER

The Computer's Built-in Actions

A car has a number of built-in actions that are common to all motor vehicles. For example, the car speeds up when the accelerator is pushed and slows down when the brake is pressed; its wheels turn with the rotation of the steering column; and a movement of the gearshift to neutral frees the wheels from transmission control. In a similar fashion, essentially all computers share some built-in actions that you can count on as you get started as a computer-using teacher. Here are a few typical examples.

When a microcomputer is turned on, the keyboard becomes active and ready to accept the information that you type. The blinking cursor indicates the position at which any character will appear, and when a key is pressed, the resulting character appears on the display screen almost instantaneously. The <RETURN> (or <ENTER>) key is active, and a push of this key will send a signal to the microprocessor that some sort of message or command is to be handled. The computer will respond automatically to the message with its own message or action (which the user must interpret).

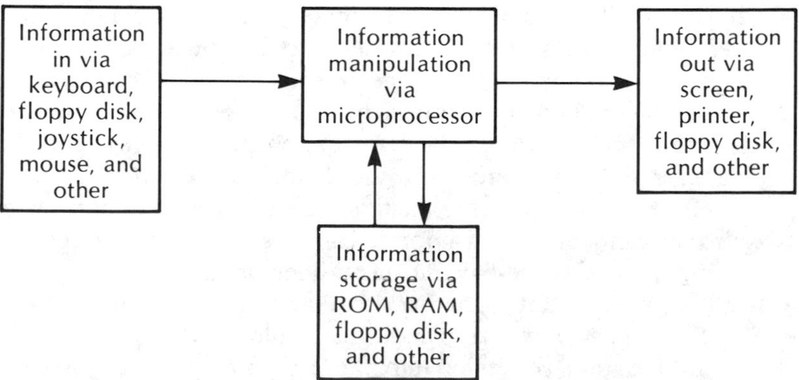

FIGURE 2.7 Expanded View of Computer Operation

The Computer's Acquired Actions

The number of actions built into a computer is limited. The reason for this is that when a manufacturer builds in a certain program (to provide a particular function to a user), it raises the cost of the machine, takes up valuable memory, and is wasteful since not everyone would want to use every built-in program. So most computers rely on input from disk storage for programs. Computer programs provide most of the repertoire of computer actions.

Disk Operating System

The task of storing and retrieving information from a diskette is a complex one for a microcomputer. To accomplish the job, it uses a program called a *disk operating system*. This program, commonly abbreviated *DOS* (pronounced *doss* by many people, and *dee-oh-ess* by others), is the set of instructions a given computer uses to control the storage and retrieval of information from a diskette, and all the housekeeping chores associated with that function. Some computers have a DOS built in, but most microcomputers used in classrooms require that DOS instructions be provided on a special diskette obtained with the computer when it is purchased.

Placing this *systems disk* in the disk drive when the computer is turned on allows the computer to retrieve the instructions it needs to conduct disk drive operation (the computer lingo is *boot*). The necessary instructions are passed along to the computer and stored in its RAM memory for use during the session.

DOS instructions may also be placed on a diskette containing other programs. Often, when you purchase a computer program, you are purchasing the DOS along with the software you want.

What happens when you turn your computer on? The microprocessor may first perform a self-check of its components, and then send a message to the disk drive, in essence asking this question: "Disk drive—do you have a disk in place, and if so does the disk have a DOS on it?" If the latter answer is "no" the computer will know this and send you an error message such as "NO DOS AVAILABLE," and you will need to supply the DOS and try again. If the answer is "yes" the computer will then put portions of DOS into RAM, for both you and the microprocessor to use when needed.

Many commercial program disks are set up to work in a fully automatic mode, and you may not realize that a DOS has been copied and is hard at work. But with other programs you will want or need to use the DOS commands. Here are some DOS commands that are self-explanatory: (1) LOAD (a program), (2) RUN (a program), (3) PRINT, (4) SAVE, (5) COPY, and (6) DELETE.

Commercial Software

By far the vast majority of programs that are used by teachers are commercial programs sold by vendors through catalogs or stores. These programs vary widely in quality and cost.

Some programs come prepared to start automatically while others require some command from the user. Educational software usually comes with a user's guide that explains how to operate the program. You need to be aware that a program is designed to run on one (and sometimes *only* one) brand or model of microcomputer. You do need to be sure the program you use matches the computer and model you use. (This situation is not as strange as it seems at first. After all, if you need a fuel pump for a 1976 Chevrolet Monza you need to get one that is specific to the brand, year, and model.)

A large portion of subsequent chapters will examine the various types of available programs, how to acquire quality programs, and how to use them effectively in the classroom. There are four basic ways to acquire computer programs: (1) by purchasing commercial programs offered for sale; (2) by copying or obtaining copies of public domain software (which is free); (3) by locating "shareware" software for which a nominal use fee is paid; and (4) by programming one's own programs. If you have only a few programs, or programs that are poorly matched to classroom needs or of low quality, then you will be unable to use your microcomputer in constructive ways.

START-UP AND MAINTENANCE OF A CLASSROOM MICROCOMPUTER

Getting a newly purchased computer up and running is about as hard as getting a new stereo out of a box and plugging it in. With electronic products, little is required beyond hooking together the components. Far fewer directions come with a new microcomputer than with a child's swing set.

A computer's "action repertoire" is no better than the software it runs.

Maintenance is almost as simple as start-up. Naturally, there are things that can go wrong. Even the simplest of switches stop switching from time to time, so problems can arise. But in general, the components of a microcomputer are hardy and can withstand most of the trials provided them, even those in the school classroom.

Disk Drives

A computer's disk drive is the most delicate aspect of the machine, and care should be exercised when inserting and removing a diskette from the drive. The most important rule to remember is not to attempt to pull a diskette out of the computer while the disk drive is running. Since most microcomputers have an indicator light that signals a "busy drive," you should wait for the light to go out before proceeding. Disk drives work simply and smoothly, so there is never any reason to attempt to force a disk into a drive. Should a disk drive stop working, the computer must be referred to an appropriate service person (often a knowledgeable teacher or student).

Diskettes

Diskettes are open to damage by poor handling and messy fingers. Though the fixed jacket that surrounds the diskette's magnetic surface provides some protection from physical damage by abrasion or touching, precautions are necessary. Keeping a diskette in its envelope when not in the machine is helpful in preventing dust from settling on the exposed portions of the surface.

Computer information is stored on the surface of a diskette in the form of magnetic spots. These magnetic spots can be destroyed quickly by bringing the diskette too near a magnet or any source of magnetism. Since almost any device using electricity produces a mild magnetic field, it is a good idea to keep diskettes away from TVs and monitors, and from the top and sides of the computer itself.

It is also best to give some thought to where you will store diskettes in the classroom. Keeping them in an area of the room where science activities take place, for example, might be courting trouble, since the use of magnets or similar items in a learning activity might result in some expensive programs being lost. The possibility of improbable events, such as some mischievous student wanting to create havoc by waving a magical wand (magnet) over the storage box, should not be dismissed outright. Losing all your programs is not a pleasant prospect, and you will need to decide how to protect your diskettes.

Here are a few rules that can serve as general guidelines for minimizing problems with diskettes:

- Avoid denting or bending the diskette.
- Avoid placing any weight or pressure on it.

- Never touch the recording surface.
- Use a felt-tip pen to write on the disk label.
- Stay away from electrical devices and magnets.
- Keep away from dust.

Even a tiny dent or scratch can cause the loss of program information. But, by storing diskettes in a container suited to the purpose, by exercising moderate caution whenever handling a diskette, and by training students how to do the same, you will experience few problems.

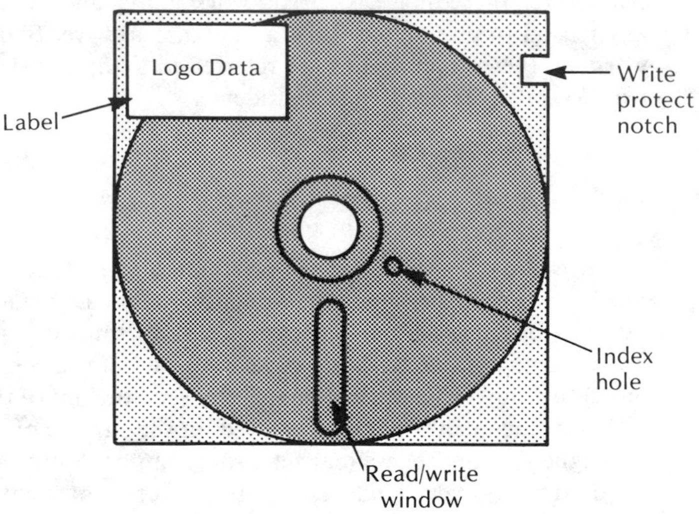

DOs	DON'Ts
Hold the disk with thumb on the label.	Touch the disk surface.
Insert the disk carefully.	Force the disk into the drive.
Keep disk in the protective envelope when not in use.	Bend or fold the disk.
Keep in a place where it is in a moderate temperature range (50° F to 125° F).	Write on the label with a ballpoint or pencil.
Store in a vertical position in a container that protects it from dust.	Place the disk near a magnet or magnetic field.
	Use a paper clip on the disk.

FIGURE 2.8 The Dos and Don'ts of Handling and Storing a Computer Disk

SUMMARY AND REVIEW CHECKLIST

In this chapter, we've tried to provide the basic information a computer-using teacher needs to know to talk knowledgeably about computers and to exercise some elementary maneuvers in operating a microcomputer.

If you are fairly new to computer use, you may not feel ready for the Indianapolis 500 of microcomputing quite yet, but with an understanding of this chapter and some hands-on experiences such as those suggested in the activities that follow, you'll be able to use a microcomputer.

Check to make sure you have mastered the following objectives as a result of your study thus far. Check off the ones you are sure of, and restudy those that are still unclear.

Checklist

[ ] I can name the basic components of all microcomputers and state the function of a microcomputer's major operating parts.

[ ] I know some ways in which basic microcomputer components vary and can identify how these are relevant to a user.

[ ] I can describe the functions of the most common peripheral devices for school microcomputers.

[ ] I can look at a typical classroom computer with its peripherals and name their important parts.

[ ] I know the difference between computer hardware and software.

[ ] I can describe in a general way how software programs influence a microcomputer's actions and use.

[ ] I can describe the importance of a disk operating system to computer operation.

[ ] I can portray in general how to care for microcomputer hardware and software.

SUGGESTED ACTIVITIES

1. (for first-time computer users) Rehearse the process of placing a diskette inside a disk drive. You will need a diskette (in its envelope) and a computer. Practice the "Do's" of diskette handling as you remove the diskette from its envelope, insert it, label side up, into a disk drive slot in the computer, and lock it in. Reverse the procedure and return the diskette to its envelope.

Extension. If various types of machines are available, practice the diskette handling exercise with computers that have slots in different positions and different kinds of locks. Don't do any "Diskette Don'ts!"

2. (new or stale computer users) Cold turkey—run a program on a microcomputer. Ask someone who is knowledgeable for recommendations on a program to use. You definitely want your program to be user-friendly. You'd also like to be able to exit (quit) the program whenever you wish.

Don't fret, even if you have never used a microcomputer before. Just be sure to handle the diskette appropriately. You may benefit from help from someone who has experience with the machine, but, if you prefer to go it alone, you can read the directions from a manual, or just take a do-it-yourself approach using the scenario on pages 14 and 15 to give you the general steps to use to run a program.

Extension. To become comfortable with the procedure for operating a computer, try repeating the steps several times with the same program. Then, if the occasion permits, try the procedure with another program on a different diskette.

3. Locate on a microcomputer each of its major operating parts, name the parts, and be able to briefly describe their functions. Try this activity with a variety of microcomputers. Notice that although the parts on the microcomputers you examine may be arranged quite differently, the basic operating parts are similar in noticeable ways. Make sure you locate:

a. The monitor (or TV) and its power source, its off/on switch, the monitor cable leading to the computer, and the brightness and contrast adjustments.

b. A disk drive or pair of drives, the door latch and, if the disk drive is outside of the computer, the power cable and the disk drive cable leading into the computer.

c. The main body (encased) of the computer, the main computer reset switch, power cable, and off/on switch.

d. The keyboard and, if the keyboard is separate from the body, its cable to the computer.

Extension. Although all of these will not be attached to all computers, look to see if the computer is plugged into either of these devices: a voltage surge suppressor (follow the computer's power cable to an outlet); or a printer (the printer cable coming from the computer is very often flat). If you locate one of these, identify its power cable and off/on switch.

Extension. If possible, look inside the main computer case of some computer. With the guidance of someone who knows about the computer, or with a user's manual, try to find: the microprocessor; some memory boards and chips; connections (called ports) for input and output cables; slots where electronic cards are plugged to increase the memory or capabilities of the computer.

Extension. Examine as many different computer peripherals as are easily accessible in your situation.

Extension. Visit a local computer store to broaden your perspective on and understanding of the various computers and hardware available.

4. Run a few user-friendly programs that are available on diskettes. (Make sure that your program diskette is labeled for the model of computer you are using!) If the program does not start automatically, you may need to refer to the microcomputer user's manual to locate the instructions on how to start up a program. Also, you may need to refer to the user guide that comes with the program to learn how to operate that particular program.

5. Using a microcomputer manual or other source, find the procedure to *copy a program* (have it appear on another disk that has space to contain the program) on the computer you are using.

   Then, copy a selected program from one diskette to a second diskette (the receiving diskette should already be formatted or initialized to work on the computer you are using). Use a public domain program, or be certain that the copying of the program is permissible (within the bounds of the copyright provisions that accompanied its purchase or lease) before you attempt the procedure. To duplicate a copyrighted program outside of the purchase/lease agreement's provisions is a violation of law.

   After you copy the program, run it to make sure it is working correctly. When you are satisfied that you have actually duplicated the program, erase it. (You may need to use the manual to learn the specific erase procedure.)

6. Use and review selected items of software from the following "Worth A Look: Software."

WORTH A LOOK: SOFTWARE

Learning About Computers

Understanding Computers. Encyclopedia Britannica; Apple II family computers. An interactive introduction to computers for the novice. It covers the history of computers, fundamental applications, hardware, software, programming, and future uses.

Computer Discovery: A Computer Literacy Program. (See Chapter 1 software.) Designed for beginners. Topics covered include computer history, hardware and software, simple programming, and the computer's role in society.

For Teachers Only. (See Chapter 1 software.) An introductory program for teachers who are inexperienced in using a microcomputer.

The Friendly Computer. (See Chapter 1 software.) An introductory program for primary children to acquaint them with the computer.

Mastering Computer Keyboards

Success with Typing. Scholastic; Apple II family and IBM/MS-DOS computers. Designed for grade levels 5 through 12, this program includes eighteen lessons, exercises, and tests to develop touch typing skills.

Most microcomputer users make extensive use of their computer keyboards. If you need help in learning to type, there are a number of good computer programs you can use to develop and hone your skills at the keyboard. In addition to the one above, you will find several programs listed under the topic "keyboarding/typing" in the "Worth A Look" sections at the ends of Chapters 3 and 5.

READINGS

Ahl, D. "Floppy Disk Handling and Storage." *Creative Computing*, December 1983: 205–206.

Baskin, L. *Teaching Early Childhood Educators and Other Adults How to Use Computers.* Urbana, IL: ERIC Clearinghouse on Elementary and Early Childhood Education, 1985.

Cowper, O. "All About Adding Peripherals." *Compute!* March 1984: 24–36.

Eadie, D. *Users' Guide to Computer Peripherals.* Englewood Cliffs, NJ: Prentice-Hall, 1982.

Pantiel, M., and Patterson, B. "Understanding Computerese." In *Kids, Teachers, and Computers*. Englewood Cliffs, NJ: Prentice-Hall, 1984.

Roberts, J. L. *Scholastic Computing: An Introduction to Computers.* New York: Scholastic, 1984.

Roth, A. J. "How to Become an Instant Computer Expert." *Teaching English in the Two Year College* 13(1): 20–24 (February 1986).

3

Exploring What Microcomputers Can Do

OBJECTIVES

- List and describe six major technical capabilities of a microcomputer as they relate to the computer's potential for classroom use.
- Describe examples of a typical classroom computer's technical capabilities, with and without attachments.
- Characterize two broad roles of a microcomputer playing "teacher's helper."
- Describe five features of a computer program that tend to make it most useful to a prospective user.
- Identify the two categories of computer programs that best enable a computer to assist a teacher in performing teaching-related tasks.
- Name and describe examples of the specific capabilities that a word processing computer program may offer to a teacher.
- Define the concept of a teacher utility program and list at least four common types and how they can help a classroom teacher.
- Identify factors that sometimes limit the usefulness or contribution of a teacher utility program.

INTRODUCTION

Until computers became the small and powerful packages we have today, they were not very common in schools. Just a few years ago it was unusual for a visitor on a school tour to see any computers. A large junior high might have had a computer in the math department, or there might have been a cluster of terminals for high school computer science, but in the typical school computers were sparse and few categories of people were computer users. Even when microcomputers were beginning to be used at the secondary level, it was unusual for an elementary school to have any machines at all, and any elementary teachers who used computers could comfortably think of themselves as progressive.

Today however, it's getting harder to visit a school and *not* see a microcomputer somewhere. Often one will see many! And, chances are, a glance at each one's screen will reveal a common story: the computers in today's schools are on active duty!

You may ask, "Just what are all these computers doing?" In this chapter we will begin to examine what it is that computers *can* do that makes them welcome in so many schools. We will focus first on the capabilities of computers themselves, and then move on to explore a few specific ways a teacher can use them.

Goals

- What are the major technical capabilities of a microcomputer?
- How can these capabilities be tapped to serve teachers?
- What kinds of commercially prepared programs can make a computer really useful to a teacher?

THE TECHNICAL CAPABILITIES OF A MICROCOMPUTER

Think of a microcomputer as a multipurpose tool. It can be used in a variety of ways by diverse users because, although its functions are limited by its electronics, it can be directed to do many different tasks. The school-related tasks a microcomputer can do are determined in part by the genetics of the computer (specifically, its ROM) and in part by how it is directed to behave by its DOS and programs.

A good computer program enables a user to accomplish a given task in a straightforward and simple fashion. The features of a program that tend to make it most useful to a prospective user are these: (1) the program is prepackaged and ready to use, (2) it runs flawlessly, (3) it has been extensively tested with typical users, (4) good instructions are provided, and (5) the program's purpose is well defined and described.

Most microcomputers have six categories of built-in capabilities that a programmer can draw upon when writing a program. Below we will describe, for each of the six categories, the range of capabilities a programmer would be able to exploit on typical school computers. Within any one category, there will be some particular brands and models of computers that offer more features than others.

Imaging

A microcomputer has the technical capability of producing and manipulating images on a screen, including the ability to make an image in full color or in monochrome. The image may be pictorial, or it may be or include letters, numbers, and other characters, sometimes in a selection of sizes. The image on a computer screen can be made to remain static or to move either in animation or with a natural motion such as one would see using a video tape player with a TV.

Although you may have seen examples of computer-produced graphics on TV and in action films, the standards for classroom computers are generally far below those that appear commercially. Classroom computers display an imaging capability that usually equals and may exceed the following: (1) a standard set of letters and numbers, available in one or two sizes, (2) both color and monochrome images, (3) some degree of image movement.

Certain models of computers have the ability to produce various sizes and shapes of text and numerical characters. When it comes to pictorial images, however, the story is similar on most of the models of computers commonly found in schools. Images are usually simple and like cartoons, and their movement limited—either stilted or jerky or time-consuming. High-image resolution, complex coloration, and naturalistic motion are features far less widely seen.

Sound

Many microcomputers have the capability of producing and storing sound. In most cases the classroom microcomputer can produce a variety of beeps and buzzes the moment it is lifted from its packing box. Beyond this standard capability the classroom microcomputer can, through the addition of fairly inexpensive accessory equipment, be made to produce and even to "understand" some human speech. It is becoming increasingly common for some sound production capabilities to be built into classroom computers. Musical tones, chords, words, and sentences are the most common features being made available.

Information Storage

The classroom microcomputer has the capability of storing and retrieving large amounts of information, whether it occurs in the form of words, numbers, characters, or images. In fact, the major strength of the modern microcomputer is this very capability.

Even the most ordinary and inexpensive classroom computer is power packed in terms of the overall amount of text and images it can store away (on floppy disks, for example) and then retrieve upon demand. But when compared to a more expensive computer, the limitations of the less costly model would become obvious. Indeed, microcomputers can vary quite noticeably in their speed at the storage/retrieval task and in the quantity of the information they can handle at once.

Depending on its electronics a classroom computer may fall short in both these categories. A wide variety of computers may be able to display a complex and colorful graphic. But on a low-cost computer, the time required to display such a screen may test the patience of the person at the keyboard. Storing certain information may also require more time than one would wish in a classroom situation. These are factors that set clear limitations on the programmer.

Logical Decisions

A microcomputer has the capability of making logical decisions. We can, in fact, view a microcomputer as a logic machine that processes information using patterns that have been built into its electronic circuits. Let's examine this logic machine at work.

If a student is working with a program that teaches how to multiply two two-digit numbers, the student may be asked to enter an answer to a problem. The student types into the computer the answer <3003> and pushes <RETURN>. The computer has the capability of comparing the student's answer with a correct answer stored in its memory. In effect, the computer can answer the logical question: Is the student's answer the same or different from the correct answer? Other logical abilities include evaluating larger/smaller/equal numerical statements, evaluating equalities (for example, deciding if the word "bigger" is the same as the word "bugger"), and following directions in the form of "if the student types <x>, then do <y>."

The same logical capability is built into each and every computer. You can rest assured that all microcomputers think in exactly the same way. Although the logical structure is built in, the given rules for any specific set of actions must be programmed in, of course. And, as we mentioned with respect to retrieval and storage limitations, lower cost classroom computers will often hinder the programmer in terms of the overall quantity and sophistication of the decisions that the computer can be made to perform in a reasonable period of time. Good programmers become expert at finding ways to maximize the decision-making capabilities of computers.

Computation

The computer originated as a computing device more akin to our modern calculators than to our present classroom microcomputers. Essentially every classroom micro*computer* today will be able to live up to its name. It will be able to perform with enormous rapidity any calculations normally associated with mathematics that would be needed in a classroom situation. By relying on this capability, a programmer could write a program instructing the computer to compute the correct answer to a multiplication problem rather than having to store all of the answers to all of the problems that might be presented. (The computer could actually be made to generate the problems, too.)

Other Capabilities

A microcomputer possesses many other capabilities that may or may not be important to a classroom teacher. It can tell time down to a tiny fraction of a second and accept and display data from environmental sensors. It has the ability to control external devices, such as a school's alarm system, heating system, and lighting system. In fact, when attached to other devices, a microcomputer can become very talented indeed. For example, a microcomputer can be connected to and made to control a number of different types of robots. A robot is an electromechanical device that is capable of motion and is under the control of a computer. Robots for educational use may be fashioned to look like robots, or they may be models constructed from components, such as Lego-like pieces.

To many students, the area of endeavor called robotics is a fascinating one. Learning to control an object's physical movements through a computer program provides students with insights into the process of programming and into how machines work. Industrial robotics is causing important changes in current manufacturing processes, so the concepts associated with the computer/machine interface are important. Still, robots do not currently have broad curricular applicability, and so they are unlikely to make a very profound impression on most teachers.

A teacher's eyes are likely to sparkle when an auxiliary device is attached to an ordinary classroom computer if the resulting technical capability has obvious relationship to the instructional program or evident potential for student learning. Three attachments in particular can bring some quite impressive features into play in a school environment. We suspect these will become increasingly important educationally.

One device that can dramatically extend a computer's potential usefulness in a classroom is the CD-ROM (compact disk read only memory). The CD-ROM is akin to the CD music disks that created a veritable revolution in the recording industry. Today one can plug into a microcomputer a compact disk player that is designed to be read by the computer. A CD-ROM disk is placed in the player and the computer can read the information from the disk.

By using CD-ROM, a computer can extend its retrieval capabilities and tap into vast amounts of information. For example, one CD ROM being offered to schools is the "Writer's BookShelf" (Microsoft, 1988). Items in this writer's reference library include *The American Heritage Dictionary*, *The World Almanac and Book of Facts*, *Roget's II Thesaurus*, *Bartlett's Familiar Quotations*, *The Chicago Manual of Style*, Houghton Mifflin's grammar checker *User Alert and Spelling Verifier and Corrector*, the U.S. Postal Service's *U.S. ZIP Code Directory*, the University of California Press's *Business Information Sources*, and a collection of model letters and forms called *Forms and Letters*. All these volumes are unabridged, and yet the entire set of writer's reference works are all to be found on one CD-ROM.

A second special capability is gained when a microcomputer is attached to a videodisc player. In this mode, the classroom microcomputer can readily access and display on its screen all types of video images, just like those displayed by a television or video tape player.

However, a microcomputer has the capability of displaying in slow motion, or searching and finding specific still images on the disk. In fact, one can access as many as fifty-eight thousand such slides from a single videodisc record. Videodiscs are available that include all the pictures in the New York Museum of Art, a multitude of NASA space mission photos, and documentaries from all over the world (National Geographic, 1987).

Another important capability of the microcomputer lies in its ability to communicate with the outside world via telephone lines. The microcomputer can be plugged into a device called a modem, which is then plugged into a standard telephone jack. Using telecommunication software, the computer can then be made to telephone other computers, or to contact various service providers (such as Compuserve® and PRODIGY®) around the country. Using telecommunication, it is also possible to be in computer contact with other teachers in other schools and even other states. Bulletin boards of educational information are only a local telephone call away in most areas of the nation.

It isn't necessary, of course, to hook a classroom computer up to external devices to sense the power of the machine itself. What kind of a program best demonstrates what a microcomputer can do on its own? We think that simulation is something the typical microcomputer can do extremely well.

Sampling Microcomputer Power: Simulation Programs

A *computer simulation* is a program that attempts to model some portion of the world that, in general, cannot be experienced due to limitations of time, circumstance, money, or physical resources. The challenge of flying an airplane, for example, is an experience that large numbers of people would like to have. Only a fraction have any hopes of ever actually taking the controls of a real plane.

There are a number of flight simulation programs available that permit a computer user to approximate the piloting experience. These programs have little or no classroom value, but they are worth mentioning due to the fact that they make use of so many powerful features of the computer. Flight simulation is also interesting from the standpoint of putting the microcomputer user into nonstandard situations. The program exemplifies the capability of the computer to model the physical world.

In such a program, the user learns how to fly an airplane, but not necessarily in the same fashion as in reality. In simulation, often the screen turns into a cracked windshield! But the simulation has the realistic sounds of the engine as it speeds up, slows down, or is put under stress; it has the view of the horizon changing at a rate proportional to the speed of the plane; the controls work accurately and respond exactly to conditions as they would in a real plane; various airports of the world are pictured, and one can fly into Paris, with appropriate runways and views. It has been reported by pilots that one indeed gets the real feel of flying an airplane with this simulation.

A simulation program can bring out in the computer all its best traits. The computer's logic and decision-making capability, coupled with its ability to store what users have previously done, make it possible for the computer to structure future events based on past user performance and current user decisions.

With the power of simulation, a microcomputer can take a student into situations that could never occur in the real classroom, and it can bring a piece of the world into the classroom that could never be there in reality. In the next chapter we will examine the use of computer simulation for classroom instruction and offer examples of how educators can make valuable use of such programs.

PUTTING A MICROCOMPUTER'S TALENTS TO WORK

As more microcomputers are introduced to schools each year, more and more teachers are answering these questions: What will you be doing with the new computer in your classroom? Are you turning it over to your computer whizzes? Will the students be playing games on it? What programs in (subject) are you planning to use?

We would like to argue that any teachers getting a new classroom computer should first of all think selfishly and keep the micro for their own use. Then, after becoming comfortable with how it works and getting it busy working for them, they can better make the transfer to other uses.

Two Ways of Helping a Teacher

If you could have a classroom assistant, what kind of helper would you like to have? Would you like to have someone to help you prepare tests and work sheets? How about someone to create crossword puzzles out of this week's spelling words? Perhaps you would like someone to write notes home to parents about student progress and problems? Would you enjoy having someone, at grading time, sum up and calculate all your students' grades? Most teachers would appreciate assistance with tasks such as these. Helping a teacher to accomplish teaching-related tasks is one role for a classroom assistant.

Maybe you would rather assign to a new classroom aide tasks more directly connected to instructional aspects of your job. For example, you might appreciate having someone to help the students who are behind others catch up. On the other hand, perhaps you'd like someone to take students who are ahead on some challenging excursion. And how about those students who would welcome an opportunity to delve into a new topic area? Maybe someone to guide a group project is called for, or someone to review previous skills before introducing the new material. These are things you would do more of yourself if only there were more of you to go around! You might like to have someone help out by working directly with students in your own role of teaching and managing learners' progress.

If you already suspect that the someone we are talking about your acquiring is really a something, then you're right. A microcomputer's features make it a strong candidate to serve as a classroom assistant in either or both of the two roles.

In the latter role—teaching and managing students' progress—any classroom assistant, be it human or computer, is heavily involved with curriculum matters. Examining the computer in this role will require several chapters of our attention. Right now, we would like to focus on some of the things computers can do as teachers' helpers across all subject areas and at all levels of schooling.

Some Programs That Are Popular with Teachers

It is in the capacity of helping teachers perform teaching-related tasks that computers have become immensely popular with a very broad spectrum of teachers. With the ready-to-run programs now available, there are a number of tasks a microcomputer can help almost any teacher to accomplish, regardless of the subject matter or level taught.

Many of the computer programs teachers find most useful were not originally designed for use by teachers. The *general purpose tool* programs, which include word processors, number processors (spreadsheets), and information processors (database managers), were developed to serve a broad audience in business and industry. Still, these computer programs have proved their value in helping many teachers perform aspects of their job, and few computer-using teachers are without at least one of these programs.

In addition to general purpose programs, there are more specialized *teacher utility* computer programs designed to do specific jobs that teachers routinely perform, such as grading or testing.

Here we will focus on teacher use of word processing, which is without

A computer in the teacher's hands may be used for teaching-related tasks.

doubt the most popular general-purpose tool, and on a selection of teacher-utility programs. We will cover teacher utilization of spreadsheets and database programs later, when we discuss their use by students. It is important to note that the general purpose tools (word processors, number processors, information processors, and communications software) can all be employed by a teacher for personal use, or with students as instructional tools. For the remainder of this chapter, our focus is only on the former.

A VERSATILE VALET: COMPUTER AS WORD PROCESSOR

There is one category of ready-to-run programs that displays the tremendous versatility one would look for in a classroom helper. This program category is *word processing.* It can turn your microcomputer into a general purpose assistant for many of the writing tasks you face in your professional role.

There is a wide variety of word processors, ranging from those developed for use by prewriting children through professional level word processors used in publishing.

No matter how simple or complex, a word processor commonly enables the user to:

- produce text
- save text

- retrieve text
- edit text
- print text

How a Word Processor "Works"

Word processors have revolutionized the writing and rewriting process. A word processing program turns the computer's screen into an electronic sheet of paper. The screen accepts the characters you type, automatically making appropriate length lines, and moving the "paper" along as you type. If you wish to correct an error or change any part of the document by adding or deleting words, the word processing program makes it a breeze. And, when you are done with the document, it can be stored for future use or reference, or copied, edited, and revised to create a second, or third, or fourth version of the original.

In order to describe the usefulness of a word processor for a teacher, let's use an example. Julia Hernandez is a sixth grade teacher at Fieldsworth Elementary. Her principal feels it is important for teachers to keep in constant contact with parents, and recommends that they send parents notes regarding each student's progress, as well as a grade card. Julia uses a word processing program on her computer to do the task.

When Julia got her word processing program, the first letter she produced with it was a general form letter regarding student progress. She typed it into the computer, corrected the errors, and left blank spaces for places into which she could put comments for individual students. Her computer screen looked like the one in Figure 3.1

Julia then stored the letter on a diskette under the file name of "Absence.ltr." When the time came to write letters, she could then retrieve this letter, add individual comments, print it, and store the individual's letter in a new file under the student's name (the file could be called "Barkleys.ltr"). In this manner she could write, print, and save personalized letters to each student's parents. Figure 3.2 is an example of a personalized letter developed from the form letter.

When preparing a personalized version of her form letter, Julia might choose to use her word processing program's FIND function to speed the process of replacing the text in parentheses with the specific information that applied. With that function, Julia could move her cursor quickly from one arrow mark to another to be in correct position for typing the information. She could also use a word processing function called BLOCK COPY to insert often used comments into her letter. Let's take a close look at how she would do this process.

Julia's word processor allows her to work on two documents simultaneously, one at the top of her screen and one at the bottom. She retrieves her letter to the top screen, and a set of paragraphs she often uses to the bottom screen (see Figure 3.3). She first highlights the paragraph she wants to include

FIELDSWORTH ELEMENTARY SCHOOL
1409 RIVER ROAD
CENTRAL CITY, NEBRASKA

→(space for date here)

→(space for address here)

Dear Parent→(type "s" when appropriate)

I have recently noticed that your→(type son/daughter)→(type first name) has been missing quite a bit of school lately. Our records show that→(type she/he) has missed→(type number of days missed) days of school in the last four weeks.

If I can do anything to keep→(type first name) up with the class, please let me know. We do have a special tutoring program that will help→(type first name) to catch up, and→(type she/he) can enroll in it by contacting Ms. Johnson in the Learning Resource Center.

Sincerely yours

Julia Hernandez
Teacher

FIGURE 3.1 Typical Word Processing Page

in her letter (Figure 3.4). Next she moves her cursor into her letter at the place she wants the paragraph to be (Figure 3.5). Finally, she issues a command (taps a key) and the paragraph appears in the form letter (Figure 3.6).

The blocking function can be used to do a variety of things to a unit of text. For example, a unit of blocked text can be moved, printed, stored, turned to bold, underlined, centered, or deleted.

A good word processor will offer many more features than what we have described thus far. Some of the common word processor functions are illustrated in Table 3.1. More esoteric features include searching an entire document for a word and automatically replacing it with another word, creating automatic merges of children's addresses with a form letter, creating automatic footnotes for a paper, creating newspaper type columns, incorporating graphics into a document, automatically creating a table of contents, making boxed text, automatically creating an outline, numbering sentences and paragraphs,

FIELDSWORTH ELEMENTARY SCHOOL
1409 RIVER ROAD
CENTRAL CITY, NEBRASKA

October 16, 1989

Mr. and Mrs. Albert Barkley
4536 Winding Way
Central City, Nebraska 76234

Dear Parents

I have recently noticed that your daughter Carla has been missing quite a bit of school lately. Our records show that she has missed nine days of school in the last four weeks.

If I can do anything to keep Carla up with the class, please let me know. We do have a special tutoring program that will help Carla to catch up, and she can enroll in it by contacting Ms. Johnson in the Learning Resource Center.

Sincerely yours

Julia Hernandez
Teacher

FIGURE 3.2 Personalized Letter to Parent

doing alphabetic sorts of information, checking the spelling, and presenting a thesaurus. An even more sophisticated function is available called a *macro*. The macro function allows one to combine a number of functions into a single complex function.

Common Teacher Uses for Word Processing

How many ways can a teacher use a word processor? We have illustrated using it to generate personalized reports. It may also be used to make tests. First, the test creation process becomes more flexible on a word processor. Second, the tests are easy to modify by using the program's capability to copy and to move blocks of text, so alternate forms of a given test become easier to produce. Third, in subsequent years a test can be quickly modified to incorporate new test items and drop items not covered.

Top Screen

Dear Mr. and Mrs. Franzetti

I have recently noticed that your son Tim has been missing quite a bit of school lately. Our records show that he has missed five days of school in the last four weeks. ▮

Item 1: Our principal, Mr. Brandice, would like to talk to you about→(name)'s absence. Please give him a call at 875-7854.

Item 2: Our nurse, Mr. Bodine, would like to talk to you about→(name)'s absence. Please give him a call at 875-7855.

Item 3: I would like to talk to you about→(name)'s absence. Please give me a call at 875-7857 after 3.

Bottom Screen

FIGURE 3.3 Using a Split Screen and Two Documents

Dear Mr. and Mrs. Franzetti

I have recently noticed that your son Tim has been missing quite a bit of school lately. Our records show that he has missed five days of school in the last four weeks.

Item 1: Our principal, Mr. Brandice, would like to talk to you about→(name)'s absence. Please give him a call at 875-7854.

Item 2: Our nurse, Mr. Bodine, would like to talk to you about→(name)'s absence. Please give him a call at 875-7855.

Item 3: I would like to talk to you about→(name)'s absence. Please give me a call at 875-7857 after 3.

Block of text highlighted

FIGURE 3.4 Marking a Block of Text to Be Copied

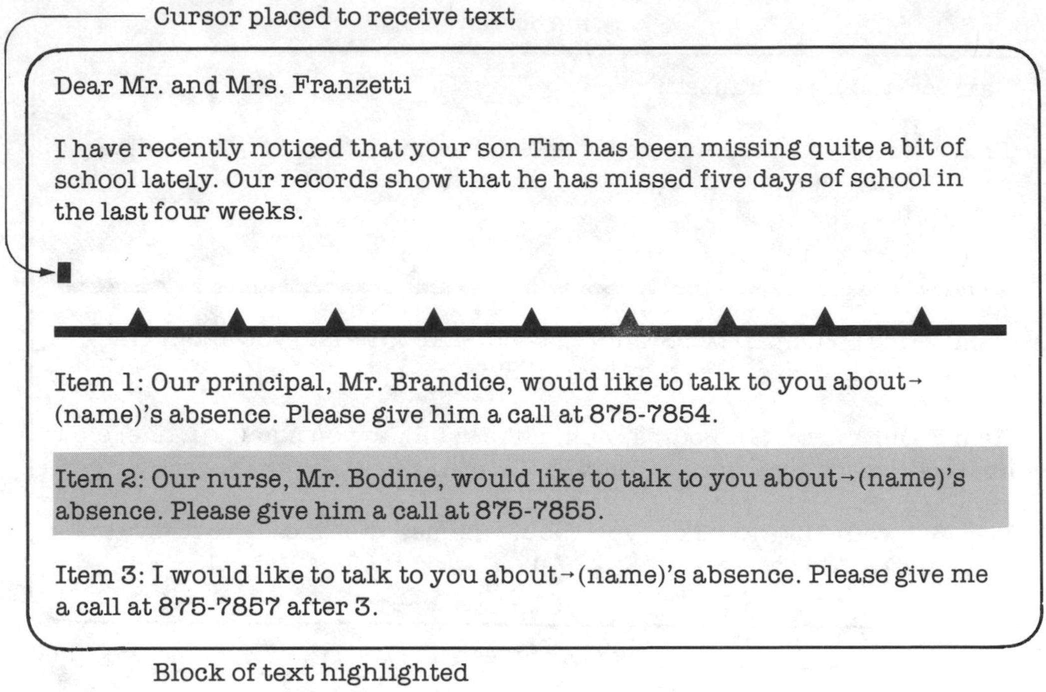

FIGURE 3.5 Indicating Where to Place a Block of Text

TABLE 3.1 Common Word Processing Functions

Item	*Function*
Delete	Removes from a document a character, word, sentence, paragraph, or page
Insert	Puts into a document a character, word, sentence, paragraph, page, or another document
Find	Locates in a document any set of characters, such as a word or number
Move	Moves the typing cursor to a new place in the document by a character, sentence, paragraph, or page at a time
Save	Stores a document to a diskette or hard disk
Retrieve	Gets a stored document from a diskette or hard disk
Rename	Gives a stored document a new name
Print	Prints the document being worked on, using a dot matrix, daisywheel, laser, or inkjet printer
Set Margins	Sets the right and left margins of a given document
Set Spacing	Sets spacing between lines of a given document

Item #2 copied into letter

Dear Mr. and Mrs. Franzetti

I have recently noticed that your son Tim has been missing quite a bit of school lately. Our records show that he has missed five days of school in the last four weeks.

Our nurse, Mr. Bodine, would like to talk to you about Tim's absence. Please give him a call at 875-7855.

Item 1: Our principal, Mr. Brandice, would like to talk to you about→(name)'s absence. Please give him a call at 875-7854.

Item 2: Our nurse, Mr. Bodine, would like to talk to you about→(name)'s absence. Please give him a call at 875-7855.

Item 3: I would like to talk to you about→(name)'s absence. Please give me a call at 875-7857 after 3.

FIGURE 3.6 After Copying (and Editing) the Block

Filing of various school reports can be facilitated with word processing. Once a given form is placed into the processor, the unique information is easy to add. If the teacher needs to complete reports on a regular basis, the word processor can store and provide the blank form ready to retrieve whenever needed.

Classroom and school newsletters are easier to produce with a word processor, too. Some specialized word processors facilitate this task by providing various newsletter formats and a set of special graphics (pictures that may be incorporated into the written material) from which selections can be made.

Perhaps the most fruitful use for a word processor is in the preparation of instructional materials. As experience with a lesson or work sheet reveals its imperfections or causes the teacher to wish it slightly altered, a modified version of the item can be swiftly produced. Uses for word processing abound (refer to Table 3.2).

Because we are focusing on teacher computer use in this chapter, we have not touched on the use of word processing by students. It is our belief, however, that this application in schools has a lot of potential. Much of education deals with reading and writing, and a word processing program is a powerful item in a teacher's toolbox.

TABLE 3.2 Illustrative Teacher Uses of Word Processing

Creating form letters into which student-specific information can be inserted
Doing mail merges that combine a list of student or parent addresses with a single form letter, creating a personalized letter automatically
Developing tests that can be easily modified, or rearranged into various forms by using block moves
Developing tests by having a file of test questions, and using block moves to select specific questions to incorporate into a test
Developing work sheets by having a file of practice problems, and using block moves to select specific problems to include
Using spelling checking to produce error-free tests, letters, handouts, and reports
Using automatic outliner to produce the outline for a workshop presentation
Using footnote generator to automatically format a graduate level paper
Using the capability of a word processor to fill out required forms, placing the words at the proper locations automatically
Keeping records of school projects or inventories, using the capability of the word processor to add columns and rows of numbers
Keeping classroom records, using the capability of sorting to select categories of information
Saving student information in files that can be sorted or merged into letters
Printing out announcements for the bulletin board using very large letters
Using large type to produce overhead transparencies
Creating an individualized work sheet for a specific student by modifying the standard work sheet and printing it while the student waits
Using a split-screen technique to translate a student form in English on the top screen to a second language on the bottom screen

TEACHER UTILITY PROGRAMS

Teacher utility programs are microcomputer programs that are specifically designed to facilitate some professional task. They do not involve students. Such programs are designed for such purposes as: (1) recording grades, (2) preparing tests, (3) judging level of reading material, (4) generating puzzles, and (5) scheduling appointments.

Sometimes a utility program facilitates a task that cannot easily be done without a microcomputer. For example, if you have a large number of students and you like to weight scores, a "grade book" program may be the very thing for you. But even though a program is available and works well, you may find that using it just makes your life more complex. For example, rather than use a test-generator program on your classroom computer, you may find it easier to write out your quiz on the night before, sitting down with a sheet of ditto master paper. Many teacher utility programs cannot be modified once you buy them, and they may not exactly fit your specific needs. For each utility you consider, you must review what the program can and cannot do for you, and decide whether it makes your life simpler or more complex.

Grade Book

There are dozens of *electronic grade book* programs on the market, with names such as "GradeBook," "ScoreKeeper," "RecordBook," and "Easy Grader." An electronic grade book mimics the function of a regular paper and pencil grade book, but generally has capabilities that far exceed the traditional method of keeping grade records (refer to Figure 3.7). A grade book utility program provides such features as: (1) organized entry of student names by class or groups, (2) easy entry of test scores or any other performance measures (letter grades), (3) the ability to print the stored information, and (4) the ability to make changes quickly. In addition, a microcomputer grade book will be able to perform miracles at the end of a grading period, such as: (1) summing up all scores, (2) weighting individual scores before summing, (3) averaging class scores, (4) assigning grades, (5) flagging students who are in trouble, and (6) dropping selected scores, such as the lowest test score, before final tabulation. There are grade books designed to facilitate individualized programs and mastery learning approaches, as well as traditional and norm-referenced scoring and grading.

With such marvelous programs, you might expect all teachers with microcomputers to use them. But, there are drawbacks. For example, many teachers feel the need to maintain a pencil and paper grade book in addition to their electronic one. This redundancy makes for twice the work. As another example, to use a paper and pencil grade book, one simply reaches into a drawer and presto, there it is. To use an electronic grade book means one must first fire up the computer and load the program. Finally, often papers are graded at places other than school, and a paper and pencil must be used to record the scores for entry at a later time into the computer.

	A	B	C	D
STUD. NAME	QUIZ 1	QUIZ 2	ATTEND.	HOMEWRK.
ABELARD, JOY	79	82	95	92
BAKER, BOB	76	96	97	90
CHUNG, LEE	67	87	91	85
ELBERT, JOYCE	98	87	89	
FINDER, MARTIN	67			

FIGURE 3.7 Sample Page from an Electronic Grade Book

So what is the advantage of an electronic grade book? For the teacher who has lots of students, likes to weight scores on tests, and has a lot of scores that require manipulation and calculations to process at grade time, the electronic grade book is valuable. Imagine, on the last day of class being able to push one key and have all your scores weighted, summed, averaged, and grades assigned! In addition, many teachers like to use the gradebook as a way of keeping students well-informed on their progress on an ongoing basis.

Test Writing Programs

A *test authoring* program is a special type of word processor. It has the structure for entering test items and answers into ready-made multiple-choice, matching, and true/false formats. After entering items, perhaps coded to performance goals and objectives, you may have the program print out a test. In some cases the test items may be used to generate practice sheets. In other cases alternative forms of the same test may be printed. In all cases addition and deletion of items is a snap.

There are only a few disadvantages to test authoring programs. For one thing, you need to enter your tests into the program, and this requires advance planning. A test writing program may require a certain number of test items for one instructional objective (in order to create alternate forms). Perhaps more importantly, a test format may be quite fixed, and you may like to write more creative test items that don't fit the program format. You need to select a test writing program with care to match the type of tests you like to write.

Many schools use a test writing program to develop and produce larger grade-level tests. A number of teachers, perhaps all at the seventh grade level, may cooperate to develop an end-of-unit test. Everyone supplies questions related to the unit's objectives, and then the test authoring program is used to generate alternative forms of the test, each teacher receiving a different test, with all the tests being parallel.

Text Analysis Programs

A very common problem with textbooks is that they are written at levels that are too high. Although a text may be sold as a fourth grade text, the reading level in many sections may be one or two grades higher. Students would be likely to benefit if their teacher only knew which sections of the text were more difficult. Prior to the advent of the classroom microcomputer, checking the reading level of a text was laborious. There are now available a number of text analysis programs that include aspects such as checking the reading level of text.

Text analysis programs are designed to accept a typed-in passage, and then to identify designated features (such as grammatical constructions) or determine standard indices (such as reading level coefficients) pertaining to the passage. These programs are easy to use and very accurate. To check on the reading level of a book, you simply type in random passages of a few hundred words from it, and then ask the program to analyze the passage. It will yield the results quickly. With such a program, you could check newspaper and magazine articles, trade books, or other resources that you might wish to evaluate for appropriateness to target students.

Puzzle Generators

Many teachers use puzzles to interest students in the learning of bodies of words, such as for a French lesson or an exercise in learning map terminology. A *puzzle generator* program allows a teacher to enter a set of words and the format for a crossword puzzle, and have the computer figure out how to best fit them into the puzzle.

Puzzle generators do have some problems. The number of words used must be kept fairly low or the computer will have difficulty finding places for all of them. Then, too, the final crossword puzzle may not look exactly as well done as the ones you would see in a newspaper. Still, many teachers find the resulting puzzlers do interest students. The puzzle generator programs enable these teachers to present study vocabulary without the time or bother of constructing the crosswords by hand.

Appointment Book

If you have a busy schedule and would like a reminder each morning of what the day holds in store, an *appointment book* program might prove useful. A computer appointment book allows you, at any point in time, to enter dates and events into an electronic calendar. The program then watches the date and your schedule, and when you start using the computer for the day, it will remind you of your appointments for that date.

Most appointment book programs also allow you to write notes to yourself about the event. And of course, you can enter reminders about events before they happen, so that one week before Valentine's Day your computer will remind you to get a card.

Appointment book programs are of little value if you don't turn on your computer at the start of the day, or at least on a regular basis. In general, this type of program serves best the individual who starts off the day by turning on the computer, seeing what appointments are on for that day, and entering new ones for the future.

SUMMARY AND REVIEW CHECKLIST

In this chapter we have examined the various technical capabilities a typical microcomputer provides and have provided clues to its power and to its popularity with educators. More specifically, we have examined the computer's appropriateness as a classroom aide, particularly to the teacher who uses it as a tool to accomplish typical teaching-related tasks, rather than for directly teaching or managing students. We mentioned a number of different types of programs available to help teachers with such tasks.

Of the general purpose tools, we have given word processing the emphasis since it has by far the widest range of uses. The teacher utilities are much more specific in the tasks they perform, and each teacher will need to decide whether a given utility would be a classroom helper, or would make life more complex. Of course, we have not exhausted all the utilities that exist for teachers, but if you keep an eye open for new programs as you are reading computer and professional journals, you will probably spot some that interest you that you will want to review.

Checklist

[ ] I can list six major technical capabilities of a microcomputer and describe how each relates to the computer's potential for classroom use.

[ ] I am able to describe several examples of the typical classroom computer's technical capabilities, with and without attachments.

[ ] I can characterize the major "teacher's helper" roles that a classroom computer could play.

[ ] I can describe five features of a computer program that tend to make it most useful to a prospective user.

[ ] I can identify two main categories of computer programs that assist a teacher in performing teaching-related tasks.

[ ] I can name and describe in general what a word processor does and some of the things a teacher can use it for.

[ ] I can describe four teacher utility programs and some of their advantages and drawbacks.

SUGGESTED ACTIVITIES

1. Choose a word processing program designed for lower elementary grades. Place the diskette in the drive and start your computer. Follow these steps to get acquainted with the program. Feel free to play with the word processing program as you go along!

a. Type enough text to see what happens on the screen. Specifically, watch what happens when you reach the right side of a screen and keep on typing, when you hit the <RETURN> or (<ENTER>) key between paragraphs, and when you reach the bottom of the screen. If you don't type well, simply hit miscellaneous letters and spaces to fill the screen with characters and words, and type beyond the screen's allotted space.

b. Try these functions: (1) use arrow keys to move the cursor around on the screen, (2) use a delete key to see what it does, (3) use a backspace key (if there is one) to see what it does, (4) purposely delete (erase) a letter, and then a whole word, (5) try to insert (add) a word between two existing words (if your machine is in typeover mode, it will type over instead of insert), (6) move the cursor to the start of the document, (7) move the cursor to the end of your document, and (8) delete and/or insert (or type over if machine is in that mode) characters and words of your choice.

c. As you gain control over the above simple actions, you are beginning to actually learn the program. If you are interested in continuing on to learn the more powerful functions—learning to save what you type onto diskette, moving text around and exploiting the program's significant features, retrieving what you type from diskette, etc.—there are a number of pathways you can follow. These include using a self-instructional tutorial program that accompanies a word processing package, attending classes offered by colleges and business schools, or just getting started on the do-it-yourself pathway that many teachers before you have used—using the manual for the program. Whether you can type or not, mastering some functions in a word processing program will give you a feeling for the computer's capabilities. Using such a program is also a good way for you to become familiar with a computer and begin to see how you might get it to apply its capabilities to your purposes.

Extension. If you enjoy and experience great success in the word processing actions above, you may wish to experiment further with the following activities. You will find the directions on how to do these things in one or more of three places. First, directions may appear on your screen by using a <HELP> key. Second, you may be able to move to a *"menu"* page, where the functions will be listed. Third, there will be a user's guide telling how to make the word processor work. You can check off each action that you accomplish.

1. Work with these functions when available:
   [ ] delete text in a block, [ ] move text as a block, [ ] use both text modes (insert vs. typeover), [ ] quick cursor move to start of document, [ ] quick cursor move to end of document.
2. Use your word processor to name and save on the diskette whatever document you have typed. Then erase the document on the screen. Is it gone? Retrieve the original document. Work to master: [ ] save a document, [ ] retrieve a document, [ ] clear screen.

3. Master the above, and you are ready for printing. It requires that you have a printer ready to go. Check that the printer has paper and ribbon properly aligned and is turned on. Use your program's print function to produce a paper copy. To do this you may need to set margins or line spacing. Resort to the user's guide when necessary. If you succeed, check off: [ ] print.
4. Accomplishing 2 and 3 means that you could make good use of the word processor to create a form letter and then individualize it for special students. Start a new document and write a brief note for parents advising them of current class events. Save this document. Then, bring back the form letter and individualize it for one student by adding a brief note about how well that student is doing in class. Save this document under the student's name. Bring back the form letter and create a second student note. Save it too.

2. If you find your typing skills need improvement, get a keyboarding (typing) program to help you upgrade your skills. There are some excellent typing tutor programs.

3. Choose one or more of the following utilities, and follow the steps for reviewing how they work:

grade book
test writing program
text analysis program
puzzle generator
appointment book

Step 1. Read the introduction to the user's guide to the program. (Scan further as necessary.)
Step 2. Put the diskette into the computer and run the program.
Step 3. Play with the program until you are familiar with its operation.

Extension. If interested, master the operation of the program.

4. Use and review selected items of software from the following "Worth A Look: Software."

WORTH A LOOK: SOFTWARE

Word Processing and Language Processing

WordPerfect. WordPerfect Corporation; most computers. For grades 9 through adult. This *almost* perfect word processor is powerful yet easy-to-use. It includes a speller, a thesaurus, math functions, and all the other functions found in a professional-level word processor. Liberal discount available on purchase for educators and students.

Bank Street Writer III. Scholastic; Apple II family and IBM/MS-DOS computers. Applicable from first word processing efforts through grade 12, this word processor has been long recognized as a school writing tool. It includes some teacher tools and management features, as well as a spelling checker and a thesaurus.

Bank Street Writer (Broderbund Version). Broderbund; Apple II family and IBM/MS-DOS computers. Useful from first word processing efforts and up, this word processor includes an on-disk tutorial that helps in learning the program.

Magic Slate. Sunburst; Apple II family computers. A word processing program that offers varied formats (20-column, 40-column, and 80-column) and features that change as students gain proficiency. Applicable to grade level of earliest word processing efforts and up.

Writer's Helper. CONDUIT; Apple II family and IBM/MS-DOS computers. This aid-to-writing program checks reading levels, has a readability index, does word counts, and has other useful features for evaluating text. It works with any word processor that can accept standard text files (such as WordPerfect and Bank Street Writer III).

Fun Features

Reader Rabbit (Talking Version). The Learning Company; Apple II GS and Tandy 1000 computers. Recorded human voice pronounces words for animated games and provides children aged four through seven with practice in letter and word recognition.

Stickybear Town Builder. Weekly Reader Software; Apple II family and Commodore computers. This simulation introduces map reading skills to students in grades 1 through 4. The users build towns, take trips, and hunt for missing keys. They practice map reading and use a compass and directional clues to locate mystery keys hidden in town.

The Music Studio. Activision, Inc.; Apple IIGS computer. Allows users from intermediate grades to adult to compose, play back, and print out music, even with lyrics. Beginners can play around in a music "paint box."

Music Construction Set. Electronic Arts; Apple II family, Atari, and Commodore computers. This is an interactive music learning set for ages six and up. Good use of computer sound.

Deluxe Music Construction Set. Electronic Arts; Macintosh and Amiga computers. Designed for grade 5 and up, the program lets students listen to music of their own creation and produces sheet music as well.

Picture Perfect. MindPlay; Apple II family, IBM/MS-DOS computers. This program, for ages four and up, lets students illustrate the stories they create. Program provides library of graphics and means for limited text production.

Muppet Slate. Sunburst; Apple II family computers. Designed for use with the Muppet Learning Keys (alternative keyboard), this program lets children in grades K–2 produce and illustrate simple stories using a built-in library combined with word processing features.

Create with Garfield! DLM Teaching Resources; Apple II family and Commodore computers. With this program, students from grade 3 and up can design and create cartoons, labels, and posters. By sequencing cartoons creatively, one can produce an interesting "slide show" to accompany a presentation or story.

Deluxe Paint II. Electronic Arts; Apple II family, Commodore Amiga, and IBM/MS-DOS computers. Students in grade 4 and up can create graphic designs using paint, text, and magnification features.

Fantavision. Broderbund; Apple II family, Amiga, IBM/MS-DOS computers. Program teaches animation techniques. The computer fills in between frames drawn by the student so that images appear to be in motion when shown in rapid sequence.

816/Paint (school edition). Baudville; Apple II family computers. An icon menu makes this graphics and art program easy to use.

Paintworks Gold. Mediagenic; Apple II GS computers. A paint program with lots of features such as rotation of objects in fine increments and gradient color blending.

Chess. Odesta; Apple II family, Atari, Commodore, IBM/MS-DOS computers. The computer at its logical best. If you have any doubts about the computer's ability to "think" about problems, chess programs should put your mind at ease.

Teacher Tools

Classmate. Davidson and Associates, Inc.; Apple II family and IBM/MS-DOS computers. A program that records grades, attendance, and comments; computes final grades on total points or weights; graphs distribution curves; and prints reports.

Teacher's Quiz Designer. IBM; IBM/MS-DOS computers. Allows teachers to design, print, and/or give multiple choice tests on the computer. The program includes record keeping and a number of options, including maintaining a database of questions.

Crossword Magic. Mindscape; Apple II family, Atari, Commodore, and IBM/MS-DOS computers. Generates crossword puzzles from teacher's or student's words. Puzzle can be played on screen or printed and duplicated for student desk work.

Certificate Maker. Springboard; Apple II family, Atari, Commodore, IBM/MS-DOS, and Macintosh computers. A library of predesigned certificates, awards, licenses, diplomas, and so on that can be personalized and customized.

Report Card. Sensible Software; Apple II family and IBM/MS-DOS computers. A management system for use by teachers at any level. Program allows weighting factors for calculating grades and also the printing of a varied assortment of reports useful in monitoring students' progress.

Calendar Crafter. MECC; Apple II GS computers. User can design calendar pages for a day, a week, a month, or a year. Package has prepared categories of events, different languages, and more.

Partner 64. Timeworks; Commodore computers. Several handy accessories: calendar/date book, memo pad, phone list and dialer, calculator, typewriter, label maker.

Keyboarding/Typing Instruction

Mavis Beacon Teaches Typing! The Software Toolworks; IBM/MS-DOS computers. A program that uses artificial intelligence and very good graphics to produce an outstanding keyboarding program for adults.

Success with Typing (see Chapter 2 software). Though intended for grade levels 5 through 12, this program can be used by adults, too.

Type! Broderbund; Apple II family, IBM/MS-DOS, and Macintosh computers. Typing instruction for beginning, intermediate or advanced typists, grades 5 through 12. Makes recommendations of exercises based on diagnosis of speed and accuracy.

READINGS

Adams, R. C. "Why I Moved My Micro to the Teacher's Desk." *Instructor*, January 1985, 56–58, 62.

Bork, A. *Learning with Personal Computers.* New York: Harper and Row, 1987.

Bullock, D. W. "Word Processing for Teachers: Professional Results." *The Computing Teacher* 16(8): 9–11 (May 1989).

Daiute, C. "Computers and the Teaching of Writing." In *The Intelligent Schoolhouse: Readings on Computers and Learning*, edited by D. Peterson. Reston, VA: Reston Publishing Co., Inc., 1984.

Feldstein, S. "Technology for Teaching." *Music Educators Journal* 74(7): 33–37 (March 1988).

Freiberger, P. "The Videodisc Connection." *Popular Computing*, September 1984, 64–71.

Futrell, M. K. "Hardware Technology in Bionic Perspective." *Educational Technology* 22(11): 1982.

Futrell, M., and Geisert, P. "Wielding the Wand: Electronic Information for the Individual." In *Humanizing the Computer*, edited by D. Flaherty. Belmont, CA: Wadsworth Publishing, 1986.

Lodish, E. "Test Writing Made Simple: Generate Tests and Worksheets Electronically." *Electronic Learning* 5(5): 28, 30, 68 (February 1986).

National School Boards Association. *The Electronic School: Innovative Uses of Technology in Education.* Alexandria, VA: Institute for the Transfer of Technology to Education, 1987.

Office of Technology Assessment. *Power ON! New Tools for Teaching and Learning.* Washington, DC: U.S. Government Printing Office, 1988.

Olds, H. J. "Teachers vs. Students: In Whose Hands Should We Put the Computers?" *Classroom Computer Learning* 9(7): 32–42 (April 1989).

O'Malley, C. "Going Beyond Word Processing." *Personal Computing*, December 1985, 113–115, 117, 119, 121.

Riedl, R. "Computer Communications Potentials for Library Media Centers: An Introduction." *School Library Media Activities Monthly* 3(3): 28–31 (November 1986).

REFERENCES

Microsoft Corporation. *Writer's Bookshelf* (CD-ROM). Redmond, WA: Microsoft Corporation, 1988.

National Geographic. *National Geographic Documentaries* (CD-ROM). Washington, DC: National Geographic, 1987.

—4—

Promoting Learning at the Keyboard

OBJECTIVES

- Define computer-assisted instruction and identify common types of computer programs that produce student learning in a classroom setting.
- List and describe functions the microcomputer can and cannot perform in an instructional role and specify factors that relate to the appropriateness of using a microcomputer for an instructional task.
- Explain the value of performance objectives in microcomputer lessons.
- Describe the tasks of a computer program that provides drill and practice.
- Describe the structure of a typical drill pattern and identify elements to look for in a quality drill and practice program.
- Describe the design features of a computer tutorial lesson that make it effective in promoting the student learning it is supposed to produce.
- Describe the features of a computer simulation that make it of instructional interest.

INTRODUCTION

In this chapter we begin our discussion of the use of microcomputers specifically to help students learn. As a teacher, promoting learning is your primary professional responsibility. There is a broad diversity of computer programs available to assist you in this role.

With computers, you can foster learning in different ways and to different extents. For example, some programs serve a tutorial function. They are usually designed around specific content, and you can use such programs to promote substantial new learning in your students. Other types of programs are useful for assisting students in reviewing and refreshing previous learning, and still others feature strategies to enhance or fine-tune learner skills. Numerous programs serve more as tools you can have students make use of in a teacher-directed learning situation.

Programs specifically designed to help students to learn are called *computer-assisted instruction* (CAI) software. Other terms, such as computer-assisted learning (CAL) or computer-based learning (CBL) may also be applied to such programs. They have as their raison d'etre the promotion of student learning.

In order to create a framework of understanding of how the microcomputer can be used to promote learning, we will first present some ideas about teaching and learning—in general, and with computers—and then expand those ideas via a spectrum of CAI programs.

GOALS

- How do microcomputers promote student learning?
- What are some of the types of learning that microcomputers are successful at promoting?
- What types of computer programs foster student learning?

MERITS OF MICROCOMPUTER-BASED INSTRUCTION

When you use computers to teach your students, can you be sure the time and effort it takes will be well spent? The research is rather clear on the question of students learning with computers.

A meta-analysis of the major research on the topic draws five major conclusions (Kulik, 1983; Kulik et al., 1983, 1985; Kulik and Kulik, 1986, 1987a). First, computer-based instruction has been effective in improving student achievement at all levels of schooling. Second, computer-based instruction has been most effective in improving student achievement at the elementary level, followed by secondary, and then college level. Third, it has had positive effects on student attitudes toward subject matter, toward instruction, and toward computer technology. Fourth, computer-based instruction has yielded substantial savings in instructional time. And fifth, the research findings are very robust, emerging consistently in study after study in spite of methodological differences and differences in the setting of the studies.

These conclusions are important to the teacher. Computers *can* promote learning ("teach"!). For example, at the elementary level the average effect in twenty-eight studies of computer-assisted instruction was an increase in pupil achievement scores from the 50th to the 68th percentile. That is to say, the average student using traditional study methods would have been at the 68th percentile, had that student utilized computer-assisted instruction to reach the same goal.

From the standpoint of current information, choosing to use computers with your students appears likely to be an instructionally wise decision.

DEFINING THE TEACHING TASK

When you use CAI programs with students, you are, in effect, turning over portions of your teaching role to computers. If you know precisely what portion of the teaching role you want a computer to do, you can then readily check to see how well it actually accomplishes whatever teaching job you assign it. Being able to identify and clearly state your teaching intent is a valuable first step toward effectively using a computer to teach.

Using Objectives to Describe Teaching Aims

Educational goals are broad statements of educational intent. Specific statements of educational intent, voiced in terms of student performance, are called objectives, or *performance objectives.*

The characteristics of performance objectives have been widely discussed and their strengths and weaknesses well documented (Futrell and Geisert, 1984; Gagne and Briggs, 1979). They are used to clarify what *learning outcome* (behavioral performance change) one seeks to produce and to help to guide the planning of instructional strategy. Since a computer can interact with a student only by way of the student's behavioral performance, performance objectives are a requisite aspect of computer-based teaching.

Objectives are written in different formats. One easy-to-remember format uses the acronym ABCD. The four main elements of an ABCD performance objective are:

1. The *A*udience that is targeted for learning,
2. The *B*ehavioral action of the student,

3. The *C*onditions under which the learner will demonstrate the behavioral action, and
4. The *D*egree of acceptable student performance.

The following is an example of a performance objective in the area of mathematics instruction:

> **PERFORMANCE OBJECTIVE:** When a fourth grade student (audience) is presented with a proportion word problem utilizing the integers from one to nine (conditions), the student will write a fraction that represents the proportion (behavioral action), getting at least nine of ten problems presented correct (the degree of performance acceptable).

Performance objectives are mandatory because they provide a clear picture of the desired result of any teaching effort. It doesn't matter who does the teaching—the teacher, the computer, or the two in combination. By using performance objectives, a teacher can state with certainty just what learning she or he hopes to promote. Then the teacher can decide how to go about it (and whether or not the computer can handle any of the job).

Kinds of Learning

Learning to spell is not the same kind of learning as comprehending a reading passage. Robert Gagne (1977), a well-regarded learning theorist, has studied various learning patterns and has developed a relatively simple and yet comprehensive way to distinguish among various forms of learning. Gagne states that learning can be classified into five major categories: (1) attitudes, (2) motor skills, (3) cognitive strategies, (4) verbal information, and (5) intellectual skills. For each category we will provide a brief description and an example performance objective for learning within the category, and then we will relate the learning to tasks the computer can perform to support the learning. In the interest of brevity, subsequent objectives we describe will omit reference to the intended audience.

Attitudes

Attitudes and feelings toward some aspects of life can be and are taught in school. Music appreciation, for example, attempts to go beyond teaching the means for interpreting what is heard and tries to instill in a student a behavioral pattern of listening to and enjoying music, certainly an affective objective. In health and physical education classes, instruction often is geared toward instilling attitudes that will translate into appropriate behavioral practices in personal hygiene or sportsmanlike behavior on a playing field.

Here is an example of a performance objective in reading that stipulates the educational intent of increasing a student's desire to read.

> **PERFORMANCE OBJECTIVE:** Given the option of playing a game or reading interactive fiction on the computer during preferred activity time, the student will choose to read at least 80% of the time.

Research has demonstrated that a positive attitude toward subject matter and toward computers can be generated by having students learn something on a computer (Kulik et al., 1983; Kulik and Kulik, 1986, 1987a, 1987b). In general, though, there are few if any microcomputer programs designed to promote the learning of attitudes directly.

Motor Skills

When an individual learns to skate, ride a bicycle, leap for rebounds in basketball, or type on a keyboard, the person is learning to change a behavior pattern to master behavior involving muscles and body movements. The sample objective below is from a high school computer literacy program:

> **PERFORMANCE OBJECTIVE:** Given a computer with a mouse and graphics program, the student will produce a diagram having a sweeping arc of speckles that increase and decrease in density but do not reach the edges of the screen.

Teaching the above objective would involve demonstration of proper movement technique and coaching of the learner's practice. Computer teaching endeavors for motor skills are restricted to a fairly narrow range of promoting new muscular activities, such as in keyboarding.

Cognitive Strategies

How do students learn to solve word problems in math? What is a good general approach to deciphering word meaning from context? These questions involve the concept of "how to think about problems." The term "cognitive strategies" refers to the thinking approaches that govern an individual's learning, remembering, and thinking behaviors. Enhancing such approaches is a desirable end of education. Consider the cognitive strategy objective below:

> **PERFORMANCE OBJECTIVE:** Given a problem concerning air pollution, the student will originate two different approaches to solving the problem, communicating adequately the components of the two strategies.

There is a growing interest in this area of instruction, which has been long neglected in education. Most everyone realizes that *learning how to learn* is very important to academic success, but little systematic training for the set of skills called cognitive strategies takes place in schools.

Computers have been used in a number of recent educational endeavors aimed at teaching students how to think, and how to think about thinking. Most recently, greatest interest in this worthwhile, but often neglected, area has centered around programs of the types we will examine in Chapter 5. Another computer area that focuses on cognitive strategies is the teaching of Logo, a programming language that will receive attention in Chapter 11.

Verbal Information

All students learn great amounts of verbal information in school. Kindergarten students learn their names and addresses, the days of the week, and the names of letters and numbers. High school and college students learn such things as the names of the parts of a cell and the important nineteenth century poets. Here is an objective representing the type of information a teacher might seek to impart in elementary science:

> **PERFORMANCE OBJECTIVE:** From memory, a student recites the names of all the planets in the solar system in sequence (from the sun), with no more than one omission or reversal.

In addition to learning simple verbal information, such as word associations and names, as students progress in their studies they store in their memories more complex and highly organized verbal information, such as the forms of government, major experiments in physics, and how an economy works. Often such information is not stored verbatim for instant recall, but the gist of the information can be recalled when the occasion demands.

Microcomputers are used extensively in having students learn verbal information. Certainly the simpler forms of this type of learning are easy to measure by having students type or choose words to demonstrate they know the meaning of a term, or have memorized a poem, passage, or list.

Intellectual Skills

Having an intellectual skill means knowing how to do something and being able to demonstrate the action, like how to subtract three-digit numbers, or how to identify a musical pattern from its beat, or how to analyze a chemical formula to determine how many carbon atoms are present in a molecule. Here is an example of an objective related to the learning of an intellectual skill.

> **PERFORMANCE OBJECTIVE:** Given outline drawings on the computer screen of plants typically found in a forest, the student will correctly identify the plant as a tree, shrub, grass, or fungus, with 80% accuracy on ten items.

Many programs available for the microcomputer in the classroom are involved with attempting to teach intellectual skills. Such programs will have titles such as: "Learning How to Capitalize Words," "Multiplying by Zero," "Identifying Topic Sentences in Paragraphs," "Word Finder," and "The Periodic Table of Elements."

Table 4.1 provides a listing of a computer's typical involvement with each of the learning categories.

COMPUTER AS TEACHER

We pointed out earlier that using CAI programs means turning over some aspects of teaching to the computer. It's important for you to adequately understand your teaching partner before you look to it to do any teaching. This means knowing how a computer, though powerful in some ways, is limited by its own nature.

TABLE 4.1 Five Categories of Learning

Kind of learning	*"The student will" (behavioral action)*	*Computer's teaching involvement*
Attitudes	choose something to do	Indirect, rather than direct. For example, a math game drill and practice program tries to make practice enjoyable and something the student would choose to do.
Motor skills	move fingers, body parts	Limited; examples are students learning to use the keyboard and possible teacher use with handicapped children to teach special motor skills.
Cognitive strategies	efficiently or incisively do one of the other categories of learning	Potential for use in creative problem solving, such as creating programs in Logo, or inventing a design or work of art or music, or devising a plan for searching a data base.
Verbal information learning	state, describe, list, name	Very heavily used; drill and practice, and tutorials.
Intellectual skills (five major subcategories)	discriminate, identify, classify, demonstrate, generate	Can do well in tutorials, drill and practices, simulations, and problem-solving programs.

How Computers Make Judgments

As a teacher, you carry into the classroom the ability to make intuitive judgments about students' attention or mood and about how well a given lesson is progressing. Whereas a teacher can act on feelings and concerns about students well beyond the bounds of the actual instructional time and setting, computers can only deal with what a student does while seated at the keyboard. They can respond only to the student's behavior in the forms of key presses or actions with a light pen, joy stick, mouse, or other input device.

To make decisions about whether or not the student needs to learn a performance objective, or how well a student is progressing in a lesson, or when the student no longer needs instruction, the computer must use the information it gets from the student's actual interactions with the computer.

When a Computer "Teaches"

If a student walks up to a computer, sits down, and starts up an instructional computer program, then the computer can begin to make decisions. For example, by giving a short test, the computer can find out whether or not any teaching needs to be done.

A computer judges learner performance and progress solely on the basis of a student's actual interactions with the computer.

Suppose a CAI program entitled *Interpreting Graphs* has the following objective as its teaching task:

> **PERFORMANCE OBJECTIVE:** Given a labeled line graph displaying any of five data relationships and a set of generalizations, the student can select the sentence that properly generalizes the data presented, getting 90% of the data relationships presented correct.

By presenting a few instances of data displayed on graphs, the computer program may gather evidence that the student cannot make sense of the data and needs instruction, or (if she meets the performance standards of the objective) that the student needs no instruction. Its diagnosis would be based on the selections made by the student.

From this example, you can see that a computer program would determine a student's learning from movement in student behavior toward the desired performance level. If a student goes to the computer not meeting the performance objective, but works with the computer for a while and gets closer to the performance objective's standards (for selecting generalizations when presented practice graphs to interpret), this change would represent progress, which the computer could recognize by sampling the student's performance during the lesson. If, after forty minutes, our student walks away from the computer being able to identify valid generalizations when shown graphs of the types earlier presented, the student would have demonstrated achievement of the performance objective.

Having viewed the situation, a teacher would very probably say: "The computer taught the student to interpret graphs."

Microcomputer-based Learning and Performance Objectives

When you put a student in front of a computer to learn, you need a means to ascertain behavioral change, since, rather than promoting intended learning, a computer lesson might just as easily produce unanticipated outcomes or simply occupy students' time. A microcomputer truly teaches for you only when it changes student behavior as you intend . . . that is, when it moves a learner's behavior toward a known performance goal. To put the concept more bluntly, if you put a student on a microcomputer to do a lesson, and after the lesson you do not know how his or her behavior has changed, then you really do not know what, if anything, the computer has taught (or the student has learned).

A performance objective can serve as a focal point for communication between a teacher and the computer on the topic of student learning. For example, the performance objective of the graphing lesson we described earlier could be quite useful to a teacher. For one thing, it would make the program's teaching intent quite clear, so one could decide whether or not to use the program in a given curriculum or with any given student. Second, because it would communicate the targeted learning outcome very precisely, its presence would better enable one to ascertain the extent to which the program actually achieves its stated intent when engaging students with the lesson. A computer lesson that states its objective(s) in performance terms and measures movement toward the targeted behavior(s) is far more likely to really teach than is a lesson that fails to communicate its intent or to offer any means for assessing behavioral change.

DRILL AND PRACTICE: FRIEND OR FOE

In the past, drill and practice on computers developed a bad name. Critics of these programs claimed that the learning they produced was trivial and boring, that they taught students that the computer was just another uninteresting aspect of the classroom, and that they merely allowed the students to look busy. In many cases, the critics of drill and practice were right.

Many (if not most) of the early educational programs produced for microcomputer use were trivial and badly done. Some of them were programmed by non-educators and were pedagogically unsound, and the programs developed by teachers for use in their own classrooms were usually quite primitive. Increased commercialization of the educational microcomputer field brought a number of these inferior programs to the market; some are still being sold. As educators gain better understanding of what a good drill and practice program should do, the software situation will improve.

Drill: Its Purpose and Pattern

It is important for a teacher to recognize that drill and practice software does not instruct the learner in a new behavior. Rather, drill programs are useful for sustaining, refining, or perfecting performance in some category of behavior already learned by another method. Usually, drill and practice is employed to increase the speed or accuracy of student performance of certain tasks. Since the student's behavioral performance does change with practice, it is important to remember that the software does indeed promote real learning.

In computer drill and practice, the usual job of the computer is repetitive and follows a pattern (refer to Figure 4.1). The routine is commonly quite simple: (1) the computer presents to the student a question, problem, or situation that corresponds to the target category of behavior, and (2) it requires the student to make a response that is then evaluated for adequacy. For example, suppose a program is to drill a multiplication behavior (multiplying two 2-digit numbers). The computer presents the math problem "24 × 17." The student types in an answer, either by choosing the correct answer from a multiple choice format, or by typing in an answer. The computer evaluates the answer, and provides immediate feedback on the correctness (or quality) of the response. If the answer is wrong (or inadequate), the student can try again. If right, the student is presented with another problem.

The speed with which a computer can provide the knowledge of results for each practice item is something that a teacher, using paper/pencil exercises, cannot match. In addition, computer graphics can, if used appropriately, enhance a drill (refer to Figure 4.2).

Note that the computer does not teach the student how to multiply the number or how to name a fraction in the examples presented here. If it did that, it would be a tutorial type activity. These drill and practice programs help students to perfect actions that they already know how to execute. Through the practice, they learn to reach higher degrees or levels of behavioral performance.

Reasons for Using Drill and Practice Software

Since the purpose of drill and practice is not to teach new material, what then is its value? There are at least three ways a teacher can make very profitable use of this software in a curriculum: (1) to maintain a performance level previously reached by a student, (2) to automatize skills already demonstrated by the student, and (3) to remind the student of some information or skill that is prerequisite to a new lesson.

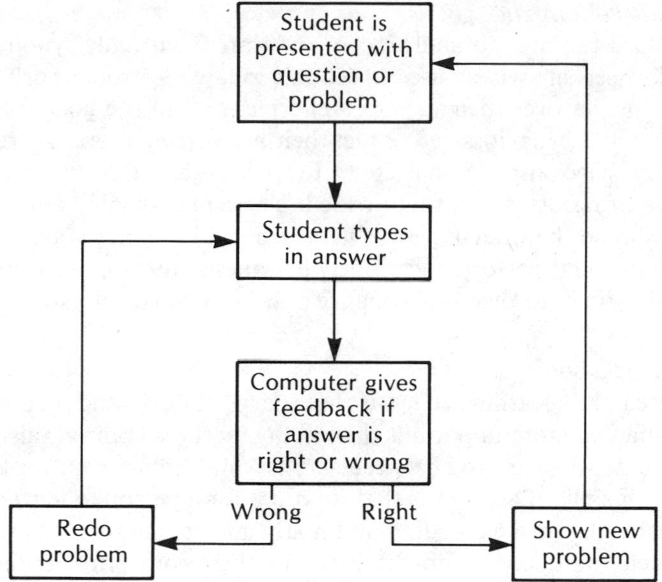

FIGURE 4.1 Simple Drill and Practice Pattern

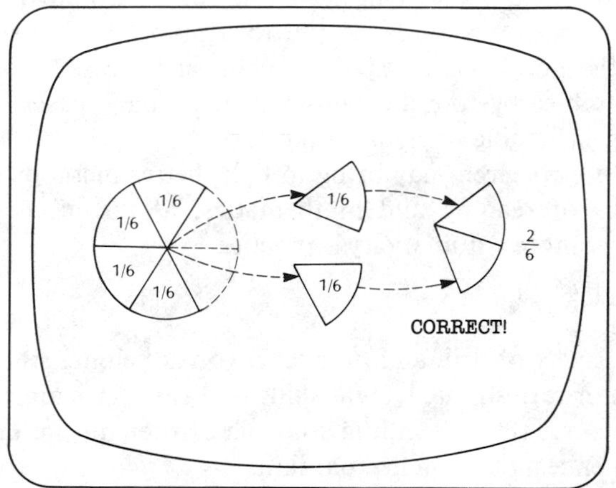

FIGURE 4.2 Graphic Enhancement of Feedback for a Correct Response

Maintaining Performance Levels

One standard use of drill and practice software is virtually synonymous with how work sheets are widely used in schools today. Electronic work sheets have some advantages over their paper counterparts when the goal is helping students to practice behaviors and not let their performance level get rusty on materials they have already mastered. Responses are quickly evaluated and knowledge of results promptly provided. There may or may not be corrective feedback should the student get the item wrong, and scores may or may not be kept on individual performance, but when these latter options are available, they help in efforts to keep performance polished or to reach established levels.

Automatizing a Behavior

Recent research in learning suggests that the role of drill and practice in school learning may be more important than many teachers realize (Salsbury, 1984). Drill and practice seems to be a necessary learning component for the automatizing of sub-skills. This view is that, in order for a person to perform complex intellectual tasks such as reading and mathematics, many of the sub-skills involved need to become automatized. In other words, to do the task successfully, the learner must be able to perform certain sub-tasks without consciously thinking about them.

It has been shown that in reading, speedy and efficient word recognition and word understanding is critical in order to allow the reader to concentrate on such things as concepts and themes. Also it has been known that typing skills improve in direct correspondence (up to a point) with the amount of practice. And in the good old days, the repetition process associated with learning the times tables by rote did automatize (in many cases for life) the capability of saying each table without thinking.

Although future research may bring to light better methods of automatizing the sub-skills of reading and mathematics, at the moment the best method known to promote automaticity is practice.

Review

A third important aspect of drill and practice involves helping students review verbal information or refresh intellectual skills that they have already learned. Gagne (1977) points out that reminding students of prerequisite knowledge is an essential step when teaching intellectual skills.

Using Drill and Practice Software: An Example

Suppose you have the task of automatizing the addition of the numbers from one to nine. Here is your performance objective:

> **PERFORMANCE OBJECTIVE:** Given ten addition problems of any two numbers between one and nine, the student will add the numbers, typing in all answers within 25 seconds and with 100% accuracy.

What you really desire here is that students can do their additions quickly and automatically—a job of skill refinement and one that clearly calls for drill and practice in a form computers can do well. Before aiming for the automaticity level, you really would want the addition behavior itself to be at a satisfactory level of accuracy. In fact, to get students to a point where computer drill and practice of this behavior would really be helpful, you would need to have taught a number of prerequisites, including: (1) the concept of a number, (2) the concept of addition, and (3) the action itself: specifically how to add the numbers from one to nine to each other. Once students have reached a satisfactory accuracy level, you can begin to employ drill and practice software to help students maintain and enhance the performance level reached.

As a general rule, whatever the skill of interest, students need adequate instruction to learn to perform a skill correctly, no matter how slowly, before automatization efforts begin. Only when you are certain they can consistently perform a skill correctly should you engage a computer in speeding the process up to the point where it becomes automatic. With an appropriate practice program, students can review the skill periodically to sustain their accuracy and can perhaps continue to enhance, to some degree, their speed.

What a Good Drill and Practice Lesson Should Be

How can you avoid purchasing some of the computer drill programs available on the commercial educational market that are poorly designed or don't do what they claim to do? The best way is to know clearly what a good drill and practice lesson on a computer should be like. At minimum, it should have a clear statement of purpose (included in a user's guide), so that you can readily decide whether or not to employ the program in the curriculum. In addition, it should be systematically structured, so that you can depend on it to promote the review and/or automatizing of the learning stated in the purpose.

Clear Educational Intent

A quality drill and practice will make clear the category (or categories) of behaviors that it is designed to promote. It is to the teacher's advantage if the program can be manipulated, so that the teacher can select from among available categories of behavior or adjust other program variables, such as timing of feedback or pacing of presentation. For example, a multiplication program might be set just at the sevens, or inclusive of one to seven as the teacher chooses. At the least, however, the program should state its specific intent in writing for the teacher to read.

In a high quality program, you will be able to locate a performance objective for each targeted behavior (there may be several in the program package). Such a program will be labeled as to the type and age range of student for whom it has been shown to work best (highly effective programs are tested with target learners).

Though you would usually find performance objectives for computer drill and practice in the guide, sometimes they are instead within the student program itself, since an effective teaching technique for use with an older student is to present the performance objective that the student is to work toward demonstrating.

Systematic Structure

Typically the developers of drill and practice programs do not pay attention to what research has demonstrated. Whether their goal is teaching verbal information or motor skills, or enhancing an intellectual skill, it is clear that CAI programs should be structured around four major concepts that have been extensively studied by psychologists (Salsbury, 1984). These four concepts are: (1) interference, (2) spaced practice, (3) spaced review, and (4) the capacity of short-term memory.

Interference is the concept that previously learned information can interfere with the learning of new information. Information presented in drill and practice sessions should not interfere with previously learned information. The designer of a quality computer drill takes into consideration the body of knowledge the student brings to the lesson, and identifies aspects of the lesson that may cause learning interference. In the development of computer typing lessons, for example, the designer would pay attention to sequence, taking care not to include certain new keystrokes before adequate evidence of mastery of previous keystrokes. Careful sequencing to minimize interference is a design challenge that quality drill and practice programs will work on.

Research also shows that short, spaced periods of practice give better results than long, concentrated practice periods. This implies that a computer program should allow a student to progress in short sessions, rather than in a single concentrated session. It may mean that the program will have to remember what a student has and has not accomplished, and provide sub-lessons that progress toward a main goal over time. In presenting an alphabet review to kindergarten students, for example, it would be best to structure the program to support short study periods of small groups of letters rather than attempting to extend the session in order to accomplish all the letters at one sitting.

Spaced review has been shown to be a significant means of enhancing retention of learned material. Rather than using a computer drill only once, the more effective approach is to have a program that will periodically review knowledge. For example, by keeping track of a child's performance, the alphabet program could automatically withdraw presentation of those letters a child already knows in order to concentrate practice on those still to be learned. The program should reintroduce the former letters into practice sessions at spaced intervals to maintain proficiency.

In order to make drill and practice effective, a program should recognize that students are limited in the amount of information they can mentally handle at one time. Research shows that the typical student can only work with up to seven stimuli simultaneously. For example, a student will typically be able to remember a seven-digit number for a few seconds, but not a ten-digit one. The limited capacity of short-term memory suggests that only a few items or meaningful chunks of information should be presented to a learner at once. By concentrating new items for practice in the smallest clusters feasible, rather than drawing randomly from all available items, the program designer expedites the learning process and reduces practice time needed to achieve desired performance.

TUTORIAL PROGRAMS: TEACHING NEW KNOWLEDGE OR SKILLS

Whereas drill and practice helps a learner refine or enhance performance, a *tutorial program* can teach something altogether new. Microcomputers can be very effective at promoting new learning, and tutorial software is designed for this purpose. In schools, the new behaviors acquired by the student using a tutorial will tend to be in the learning categories of verbal information or intellectual skills.

For some select aspect of the curriculum, you may wish to use a tutorial to supplement or replace you in the task of teaching a specific type of behavior. In science, for example, you might want to teach the concept of "balancing an equation" using a computer program. On the other hand, you might choose to use a tutorial for some special situation. A student who is temporarily homebound from a primary classroom could use a tutorial program to learn to subtract. The computer would serve as a one-on-one tutor to teach the skills that would keep the student up with the class. Whatever your purpose in using a tutorial—whether for your regular program or a special need—you will be relying on the program to do its teaching job effectively.

Effective Lesson Design

To be effective in promoting the sought-after student behavior(s), a tutorial program must be well designed. The essential elements of a good design are: (a) performance objectives, (b) performance measures, and (c) effective instructional processes (see Figure 4.3) (Futrell and Geisert, 1984).

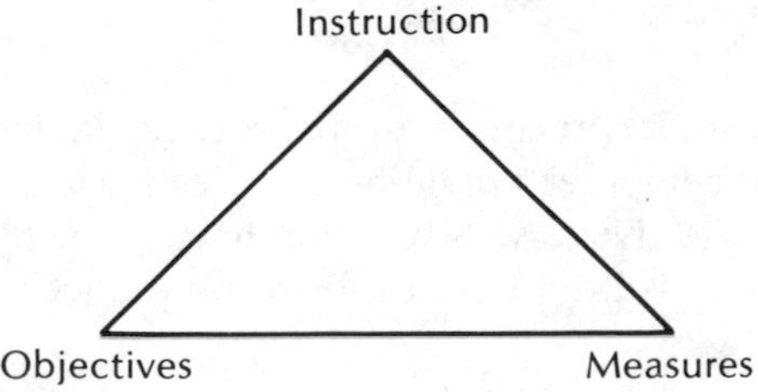

FIGURE 4.3 Design Elements for Effective Lessons

Performance Objectives and Measures

A tutorial lesson should be designed to reach one or more specific performance objectives, and those objectives should be included in a teacher's guide or in the program itself. In addition, a well-designed tutorial should include measures (tests) that can be used to determine if the performance objective has been reached by a student.

If you acquire a tutorial program that has no performance objectives, you will have a hard time determining what the computer program is supposed to do. (Topic covering is *not* the same thing as teaching.) Without performance measures, you will find it difficult to ascertain what students gain from the lesson.

Effective Instructional Processes

Given that a program has a performance objective and measures, the third component of an effective tutorial is a complete set of instructional events to produce the desired learning. The features of effective lesson presentation have been described in detail by Gagne and Briggs (Gagne, 1977; Gagne and Briggs, 1979). In an effective computer lesson, these processes will be in evidence. The computer:

1. gets the student's attention and provides motivation.
2. presents the lesson objective (in a form that takes into consideration the student's age and learning maturity).
3. reminds the student of relevant background information that must be remembered in order to be successful in the forthcoming lesson.
4. presents instruction in the form of narrative, explanations, simulations, graphics, and so forth, to implement the elements of an instructional strategy.
5. provides examples of expected student performance (the same type of problems that the student is called upon to do in the objective).
6. presents practice items on the lesson objective.
7. provides feedback on the student's performance on practice items, including right and wrong, and if wrong, offers hints for improved performance and the possibility of redoing the item.
8. assesses the student's performance using a test that measures whether or not the student has reached the objective.
9. implements transfer and retention strategies, pointing out how the information learned will be used in future programs (if the program is a portion of a series of learning programs).

The utilization of the nine processes of instruction in lesson design boosts the probability of the computer providing an effective lesson presentation. They are indicators of effectiveness. A program having less than the nine elements should be suspect unless it had been shown to produce results in actual tryouts with learners.

An Example of a Quality Tutorial Lesson

What would a good tutorial lesson look like? The example we will present is the teaching of the concept "triangle." Our model lesson will need to display two major attributes. It will need to lead a learner to be able to identify any presented figure as a member or nonmember of the group of objects having the name "triangle." Secondly, the model lesson will need to display all of the events of instruction.

The objective to be taught, in technical terms, is:

> **PERFORMANCE OBJECTIVE:** Given on the screen several plane geometric figures, some triangles and the others not, the student will identify all the figures that are triangles with no identification error in seven successive tasks.

In order to be able to learn the concept of triangle, the student will need to have mastered a number of other learning tasks, such as discriminating straight lines from curved ones, counting the number of straight lines in a geometric figure, and discriminating if the ends of two straight lines are touching each other or not (i.e., whether they actually form an angle). Presuming the prerequisite knowledge, the student could make use of a computer lesson to learn the concept of triangle. The following are the illustrated steps in the nine events of instruction.

1. The computer gets the student's attention and provides motivation. For this lesson a graphic introduces the lesson. A cartoon character stands to the left of the screen and from the right of the screen comes a stream of small geometric figures. As each approaches the character he boots the figure into one of two areas of the screen. One area is reserved for triangles. All the other shapes land in a jumbled pile. (See Figure 4.4). As the triangles accumulate, they eventually take over the screen, obscuring the kicker and everything else.

2. The computer presents the lesson objective (in a form that takes into consideration the student's age and learning maturity). In this case, the cartoon figure speaks and demonstrates (see Figure 4.5).

3a. The computer reminds the student of relevant background information. In a series of action screens the cartoon character points out to the students the difference between straight lines and curved lines, emphasizes the nature of an angle formed at the juncture of two straight lines, and counts the number of straight lines in various figures, from one through eight (see Figures 4.6–4.7).

3b. (Diagnostic Check) In order to determine if the student already knows the concept of "triangles" the computer lets the student do a little kicking. Various geometric figures are tossed toward the leg slowly, and the student must decide which location to kick the figures into. The computer monitors

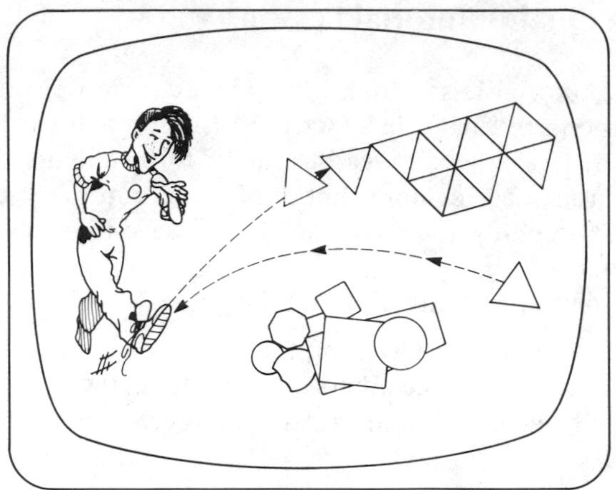

A character kicks the shapes differently.

FIGURE 4.4 Computer gets the student's attention and provides motivation.

The character speaks.

FIGURE 4.5 The objective of the lesson is presented in spoken words.

The character presents several figures not closed then closes them.

FIGURE 4.6 Background information is presented.

The character numbers the sides while pointing to each one.

FIGURE 4.7 More background information is presented.

the performance and makes a decision as to how much instruction the student needs (if any).

4. Given that the student does not know the concept, the computer presents instruction (in the form of narrative, explanations, simulations, graphics, and so forth) to implement the elements of a lesson strategy. The cartoon character teaches, through a series of screens, that the reason why he kicked the triangles together into a cluster was based on his observations that triangles have three sides, all of which are straight, and that these sides are attached at the ends to form three angles. He kicked everything else into the "not-triangle" pile (see Figures 4.8 and 4.9).

5. The computer presents examples of expected student performance as the cartoon character repeats the performance of kicking shapes correctly, in each instance telling why he is making the choice he does. One screen illustrates "has four sides—into the not-triangle" pile, while another tells "three sides, but not a closed figure." (Refer to Figure 4.10)

6. The computer presents practice items on the lesson objective by having the student again control the leg of the animated figure.

7. The computer provides feedback on the student's performance on practice items. If an error is made, the cartoon character demonstrates puzzlement. He then attempts to match the properties of triangles with the figure in question and then finally succeeds in placing the object in the correct pile. If a match is made by the student, then the object goes to the pile directly as the figure leaps into the air with glee.

8. After a suitable number of practices (the student is getting 90% right) the computer measures performance on the objective. The figure informs the

The character accepts a figure (example).

FIGURE 4.8 Instruction is presented.

Character rejects a figure (non-example).

FIGURE 4.9 More instruction is presented.

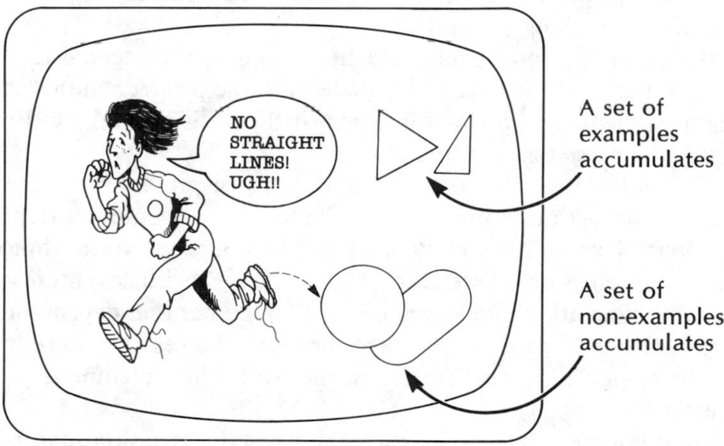

Character models the performance.

FIGURE 4.10 The desired performance is modeled.

student that the next seven figures will constitute a test, and to be as careful as possible in making kicks.

This program is a portion of a series of learning programs, so the computer performs an additional step.

9. It implements transfer and retention strategies, pointing out how the information learned will be used in future programs with other shapes. In the next portion of the series the student will learn the concept of "square," so to enhance transfer the student is reminded to count carefully the number of sides when viewing figures and to pay close attention to the number of "corners."

INSTRUCTIONAL SIMULATIONS

Some of the most effective uses of computers for teaching revolve around simulation—the computer's ability to artificially create on its screen a model of some "reality." This type of computer program enables a teacher to involve students in activities they could not otherwise experience. It would be nice, for example, to be able to take a social studies class on a wagon train adventure, reliving the exploits of the pioneers as they moved westward, but of course that can't be done. It is possible, however, to approximate the venture, and for students to learn (be changed) by the experience.

How a Simulation Teaches

In one popular computer simulation students are given a finite amount of resources (money, food, water, horses, etc.) and assigned the challenge of traveling, as they did in the days of covered wagons, to California over the Oregon Trail. Along the way they have various adventures, and each adventure costs them something in terms of their resources. If someone becomes ill, time will be lost if the party stops, and time requires the expenditure of food. If Indians attack, decisions must be made as to the proper action to take. In this fashion, students are involved in some of the decision-making situations that the real western settlers experienced.

In a simulation the computer does not just present predetermined situations. The strength of a simulation is the fact that a computer responds to student input. That is, the computer's responses depend on the choices students make, and there is no set scenario of what the westward adventure will turn out to be. The simulation mimics reality, with outcomes that depend on the adventurers' actions. Some travelers make the right choices and make it to California; others perish somewhere along the way. The outcome depends on the students' decisions.

In computer simulations students are active decision makers. But what do they learn? Are students changed by the process of engaging in simulations?

Indications are that many programs not only effectively meet their stated instructional goals, but may well modify to advantage how students approach data and decision making. In a series of simulations on historical events, for example, students make the important political decisions. At the start of each simulation the students establish their priorities; later they base decisions on those priorities and the program proceeds on the basis of how well they meet their own goals. The computer has the capacity to present "advisors" at appropriate times, and students read advice from a reference book and make new decisions. As students work their way through the simulation, they learn not only about the history of the United States, but also that decisions are not always clear-cut.

The Instructional Value of Computer Simulation

Numerous teachers in many subjects have found computer simulations extremely helpful in making their subject matter come alive. For a biology teacher who would like to convey the multiplicity of factors involved in the life and death of a pond in the classroom, nothing beats an instructional simulation designed for this purpose.

There is another reason that computer simulations have not been ignored by teachers: many such programs lend themselves readily to cooperative and large group learning. Consider this example: a simulation of the growth of a deer population in an urban area. In it, students are presented with the situation that deer can be allowed to remain in the urban neighborhood, or they can be trapped or killed. Decisions must be made.

If the students allow the deer to remain in close proximity, they are presented with the situation that happens in real life—the deer population begins to grow until it becomes a distinct nuisance, and people begin to demand that the population be put under some sort of sanction and control. At this point community groups begin to form, some trying to "save the wildlife" and others wanting to "harvest the deer for food." The students are carried through a decision-making process that simulates what would happen in real life, and the results of their decisions are shown on the computer screen.

Because the heart of the computer simulation is that it can be modified by student interaction with the program, the teacher who uses the program gains considerable flexibility in its use. Individual students might use the program and make their own decisions. Partners or a small group can debate the issues and make decisions by consensus. Better yet in the view of many teachers, an entire class can engage the problem with the teacher fully involved. For teachers in "just-one-computer" classrooms, this last feature is important. With no other type of CAI software can they as readily exploit three-way interactions (students, teacher, and computer) and teach their subject matter.

OTHER WAYS TO PROMOTE LEARNING

By comparing the three types of CAI programs we have presented thus far, you can readily see that a computer assist to instruction can take place in quite different ways. Each of the three—drill and practice, tutorial, and simulation software—has something different to offer to your teaching endeavor.

Needless to say, there are a host of other approaches you can use to involve the computer in promoting learning in your classroom, and a number of marvelous programs are available to support your efforts. Two additional types of CAI programs are certainly worthy of mention here, since they combine with the above three program types to encompass by far the vast majority of available CAI software in schools today.

Problem-Solving Software

Quite a large number of CAI programs are advertised and cataloged as problem-solving software and are generally intended for use by teachers to provide creative problem solving opportunities, and to encourage development of higher order thinking skills. As is true of the drills, tutorials, and simulations, such programs can vary tremendously in the degree to which they (1) specify clearly what they are intended to do, (2) provide a means for teachers to measure their effects, and (3) are structured effectively to deliver.

In one program for young children (ages 4–7), a goose leads students into puzzles that require students to see similarities and differences, a skill that is needed for learning numbers patterns and for reading words that look almost alike. As they become more proficient in solving puzzles, the students learn to generalize the concepts of similar and different.

Instructional Games

Almost all games have a win/lose element, and computer games are no exception. Instructional games are designed to be highly motivational and to engage a learner in purposeful activity to accomplish a goal, prize, or winning score.

Graphics are typically a key element in game design, though in many programs they are not used to educational advantage or in the most constructive manner. Elaborate graphical displays, for example, can be time-consuming and subtract needlessly from limited learning time. Fast motion or dramatic action graphics can distract seriously from, rather than complement, the instructional aspects of a program. Sound effects, too, are often emphasized to a greater extent than is appropriate, and it can be problematic when the bells and buzzers cannot be turned off, as is the case with some programs. Still, games are fun and can be used to great advantage, and schools and teachers continue to purchase them in high volume.

Computer drills and practice are often couched in a game format. For example, words may fly out of space ships, spelled correctly or incorrectly, and the student must fire his rocket to destroy the misspelled ones. Generally the game keeps some kind of score, and there are provisions to modify the speed of presentation. The same format may be used with number sentences instead of words, and the student must blast incorrectly multiplied numbers. The tendency of computer games to rely on aggressive action has received much comment, and it is a welcome fact that software producers are responding with more varied and appealing game formats.

Many CAI programs exist and are available to the classroom teachers at all levels. The instructional software spectrum ranges from simple drills through skill developers to programs that foster creative artistic thinking and even "thinking about thinking." To use CAI effectively, though, necessitates finding and integrating into the instructional program just those high quality programs that are appropriate to teaching needs.

SUMMARY REVIEW AND CHECKLIST

The computer has been shown by research to be an effective teaching tool. Whether you employ one to provide students with new verbal knowledge, concepts, or capabilities, or to review or make automatic existing intellectual skills, or to present new or different challenges via the myriad of simulations and games and problem-solving programs available, a computer can effectively promote student learning.

Appropriate decision making on your part, including the careful choice of software, is necessary if you are to have confidence that when you turn over some teaching to a computer, it will live up to your expectations. Only when teaching tasks are appropriately assigned will computers perform them responsibly.

Checklist

[ ] I can define computer-assisted instruction and identify common types of computer programs used to contribute to student learning in a classroom setting.

[ ] I can list and describe functions the microcomputer can and cannot perform in an instructional role and specify factors that relate to the appropriateness of using a microcomputer for an instructional task.

[ ] I am able to explain the value of performance objectives in microcomputer lessons.

[ ] I can describe the specific responsibilities of a computer that is charged with the instructional task of drill and practice.

[ ] I can describe the structure of a typical drill pattern and identify elements to look for in a quality drill and practice program.

[ ] I am able to describe the design features that indicate a computer tutorial lesson will be effective in promoting the student learning it is supposed to produce.

[ ] I can identify some features of instructional simulations that make this form of computer program attractive to educators.

SUGGESTED ACTIVITIES

1. Use a microcomputer drill and practice program to refresh some skill you previously learned. Some examples might be: (1) math computations, (2) foreign language vocabulary, (3) spelling, and (4) typing "tutorial" for keyboarding skills.

2. Analyze a drill and practice program to see if any of the following elements have been given consideration: (1) spaced review, (2) spaced presentation, (3) lowering of interference, and (4) presentation of correct amount of new material. Look to see if the program knows who is using it and, if it does, then if it cares (uses the information to decide program content). Rerun the program to see how it differs (if it does) the second time through.
3. Learn something totally new, using a tutorial program.
4. Analyze a tutorial program for the clarity of its teaching intent. Does it have a clear performance objective? Analyze the program for the nine design features that have the potential to increase its effectiveness. Which ones does the program seem to have? Which does it lack? Does it track the progress of a learner toward accomplishing the program's intent?
5. Analyze an instructional simulation program and try to identify some specific instructional goals one could achieve through use of the program (if not already specified in the program documentation).
6. Use and review selected items of software from the following "Worth a Look: Software."

WORTH A LOOK: SOFTWARE

Drill and Practice Software

Guesstimation. Educational Materials & Equipment; Apple II family and Commodore computers. Students view a marker on a line with numbered endpoints (integers, whole numbers, decimals, and fractions) and estimate the number where the marker is located. Different difficulty levels.

Spell It! Davidson & Associates; Apple II family, Atari, Commodore, IBM/MS-DOS computers. This program has a number of activities that remind students of spelling rules and drill them on the 1,000 most commonly misspelled words.

Fay: That Math Woman. Didatech; Apple II family and Commodore computers. Program provides a graphic illustration of how arithmetic equations work. Children in grades K–3 view examples and practice whole number manipulations.

Money Works. MECC; Apple II family computers. This program enables primary students to practice recognition and counting of currency. Many teacher options are available (for example, setting denominations, maximum amounts, and type of monetary expression).

Dividing Fractions, Adding Fractions. Mindscape; Apple II family, Commodore, IBM/MS-DOS computers. Part of the *Success with Math* series. Students practice dividing and adding fractions. This series includes a management system.

Math Blaster Plus! Davidson & Associates; Apple II family and IBM/MS-DOS computers. For grade levels 1 through 6, this arcade style program drills students on basic math skills.

Math Shop. Scholastic; Apple II family and IBM/MS-DOS computers. Middle school students play clerk in one of ten different stores to solve problems of a particular category and fill a customer's order. (A similar program, *Algebra Shop*, has ten shops focusing on pre-algebra/algebra skills for students in grades 7 through 10.)

Tutorial Programs

Comparison Kitchen (see Chapter 1 software). Students at grade levels K through 3 learn to discriminate and conceptualize sizes and amounts.

Dinosaurs. Advanced Ideas; Apple II family, IBM/MS-DOS, Commodore computers. Classification and discrimination skills for early childhood education are emphasized as young students practice matching five different dinosaurs with various traits.

CORE Reading and Vocabulary Development. Educational Activities; Apple II family, Commodore, IBM/MS-DOS computers. A teaching program with computer management and reentry into program. This program is designed for older students who are beginning readers, but it is also usable with primary students.

Geometry Alive. Educational Activities; Apple II family and IBM/MS-DOS computers. This is a three-part program that is highly tutorial and progressive on the topics of geometry, areas of triangles and quadrilaterals, and circles.

Hydrologic Cycle. IBM; IBM/MS-DOS computers. In this interactive tutorial, secondary level students and up can learn how water moves in its various forms and how humans modify the workings of the global water cycle.

Subject-Verb Agreement. Mindscape; Apple II family computers. Rules of agreement are explained and illustrated. Diagnostic testing followed by work at appropriate level of difficulty is part of this tutorial program for junior high.

Simulations

Oh, Deer! MECC; Apple II family computers. A simulation of the growth of deer populations in a suburban community, and pathways to the solution of various problems.

Botanical Gardens. Sunburst; Apple II family computers. Secondary level students learn the importance of controlling variables and interpreting graphs as they experiment with culturing plants under various conditions. Plants wilt or grow on screen in response to student decisions.

Go Fish. HRM/Queue; Apple II family computers. Users decide where to fish, how to navigate, and where to sell the fish in this simulated fishing expedition for secondary level. Uses imaginary port or one in Great Britain.

Chem Lab Simulations. High Technology; Apple II family computers. Simulations of the ideal gas law, kinetic-molecular theory, and the principles of diffusion.

Golden Spike. National Geographic; Apple II family computers. Students in grades 5 through 9 do everything to build the transcontinental railroad of the 1860s, from surveying the land to driving the spike in the last rail.

Car Builder. Weekly Reader; Apple II family computers. Users from grades 3 up can test (for example, in wind tunnel or around test track) automobiles they design and construct from various mechanical components (chassis, suspension, and so on).

Standing Room Only? Sunburst; Apple II family computers. Program lets anyone from grade 8 to adult study population dynamics by altering population statistics for seven countries.

Haber: Ammonia Synthesis. CONDUIT; Apple II family computers. A highly regarded simulation that high school or college students can use to study how conditions affect the course of a chemical reaction.

Sampling: Probability and Prediction. D.C. Heath/Collamore; Apple II family computers. Program helps students in grades 7 through 9 develop an understanding of statistical analysis and the effects of sample size.

Air Pollution. Educational Materials and Equipment Co.; Apple II family and TRS-80 computers. A simulation of carbon monoxide pollution in an urban environment, with student in the role of environmental planner. Most useful for secondary level instruction.

Oregon Trail. MECC; Apple II family computers. Relive the days of pioneers. A simulation of the trek westward, as students practice decision-making and problem-solving skills and learn about U.S. history.

"And If Re-Elected . . ." Focus Media; Apple II family and IBM/MS-DOS computers. Secondary level students assume the role of an incumbent president and try to resolve crises to win reelection. Impact of decisions made on popularity within various interest groups is displayed via graphs of poll data.

Odell Lake. MECC; Apple II family computers. A simulation designed to teach upper elementary students about predator/prey relationships and food chains. In the "go exploring" mode, the student plays the role of a particular type of fish trying to stay alive while encountering other organisms.

Operation: Frog. Scholastic; Apple II family and Commodore computers. Students dissect and reconstruct a frog in this simulation of laboratory procedures for grades 4 through 10.

Catlab. CONDUIT; Apple II family computers. A genetics simulation for high school or college use. Students mate domestic cats selected by coat color and pattern and grow in experience in generating, testing, and revising scientific hypotheses.

Crosscountry USA. Didatech; Apple II family computers. Students in intermediate grades up can assume role of truck driver picking up and delivering products across the United States.

The Observatory. Mindscape; Apple II family computers. Interested computer users from grade 7 to adult can zoom in on solar events of their choosing with a software "telescope."

Discovery Lab. MECC; Apple II family computers. Students (grades 6 through 9) can investigate variables involved in growth of imaginary organisms. Labs at three levels of difficulty.

The Other Side. Tom Snyder Productions; Apple II family and IBM/MS-DOS computers. A game of global conflict resolution for grade 7 to adult. Student(s) assume roles of nation engaged in making decisions individually to promote national interest or along with another nation to work toward a common goal.

Decisions, Decisions Series. Tom Snyder Productions; Apple II family and IBM/MS-DOS computers. Seven program titles on varying topics (for example, foreign policy, television, immigration, colonization, and urbanization) for grade 5 and up. Programs have as a common objective informing students about aspects of issues surrounding the topic and engaging them in making decisions within a simulated situation.

Problem Solving Software

Royal Rules. Sunburst, Apple II family and IBM/MS-DOS computers. Students (grade 6 and up) generate and test hypotheses based on data provided at several levels of difficulty.

Gertrude's Secrets. The Learning Company; Apple II family, Atari, Commodore, IBM/MS-DOS, Compaq. Though designed for pre-K to grade 4, this problem-solving program is fun for everyone. Focus is on classification skills and attribute challenges.

Gnee or Not Gnee. Sunburst; Apple II family, Commodore, TRS-80, and IBM/MS-DOS computers. Intermediate level students generate and test hypotheses about shapes and patterns to decide the secret rule that distinguishes the "gnees" from the "not gnees."

Mystery Matter. MECC; Apple II family computers. Students from grades 3 through 9 investigate physical and chemical properties of substances using animated testing tools and compare their results with the program's database.

Super Factory. Sunburst; Apple II family and IBM/MS-DOS computers. Users rotate and flip a series of cubes, attempt to duplicate designs, and create designs to challenge others in this program focused on three-dimensional properties. Most useful at secondary level up.

Zoyon Patrol. MECC; Apple II family computers. Secondary level students track an endangered species called zoyons using computerized tools (database, glossary, maps, and weather reports). Goal is to return organisms to natural habitat.

Safari Search. Sunburst; Apple II family, Commodore, and IBM/MS-DOS computers. Anyone from grade 3 up can get involved in this program to exercise thinking skills. Users go on a safari and must decipher clues to locate "mystery" animals.

Bounce. Sunburst; Apple II family computers. Students in grades K through 8 gather data on bouncing balls, recognize patterns, and make predictions.

Dinosaurs and Squids. Scott, Foresman; Apple II family computers. Students from grades 4 through 8 learn to use data tables to solve word problems on attributes of objects.

Instructional Games/Combined Strategies

Stickybear Town Builder (see Chapter 3 software). Program introduces map reading skills to students in grades 1 through 4. The users build towns, take trips, and hunt for missing keys using a compass and directional clues.

Fun from A to Z. MECC; Apple II family computers. This program for early childhood targets letter discrimination, alphabet sequence, and matching of upper and lower case letters.

The Voyage of the Mimi: Maps and Navigation. Holt, Rinehart and Winston; Apple II family computers. Four games with which intermediate and middle school students can learn basic navigational concepts.

Where in the World is Carmen Sandiego? Broderbund; Apple II family, Commodore, IBM/MS-DOS computers. For grades 4 through 12, social studies. This is an adventure game that draws students into using geography skills and various types of reference materials. The student uses *The World Almanac* to help find one of ten suspects in cities of the world.

Sound Ideas: Consonants. Houghton Mifflin; Apple II family computer (with speech synthesizer). A speech-based early reading program to help youngsters in grades K through 3 master decoding of consonants and the "th," "sh," and "ch" sounds. Employs tutorial and drill strategies.

Exploring Tables and Graphs. Weekly Reader; Apple II family computers. A two-volume program that teaches students with examples, quizzes, and games. It gives practice in making, saving, and printing tables and graphs.

Anagramas Hispanoamericanos. Gessler; Apple II family computers. Game designed for secondary or college students in Spanish language classes to use in reviewing the names, capitals, and locations of Latin American countries.

High Wire Logic. Sunburst; Apple II family, IBM/MS-DOS computers. This is a learning game of logic in which students learn how to develop rules concerning dividing objects into two groups.

Remember. DesignWare; Apple II family, Commodore, IBM/MS-DOS computers. This program helps students at grade levels 9 through 12 in studying and remembering information common to schoolwork, including lists, sequences, facts, and relationships.

READINGS

Bork, A. *Personal Computers for Education.* New York: Harper and Row, 1985.

Chambers, J. A., and Sprecher, J. W. *Computer-Assisted Instruction: Its Use in the Classroom.* Englewood Cliffs, NJ: Prentice-Hall, 1983.

Flake, J. L., et al. "Developing Thinking Processes." *Classroom Activities for*

Computer Education. Belmont, CA: Wadsworth Publishing Company, 1987.

Hazen, M. "Instructional Software Design Principles." *Educational Technology*, November 1985, 18–23.

Kellogg, T. M., and Leonard, C. *Teacher Behavior in Whole Class Computer-Mediated Instruction.* Paper presented at the Annual Meeting of the National Association for Research in Science Teaching, April, 1987 (ERIC Document #284723).

Merrill, M. D., and Tennyson, R. D. *Teaching Concepts: An Instructional Design Guide.* Englewood Cliffs, NJ: Educational Technology Publications, 1977.

Moursund, D. *Teacher's Guide to Computers in the Elementary School.* La Grande, OR: International Council for Computers in Education, Eastern Oregon State University, 1980.

Pea, R. D., Kurland, D. M., and Hawkins, J. "Logo and the Development of Thinking Skills." In *Mirrors of Minds: Patterns of Experience in Educational Computing*, edited by R. D. Pea and K. Sheingold. Norwood, NJ: Ablex Publishing, 1987.

Ploeger, F. D. *The Effectiveness of Microcomputers in Education: A Quick Guide to the Research.* Austin, TX: Southwest Educational Development Laboratory, Division of Educational Information Services, 1983.

Poppen, L., and Poppen, R. "The Use of Behavioral Principles in Educational Software." *Educational Technology* 28(2): 37–41 (February 1988).

Roblyer, M. D., Castine, W. H., and King, F. J. "Assessing the Impact of Computer-based Instruction: A Review of Recent Research." *Computers in the Schools*, 1988, 5(3/4).

Rooze, G. E., and Northrup, T. *Using Computers to Teach Social Studies.* Littleton, CO: Libraries Unlimited, 1986.

Rupe, V. *A Study of Computer-Assisted Instruction: Its Uses, Effects, Advantages, and Limitations* (ERIC Document #282513).

REFERENCES

Futrell, M. K., and Geisert, P. G. *The Well-Trained Computer: Designing Systematic Instructional Materials for the Classroom Microcomputer.* Englewood Cliffs, NJ: Educational Technology Publications, 1984.

Gagne, R. M., and Briggs, L. J. *Principles of Instructional Design.* 2d ed. New York: Holt, Rinehart, and Winston, 1979.

Gagne, R. M. *The Conditions of Learning.* 3d ed. New York: Holt, Rinehart, and Winston, 1977.

Kulik, C. L. C., and Kulik, J. A. "Effectiveness of Computer-based Education in Colleges." *AEDS Journal,* 1986, 19(2/3):81–108.

Kulik, J. A. "Synthesis of Research on Computer-Based Instruction." *Educational Leadership* 41(1): 19–21 (September 1983).

Kulik, J. A., Bangert, R. L., and Williams, G. W. "Effects of Computer-Based Teaching on Secondary School Students." *Journal of Educational Psychology*, 1983, 75(1): 19–26.

Kulik, J. A., and Kulik, C. L. C. *Computer-Based Instruction: What 200 Evaluations Say.* Paper presented at the Annual Convention of the Association for Educational Communications and Technology, Spring, 1987 (ERIC Document #285521).

Kulik, J. A., and Kulik, C. L. C. "Review of Recent Research Literature on Computer-Based Instruction." *Contemporary Educational Psychology*, 1987, 12(3):222–30.

Kulik, J. A., Kulik, C. L. C. and Bangert-Drowns, R. L., "Effectiveness of Computer-based Education in Elementary Schools." *Computers in Human Behavior*, 1985, 1(1):59–74.

Salsbury, D. F. *Cognitive Psychology and Its Implications for Designing Drill and Practice Programs for Computers.* Florida State University, Tallahassee, FL: Presentation at the American Educational Research Association, New Orleans, April 1984.

5

Teaching with Applications Programs

OBJECTIVES

- Describe the form and function of three major types of computer applications programs: word processing, spreadsheet, and data base programs.
- Give examples by subject of classroom applications of word processors, spreadsheets, and data base programs.
- Explain what is meant by the term "information-free" when it is ascribed to a computer program.
- Describe the types of learning that one could expect to achieve through the use of applications programs.
- State problems and limitations a classroom teacher is likely to encounter when implementing an applications program in instruction.
- Identify additional information-free applications programs that serve as useful tools in certain curricular areas.

INTRODUCTION

In the 1980s the microcomputer created a revolution in how information was handled within the business world. Will there be a similar revolution in the classroom?

Much of the business revolution was caused by three types of power-packed computer programs: (1) word processors, (2) number processors (spreadsheets), and (3) information processors (data base programs). The word processor revolutionized the production of printed materials; the spreadsheet revolutionized bookkeeping, accounting, and financial processes; and data base programs revolutionized the storage and retrieval of information. The new programs saved money by making it possible to accomplish tasks in a much more effective and efficient manner than was previously attainable, so they were integrated quickly into countless everyday business operations.

The classroom is not a business. Although many classroom tasks could be performed more efficiently or effectively using programs similar in nature to business applications, such programs were designed to accomplish business-related tasks. Hence teachers do not find their transfer to a classroom to be clear-cut and simple.

This chapter will explore ways teachers can put word processing and other powerful applications programs to use in the educational setting.

Goals

- What types of applications programs are available for educational purposes, and what are some of their uses in the classroom?
- How can a microcomputer program be free of content, and of what value is that attribute?
- What kinds of learning outcomes are likely to take place when students use applications programs?

A DIFFERENT TYPE OF TEACHING TOOL

Although the ultimate effect on schools of the "Big Three" applications programs—word processors, spreadsheets, and data bases—remains to be seen, one thing seems clear: a classroom revolution might take place if and when teachers recognize that these programs can provide the means to do something all too rarely accomplished in schools—teach students how to create, organize, store, and manipulate information.

An important attribute of each of these three applications programs is that they are "information-free" by design. Unlike tutorials and most other forms of computer-assisted instruction (CAI), there is no content inherent in these programs. Rather, the content comes from the user of the program, and it is handled as the user directs. Such programs are like a scaffold upon which information can be placed and manipulated in various ways. For example, by itself a word processor contains virtually no information, but it may be used to write and store stories, lists, tests, letters, poems, or newsletters.

Another attribute distinguishes these three programs from most CAI: the power provided by the program is very dependent on user proficiency with the program itself. That is, one must learn how to use an application program to receive the payoff it offers in task performance. For example, a teacher who wishes to make use of a word processing program must invest time and effort in learning the program. The more features the teacher masters and the more fluent the teacher becomes, the more useful the program will be for writing tasks.

As a result of these two characteristics, a classroom teacher who wishes students to use an applications program may face initial barriers: (1) students may not be able to enter information to the program because of inadequate keyboarding skills, and (2) precious time may need to be spent in teaching pupils how to use a program and developing an adequate proficiency level.

The keyboarding problem cannot be solved by an individual teacher. Although it is fair to expect teachers to provide a model of proper technique, the school system should provide the pattern whereby all students learn proper keyboarding and are ready to benefit from any applications programs that require keyboarding skills.

By selecting a simple and easy-to-learn applications program, a teacher can minimize the time required for teaching students to use it. Still, choosing a sophisticated word processing program or spreadsheet may be preferable if the program provides greater usefulness in the long run.

As is the case with using CAI, teacher decision making is critical. When you use spreadsheets, word processors, or data base programs in instruction with students, the computer becomes a working partner in your teaching process. Its share of the load may be tiny or tremendous, but your decisions can make or break the computer as a promoter of student learning. So, examine well what your "colleague" can do as we proceed in this chapter. You will find that, with applications programs, the computer can help you promote forms of learning quite different from what traditionally takes place in a classroom.

USING WORD PROCESSORS IN TEACHING

You are familiar with the operation of a word processor and know some of the ways you can use it as a tool for your own teaching-related tasks. What are some worthwhile ways to involve students with this application?

Since one of the major aspects of schooling is teaching students to deal with the written word, the word processor can become a ubiquitous partner in the process. One of its strengths lies in its ability to help us do what English teachers have always wished we other teachers would do more of: involve our pupils in *writing*.

It is clear that students do not write as much as they should, but the task of assigning, collecting, reading, and passing back numerous writing assignments is a burdensome one. And, unless they have a writing bent, it is not easy for students, either. Although some students do enjoy an authoring challenge, large numbers find writing to be laborious, dull, and lacking in rewards.

If writing is problematic, *re*writing must be worse, because it is clear we have our students rewrite much less often than we ask that they write. After all, a second draft means a second round of reading for the teacher, with the content no longer fresh. While some students appreciate opportunities to mold their ideas through rereading, rethinking, and rewriting, others view any revision as a taxing process. Rewriting becomes particularly arduous for students for whom error-free composition seems out of reach.

Word processors, as facilitators of text production and modification, have much to offer both teachers and students in the writing and rewriting process.

Generalizations about Word Processors in the Classroom

Although research on the use of word processors in the classroom is far from complete, some generalizations can be made (Wresch, 1984). When students use word processors, they tend to write more, revise more, and develop a better attitude toward the writing process.

Word processors seem to improve students' attitudes toward writing for three reasons. First, the use of computers is still surrounded with an air of

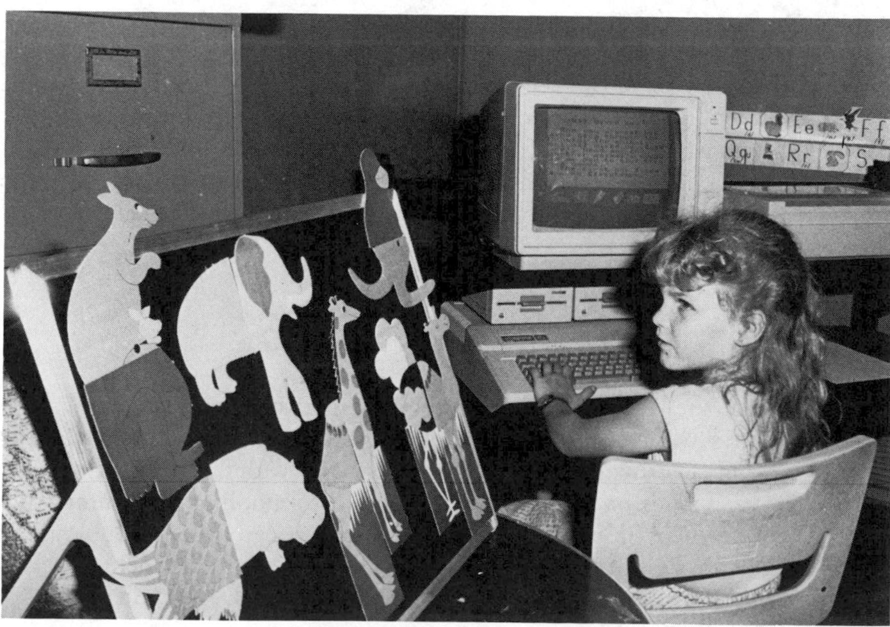

A computer can facilitate a student's writing and rewriting efforts.

mystery, and hence is novel and interesting. Second, students may feel they are engaged in an important idea, since it warrants the use of a computer to fulfill the task. Third, the products of their endeavors are neatly printed papers with the appearance of professional documents.

Because the writing process is simplified, and corrections are easy to make, the research shows that students tend to do more of both. This does not mean, of course, that students produce better writing.

Many educational innovations have been shown to have little or no educational effect. At least word processing produces students who have a better attitude toward writing in general and do more of it. Keith and Glover, in their book titled *Primary Language Learning with Microcomputers* (1987), point out a number of advantages that word processing brings to learners and teachers. For learners it:

- Enhances their perceptions of themselves as "real" writers.
- Gives their text a better public image.
- Brings their writing closer to public forms of communication and adult models.
- Gives them a new perspective on spelling and punctuation errors.
- Enables them to reflect on the thinking that goes on behind the writing.
- Makes it easier for them to share their work with others.
- Encourages and facilitates collaborative writing.
- Gives them control over the pace and direction of their own learning.
- Helps them adopt an appropriately self-critical distance from their writing.
- Encourages experimentation and risk taking.
- Provides a focus for group discussion.

For teachers, the word processor:

- Permits them to spend more time on individual supervision and tutoring.
- Directs and controls the work of small groups.
- Gives them a store of information on children's writing and thinking.
- Makes compositions easier to read.

Given that the word processor has a great potential for making improvements in writing, how can this tool be incorporated into teaching? Let's examine a sampling of teaching activities.

Some Sample Classroom Word Processing Activities

Student Editing

One technique for working with word processors in classroom instruction involves students in editing and correcting other students' work—anonymously.

To accomplish this technique, you first give students an assignment to write something on the word processor, asking them to save their draft in a file with a code number that you provide.

For the next activity, each student edits another student's file. You as teacher make the assignment, but the editor is unaware of the author's identity. You give the students the rules for editing and teach them how to include comments in a writer's file by marking the comments with a series of five asterisks. The editor saves the edited file on the same disk with the original file for return to the author.

In a follow-up activity, the author looks at the original document and at the comments and makes a second draft of the work. Repeating the editing and response exercise can lead to better and better drafts of an individual's written work.

Collaborative Projects

Cooperation at the keyboard, a useful technique with certain CAI programs, can also be extended to the writing process. For example, a teacher can have students pursue a team approach, using word processing, to the writing of papers or the development of oral presentations. The word processor's ability to segment and/or merge portions of a document in various fashions facilitates such joint development processes.

Were you teaching social studies, for instance, you might ask teams of students to cooperate to develop a position paper on a controversial topic to be

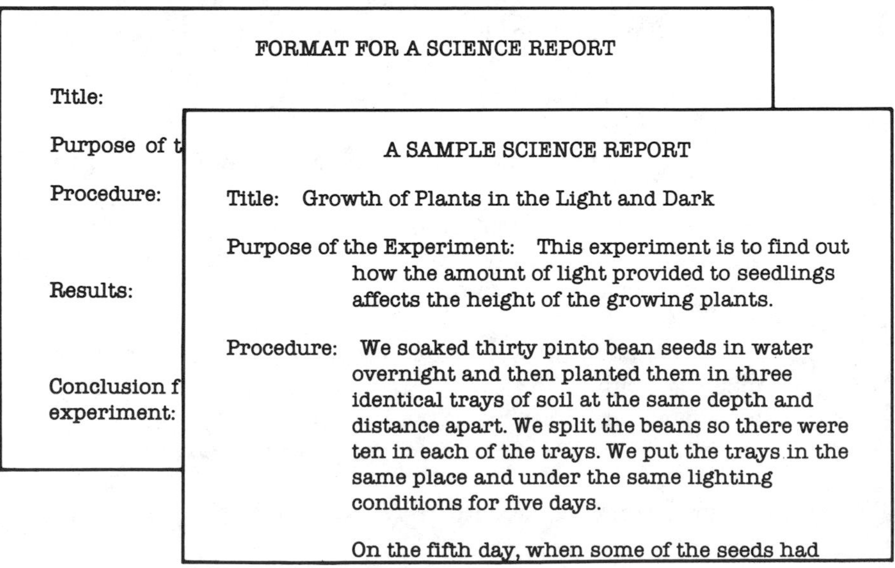

FORMAT FOR A SCIENCE REPORT

Title:

Purpose of t

Procedure:

Results:

Conclusion f
experiment:

A SAMPLE SCIENCE REPORT

Title: Growth of Plants in the Light and Dark

Purpose of the Experiment: This experiment is to find out how the amount of light provided to seedlings affects the height of the growing plants.

Procedure: We soaked thirty pinto bean seeds in water overnight and then planted them in three identical trays of soil at the same depth and distance apart. We split the beans so there were ten in each of the trays. We put the trays in the same place and under the same lighting conditions for five days.

On the fifth day, when some of the seeds had

FIGURE 5.1 Science Report Form and Sample of Model Report

used as the basis of a class debate. Each student team develops a first draft of their position based on text and reference study, subjects their draft version to joint and/or individual scrutiny, and then devises a revision procedure and final product.

Writing Frameworks

The word processor can be used in any situation where there is a standard format or structure underlying a writing endeavor. For example, you could use it in a science class to help teach students how to write laboratory reports for their experiments. With the program, you produce a framework for this task by storing a model report in one file and a blank model form in a second (see Figure 5.1). The student reads the model report to view an example of the type of report you would expect to receive. The blank model form provides the headings and format, but is empty and ready for the student's own work.

The student would be able to enter information, but also to refer to the sample report at any time. (Some word processors even have a split screen that allows a student to view the completed model and complete the blank model at the same time.) The student would save the developing report on a disk in a third word processing file, so that the blank form could still be available for any restarts or for additional lab reports. The third file would be the location of the student's report in progress, and as such would be always available for easy reading by you and/or rewriting by the student.

Additional files might be useful in the report development process. For example, to enhance the clarity of the task instructions, you could make available a *directions file* that included, within the format of a "blank" form, specific directions for completing each segment of the lab report. To further guide each student, you could also create a *feedback file* as you scan the student's work. To create it, you simply add in comments and suggestions to the student's file, and then record this new file separately for later viewing by the student.

Individualized Spin-offs

Some word processing programs incorporate a *spelling checker* and a *thesaurus*. These adjunct capabilities offer additional instructional opportunity to any teacher interested in enhancing students' vocabulary and spelling skills.

Students who write on the word processor can use the spelling checker to highlight (and correct) their misspelled words. This function also provides a means for teachers to create customized spelling lists for students. To do this, you would have the student on the word processor use the copy function to transfer the words identified into another file. The student would then be able to use that file as a personal spelling list for study.

The electronic thesaurus allows the students to examine synonyms for words they are using in reports, and to choose more varied language. Were you seeking to promote expansion of the students' written vocabulary, you could ask students to store these in another file as their personal "growth words" list to be studied and/or incorporated in subsequent written work.

Using Adjunct Programs

Text analysis programs have the capability of analyzing grammar and providing automatic advice on sentence, paragraph, and composition construction. If such a program were used regularly as a *grammar checker* in your classroom, you could be informed regarding selected aspects of students' writing, such as the number of words produced, the reading level, and the average word length, sentence length, and paragraph length. Better yet, with the program handy to spot the overuse of the passive voice or of pronouns or the presence of inappropriate idioms or clichés, you would be better able to set aside your red pencil and assume a more facilitative role in guiding students' writing efforts.

An *electronic outliner* can help a student to organize the content of a paper. The outliner program allows the student to place ideas in an outline form easily, with the outliner doing the format work and the student the thinking. After creating an outline, a student may add or delete ideas, and the outline will reconfigure itself to contain the new ideas.

A writer's style and usage manual is available as a *pop-up program.* While working in a word processor, if a question arises regarding word usage, the student can "call for" a usage manual. A section of the screen is used to present a menu of choices that leads to explanations and definitions of proper usage. For example, if a student is writing about the Pope, but does not know the appropriate title for this office, the student can call for the usage manual and look it up. An even more sophisticated adjunct to a word processor is a *writer's reference library* available on CD-ROM.

Schoolroom Newsletters and Desktop Publishing

Although students are normally recipients of information, the notion of having students organize and disseminate information is one that merits consideration. One special type of word processor can be used to great advantage in such an endeavor.

A "newsletter program" (or *desktop publisher*) transforms the chore of producing a newsletter, complete with pictures and print in columns, into an easy task. The program facilitates the typing of columns of information and the production of various sizes and styles of headlines. Just as important, it makes the incorporation of graphics into print exceedingly simple. The result is an almost professionally printed document – all "published" on the desk top.

In the classroom, students can publish newsletters in diverse forms and for various purposes. For example, an elementary class can create a "science project news" or "mathematics monthly" newsletter, describing to parents the important activities being accomplished or topics being studied. A geography newsletter focusing on one country, produced in one classroom, could be exchanged with a sister classroom focusing on a different country.

A high school social studies class could produce a newsletter on a given societal topic, such as "the status of television news" or "nuclear *versus* solar energy," to demonstrate the students' understanding of all the ramifications of the topic. A history class could demonstrate its ability to research a topic and present historical ideas in a relevant manner by producing a "newspaper" of a certain era (for example, a newspaper that could have been issued on the day the Magna Charta took effect). A drama class could drum up interest in a forthcoming play by issuing a weekly newsletter of how the play is progressing and all the latest information on those involved in the production.

THE SPREADSHEET

Just as a word processing program creates an electronic blank page upon which one can write and make changes in text, a spreadsheet is an electronic blank page upon which one can manipulate numerical quantities. In the world of business, accountants and bookkeepers have taken to spreadsheet programs in much the same way that managers and secretaries, not to mention novelists, poets, and journalists, have adopted word processors. Before we consider how educators might find this tool useful, let's look carefully at how this particular scaffolding for numerical information is constructed.

The Form of a Spreadsheet

A spreadsheet is a framework into which you can place words, numbers, and formulas. What appears on the screen at the beginning of a spreadsheet program is nothing more than a set of numbered rows and alphabetized columns. The user can identify it with, for example, a work sheet name and date. The intersection of each row and column is called a *cell* (see Figure 5.2), each hav-

WORK SHEET NAME ( )
DATE ( )

	A	B	C	D	E etc. →
1					
2					
3					
4					
5					
6					
7					

etc.

Row 7 — Column B — Cell D5

FIGURE 5.2 The Framework of a Spreadsheet

ing a unique name (such as C4). It is into these cells that a user puts information to produce a particular work sheet.

Words

Words are used to label columns and rows and to name or describe specific portions of the spreadsheet. In Figure 5.3 four rows of the sample spreadsheet represent student groups, and two columns have been named "soil damp" and "soil moist."

Numbers

Numbers (integers or decimals) appearing on a spreadsheet can get there in one of two ways. First, a user can type the number into an appropriate cell. Second, the user can enter a formula to calculate a number (such as a sum) and the result of the calculation will appear in the cell. In Figure 5.4, the numbers in columns B and C, from row 2 to row 5, were entered by a user who is recording data from an experiment.

Calculation Formulas

Any given cell on a work sheet may contain a calculation formula that produces a number value. The calculation formula is a mathematical statement of how the computer is to manipulate some other aspect of the spreadsheet to produce a number for the cell. For example, some typical calculation requests for an imaginary spreadsheet might be: (1) add all the numbers in column G, (2) average the numbers in row 4, (3) find the highest number in column J, and (4) multiply column C times column D, divide by 100, and put the result into column K.

In Figure 5.5 calculation formulas for columns B, C, and D and for rows 2, 3, 4, and 5 have been entered. The spreadsheet is prepared to sum and average the three columns of numbers, and find the difference between two columns for each row.

WORK SHEET NAME (seed experiment)
DATE (lab number 17)

	A	B	C	D	E
1		SOIL DAMP	SOIL MOIST		
2	GROUP 1				
3	GROUP 2				
4	GROUP 3				
5	GROUP 4				
6					
7					

FIGURE 5.3 Spreadsheet with Some Rows and Columns Labeled

WORK SHEET NAME (seed experiment)
DATE (lab number 17)

	A	B	C	D	E
1		SOIL DAMP	SOIL MOIST		←row 1
2	GROUP 1	3	9		←row 2
3	GROUP 2	2	6		←row 3
4	GROUP 3	0	8		←row 4
5	GROUP 4	4	7		←row 5
6					←row 6
7					←row 7

FIGURE 5.4 Spreadsheet with Numbers

WORK SHEET NAME (seed experiment)
DATE (lab number 17)

	A	B	C	D	E
1		SOIL DAMP	SOIL MOIST	DIFFERENCE	
2	GROUP 1	3	9	B2–C2	
3	GROUP 2	2	6	B3–C3	
4	GROUP 3	0	8	B4–C4	
5	GROUP 4	4	7	B5–C5	
6	TOTAL	SUM (B2·B5)	SUM (C2·C5)	SUM(D2·D5)	
7	AVERAGE	AVG (B2·B5)	AVG (C2·C5)	AVG(D2·D5)	

The calculation terms used are:

SUM (B2·B5) = sum cells B2 through B5
AVG (C2·C5) = take the average of cells C2 through C5
B3-C3 = subtract the number in column C from the number in column B in row 3

FIGURE 5.5 Spreadsheet with Calculation Definitions in Place, Ready for Calculations

An Example Lesson Using a Spreadsheet

The following is an example of how a high school biology teacher developed the spreadsheet we have been describing. Her students completed a laboratory activity in which they worked in groups of five to measure how many bean seeds germinated in damp and moist soil. There were four groups of students, and each group planted ten seeds in damp soil and ten in moist soil. The teacher uses one computer attached to a projection monitor on an overhead projector with a screen.

With the students watching the screen, the teacher brings up a blank spreadsheet and labels it, typing in information to identify the worksheet of interest. Then she types directly into column A the names of the four groups, and into row 1 the two soil conditions. The class's spreadsheet now looks like Figure 5.3.

Next, one representative from each group comes up to the computer and types into the spreadsheet the data for the group: the number of seeds that germinated out of the ten planted in each type of soil (see columns B and C of Figure 5.4).

The teacher writes at the top of column D the label "DIFFERENCE" and places in rows 2, 3, 4, and 5 a *calculation formula.* The teacher specifies that the number in column D should be equal to the difference of the numbers in column B and column C (refer to Figure 5.5). At the bottom of the page the teacher states that the number in row 6 should be the sum of all the numbers in columns B, C, and D, and that row 7 should be the average of the numbers in columns B, C, and D. The spreadsheet is now ready to do the number processing for which spreadsheets are noted.

One push of the "calculate" key (a function key) on the computer replaces the formulas with the results of the formulas. Instantaneously the worksheet shown in Figure 5.5 transforms itself to look like Figure 5.6.

The power of the spreadsheet lies in its ability to calculate almost any formula using any combination of cells. Continuing the biology example, an advanced biology class might calculate means and standard deviations for the data, in order to decide the amount of variability in the measured numbers. Although standard deviation requires a number of calculations, most spread-

WORK SHEET NAME (seed experiment)
DATE (lab number 17)

	A	B	C	D	E
1		SOIL DAMP	SOIL MOIST	DIFFERENCE	
2	GROUP 1	3	9	6	
3	GROUP 2	2	6	4	
4	GROUP 3	0	8	8	
5	GROUP 4	4	7	3	
6	TOTAL	9	30	21	
7	AVERAGE	2.25	7.5	5.25	

FIGURE 5.6 Spreadsheet with Calculations Automatically Performed

sheets have built-in formulas, including ones for mean, variance, and standard deviation.

Spreadsheets have other advantages. When attempting to interpret data, one often wants to develop and examine a graph of the information. Many spreadsheets have the graphic power to draw a line, bar, and/or pie graph directly from the data in the sheet. At a more sophisticated level, a spreadsheet can be utilized as a data base (described later in the chapter) and can be used to pose and solve hypothetical questions.

Spreadsheet Versatility

Here are some examples showing the versatility of spreadsheets. Figures 5.7 and 5.8 show information that might be gathered and analyzed by a home economics class.

The third example, a teacher-prepared grade book (see Figure 5.9) may bring more possibilities to mind. With a spreadsheet, you can develop a custom-made grade book. You set up the spreadsheet so it is possible to make your gradekeeper suit your class scoring and grading procedures exactly.

Some newer forms of spreadsheets possess the capability of having two or more dimensions. That is, any cell in a spreadsheet may hold a number that is the result of some other spreadsheet's calculations. As an example, in the case of the biology class's spreadsheet, the class could have created one spreadsheet for damp soil, a second one for moist soil, and a third to combine the results of the other two sheets.

This feature is useful especially where one wants to combine the information from a number of different spreadsheets. In a class setting, perhaps this could be employed by a teacher with cooperative learning groups. Each group

WORK SHEET NAME (compare burger joints)
DATE (January)

	A	B	C	D	E
1		King-Brg.	Dandy Dog	Brg. Shack	Big Brg.
2	Burger	1.85	1.35	0.99	1.75
3	Shake	1.25	1.39	1.00	1.10
4	Fries	.55	.85	.65	.85
5	Lg. drink	.79	.85	.65	.88
6					
7	TOTAL	4.44	4.44	3.29	4.58

FIGURE 5.7 Food Prices in Fast-Food Restaurants

WORK SHEET NAME (Sally's budget)
DATE (February 12, 1990)

	A	B	C	D	E	F
1		JANUARY	FEBRUARY	MARCH	APRIL	MAY →
2	RENT	375	375	375	375	395
3	HEAT	85	76	55	37	14
4	ELECT	11	11	9	8	8
5	WATER	8	8	9	8	8
11	TOTAL	657	602	589	607	617

FIGURE 5.8 A Home Budget Sheet (Abbreviated)

WORK SHEET NAME (Grade book)
DATE (Social studies #2)

	A	B	C	D	...	J
1		QUIZ 1	QUIZ 1	REPORT	→	STD. AVG.
2	BELSON	89	92	95		92.4
3	BRANSON	76	79	65		73.6
4	DOUGLAS	87	89	78		85.8
5	HENNING	76	83	69		76.9
33	VERNER	91	83	88		87.5
34	CLASS AV	82.6	79.4	79.1		82.1

FIGURE 5.9 A Teacher's Grade Book (Abbreviated)

could prepare its own spreadsheet of data, and the results would be accumulated on the teacher's spreadsheet for class presentation and discussion.

Curricular Uses of Spreadsheets

Spreadsheets are a natural for many of the educational activities in science, mathematics, and business courses. Business teachers in particular will be likely to involve students in studying the spreadsheet because it is now such an integral tool in commercial bookkeeping and in the making of budgets and financial projections. An elementary math class can use the same tool to develop addition, subtraction, multiplication, and division tables. The high school trigonometry class can use it to generate angle function tables. The physics class can use it to develop a solution to an equation for how gravity affects a falling body.

Please don't think that the usefulness of a spreadsheet is limited to such classes, however. Any class that looks at or uses numbers is a candidate to make interesting use of a spreadsheet program. For example, a home economics class might, while conducting an analysis of the local economy, use spreadsheets for such comparisons as are illustrated by Figure 5.7, which shows food costs for four fast-food restaurants. The same home economics class can use spreadsheets to produce individualized dietary and nutrition plans for the students in the class. A social studies class may use the spreadsheet to record student survey data on a variety of current topics, generating a picture of totals, averages, and a progression of results over time. A government class could use it to analyze data from past elections. Wherever numbers are manipulated in a class, the spreadsheet has the potential to add interest and power.

DATA BASE APPLICATION PROGRAMS

Data base programs are designed to solve the problem of storing, organizing, accessing, relating, and changing large amounts of information. They are information processors. The simpler forms of data base programs act as file managers that catalog information. In their more sophisticated versions, the programs become the means for answering questions where the answers are based on the analysis of extensive banks of data.

Form and Function of a Data Base Program

The heart of a data base is a set of electronic file cards of information. The data base file might look like Figure 5.10, which is a part of a data base provided by a publisher to augment its textbook series. Each file card is one

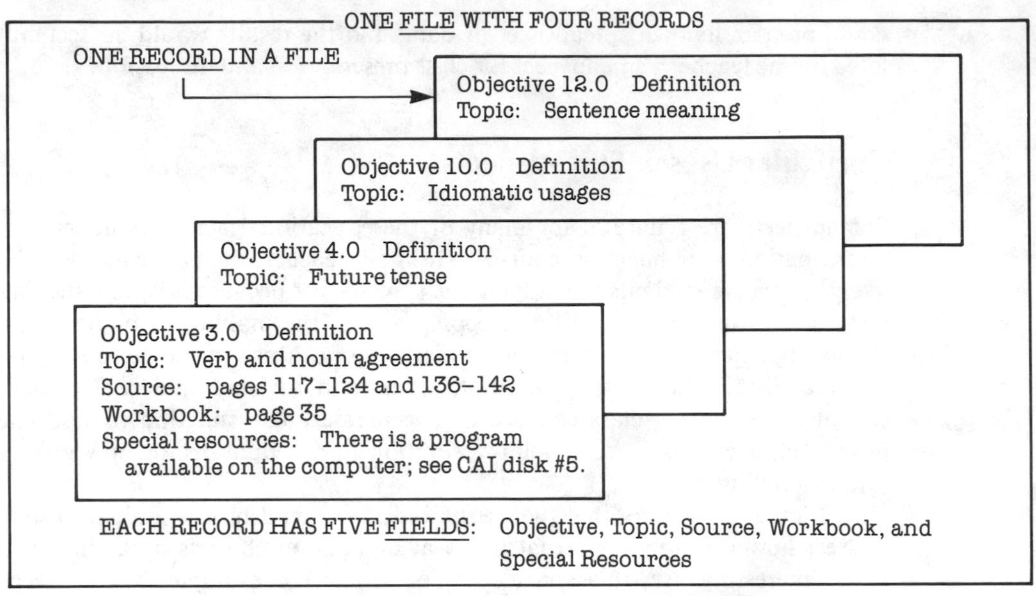

FIGURE 5.10 A Small Data Base File

record, and each category of information on the card is one *field.* A set of records would be a *data base file.*

Arguing the benefits of having a file of records on a microcomputer instead of on paper is easy, and the argument resembles the one favoring a word processor over a typewriter. A file, record, or field can be changed with ease, and additions and deletions readily made. More important, locating information within a data base is dramatically simpler than searching for information in customary ways, since a computer can respond so quickly to requests to find, sort, or select data. For example, when building a teaching unit, you can ask the computer to: "Find all the teaching objectives related to pronouns," and the computer will respond instantaneously with the information you see displayed in Figure 5.11.

Organizing information by records and fields provides opportunities to quickly view the same file of information in a multiplicity of ways. As an example, consider the actions of a social studies teacher who developed a data base of information on the United States presidents. She included in the data base the following fields: name, year of birth, political party, age at death, date of inauguration, and number of years served. The data was entered into the data base in chronological order of the presidential term (see Figure 5.12).

Out of curiosity, she decides to arrange the information in the data base file using the category (field) of AGE. All she does is select a simple command from the program's menu, and the computer rearranges all the data within seconds, listing the presidents in order by their age at death (see Figure 5.13).

Sorting the file first by PARTY and then again by INAUGURATION, the teacher creates a listing that groups the presidents by party affiliation and within party by the dates of their inaugurations. Figure 5.14 shows her com-

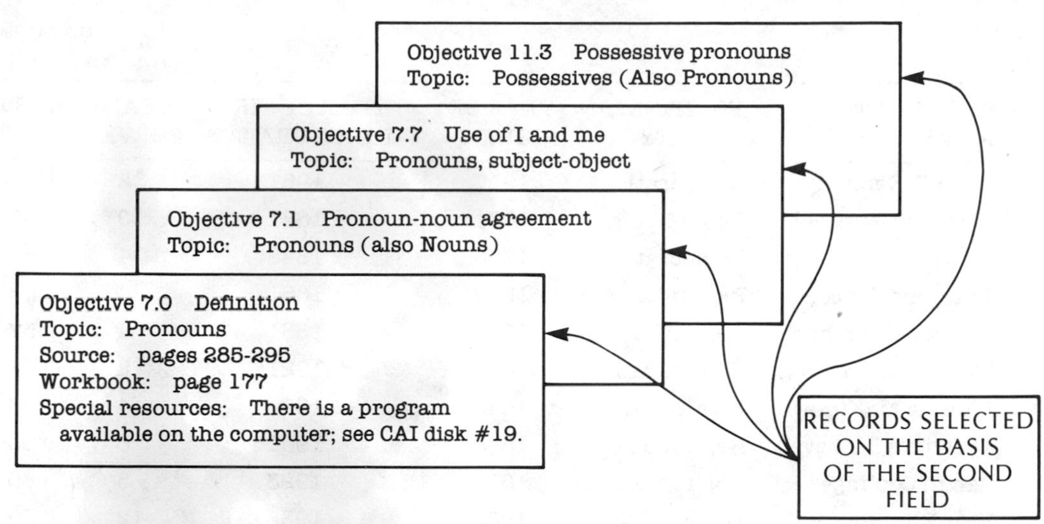

FIGURE 5.11 A Data Base Sorted by Topic

Field ↓ Record

PRESIDENT'S NAME	POLITICAL PARTY	YEAR OF BIRTH	YEAR OF FIRST INAUGURATION	YEARS SERVED	AGE AT DEATH
George Washington	Federalist	1732	1789	8	67
John Adams	Federalist	1735	1797	4	90
Thomas Jefferson	Dem.-Rep.	1743	1801	8	83
James Madison	Dem.-Rep.	1751	1809	8	85
James Monroe	Dem.-Rep.	1758	1817	8	73
John Quincy Adams	Dem.-Rep.	1767	1825	4	80
Andrew Jackson	Democratic	1767	1829	8	78
Martin Van Buren	Democratic	1782	1837	4	79
William H. Harrison	Whig	1773	1841	0	68
John Tyler	Whig	1790	1841	4	71

FIGURE 5.12 Presidential Information in Chronological Order

puter screen after the second level is completed. Only a few taps of the keyboard were required to make all the rearrangements in the file. The teacher has viewed these data in three ways in only a couple of minutes, and many more manipulations are possible (and just as easy). The standard data base program typically supports such operations as searching through records quickly, counting and reporting instances of data, and arranging or selecting by a specific attribute or combination of attributes; but a sophisticated program will enable a user to perform an even more impressive array of manipulations of the information.

Some spreadsheets have the power to find, sort, and select information.

Records Sorted on this Field ↓

PRESIDENT'S NAME	POLITICAL PARTY	YEAR OF BIRTH	YEAR OF FIRST INAUGURATION	YEARS SERVED	AGE AT DEATH
John F. Kennedy	Democratic	1917	1961	2	46
James A. Garfield	Republican	1831	1881	0	49
James K. Polk	Democratic	1795	1845	4	53
Abraham Lincoln	Republican	1809	1861	4	56
Chester A. Arthur	Republican	1829	1881	4	57
Warren G. Harding	Republican	1865	1921	2	57
William McKinley	Republican	1843	1897	4	58
Theodore Roosevelt	Republican	1858	1901	8	60
Calvin Coolidge	Republican	1872	1923	5	60
Franklin Roosevelt	Democratic	1882	1933	12	63

FIGURE 5.13 Same File Arranged by Presidential Age at Death (Youngest to Oldest)

First Sort ↓

PRESIDENT'S NAME	POLITICAL PARTY	YEAR OF BIRTH	YEAR OF FIRST INAUGURATION	YEARS SERVED	AGE AT DEATH
Andrew Jackson	Democratic	1767	1829	8	78
Martin Van Buren	Democratic	1782	1837	4	79
James K. Polk	Democratic	1795	1845	4	53
Franklin Pierce	Democratic	1804	1853	4	64
James Buchanan	Democratic	1791	1857	4	77
Andrew Johnson	Democratic	1808	1865	4	66
Grover Cleveland	Democratic	1837	1885	8	71
Woodrow Wilson	Democratic	1856	1913	8	67
Franklin Roosevelt	Democratic	1882	1933	12	63
Harry S. Truman	Democratic	1884	1945	8	88
John F. Kennedy	Democratic	1917	1961	2	46

↑ Second Sort

FIGURE 5.14 Information Sorted at Two Levels

In a very real sense these spreadsheets act like (and can be thought of as) data base programs. The work sheet becomes a file, the rows become records, and the columns are the fields (refer to Figure 5.15).

Types of Data Base Programs

Hedges (1984) categorizes data base programs into file management systems, relational data base management systems, and network/hierarchical data base management systems.

The *file management system* facilitates file definition, data entry, simple sorting, and report production, and is the simplest of the three categories. It might be found in the school library serving as a catalog file or in a classroom as a materials reference source. The *relational data base* has data stored in the form of files, records, and fields and is the most useful for the organizing and relating of one set of data with another. For example, AppleWorks® is a relational data base that can be used by classes to manipulate information (Luehrmann & Peckham, 1987). The *network/hierarchical data base* consists of huge information files accessed via modem and telecommunication. This type of information resource might be used by a teacher or a school librarian, using Compuserve®, The Source®, PRODIGY℠, or some other commercial source for data retrieval.

Teacher Use of Data Bases

Here is a sampling of data base files a teacher might be interested in having handy: (1) curricular objectives keyed to learning materials, (2) encyclopedic information related to a particular subject area, (3) lists of spelling words with sample sentences, (4) classes available for in-service training, (5) commercial sources of learning materials and books, (6) community resources available for

Using the spreadsheet to store class information

	A	B	C	D	E	F	G
1	LAST NAME	1ST NAME	AGE	SEX	PARENTS	PHONE #	
2	NGUYEN	HIEN	12	M	VINH NGUYEN	456–7865	
3	ESTRADA	MARTINA	12	F	NINA REYES	567–8976	
4	BRAMSON	TIM	13	M	TARA BRAMSON	567–8765	
5						431–9207	

FIGURE 5.15 The Spreadsheet as a Data Base

classroom teachers, (7) student and parental information, (8) trade books in the school library keyed to units regularly taught, and (9) test questions and answers related to topics taught.

Student Uses of Data Bases

Hunter (1985a; 1985b; Hunter and Furlong, 1985) has been especially interested in the utilization of the data base in the classroom. A few of the different purposes she identifies for using computer data bases are discovering commonalities and differences among groups of events or things, analyzing relationships, looking for trends, testing and refining hypotheses, organizing and sharing information, keeping lists up-to-date, and arranging information in useful ways.

One use of a data base at the elementary level is the development of personal data bases. For example, elementary students can build computer files of the spelling words they have learned, the definitions of the words, and synonyms for each word. As time progresses, each student would begin to have a personal vocabulary data base that could be used for the purposes of review. This approach could also be used with vocabulary from a school subject, such as science.

One use the authors have made of the AppleWorks® data base is to have students (college level, but the idea is applicable to any level) write their own tests. For each reading assignment in the course, students were assigned to write from two to five multiple-choice questions regarding the details of the assignment, and one broad essay question on the big issue of the lesson. A computer was set up in the back of the class, and a data base established that easily accepted the topic name, the student's name, the multiple-choice questions, and their correct answers.

As test time approached, the teacher first sorted the data base records by student name, and got a listing of all the questions written by a given student. This provided a basis for a grade on the assignment since the teacher could tell whether all the assignments had been done and assess the level of the work.

Next, the teacher sorted the records by topics, omitting the student name and the answer fields. This provided a listing of all the questions on a given topic, which was edited, printed, duplicated, and handed out to students as a study guide for the test. At class meetings questions were discussed as students reviewed them.

Finally, the teacher scanned the data base records, selected the best questions, and printed them directly from the data base in the form of a final test (along with an answer key for the teacher).

The result was that students started writing better and better questions and enjoyed their participation in the test writing processes. The teacher had to spend less time writing test questions (but more time manipulating them).

Some publishers caught on quickly to the value of a data base program for the electronic retrieval of information for students. Commercial data bases available for classroom use have appeared in life and physical science, history, and U.S. government. These come with files already filled with information rather than being "empty shells" requiring the teacher or student to input information. For example, there is available a relational data base that contains all the following totally related information: the names and areas of all the United States; the names, lengths, and states traversed by major rivers; the names, sizes, and locations of almost all United States lakes; the state and national roads by name, length, and location; state boundaries, capitals, highest and lowest points, cities, and city and state populations (Borland, 1986). This "artificial intelligence" data base allows a student to ask questions of it in English.

Here are examples of the types of questions one could ask and have answered: What is the highest peak in New York? What are the populations of the five largest cities in the United States? What states border on Utah? What is the capital of West Virginia? Through what states does the Mississippi River flow? What are the five longest rivers in the United States? Using a program of this type, a teacher could involve students in actively exploring the geography of the United States rather than simply reading about it.

The Class Data Base Project

Projects can be an ideal vehicle for student learning. One such example of project-based learning using a data base is in social studies on the topic of surveys (Hannah, 1986).

Surveys are an ever-present aspect of today's society. A high school data base project on this topic could be "A Survey of School Interests" and could focus on answering questions of the following types: "How do the interests of high school students change from freshman to senior year?" "In rank order, what are the major areas of interest of the students of our school?" "Do males or females have more interest in Topic X?" and "Do students who excel in math and science have different interests from those who excel in sports?"

In such a project the teacher would first need to direct students to decide what categories of data would be stored in a data base. For example, whatever information was gathered would need to be cross-indexed with grade level, sex, and science, math, and sports activities if it were to be used to answer the questions in the previous paragraph.

The students would also need to decide what survey information they needed in order to find out the interests of the respondents, and then the survey would need to be conducted. This would generate the information for the data base, which could then be queried to answer the questions.

APPLICATIONS PROGRAMS AND KINDS OF LEARNING

Schools place great emphasis on students acquiring knowledge, but very little on teaching students how to produce new knowledge or to organize existing knowledge into new patterns. Applications programs open up opportunities for teaching in some areas that are typically not well developed by teachers. Of the five domains of learning (attitudes, motor skills, cognitive strategies, verbal information, and intellectual skills), the usual forms of CAI seem to relate most often to the teaching of verbal information and intellectual skills objectives. It appears to us that applications programs will prove valuable for objectives in both these categories, and indeed will add an additional one—cognitive strategies. Let's start with that one.

Cognitive Strategies

Cognitive strategies are the skills that a student uses to govern his or her own learning, remembering, and thinking behaviors. They are like a set of behind-the-scenes organizational rules, which direct and govern how a student approaches the solving of a problem. The word processor, spreadsheet, and data base applications programs are all tools with which teachers can begin to unlock this domain.

Knowing how to do a spreadsheet is only the start of a learning endeavor. Since a spreadsheet is initially information free, it is a playground upon which any set of numbers can be manipulated. In order to use a spreadsheet for a given problem, a student must figure out how to structure it in order to produce a specific outcome. Investigation of *how* students solve spreadsheet problems may well provide a field for learning about cognitive strategies.

Similarly, how do students design their own data bases? A data base is not automatically created by a program. Decisions must be made on questions such as: (1) what information needs to be stored, (2) how much information will be stored, (3) what categories need to be created, (4) how many records will be created, (5) who will get access to what information, and so forth. The creative aspect of the data base design is the planning that goes into the structure of the data base even before any information is typed into it. In this type of decision making, cognitive strategies can be exercised.

And, what about the exercise students get in using the ready-made relational data base programs? For example, how do they go about analyzing these data bases, generating applicable questions, or searching for answers to questions using such a program? Much remains to be learned, but there is no doubt that, with the coming of applications programs, new opportunities seem to have opened up for those educators—be they researchers or teachers—who have been desirous of promoting learning in the area of cognitive strategies. Some potentially valuable tools have appeared in their tool boxes.

Verbal Information

This domain of learning deals principally with knowledge or knowing, mainly verbal knowledge. Although the word processor allows the almost unlimited manipulation of words, it probably is not the most powerful application in re-

Applications programs offer students new and different learning opportunities.

gard to verbal information. The data base program seems to hold the most potential in this area.

Designing a data base requires a student to organize verbal information. Given the task of creating a data base of information on plants, an elementary student must make decisions concerning what to store, how much verbal information to store, where to locate the information, and the relative importance of various kinds of information. This type of activity is far different from having the student memorize the names of the phyla of plants or capitals of foreign countries.

Intellectual Skills

The utilization of a data base program certainly requires a high degree of skill in the area of concept learning. The data base program is organized around specific groupings of words and numbers. Opportunities for new concept learning abound as students manipulate information and identify it by category labels.

The spreadsheet exemplifies rule-using learning and the application of rules, since all the numerical quantities of the spreadsheet are interrelated via various calculation rules. Both the spreadsheet and the data base program present ample opportunities for building of higher level intellectual skills through problem-solving endeavors.

SPECIALIZED APPLICATIONS

Although our emphasis in this chapter has been on the classroom use of the "Big Three" applications programs, there are some additional information-free programs that can serve as valuable classroom tools in certain curricular areas.

Graphics Programs

One dedicated use of computers in certain businesses is the processing of pictorial information, and the value of computer aided design is well known to architects, drafters, engineers, and artists. Although professional level graphics and design programs would not have widespread applicability in schools, programs of lesser sophistication are available to permit students at various levels to produce and process images similarly.

With the aid of an appropriate application program, a student can produce some simple shape and then quickly transform it into an intricate pattern or design. The computer can shade, color, enlarge, shrink, multiply, rotate, or reverse the image at the direction of the user. These programs facilitate drawing, painting works of art, and the design of items of utility. Other programs combine artistic composition and text, allowing students to produce and illustrate their own works of literature.

Musical Composition Programs

Professional musicians are turning more and more to the computer to aid aspects of their creative endeavors. There are a number of computer programs that allow students to develop musical compositions and to exercise their creativity in this area as well. Available musical programs range from the printing of the music played by children through music transposition and arrangement. Music from an electronic keyboard can be fed directly into a computer and modified in various creative ways.

Programs to Handle Environmental Data

With appropriate software, students can use the computer as a tool to learn more about the real world, just as professional scientists do. Rather than typing in data, such as one would do with a spreadsheet, data for this application is provided to the computer via sensing devices, such as thermometers or probes, to which it is attached. The *data gathering program* displays the data, and in many cases then permits the user to perform certain manipulations to aid in interpretation.

Some companies offer an array of environmental sensors and software support for manipulating acquired data. Classes could employ such applications software to pursue a wide variety of investigations. For example, in science class students might ask this question, "Which of these types of sunglasses absorb the most light?" Using a constant light source and a light probe attached to the computer, students could test a collection of items, and the program would preserve and/or display the measurements.

On a long-term experiment, the computer might become the mainstay of data collection. For example, students could design an experiment in which they could control and measure the two variables of temperature and light on growing plants. A computer-connected thermal probe would be used to monitor the temperature conditions, and the light sensor would monitor light intensity over time.

Graphing Programs

We have mentioned that spreadsheets often offer a graphing capability. There are application programs that specialize in this feature. These *graphing programs* are particularly useful when there is a need to compare and interpret information, whether it is provided by the user, such as in a mathematics, social studies, or business class, or by environmental sensors, such as in science classes. In the above experiment, a graphing program would be very handy. After a sufficient amount of data had been gathered by the computer, the teacher could use such a program to illustrate the germination of the plants under the various conditions.

SUMMARY AND REVIEW CHECKLIST

In this chapter, we have surveyed three major applications programs as well as an assortment of adjunct programs and more specialized applications. The boost to task performance such programs provide has led to a revolution in the business world. Although they may or may not create an educational revolution, they can help the teacher provide new and valuable learning experiences for students.

There are some challenges associated with the use of applications programs in the classroom, particularly in terms of providing requisite time and resources to surmount initial barriers to student use. Still, it seems likely that the potential payoff offered by these programs will provide the thrust to overcome the problems. The ability of the programs to respond to teacher and student interests is superb, and as schools obtain more computer resources, we expect to see dramatic increases in their classroom use.

Checklist

To facilitate your use of applications programs in your classroom, you should be able to check off the following:

[ ] I can describe the form and function of each of these: the word processor, the spreadsheet, and the data base program.

[ ] I can state what is meant by the descriptor "information-free" when it is ascribed to an applications program.

[ ] I can identify the types of learning that one could expect to achieve through the use of applications programs.

[ ] I am aware of the problems and limitations I can expect to encounter when implementing an applications program in the classroom.

[ ] I can name and describe at least three types of information-free applications programs that are particularly useful in specialized curricular areas.

SUGGESTED ACTIVITIES

1. Develop a classroom activity in which you would use the word processor as a teaching tool, rather than as a simple text manipulation device. For example, the word processor could be the heart of a cooperative learning project in which groups would prepare and then share reports, each group modifying the others' work.
2. Select a simple spreadsheet program to work with and learn how to use it to make a grade book. Try to develop a pattern of grading that would not be done easily using traditional methods. For example, for tests, assignments, attendance, extra credit, and so forth, try giving each category its own weight toward a final summary score.
3. Develop a classroom activity that uses a spreadsheet as a teaching device for subject matter you enjoy. You will need to select some numerical aspect of the subject. For example, you might use the spreadsheet as an electronic blackboard to present text and data, or students might use the spreadsheet to enter and manipulate data from the body of content you teach.
4. Use a very simple filing program (data base) to organize and manipulate some data that a classroom teacher would deal with, such as classroom books by topic or subject area and/or lists of student names and characteristics.

5. Do a lesson plan (goal, objective, teaching methods) to organize a lesson for students that requires the student to use a simple data base program. The students must decide what information to store, what kind of data could be retrieved, and what kinds of questions could be answered using a data base.

6. Using your curriculum or a model curriculum from some other source identify areas that might be taught using a word processor, spreadsheet, or data base program.

7. Look at your classroom (or a typical classroom) and decide what modifications would need to be made in order to facilitate the use of applications programs by students.

8. Review other types of applications programs that may have value in your discipline (such as graphics, graphing, computer-aided design, music, or environment-sensing tools).

9. Use and review selected items of software from the following "Worth A Look: Software."

WORTH A LOOK: SOFTWARE

Word Processing Software

WordPerfect (see Chapter 3 software). A very sophisticated yet easy-to-use word processor for secondary to adult levels, including the speller, thesaurus, math functions, and other features of a professional level word processor. Takes time to learn.

Bank Street Writer III or *Bank Street Writer (Broderbund Version)* (see Chapter 3 software). The Bank Street Writer word processing program has been highly regarded for a long time as a school writing tool, and its recent versions include several added features.

Easy Working: The Writer. Spinnaker; Apple II family, Commodore, and IBM/MS-DOS computers. This easy-to-use word processor offers built-in spell-checker and standard editing features at exceptionally low cost.

Magic Slate (see Chapter 3 software). A word processing program that adds options as students grow in proficiency from earliest word processing efforts on up.

Milliken Word Processor. Milliken Publishing: Apple II family computers. Absence of format options and other so-called "standard" word processing features makes this program a marvelously easy-to-learn and easy-to-use word processor for standard writing tasks once students learn keyboarding (grades 3 up).

Kidwriter. Spinnaker Software Corp.; Apple II family, Commodore, IBM/

MS-DOS computers. This is a very simple word processor combined with colorful graphics that makes student-generated storybooks possible and fun.

Muppet Slate (see Chapter 3 software). Used with the Muppet Learning Keys by children K–2 to produce and illustrate simple stories via the program's built-in graphics library and word processing features.

Picture Perfect (see Chapter 3 software). This tool can be used by young children to create illustrated stories. Library of graphics for selection and manipulation is provided.

Writing and Production Tools

Children's Writing & Publishing Center. The Learning Company; Apple II family computers. A desktop publishing program for grades 4 up with word wrap around pictures and other nice features.

Wordbench. Addison-Wesley; Apple II family and IBM/MS-DOS computers. Tools for notetaking, brainstorming, and outlining in addition to word processing with thesaurus, dictionary, and reference manager for senior high up.

The Newsroom. Springboard Software; Apple II family, Commodore, and IBM/MS-DOS computers. Program assists user in producing newsletters, flyers, notices, logos, etc. Enables printing of text, pictures, and page layouts.

Springboard Publisher. Springboard; Apple II family computers. A Macintosh-like desktop publishing program that communicates with a laser printer.

Writer's Helper (see Chapter 3 software). This aid-to-writing program has an outline aid, checks various attributes, such as gender-based words, "to be" words, and identifies word usage errors, misused homonyms, and does a word frequency count. Its two main uses are in developing and organizing a subject, and analyzing a writing project once it is drafted. It works with any word processor that can accept standard text files (such as WordPerfect or Bank Street Writer III).

Term Paper Writer. Mediagenic; Apple II family, Commodore, and IBM/MS-DOS computers. With this tool students from grades 8 up can prepare formal papers. In addition to word processor, program has notetaker, outliner, and ability to insert footnotes and compile bibliography.

Sensible Speller. Sensible Software; Apple II family computers. An electronic dictionary that finds misspellings and works with most popular word processing programs.

Proteus: The Idea Processor. RDA/Mind Builders; Apple II family; Commodore, TRS-80, and IBM/MS-DOS computers. A prewriting utility and tutorial that assists student or teacher in generating ideas and organizing thoughts.

ETG Plus. Savtek; IBM/MS-DOS computers. An integrated tool offering word processing, drawing program, spelling checker, thesaurus, and clip art for grades 7 up.

The Print Shop / Print Shop Companion (see Chapter 1 software). Useful for producing signs, banners, cards, calendars, stationery, etc. Enables a user to produce a limited amount of text in decorative formats with varied typestyles and borders. Graphics editing capability and a library of pictures and symbols.

Super Print. Scholastic; Apple II family and IBM/MS-DOS computers. Printing program can produce graphics four feet tall; also banners, cards, signs, posters, number lines, maps.

Keyboarding/Typing Programs

Keyboarding and typing software typically combines strategies of tutorials and drills. These programs are *not* in the category of information-free software described in this chapter; however, use of keyboarding or typing skills very often precedes significant curricular application of "tool programs," particularly those that are keyboard intensive. (Adequate keyboarding skill is essential for effective word processing, for example.) Therefore these programs can play a fundamental role in teaching efforts that use applications programs for student learning.

MicroType, The Wonderful World of Paws. South-Western Publishing; Apple II family computer. Keyboarding skills development for grades 3–6. The program provides an 18-lesson sequence of short sessions guided by a cartoon cat.

Success with Typing (see Chapter 2 software). Extensive sequence of lessons to teach typing for grade levels 5 through 12. Testing included.

Mavis Beacon Teaches Typing! (see Chapter 3 software). Artificial intelligence and very good graphics combine to produce an excellent choice of keyboarding program for secondary level and up.

Type! (see Chapter 3 software). Diagnosis of speed and accuracy enables this program to provide typing exercises suitable for beginning, intermediate or advanced typists, grades 5–12.

Superkey. Bytes of Learning; Apple II family computers. Ten-lesson sequence to teach basic keyboarding, skill check, and advice.

Microcomputer Keyboarding. South-Western; Apple II family, IBM/MS-DOS, and TRS-80 family computers. This program for grades 7 up includes alphabetic and numeric keyboarding lessons.

Typing Well. Mindscape; Apple II family computers. Games that are useful for sharpening touch typing skills of beginners in grades 2 up.

Stickybear Typing. Weekly Reader; Apple II family, Commodore, and IBM/MS-DOS computers. Three games at varied levels, sequenced typing practice and timed typing tests.

Kids on Keys. Spinnaker; Apple II family, Commodore, and IBM/MS-DOS computers. Practice games focused on familiarizing children ages 4–9 with the keyboard.

Spreadsheet Software

Educalc. Grolier Electronic Publishing; Apple II family, Commodore, IBM/MS-DOS computers. A tutorial on spreadsheets with interactive practice with a simple spreadsheet. Applicable from grades 4 up.

Lotus 1, 2, 3™. Lotus Development Corporation; IBM/MS-DOS computers.

Currently the best selling spreadsheet in the country. Includes data base management and graphing capabilities.

Easy Working: The Planner. Spinnaker; Apple II family, Commodore, and IBM/MS-DOS computers. This easy-to-use and exceptionally low-cost electronic spreadsheet is handy for budgeting, financial statements, and reports. It can be used with The Filer and The Writer in the same series.

SuperCalc. Sorcim; Apple II family and IBM/MS-DOS computers. A high level spreadsheet for any application.

Data Base Software

Bank Street School Filer. Sunburst Communications; Apple II family, Commodore. A data base manager specifically designed for classroom use, with simple commands. Can be used from grades 5 up. Several data bases are available for use with the program.

Data Handler. MECC; Apple II family, IBM/MS-DOS computers. A menu-driven data base that allows the user to enter, store, modify, search, sort, retrieve, and print data in reports, mailing labels, or other formats.

d-Base IV. Ashton-Tate; IBM/MS-DOS computers. The most widely used IBM/MS-DOS-relational data base management system. Takes time to learn, but sophisticated.

Friendly Filer. Grolier Electronic Publishing; Apple II family, Commodore, IBM/MS-DOS computers. This is an introductory program for teaching data base basics to beginning students in grade levels 3 through 9. Limited in storage, but a way to get started. Data base files also available.

Easy Working: The Filer. Spinnaker; Apple II family, Commodore, and IBM/MS-DOS computers. This simple data base manager can handle the basics of storing, selecting, and reporting of information. It can be used with The Writer, (also in the publisher's "Easy Working" series) to handle mail merge procedures.

Endangered Species Databases. Sunburst; Apple II family and Commodore computers. This data base on U.S. and worldwide endangered mammals and extinct animals requires Bank Street School Filer program.

One World: Countries Database. Active Learning Systems; Apple II family, Commodore, IBM/MS-DOS computers. A data base of current information on 175+ nations grouped into social, political, economic, and geographic fields. Teacher or students can add information.

USA Profile. Active Learning Systems; Apple II family, Commodore, IBM/MS-DOS computers. This program is a data base on the fifty states and the District of Columbia. It offers teaching suggestions and six units of study.

U.S. History DataBases for Scholastic PFS:File. Scholastic; Apple II family, IBM/MS-DOS computers. Utilized with the "Scholastic PFS: File" program this program provides files on information on U.S. history. The purpose of the program is best served when it is used to develop research process skills rather than gain content knowledge.

Integrated Software (Word Processor, Spreadsheet, Data Base)

AppleWorks™. Apple Computer Company; Apple II family computers. This integrated program allows one to share information between all three aspects of the program. A widely-used all-purpose classroom tool.

AppleWorks GS. Claris; Apple II GS. Enhanced "AppleWorks" package includes page layout, graphics, and communications as well as the "big three." Takes advantage of GS features, too.

Specialized Applications—*Fine Arts*

The Music Studio (see Chapter 3 software). Allows user to compose music, play back, and print out, even with lyrics.

Music Construction Set (see Chapter 3 software). Users with diverse musical experience and skill can write, edit, and print their compositions.

Create with Garfield! (see Chapter 3 software). Students from grades 3 up can use program to design and create cartoons, labels and posters.

Fantavision (see Chapter 3 software). The computer fills in between frames drawn by the student so that images are "animated" when shown in rapid sequence.

Koala Painter. Koala Technologies; Apple II family, Atari, Commodore, and IBM/MS-DOS computers (with Koala Pad). A tool for drawing and coloring designs with a finger or pointer device. Students with special needs may find this alternative to the keyboard very helpful in their drawing activities.

816/Paint (school edition) (see Chapter 3 software). An easy-to-use graphics and art program with icon menus.

Deluxe Paint II (see Chapter 3 software). Students in grades 4 up can use program to create graphic designs.

Paintworks Gold (see Chapter 3 software). A paint program with lots of features, such as rotating objects in fine increments and gradient color blending.

Adobe Illustrator. Adobe Systems; Macintosh computers. A powerful graphics program useful from grades 9 up for freehand sketching and automatic tracing for professional quality artwork.

Deluxe Video Vol 1.2. Electronic Arts; Amiga computers. Program provides a way to make videos without a camera. This tool employs computer generated graphics and digitized sound effects.

VCR Companion. Broderbund; Apple II family computers. Adds introductions, credits, special effects, animation, and transitions to video sequences.

MacDraw (see Chapter 3 software). A graphics development tool whose several CAD (computer-aided design) features are most useful at secondary level and up.

Specialized Applications—*Sciences*

Science Toolkit. Broderbund; Apple II family and IBM/MS-DOS computers. Students can use on-screen instruments: thermometer, light meter, timer, and strip chart to plot sensory input from temperature and light probes. (Beyond basic module, other modules' toolkits have tachometer and speedometer for investigating motion, and instruments for heart rate, response time, lung capacity, etc.)

The Atari Lab Starter Set. Atari, Inc.; Atari and Commodore computers. A package for turning the computer into a tool for experiments requiring temperature data.

Playing with Science. Sunburst, Apple II family computers. With the "Temperature" program, elementary children can perform experiments with thermisters while the computer handles data storage.

Experiments in Chemistry. HRM Software; Apple II family. A package of 15 experiments to do is provided, but high school students can use probes and data analysis utility for their own investigations.

Biofeedback Microlab. HRM Software; Apple II family and Commodore computers. Students from grade 9 to adult can investigate aspects of body functioning directly using sensors for pulse, skin temperature, etc.

Precision Timer. Vernier; Apple II family computers (with photogates). Program can be used by high school or college students for timing of falling, rolling, bouncing, or oscillating objects, studying collisions, calibrating strobe lights, etc.

Frequency Meter. Vernier; Apple II family computers (with microphone input). A lab tool useful from grade 9 up in science (or music) to measure audio frequencies or demonstrate the physics of music.

Sound: A Microcomputer-Based Lab. HRM/Queue; Apple II family computers. With this program students can measure, analyze and display image of sounds recorded by sensitive microphone.

Graphical Analysis II. Vernier; Apple II family. A tool for high school and college students to use in analyzing and graphing experimental data.

Other Specialized Applications

LogoWriter. Logo Computer Systems; Apple II family, Commodore, IBM/MS-DOS computers. For grades K through 12, this combined word processor and Logo turtle graphics program allows teachers a new avenue for introducing Logo into the curriculum.

Survey Taker. Scholastic; Apple II family computers. Provides the means for creating and printing surveys, analyzing survey data, and printing tables and graphs to display results visually.

Easy Graph. Grolier; Apple II family, Commodore, and IBM/MS-DOS computers. A program that uses a short, fill-in-the-blank process for accepting information which it then displays as pictograph, bar graph, or pie chart.

Mathgrapher: A Complete Graphing Utility. HRM/Queue; Apple II family and Commodore computers. With this tool, students grade 8 and up can analyze and manipulate equations and perform a number of procedures with functions.

Function Plotter. Wadsworth; Apple II family computers. A demonstration tool to illustrate geometric concepts in algebra.

Calendar Crafter (see Chapter 3 software). Utility for designing various types of calendars for printout.

READINGS

Abruscato, J. "Relational Knowledge and High Technology." *Children, Computers, and Science Teaching.* Englewood Cliffs, NJ: Prentice-Hall, 1986.

Becker, H. J. *Microcomputers in the Classroom—Dreams and Realities.* Report No. 319, Center for Social Organization of Schools, Baltimore, MD: The Johns Hopkins University, 1982.

Binderup, D. B. "Computer Keyboard Savvy." *Instructor* 97(8):30–32 (April 1988).

Daiute, C. *Writing and Computers.* Reading, MA: Addison-Wesley, 1985.

Dalton, B. M. et al. *I've Lost My Story! Integrating Word Processing with Writing Instruction.* Paper presented at the Annual Meeting of the American Educational Research Association, April, 1988 (ERIC Document #296717).

Gadomski, K. E. *Preparing Students to Compose on a Computer.* Paper presented at the Annual Meeting of the National Council of Teachers of English, November, 1986 (ERIC Document #277044).

Hedges, W. D. "The Data Base and Decision Making in Public Schools." In *Computers in the Schools*, The Haworth Press, Inc., 1984, 91–100.

Herrmann, A. W. *Teaching Writing with Computers: Are We Being Realistic?* Paper presented at the Annual Meeting of the South Central Modern Language Association, October, 1987 (ERIC Document #288199).

Koenke, K. "Keyboarding: Prelude to Composing at the Computer." *English Education* 19(4):244–49 (December 1987).

Larter, S. et al. *Writing with Microcomputers in the Elementary Grades: Process, Roles, Attitudes, and Products.* Toronto: Ontario Department of Education, 1987.

McLeod, R., and Hunter, B. *Scholastic PFS: Curriculum Data Bases for Physical Science (and Life Science).* New York: Scholastic, Inc., 1985.

Scheifer, N. "Making the Leap to Desktop Publishing." *Classroom Computer Learning* 7(3):39–41 (November-December 1986).

Schwartz, H. *Interactive Writing: Composition with Word Processors.* New York: Holt, Rinehart & Winston, 1985.

Sullivan, D. R., Lewis T. G., and Cook, C. R. *Computing Today: Microcomputer Concepts and Applications.* Boston, MA: Houghton Mifflin Company, 1985.

Tolbert, P. H., and Tolbert C. M. "Classroom Applications of Electronic Spreadsheet Computer Software." *Educational Technology*, October 1983, 20–22.

Watt, D. "Practical Teaching Tools." *Popular Computing*, October 1984, 54, 59.

Williams, A. *What If? A User's Guide to Spreadsheets on the IBM® PC*. New York: Wiley Press, 1984.

Woldman, E., and Kalowski, P. "Make Your Own Dinosaur Data Base," *Teaching and Computers*, February, 1985, 14–17.

Woerner, J. J. "The Apple Microcomputer as a Laboratory Tool." *Journal of Computers in Mathematics and Science Teaching*, Fall-Winter 1987–88, 7(1–2):34–37.

Wresch, W., ed. *The Computer in Composition Instruction: A Writer's Tool*. Urbana, IL: National Council of Teachers of English, 1984.

REFERENCES

Borland International, Inc. "GeoBase." In *Turbo Prolog*. Scotts Valley, CA: Borland International Inc., 1986.

Hanna, L. "Social Studies, Spreadsheets and the Quality of Life," *The Computing Teacher*, December/January 1985-1986, 13–17.

Hedges, W. D. "The Data Base and Decision Making in the Public Schools." *Computers in the Schools*, Fall 1984, 91–100.

Hunter, B. "The Case for a Classroom Database" *Instructor*, 94(7): 54–56 (March 1985).

Hunter, B. "Problem Solving with Data Bases." *The Computing Teacher*, May 1985, 20–27.

Hunter, B., and Furlong, M. *Scholastic PFS: Curriculum Data Bases for U.S. History (and U.S. Government)*. New York: Scholastic, Inc., 1985.

Keith, G. R., and Glover, M. *Primary Language Learning with Microcomputers*, Wolfeboro, NH: Croom Helm, 1987.

Luehrmann, A., and Peckham, H. *AppleWorks Data Bases*. Gilroy, CA: Computer Literacy Press, 1987.

Wresch, W. *A Practical Guide to Computer Uses in the Engish Language Arts Classroom*. Englewood Cliffs, NJ: Prentice-Hall, 1987.

6

Measuring and Managing Learning with Microcomputers

OBJECTIVES

- Contrast the typical testing pattern used in classrooms with the pattern for measuring student performance that a microcomputer can facilitate.
- Identify the main elements of quality classroom instruction and the role of record keeping in relation to the other elements.
- Name at least three methods for using a computer to support classroom testing and record keeping.
- Describe the characteristics of a test-making application program that could be used with a given set of objectives.
- Describe how a computer can contribute to a diagnostic and prescriptive teaching program.
- Describe the features of a simple computer-managed instruction system that performs all basic classroom record keeping functions.
- State ways in which a computer-managed record keeping system can contribute to increased teaching effectiveness and improved student learning.

INTRODUCTION

Thus far we have principally discussed how a computer-using teacher can, by using the microcomputer before and during the process of instruction, enhance teaching effectiveness and promote student learning. Another area of instruction deals with the questions of how the teacher manages the instructional process and assesses students' progress. A teacher must make decisions about how students are performing, which students need further instruction, and when to move students on to new topics. The term *computer-managed instruction (CMI)* refers to computer involvement in these kinds of professional decisions.

With a computer and supportive CMI software, the teacher can readily ascertain answers to questions of the following type:

- Which students passed the test on Objective X?
- Which test question on the test of Goal Z are most students missing?
- What is the average grade on Topic W?

In addition, in classrooms where all students are not working on the same objectives at the same time, a teacher might be interested in the answers to the following questions a CMI program can readily provide:

- Which students are studying Objective X?
- What topics have been completed by Student Y?
- How much progress has the whole class made toward accomplishing Goal Z?
- Which students are lingering on one topic?
- What does Student V's test/retest record look like?
- What is each student's score on Topic W?

Answers to such questions as these hinge on two critical areas: the testing process and the record keeping process. In this chapter we will explore how teachers can use computers in these two areas to better measure and manage their students' learning. As we proceed through the chapter, we will examine a simple model for quality classroom instruction, and then focus on the testing and record keeping aspects of classroom computer use as experienced in three different types of school settings, one of which makes use of a sophisticated CMI system.

Although powerful CMI programs have been available since the onset of classroom computers, their capabilities have not created a great deal of interest among educators. In reporting the distribution of educational software by type, the Office of Technology Assessment (Scrogan, 1988) did not even list CMI as a category. CMI is a powerful teaching tool that deserves more attention. Tyre (1989), in compiling a directory of available CMI systems, reports a recent resurgence of interest in CMI's potential for addressing many of the concerns raised during the 1980s by a number of reports critical of education in the United States. He sees CMI as a possible solution to the quality of education issue.

Goals

- What major types of microcomputer programs are available to assist in the processes of testing, record keeping, and making instructional decisions?
- How does computer use for testing differ from computer management of instruction?
- What factors contribute to quality programs in testing and computer-managed instruction?

QUALITY CLASSROOM INSTRUCTION

If one were to make a simple diagram of what constitutes quality in classroom instruction, at least four important ideas would need to be incorporated (Futrell and Geisert, 1984). Quality classroom instruction needs to have: (1) clear and meaningful purpose, (2) effective and efficient teaching methods, (3) valid and reliable measures of outcomes, and (4) a record keeping system to keep track of what is happening and to sustain decision making in the other three areas. These four factors support and interact with each other, and provide a framework with which to define quality instruction (refer to Figure 6.1).

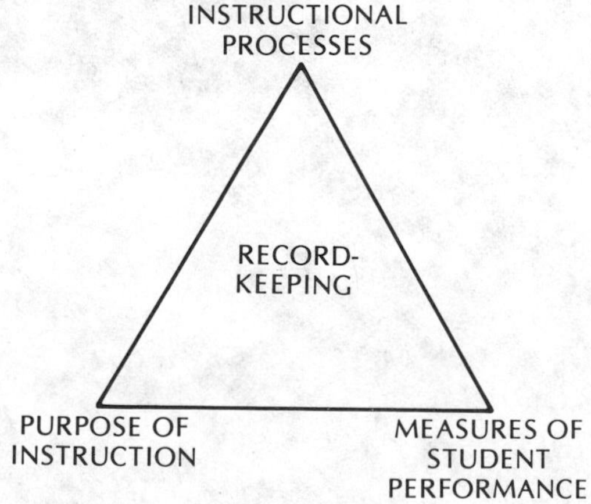

FIGURE 6.1 A Framework for Quality Instruction

Let's take a closer look at these four defining elements. We have already dealt with the topics of educational intent and teaching processes in Chapter 4. In this chapter we will only briefly touch on these two important aspects, and then go much more deeply into testing and record keeping aspects.

Educational Intent and Processes

Because it is from goals and objectives that all other instructional planning comes, developing meaningful statements of educational intent is a vital first step in the development of quality instruction.

Once the educational intent of a district or school has been established through the adoption of a set of public goals and objectives, the administration and faculty can create the school programs. The programs are to facilitate the teachers' role of implementing instructional processes that will promote learning and support students as they move toward the acquisition of the skills and knowledge they need.

Measurement

The third apex of the triangle representing quality instruction is the "measurement of student performance." The only way a district or school system will be

A computer lab can serve to meet ongoing needs in testing and instruction.

able to determine if and when its students have reached the designated goals and objectives, and if teaching methods are effective and efficient, is through some process of assessment.

School or classroom microcomputers can be valuable tools in the process of measuring student performance. Chapter 3, for example, pointed out how a microcomputer can be used to facilitate a teacher's test writing process. In addition, there are computer programs that score tests. Others test students on-line. Still others administer tests and place the test results into a computer-managed record keeping system.

The microcomputer's real power, however, lies well beyond its use for simple production of tests and storing of scores. It can be a revolutionary tool in the whole area of testing if given half a chance. But just as curricular use of the word processor, spreadsheet, and data base program requires teachers to rethink what they are teaching, efforts to utilize the microcomputer's capability to test students necessitate some rethinking by teachers of how they use tests in teaching.

For example, the typical measurement pattern for a classroom is: (1) give a unit test . . . on a specific day . . . to a group of students, (2) rank the test scores (students), and (3) make evaluation decisions (assign grades to the scores). Contrast this procedure with the type of measurement pattern a microcomputer might facilitate. For instance, the microcomputer could be used to test students on an individual basis at any point in time to determine if they have achieved some learning goal (new or old).

In a practical application of this idea, one of the authors developed a mastery learning-based biology course for college students (five hundred per semester) in which any student could take any test in the program at any time as many times as necessary to demonstrate mastery of a unit (90% score or higher) (Geisert, 1974). In the course, use was made of the computer's ability to generate different but parallel versions of the tests for each unit. This allowed unlimited testing and retesting with rapid feedback on performance provided to students on each unit objective.

Record Keeping

The fourth aspect of quality classroom instruction is record keeping. Although this concept can be as simple as the maintenance of a grade book, it can be as complex as the tracking of large numbers of students who are working on a diversity of objectives. We will present an example of the latter, with an emphasis on utilizing the computer to develop a system to keep track of what is happening in a curriculum and sustain decision making in the other three instructional areas (educational intent; instructional processes; measurement).

A paragraph or two back you were introduced to a biology course that allowed students to progress at their own rate, taking tests whenever they wanted to demonstrate mastery of a unit of instruction. How was it that a teacher could keep track of the individual performance of five hundred students, all studying different topics?

The answer lay in the use of the computer-managed record keeping system for the course (Geisert, 1974). When students took and passed a test, their names and the unit test number were entered in a computer record system. At any point in time the instructor could request a printout of who had finished what units when.

Another computer program analyzed the tests that students had taken (both tests that were passed and not passed) and identified poor questions through item analysis. As time passed, the poorer questions were dropped and better ones written to replace them, thus upgrading the quality of the *item pool,* the set of questions from which the computer constructed the tests.

The combination of computer-generated parallel tests and a computer-managed record system allowed the course instructor to make decisions on the following types of questions: Which test question(s) on the test of Goal Z are most students missing? Which students are studying Unit X? What units have been completed by Student Y? How much progress has the whole class made toward accomplishing the course? Which students are lingering on one topic? and Which units are requiring a large number of retests (perhaps not being taught as well as they should be)?

In this manner, the record keeping methodology tied together the three other aspects of the program, allowing the instructor to make decisions on course purpose and intent, methods of presentation, and testing.

A TALE OF THREE SCHOOLS

For most of the rest of this chapter we will present three different types of schools and illustrate the different ways they utilized microcomputers to solve some testing and record keeping challenges.

Our first school is Summerset High, a small senior high school organized around self-contained classrooms teaching subject-matter courses and doing most of its testing via teacher-made tests. With few resources allotted for secretarial or other assistance in the task, teachers have been spending lots of time in producing and duplicating tests. Despite a rather severe budget crunch, the principal of this school, in an attempt to help her teachers, has asked them if they would like to spend some of the materials budget for a microcomputer to help them with the task of preparing their tests.

School number two, Glenview Elementary, has been committed for seven years to the concept of mastery learning, in which students are tested and retested until all show mastery of the topic under study. The school is located in a large suburban district with a lot of attrition in the student population due to its location. Glenview has a K–6 curriculum guide and teachers are more or less expected to follow the intent, if not the letter, of the curriculum. Increasing pressures from the district related to test scores and new state mandates keep the school's curriculum committee quite active. Currently it is trying to decide if the best way to help teachers carry through the school philosophy is to implement a microcomputer-based testing program.

School number three, Fairmont School, is a central-city public alternative school for students who have completed elementary school. The school offers a very individualized instructional program that is exceedingly fluid. Fairmont deals with many high-risk students whose academic achievements to date have been minimal. Student attendance is sporadic, and turnover is high. Still, many students keep returning to the program, and teachers are strongly committed to it. Last winter, after intensively considering their challenges and resources, the faculty decided on program revisions. The school has now purchased and put into place a sophisticated computer-managed instructional system to support the program changes they have made.

The microcomputer has the potential to play an important role in each of these three schools. In each case, the role is as different as the schools themselves. Perhaps you will see a little of your school and classroom in each one as we proceed to tell the stories of what happens at Summerset, Glenview, and Fairmont Schools.

SUMMERSET HIGH

At Summerset High teachers prepare the tests for their own classes on ditto or stencil and run them off in the spacious but very-low-tech teachers' work room. The usual situation is to administer a given test to the whole class at the same time, but there is considerable diversity in the types of tests used. What kind of contribution could a computer make to the process of producing teacher-made tests? At the request of the principal, a group of interested Summerset teachers got together as an advisory committee to find out.

The committee learned that a number of different types of computer programs could be used for testing. Among other things, they found that all the following could be employed with a single computer using an inexpensive program, as long as the computer had a printer that could type a ditto or stencil: (1) word processing, (2) test-making applications programs, (3) ready-made tests on floppy disks that accompany publishers' texts, and (4) data banks of questions from which a teacher could pick and choose questions. There was considerable debate about the relative merits of these. The committee decided that, before recommending anything final to the principal, it would identify the main points and present them for consideration by other interested teachers. What follows is an informal summary by one member at an after-school meeting.

Test Construction Alternatives

Word Processing

The old standby, the word processor, seems quite versatile as a test-making program. It can save time compared to our current method of typing a test on a ditto sheet. It is neat and efficient, since errors are correctable before they hit the ditto. Once a test is produced it can be saved for future use and then easily modified. Since word processors can also move blocks of text around, it is possible to rearrange questions into multiple forms to make it harder for students to look at each others' answers. Several word processing programs have the features needed if you were to want to prepare your own formats, such as for typing in your own kind of multiple-choice questions.

We have found that every computer made has word processor programs available ranging from inexpensive through very expensive, and that on average you could learn to type a test on one in a few hours. Also, the word processor could be used for many roles other than test generation. But, we found that word processors are not specifically designed to type tests, and hence were not quite as efficient at this task as some programs that are fashioned primarily to make tests.

Test-making Programs

According to Sharon, who tried out several programs having a predesignated format into which multiple-choice, true/false, matching, and completion questions are entered, these programs seem to speed up the test development task. Generally, these test authoring programs are akin to a word processor but you have the power to pick and choose the types and numbers of questions you would like to have in a test, the entry of answers is automatic, and there are generally a variety of ways that tests and work sheets can be formatted.

In the case of a multiple-choice test-making program, you enter the question stem, the item choices, and the answers without each time having to worry about the numbering or question format. The program then generates the test from your entries and prints it onto paper or a ditto or stencil sheet so it can be duplicated and passed out to a class (see Figure 6.2).

The nice thing about some of the test generators is their power to mix various types of questions (multiple-choice, true/false, etc.); others scramble questions for alternative test forms, and still others allow you to enter questions in groups that relate to one topic, objective, or course goal (for example, five questions on Thomas Jefferson). This last feature would be handy for Dan to use in his self-paced mastery learning history course because he could get as many parallel forms as he needed, all well-organized by objectives, with no two forms having to be alike.

With most of the test generators, you enter the answer at the same time you put in each question. Then, when the generator has the printer type out a test, you can have it just print out the *teacher's key* at the same time (which is important when you're creating alternative forms).

```
MICROSYSTEMS TEST GENERATOR

TYPE TEST ITEM 1

    1.      ____________________________________
        A.  ____________________________________
        B.  ____________________________________
        C.  ____________________________________
        D.  ____________________________________
Answer:     ____________________________________

TYPE TEST ITEM 2

    2.      ____________________________________
        A.  ____________________________________
        B.  ____________________________________
        C.  ____________________________________
        D.  ____________________________________
Answer:     ____________________________________
```

FIGURE 6.2 A Sample Screen from a Test Generator

Test Item Banks

Here's something the English Department might be interested in. Remember when they discussed working cooperatively on testing? With a more sophisticated test-maker they could develop an *item bank* that would get better and better over time. They would produce a pool of test questions to select from in making specific tests. This type of system could provide a group of teachers working together (or just one teacher) a great deal of latitude in the development of tests since, as the bank of questions on a given topic grows, they'd have the ability to cull bad questions and keep those that have proven their worth. Some programs keep track of the performance of the items themselves, so the teacher could have an increasingly valid set of test questions from which to choose. In addition, there are commercial resources that provide ready-made question banks that can be tapped for use.

Ready-Made Tests

Speaking of "ready-made," several textbook publishers have produced tests for each chapter of their texts and stored them on microcomputer diskettes. You'll need to check to see if the book you use has these *text-correlated tests* available. If so, you would use the computer to select from all the publisher-written test questions the ones you want to use, and then print your own test for duplication. In some cases, the publisher produces multiple forms of these correlated tests.

One problem with some ready-made tests is that not all publisher programs allow teachers to add their own test questions. A second problem arises when the publisher does not include questions on all the topics you think are important in a unit. But there are data bases of test questions available commercially. This fact was enough to convince a couple of us on the committee that electronic test files that short-circuit the task of writing test items are worth checking into.

Our study committee also found out there are some computer grade book programs that use the computer to record grades.

Summerset's Decisions

With the funding the principal was able to supply, Summerset teachers decided to purchase one microcomputer and printer and place it in the teachers' work center alongside their duplicating machine. They equipped the computer with a test-maker that had a wide spectrum of capabilities that satisfied most teachers' needs, including creating work sheets from test items and pooling/evaluating items. Some individual teachers got diskettes from publishers and thus used the same computer to print their tests from ready-made tests.

Summerset also decided to purchase an inexpensive word processing program to fill in the gaps when a teacher wanted to create a test and to be used for general writing purposes and class handouts as well.

Finally, they decided to buy just one copy of a teacher grade book program to have a few teachers use it for one semester and report back on its effectiveness.

GLENVIEW ELEMENTARY

Resources are less a problem here at Glenview. But since the school is committed to the concept of mastery learning, the school faces a number of problems not encountered at Summerset High. Typically, when a class is given a test, not all members of the class pass the test at a mastery level and these students must be provided more instruction and then retested, while students who have passed the test are given enrichment. This process results in a fairly large number of tests and retests. To complicate matters, at this school they have a fairly high rate of student mobility with numerous students entering and leaving the program during the year. Glenview's curriculum committee finds there are a couple of microcomputer tools to help them out.

On-Line Testing Programs

The committee discovers that there are programs that will generate a test for standard use, present the test to a student on the computer, score it automatically, and save the results on diskette.

This type of program would allow a Glenview teacher to use the computer for testing in two ways: (1) to prepare a class set of printed tests for use with all students after a round of instruction, and (2) for on-line testing, on an individual basis, of those students who did not demonstrate mastery. In the first case, the teacher presents and scores the test. In the second, the computer presents the test (or a parallel version) to the student, scores the student's answers, and then saves the results for the teacher to combine with the other scores at a convenient time.

Although on-line tests are no more difficult for a teacher to prepare than computer-produced paper versions, the administration of the test requires much more computer access time because one student will be sitting at the computer for some time while taking the test. If many students have to take mastery retests, it is possible to occupy the classroom computer fully with testing. Some careful thought must go into deciding whether that is the best way to use the microcomputer.

Scoring Programs and Hardware

The Glenview curriculum committee found a second way to approach their problem—a program that automatically scores teacher-made tests. They learned that the school could purchase a device that could be attached to one computer and that would read mark-sense answer sheets (refer to Figure 6.3). A teacher could prepare and administer the tests and have students respond on special answer cards or answer sheets that would then be fed through the *mark-sense reader.* The computer would then automatically score and print out the test results. The automatic scoring procedure is very rapid and large numbers of tests can be scored and recorded in a matter of minutes. A single card reader is all that is needed to process many thousands of tests each day, a tremendous savings in teacher time at the same task.

The Glenview teachers identified some drawbacks associated with a mark-sense reader. Due to the expense, one machine is all that is purchased for a school. Though the one machine can readily handle all the tests, it means each teacher must take the answer sheets to a central office for scoring. The tests must be given on special forms used by the reader, and this means an additional expense. It also means that the tests need to be the multiple choice, true/false type. (Teachers who wished to use essay questions would have to divide their tests into parts—one part to grade themselves, and the rest for the machine to handle.) In addition, there is a special procedure required to code

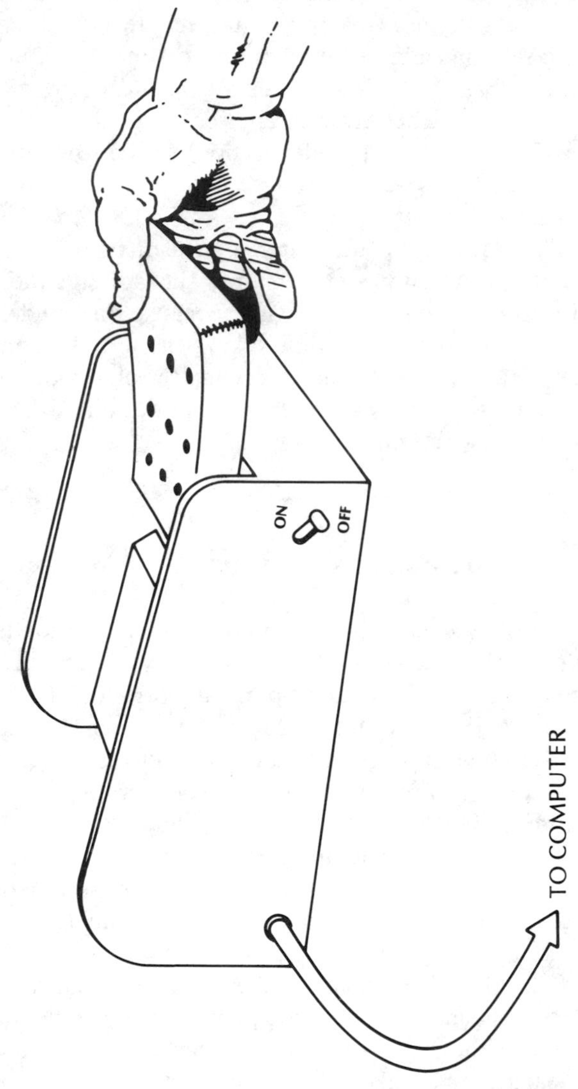

FIGURE 6.3 A Mark-sense Reader at Work

into the computer exactly which tests are being graded. This causes an initial barrier to use.

Computer-Managed Lessons

A third approach to solving the Glenview problems was discovered. It seemed to have potential in certain subjects. Some publishers of instructional materials for the elementary school produce adjunct materials for the computer that have computer-managed lessons and tests. The publisher's diskette holds one lesson along with pretests, posttests, and a capacity for keeping student records. When students use such a program, the computer asks them to enter their name or I.D. number. The students are presented with a pretest to determine if they already know the material. If the students do not know the material the computer presents CAI, followed by a mastery posttest. The program stores the results of the posttest under the students' names in a file of computer-managed records, which a teacher can access by using a password.

The curriculum committee identified a computer-managed K–6 math instructional program that was quite comprehensive and that matched their own math curriculum closely. Using the program, the teachers could teach their mastery math lesson with a whole class, and then put students who did not yet show mastery of the lesson into a computer-managed math lesson on the same objective. The computer kept the records of student progress for the teacher so that the teacher knew when students had completed the lesson and were ready to proceed on with their classmates.

Diagnostic and Prescriptive Teaching

As a possible route toward coping with their student mobility problems, the curriculum committee became quite interested in the possibility of the school implementing a *diagnostic testing program* in mathematics and language arts. This special type of testing program incorporates a set of test questions to measure student performance on a given set of objectives. The program decides, by giving appropriate test items, which specific skills and knowledge a student does and does not have, in relation to the set of objectives being tested.

A diagnostic testing program in mathematics differs in operation from standard math testing since its purpose is to identify and describe the level at which a given student is functioning. It does this by presenting to the student a hierarchy of math problems and then determining which categories and levels the student can (and cannot) answer.

The operation of the test itself is unusual. For example, the diagnostic program first presents the student with very simple problems, perhaps in addition. If the student gets two questions in a row correct, the computer will try harder problems, working its way through increasingly difficult problems. When the program starts to encounter errors, it will slow down and test more carefully the concept being measured. By this process, the computer will make a decision on which skills the student has and does not have. Then the computer will print out a statement of the objectives a student has mastered and those the student has yet to learn (see Figure 6.4).

With this type of testing available, a teacher can review objectives being studied by the class and determine where more work is required. Used on a school-wide basis, a diagnostic and prescriptive program can facilitate assignment of students to instruction that matches their level.

Glenview's Decisions

Glenview did not choose a single approach to solving their particular problems. They now have a computer in the central office that is devoted to diagnosis and prescription in math and language arts for new students. The same computer has a mark-sense scoring machine for all teachers to use. The teachers are using computer-managed mathematics lessons in their individual classrooms since each has at least one microcomputer. A few teachers are using on-line testing programs on an experimental basis to determine how well they work in the Glenview program, and they have been provided extra computing power for this purpose.

FAIRMONT SCHOOL

The four hundred students at Fairmont School range in age from twelve to eighteen, and there are twenty-seven teachers and administrators, a number of paid aides, and some volunteer and peer teachers. The Fairmont faculty is committed strongly to the concept of individualizing instruction to best meet student needs.

Prescription for Nancy Hartman, April 15th

Nancy can do the following math objectives:

    add two 2-digit numbers
    multiply a 1-digit number times a 2-digit number
    subtract two 2-digit numbers
    divide a 1-digit into a 1-digit number evenly

Nancy cannot do the following math objectives:

    add a 2-digit and 3-digit number with carrying
    multiply a 2-digit number times a 2-digit number
    —all objectives beyond this point in curriculum

FIGURE 6.4 The Results of Diagnostic Testing

The school's student body is organized by learning groups, and these groups are flexible and constantly changing. Students learn at their own rate, hence they move into and out of groups all the time. Still, this school system is required by state law to keep track of attendance and where students are during any portion of the day.

Fairmont has a very explicitly structured curriculum of learning goals and associated performance objectives. Each performance objective has a set of test items and the learning materials associated with the objective are identified. Annually the teachers have spent in-service time reviewing and updating the curriculum, and they are pleased with this aspect of the school's program. It has won them notice in the city, and last year they applied for and received a special grant to enhance retention and try to boost the percentage of students completing the secondary program.

Fairmont's Decisions

The Fairmont faculty decided not only to make some program revisions, but also to use a computer-managed instructional system.

A *CMI system* is a computer program that has the capability of storing and relating a number of different types of information files. Among a number of other things, there can be files for: (1) students, (2) school goals, (3) school objectives, (4) tests, (5) teachers, (6) learning materials, (7) volunteers and aides, and (8) administrative information such as school finances and students receiving state aid.

A CMI system might be as small as one that serves one teacher using one microcomputer, or, as in the case of Fairmont School, as large as a comprehensive system with a *network* of computers linked together and able to share information. Fairmont's network consists of numerous less powerful teacher computers linked to one central school office computer.

Elements of the Fairmont School CMI System

What kind of information does a comprehensive computer-managed instructional system control? For one thing, the school looks to its CMI system to identify who is in the school and what they are studying, and this necessitates the system handling certain student information. A sampling of such information is illustrated in the chart shown in Figure 6.5.

In addition to student information, Fairmont needs to be able to describe its instructional program. Some elements of this description are shown in Figure 6.6.

Of course the school needs to identify teachers and teacher aides and the subjects and situations they are capable of teaching. Figure 6.7 illustrates information of that type.

In short, there is a data base file for every important instructional aspect

Item	*The CMI system needs to have:*
Contact information	student's name parents' name home address telephone
Current learning group	The study group the student is a member of at present
Current learning goals	The designated learning goals the student is working on
Current objectives	For each learning goal the specific performance objectives the student is working on
Previous goals	The work previously completed

FIGURE 6.5 Information to Describe a Student

Item	*The CMI system needs to have:*
School goals	A complete listing of all goals a student could pursue
School objectives	A complete listing of all performance objectives keyed to the goals
Minicourses	A complete listing of learning segments keyed to goals and objectives
Test items	Five or more test items keyed to each objective
Learning materials	Three or more sets of learning materials that could be used to study to learn a specific objective
Learning guides	The names and locations of teachers who can work with a student or group on a given learning goal
Volunteer resource teachers	The names and telephone numbers of volunteers who will help students to reach specific objectives.
Peer teachers	Students who could help other students on specific objectives

FIGURE 6.6 Information Needed to Describe the Instructional Program

of the school, and there are designations of how these aspects relate to each other. For example, at nine o'clock on a Friday the Fairmont School CMI system could be queried for information about Robert McFerson. It would be able to provide answers to such questions as these: "Is Robert in school today, and if so, with what teacher, in which room? What language arts objective is he studying, how long has he been working on the objective, and when will he be ready to take a test to demonstrate he has mastered the objective?"

Item	*The CMI system needs to have:*
Contact information	Name Address Phone
Location schedule	Locations in school during the day and week
Subject expertise	A listing of all the goals and/or objectives person is qualified to teach
Major interests	Prioritization of all teaching and extracurricular interests
Second language	Abilities to communicate with LEP students
Special experience	A listing of special credentials or ability to work with special groups

FIGURE 6.7 Information to Describe the Teachers (and teaching aides)

What It Takes to Set Up a CMI System

It is a challenging task to establish a CMI system. The teachers and administrators at Fairmont were fortunate in that they already had in place a complete 7 through 12 curriculum listing all the learning goals for the school to a high level of specificity.

For the Fairmont CMI system, each performance objective had to have from five to ten test items written to test the objective and at least three ways a student could study to learn the objective. Each learning goal had to be associated with a teacher's name. Linked to each teacher's name was a daily schedule into which a student could be placed. All this information was entered into the CMI program, which stored and interrelated all the data.

Three main aspects are faced by users of any CMI system: (1) getting information into the system, (2) keeping the system current, and (3) getting information out of the system. Fairmont had to confront and solve all of these problems. But the energy required for the job was deemed worth it, since it allowed the school to run the type of program that the school's faculty felt was needed to serve its students.

What a CMI System Has to Offer

It is important to emphasize here that learning objectives are the core of CMI (Geisert and Futrell, 1984; Tyre, 1989). They have been from its very beginnings. Though CMI systems have evolved considerably in response to advances in technology and the demands of educators, this one constant—the focus on objectives—has clearly remained. CMI systems tie this feature very explicitly and efficiently to other elements (testing, teaching and learning resources, student information, and so on), but it is the objectives themselves that really "drive" a CMI system. Objectives underlie more than just CMI, however.

Recall that earlier in this chapter we emphasized the importance of clear and meaningful educational intent to instructional quality as well. Sound learning objectives for students are a common thread to tie CMI and instructional quality together. To the extent that educators have taken or desire to take that vital first step toward quality—clarifying worthwhile objectives to underlie the remaining instructional elements (measures, instructional methods, record keeping)—they are likely to find CMI paying off in several ways to enhance the quality of instruction provided to students, and to better ensure achievement of those objectives.

It was obvious to the Fairmont faculty that CMI would be an asset to their instructional program. For others, what CMI has to offer to education may not be so readily perceived.

Once the CMI system is set up and in place, teachers will be the first to

TABLE 6.1 Summary of Testing and CMI Features

Spectrum of testing and CMI programs available	*Brief description of the program and the computer and hardware required to use this type of program*
Word processor	Need any type of computer, printer, and word processing program. The word processor makes test typing easy; tests can be easily changed and easily stored.
Test generator	Need computer, printer, and test generation program. Need to enter test questions and answers but the form for the questions and the test is provided and there may be easy generation of alternate forms. Easy to store, change, and print tests and work sheets.
Test scoring	Need computer with an attached mark-sense reader and special program. Special test answer sheets are fed into the machine. The tests are automatically scored and the results recorded and printed out for the teacher.
Testing included with a text	Need computer and printer. Publisher provides the program and test questions for the text. No questions need to be entered, and often one can pick and choose from an item bank.
CMI included with a drill or tutorial lesson	Need lesson program and computer to run it. Teacher needs to enter student names and set any instructional parameters, such as difficulty level of items.
Simple CMI	No special hardware required, but would need a CMI program. Teacher is required to enter aspects of the curriculum such as goals, objectives, test items, and student names.
Comprehensive CMI	This requires a powerful computer and printer capability, and a special CMI program. Extensive information is required: goals, objectives, test items, learning materials, student information, and other special aspects.

benefit, because CMI reduces their paperwork and the amount of time needed to evaluate their students' performance. More importantly, their decision making, and hence their effectiveness, is enhanced by the wealth of information they can choose to examine and use. Because of the multiple measurement opportunities they are afforded and the assurance of accuracy in measuring student mastery of objectives, teachers gain confidence in their instructional planning. Students are helped since priorities for their learning efforts are clarified, and lessons can be adjusted to enable better remediation of weaknesses. CMI really can facilitate a teacher's commitment toward the individualization of instructional procedures to meet student learning needs.

Those directly involved in the instructional process—teachers and students—are not the only beneficiaries. Because curriculum goals are clarified for all concerned, parents and resource personnel and administrators can also make better decisions. A CMI system generates a great deal of hard data. The historical record of student achievement—for individual pupils, for an entire class, or even for a whole school or district—that CMI provides, helps educators in all capacities to quickly identify problem areas and adjust curriculum accordingly.

Despite CMI's many potential benefits, however, it is clear from the experiences of previous school systems that commitment to the system is a necessary ingredient to its successful implementation. CMI needs sincere commitment on the part of teachers and administrators to make adjustments. Rethinking their traditional "teach and test" patterns, for example, is an important step for teachers who wish to reap CMI's largesse.

SUMMARY AND REVIEW CHECKLIST

If there is a moral to the tale of the three schools it is this: There is a computer test-making or testing program and/or CMI system to fit every school or teacher's needs and resources and time. Testing programs can be simpler than word processing or as comprehensive as a CMI system in which the results of testing are automatically converted into student progress records and prescriptions for study.

Before checking for your understanding of this chapter, refer to Table 6.1 for an overview of the major ways that a computer program can be employed in the task of measuring and managing student learning. Perhaps you will glimpse the possibilities and potentials for what computer-based testing and CMI programs may hold for you and your students.

Checklist

[ ] I can contrast the typical testing pattern used in classrooms with the type of measurement of student performance facllltated by a microcomputer.

[ ] I can identify the main elements of quality classroom instruction and the role of record keeping in relation to the other elements.

[ ] I can name and contrast at least three methods for using a computer to support classroom testing and record keeping.

[ ] I can describe the general characteristics of an information-free test-making program.

[ ] I can describe how a school might set up a diagnostic and prescriptive teaching program.

[ ] I can identify the usefulness and the limitations of on-line testing of students.

[ ] I can state some of the elements of a simple computer-managed instruction system for simple record keeping purposes.

[ ] I can state how a computer-managed record keeping system could contribute to increased teaching effectiveness and improved student learning.

SUGGESTED ACTIVITIES

1. Use a microcomputer to take an on-line test that provides a summary performance score.
2. Use a test-making applications program to produce your own test. Produce a second version of the original test.
3. Utilize a mathematics diagnostic and prescriptive program to ascertain your level of performance in college level algebra, or some other area appropriate to your skills.
4. Use a computer-assisted learning program that stores student records. Play the role of a student and use the program for a period of time. Then play the role of a teacher and analyze what types of records the program produces.
5. Select a simple computer-managed lesson and, acting as the teacher, prepare it for use by a hypothetical class of five students.
6. Review the records provided by a sophisticated CMI system and decide what information would be of value to a teacher and what would be superfluous.
7. Use and review selected items of software from the following "Worth a Look: Software."

WORTH A LOOK: SOFTWARE

Classmate (see Chapter 3 software). A program that records grades, attendance, comments, computes final grades on total points or weights, graphs distribution curves, prints reports.

Teacher's Quiz Designer (see Chapter 3 software). Allows teachers to design, print, and/or give multiple-choice tests on the computer. The program includes record keeping and optional features such as auditory reinforcement of correct answers, second chances at questions, and automatic time control.

Grade Busters 1/2/3. Grade Busters; Apple II family computers. Grade book, attendance record, and Scan-tron/Scatsworth scoring program that can be used by teachers at most levels. Produces reports for students, parents, administrators.

TAGS: The A+ Gradebook System. COMPress; Apple II family computers. A system that keeps track of up to 288 students and 45 grade entries in a report period. Several options for reports.

Gradebook Plus. Mindscape; Apple II family, IBM/MS-DOS, and Macintosh computers. Includes recording and calculating of scores and grades, customized report-writing, and statistical analyses.

Report Card (see Chapter 3 software). A management system for use by teachers at any level. Program enables user to calculate grades and print out a variety of performance and progress reports for individuals, classes, or activities.

CORE Reading and Vocabulary Development (see Chapter 4 software). This program has a management system that keeps track of each student's performance and tracks students, putting them back into the program at the point where they left off.

READINGS

Baker, F. *Computer-Managed Instruction: Theory and Practice*. Englewood Cliffs, NJ: Educational Technology Publications, 1978.

Brodeur, D. R. "Test Generator Program Features That Facilitate Classroom Testing." *Educational Technology* 26(11):39–42 (November 1986).

Kohl, H. "Classroom Management Software: Beware the Hidden Agenda." *Classroom Computer Learning*, March 1985, 18–21.

Lippy, G., ed. *Computer-Assisted Test Construction*. Englewood Cliffs, NJ: Educational Technology Publications, 1974.

Perry, D. "Classroom Testing on the Microcomputer." *Business Education Forum* 41(4): 22–23 (January 1987).

Sleeman, D., and Brown, J. S., eds. *Intelligent Tutoring Systems*. New York: Academic Press, 1982.

Smith, R. M. *Improving Instructional Management with Microcomputers.* Portland, OR: Northwest Regional Educational Laboratory, 1981.

Wager, W. "Microcomputers and the Management of Instruction." *Educational Computer*, October 1983.

REFERENCES

Futrell, M. K., and Geisert, P. G. *The Well-Trained Computer: Designing Systematic Instructional Materials for the Classroom Microcomputer.* Englewood Cliffs, NJ: Educational Technology Publications, 1984.

Geisert, P. G. "Individualization of Student Rate, Goals, and Instructional Methods for an Introductory Biology Program." *Journal of College Science Teaching*, November, 1974.

Geisert, P. G. "Information Management In an Individualized Course." *AIBS Educational Review*, September 1974, 3(3).

Scrogan, L. "The OTA Report: New Technologies are Making a Difference." *Classroom Computer Learning*, October, 1988.

Tyre, T. "CMI Seen as Possible Solution to Quality of Education Issue." *T.H.E. Journal*, January, 1989.

7

Integrating the Microcomputer into the Classroom

OBJECTIVES

- Identify the major provisions that a teacher should make for implementing a computer application in a classroom.
- Describe environmental conditions and simple classroom practices that reduce the occurrence of problems with microcomputer hardware.
- Identify ways of storing and managing computer materials to minimize problems with classroom software.
- Identify factors of physical placement and arrangement that influence how well computers support typical student and/or teacher activities.
- Describe key equity and fair use issues in classroom microcomputer use, and state guidelines for responding to these issues.
- State ways to increase the cost-effectiveness of a classroom computer.
- Describe procedures for promoting a classroom microcomputer's appropriate and effective curricular use.
- Compare several ways to arrange for students to interact with: (1) a single or classroom microcomputer, (2) multiple computers, or (3) computers in lab settings.

- Contrast various models for student sharing of classroom microcomputer(s) to minimize problems and optimize use. optimize use.

INTRODUCTION

This chapter focuses on common computer-using situations. To maintain the focus, we have chosen to take the perspective of a teacher in a self-contained classroom. We'll be exploring some of the challenges and options associated with having one classroom computer (or multiple computers), along with access to a computer lab that offers one computer per student.

As we proceed through the chapter, there are three major ideas we will emphasize. First, the teacher needs to establish a type of "hospitality" for the resident computer(s). That is, the teacher should arrange the physical environment to simplify machine use in the specific classroom setting. Second, the teacher needs to set the stage to ensure that appropriate computer usage will be the end result. This means looking ahead to what the classroom environment should be like when computer use is in full swing. Third, the teacher needs to arrange for the computer to take on designated curricular functions, thereby helping students to reach predesignated goals and objectives.

You may notice that all three ideas connected with the computer integration process have a clear commonality: they entail our teacher planning toward envisioned ends. Planning is a key factor behind successful use of all types of media one employs in instruction, be they books, films, or, as in this case, computers.

Goals

- What key aspects underlie microcomputer use in a typical classroom environment?
- What are some of the various models for facilitating and managing students' computer use, and what are their similarities and differences?
- How does one evaluate the suitability of a microcomputer application to a given curricular goal?

THE COMPUTER IS HERE!

The "hello, computer" situation may occur when experienced teachers get their first microcomputers. It could be that of a new teacher moving to a classroom that already has a machine. Whatever the circumstance, when a teacher faces the prospect of integrating a microcomputer into classroom life, the first consideration becomes: "Where do I put the thing in order to maximize use and minimize damage?" There are some other questions to think through before deciding on a location.

Who Are the Users?

Where you put a computer depends on who is going to use it. We are assuming here that the computer has been assigned to your classroom, and that its use is entirely yours to decide. If your room has just the one machine, you will be sharing it with the students; hence the issue of proximity to users becomes important.

If your own use of the machine has a high priority (scoring and entering grades or using it as an electronic blackboard in front of the class), then consideration needs to be given to placing it in the most convenient location for such purposes. If the machine is primarily for student use, placing it farther away from your own work center makes more sense.

One strategy used successfully by many teachers is to start the year with the computer on or near the teacher's desk. As student use of the computer grows, it can be moved farther and farther away from the teacher's area. The final location can be the "computer users' area," where both teacher and students can have access.

Whatever spot is chosen, the machine should not be showcased as something special. Most people now view microcomputers as tools that are common and useful. Your integration goal is to have the computer as a fully functioning part of the classroom environment. The location of the computer should say, "this machine belongs; it's our tool." Ultimately, you will want all students to feel, "it's my tool; it's OK for me to use this machine."

Student User Licensing

There are certain aspects of computer use that do require control. Only students who exercise proper care of the disk drives, diskettes, computer software, and printer should use the computer. Thus you need to be able to limit access, especially at the start of a new year, until you finish training all your students how to use it.

Many teachers make good use of a "certificate maker" program to "license" their students. With such software, you can produce an official-looking document stating what a licensed student computer user in your class has learned (refer to Figure 7.1). Teachers report this technique to be effective especially with elementary pupils, both in motivating children toward accomplishment of skills and in imparting a sense of responsibility concerning appropriate computer use.

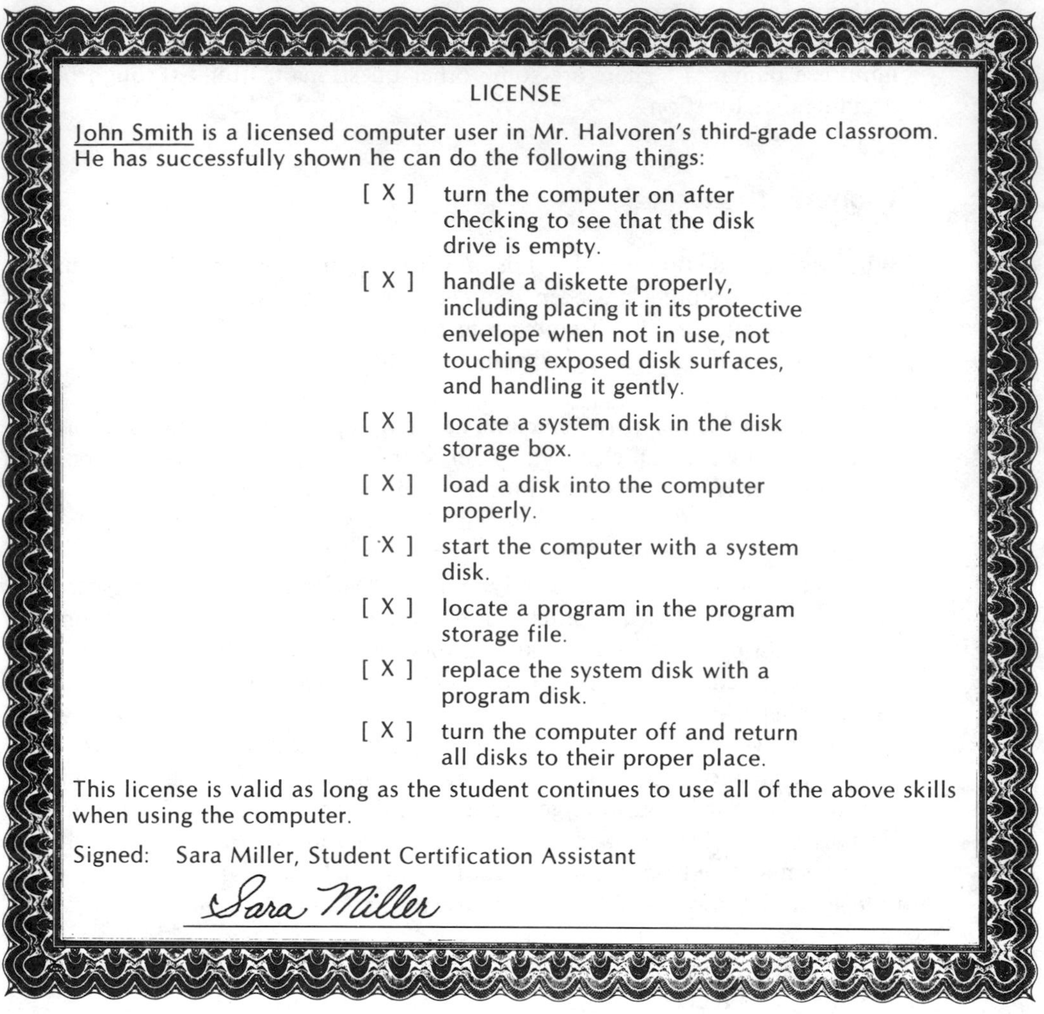

LICENSE

John Smith is a licensed computer user in Mr. Halvoren's third-grade classroom. He has successfully shown he can do the following things:

[X] turn the computer on after checking to see that the disk drive is empty.

[X] handle a diskette properly, including placing it in its protective envelope when not in use, not touching exposed disk surfaces, and handling it gently.

[X] locate a system disk in the disk storage box.

[X] load a disk into the computer properly.

[X] start the computer with a system disk.

[X] locate a program in the program storage file.

[X] replace the system disk with a program disk.

[X] turn the computer off and return all disks to their proper place.

This license is valid as long as the student continues to use all of the above skills when using the computer.

Signed: Sara Miller, Student Certification Assistant

Sara Miller

FIGURE 7.1 Sample Student User License

After certifying that necessary prerequisites to computer use have been met, you then allow a student full use of the computer as a tool. If monitoring subsequently turns up a case of a student misusing the computer, you can withdraw the license until the student again demonstrates satisfactorily the procedures you have listed on the license (or completes some renewal process). The certifying of various skill levels or designated uses is also a strategy some teachers employ.

Placement Considerations

Normally there are few limitations on the physical placement of a computer. The main considerations are heat, dust/dirt, and misuse. The following guidelines should minimize problems.

Keep the computer and especially diskettes out of hot places, such as by a sunny window or over a radiator.

Keep dust to a minimum. This means avoiding chalkboards, blowing air vents, and open windows.

Don't keep the computer in the same area as science supplies (especially near magnets).

Designate a storage location for diskettes.

Arrange wires and power cords where they won't be accidentally kicked, tripped over, or pulled out of the outlet.

Place the printer in a location where its paper feed can provide smooth operation.

Do not place archive copies of student programs with working copies. Have a separate master file in the main office, the LRC, or some other location.

Other Location Considerations

Lines of sight are worth some thought. If you plan to use the computer for demonstrating to multiple viewers, maximum screen exposure is sought. When students are using the machine, however, the sight line from nonusers to users is of greater interest. In most cases, you will want to maintain some privacy for whomever is using the computer, so it is best to position the screen where it cannot be seen by students not using the computer. You should make sure you can readily view the computer screen in order to check if a student is having problems or is off task. Classroom windows and lighting will set limits on computer positioning, because they tend to produce glare on the screen.

User comfort should not be overlooked. Height (keyboard and screen) from the floor is something to think about, particularly if users are of disparate ages or if any lengthy sessions of computer use are expected. Whatever desks are used for computers should be at a level appropriate for the size of the students involved, allowing students to work in a normal posture. A user's hands should not be reaching up to the keyboard, nor should the user's head be tilted upward to see a monitor that has been placed too high. Adequate surface area for corollary work is important, as well as sufficient floor space to accommodate whatever clustering of user chairs around the screen is expected. Movable and adjustable chairs can provide some flexibility across users and circumstances.

Up to this point, we have been considering the situation of a dedicated

Multiple teacher decisions and planning aspects underlie the successful integration of a computer into classroom instruction.

classroom computer. In finding the best spot for such a computer, you need not worry about access for users coming in from other locations; neither must you plan for the computer to be put on a cart and made handy to the door for wheeling to other locations. However, efficient school use of computers often hinges on having the machines mobile. Although each classroom may have only one computer, if the computers are easily moved, greater versatility of use by teachers is possible and higher levels of school-wide use may be gained.

In your school, there may be provisions enabling any given teacher to arrange to have multiple computers by bringing into the classroom some machines from other rooms. The idea of mobility causes a whole new set of location considerations. The movement of a computer also introduces a new set of physical variables associated with the loosening of plugs and connections that otherwise may remain stable for years.

TOWARD APPROPRIATE COMPUTER USE

Once you have tackled the issue of machine location and accessibility, a more important set of questions arises. What do you envision computer use being like in your classroom? How do you see the computer fitting into classroom action?

There is more to computer integration than finding the best physical location for the hardware and software. In some ways, bringing a computer into the classroom is like introducing a "foreigner" into the "society" that exists in your classroom. You can expect some changes to take place as a result of the newcomer's arrival. You will want to take steps to ensure that the results of these changes are just what you would wish them to be.

Some of the more important questions that you need to consider are equity in computer use, fair and legal use of software, and the extent and efficiency of computer use.

Equitable Computer Use

Research has shown that the use of computers in education has some very unbalanced features (Lockheed and Frakt, 1984; Becker, 1982). In general, the wealthier school systems are benefiting from computers more so than the poorer systems. Within schools, boys benefit more than girls, assertive students more than passive, and computer-talented more than the not so talented. Given this knowledge, a computer-using teacher can take steps to bring equity to computer use in the classroom. The key to success is an appropriate arrangement of materials and access.

Girls versus Boys

If no consideration is given by you to equity, it is probable that, in your classroom, a much higher proportion of boys than girls will be using the computer (Sanders, 1984). As in any sex-based difference, the reasons for this are many and varied, but the research is clear that, in the school setting, computers are used more highly by boys than girls. To avoid adding to the disparity, you will need to implement procedures that attempt to remedy unbalanced use (affirmative action, if you will). Here are some starter suggestions.

First, you will need to make curriculum activity on computers as appealing to girls as to boys. When selecting computer programs, you will want to be alert to the possibility of disparate gender (or other category) appeal. It is quite possible that some programs tend to invite use by one category of students and not another. For example, many games tend to use combat and high action formats. Such themes are clearly more male-oriented in society at large. You need to be cognizant of the extent to which student attitudes toward computer use may be affected by the software you are employing. Seek software that has broad appeal for the spectrum of users in your classroom so that, inadvertently, you do not reward boys more than girls for their computer learning.

Second, girls will need an appropriate role model for computer use. That is, they must be made aware that computing is a valuable endeavor for both genders. The male elementary teacher should not be the apparent source of guidance and wisdom for the female elementary teachers (if this is true, it is best kept discreetly secret). All students benefit from exposure to female teachers who are confident, knowledgeable computer users who do not view using the computer as aversive. If you are female, you can strive to educate by example, but if you are male, you could do so by arrangement or supplemental instruction. Girls (and boys, too) need to be shown roles in which women use computers and to be informed that these roles are important.

Third, you will need to make a concerted effort not to assign only to boys computer-using tasks such as duplicating disks, certifying students, caring for the computer, and so forth. Girls must be put into positions having equal (or even greater) responsibilities to the boys if typical patterns are to be averted. You should aim for a classroom that has as high a proportion of girls as boys who are "expert" users of the classroom computer.

Fourth, if there is open time for computer use, or if there is self-selection for computer study time, you should counter the usual pattern where the more assertive students—shown by research to be boys most often—will tend to dominate available computer time. In your classroom, you will want to carefully analyze how the computer is used and to develop patterns that either do not allow for open time or that promote use by individuals who would not, given the option, normally choose to use the computer. For example, you might offer tokens for computer use. Pupils would need tokens in order to do some other activity that is of greater interest to them, for example art. In this manner, less aggressive students would be rewarded for computer use by gaining access to a more favored activity.

Fifth, you should be aware that boys may dominate the amount of time the computer is in use even if you choose to make sure that everyone has equal access to the computer via some sort of logistical system, such as a chart or list of users. Boys still may, in such a situation, use the computer to the extent time allows, whereas girls will use only a fraction of the available time. This will be a difficult situation, particularly for required computer activities, since different learners will require different amounts of time on the computer to reach mastery of a given concept. A possible remedy may be to assign learning tasks to pairs of individuals, with a boy and a girl in each pair. Thus, if a boy stays engaged in the activity, the girl is still participating too, and at least the exposure to the computer activity is equal.

Also consider pairing girls together, particularly in the beginning stages of computer use, to eliminate the possibility of a girl deferring control to the boy. Since assigning activities by sex is generally to be frowned upon in education, you will probably not want to arrange "girls only" and "boys only" computer sessions. Still, these would be preferable to what seems to happen when schools do not work purposefully to ensure equity in computer use. Observers report the existence of numerous secondary school computer labs and LRC clusters that have become de facto male domains into which few females dare to tread. Without appropriate procedures to maintain equity, this "locker room" atmosphere can develop by default.

Computer-Talented versus Not So Talented

What does "computer-talented" mean? A computer-talented student may be one who has many more computer-related skills to employ than other students in the class. It may also be someone who exhibits a proclivity toward computer use.

You should be alert to the possibility that the students who seem to be so talented with the machines are those who have the advantage of access to a computer at home or previous computer instruction and therefore have mastered many of the basic competencies common to all computers. If this is the case (and it often is), then take it as a signal that most students can become computer-talented themselves if only they are given adequate exposure and training.

Be concerned lest the term computer-talented become synonymous with computer-user in your classroom. If you proceed unaware, there is a distinct possibility that this class of students will take over the use of the computer by driving out others who see that they are outclassed in terms of jargon and general operating procedures. Your task is to set up schedules and windows of opportunity so that those not so talented are not put in competition for time on the computer with those who have more skills. Most importantly, if all are to gain from computer use, it is imperative that you attempt to institute procedures that upgrade the computing-related proficiencies of all your students.

One strategy some teachers employ is to have the more skilled students teach those who are less so, thus enriching the teaching talents of one group and the computer-using talents of the other. The class as a whole benefits from the elevation of overall computer-use proficiency. As the director of this type of learning endeavor, you would need to decide what skills will be needed by everyone, who already has those skills, and then who will teach what, whom, and how.

Fair Use of Computer Software

Computer software must be protected in two major areas: (1) protection from physical abuse, and (2) protection from theft. The first has been covered already in this book. The second stems from the ease with which computer-talented students (or teachers) can copy programs that have been copyrighted by their publishers.

To discourage unauthorized copying of their software many publishers choose to *copy-protect* their material. Still, programs designed specifically to unlock the copy protection are easy to come by and quite inexpensive. For a nominal price one can obtain a program that can break through the copy protection of most other programs and allow one to duplicate them. For this and other reasons, many commercial programs, though copyrighted, are simply not copy protected and can be copied using the standard procedures available on all computers.

Why not copy educational programs? Some teachers use the "good cause" rationale. After all, from the teacher's perspective, "it would be for the benefit of the students." And, since schools do not provide enough money to buy the really good programs that are needed, why not make a few duplicates and distribute them to other teachers?

Plainly and simply, the unauthorized duplication of computer programs is theft. If someone copies a program that has not been paid for, even if for a good cause, the person has stolen money in the amount equal to the price of the program. Most of the money was stolen from the publisher of the program, which was deprived of its rights to an income from the work and investment involved in the program's development. From a societal perspective one can ask, "Should people who steal be teaching children?"

Almost all computer programs list the rights and privileges of the purchaser on the program's container or in the documentation that accompanies the program. Some programs will allow a teacher to duplicate up to a certain number of programs. Others, known as *"multiple-loading"* programs, will state that the one disk can be used in multiple computers. A teacher can move from computer to computer, loading the program on up to a certain number of machines.

There are also computer programs that are sold with *site licenses* that allow a school or a district unlimited copy rights within a time frame. A site license has a higher initial price but it provides much more flexibility in usage.

The most common rule for classroom courseware is: the purchase of one program allows you to serve one computer. If you have five computers in your classroom and need to run five word processors at the same time, you will need to buy five word processing programs.

It is accepted that you will make one backup copy of a program to store in case an accident destroys the original. But you cannot provide such an *archive copy* to another teacher to use in a second classroom. Neither can it be used to produce other copies for your classroom.

It is helpful, we think, to remember that teachers are role models in our classroom society. Students in a class soon become aware of how a teacher handles computer materials. If copies are made indiscriminantly and without rules, then students believe that this is an appropriate mode of action for all computer materials. Students should be made aware that a school buys all its computer courseware and follows all the copyright rules regarding the duplication of these materials.

In addition, you may need to set a firm tone in your classroom concerning student copying of software. Because of previous experiences, some of your students will know how to copy programs and may even have special programs to copy almost any program. You must make sure they are aware that such procedures are unacceptable with your classroom software and indeed with all copyrighted software. In extreme cases, the computer may have to be placed where you can monitor student activity and control the number of disks entering and leaving the class (such is very often the standard procedure in an open learning lab).

Perspectives on Use: Degree and Quality

To what extent is having a computer as a member of your classroom society going to be worth the time and trouble? If it just sits there and takes up space, nothing will be achieved. It must play an active and contributing role.

Since computers are thought of often as relatively expensive educational tools, one way to make sure the money for one is well spent is to try to use it in a cost-effective manner. The cost-effectiveness of a computer hinges on how many hours a day it helps in the teaching/learning process, so logistical planning is appropriate.

Efficiency—Keeping the Computer Busy

You and your class will need a plan for who will use the computer, when they will use it, and the why or how of its use. It will be easiest to make plans for computer use in a classroom where all the students do not progress in a lock step fashion. Students can be working on different projects at different times, and individuals and small groups can be assigned computer tasks while others work on non-computer activities.

Charts can help you sort through the logistical features (when, how, how long, who) and plan for efficient computer use. Since factors (e.g., imposed schedules, teaching styles) vary from classroom to classroom, the logistic variables will be different across teachers. Usually, a master chart based on the top priority variables will set the stage for further fine-tuning of logistics. For example, Figure 7.2 illustrates a weekly overview chart that shows how one teacher and her students use the computer each day during the week.

Once the when/how has been decided, it will also be necessary for this teacher to handle the notification (who/how long) aspects. Who is next to use the computer? For how long? Is the computer available yet? A visible listing of names on the chalkboard is a starter.

If set times are allotted to individuals, the person using the computer can

Ms. Bryan's Class—Schedule for the Week of January 11–16

TIME	
9–10	Free time for those finishing assignments (See free-time sign-up sheet—first come, first served.) Take a look at our new "Graph-Maker" program.
10–11	Tutorial time for the math program "Learning Simple Fractions." (See Tutorial Sheet for your turn.)
11–12	[Boys' drill use] [Girls' drill use] [Mixed time] (Use teacher assignment list for time and topics.)
1–2	Word processing teams for special report on social studies unit "Coming to the New World." Each team has twenty minutes per day. Order of use is the same as team members.
2–3	Tutorial time for the math program "Learning Simple Fractions." (See Tutorial Sheet for your turn.)
3–4	After school free-time use. Tuesday reserved for "Computer Sprites" computer club. Thursday reserved for the use of "Word Buster" to review for spelling quiz on Friday morning.

FIGURE 7.2 Charting the When and How of Computer Use

be made responsible for notifying the next user, but this may cause problems if a student gets engrossed, forgets the time, and “runs over.” Or, the next user can be responsible for telling the present user that “time is up.” A more convenient method is to place a simple kitchen timer next to the computer. Individual students are responsible for setting the time they will use the machine, and then notifying the next user.

If the computer is to be used to reach a specific target (e.g., “Finish Lesson 7”), each student needs to know exactly what the milestone for the day is, and there needs to be some sort of checking mechanism to assure the achievement of the standard. For example, in mathematics, all students could be instructed to call the teacher over to the computer as soon as “X” event (e.g., a particular message on the screen) occurred.

When students are using the computer in a self-directed fashion, they should list on the sign-up what they are going to use the computer for, and provide a projection of the maximum amount of time they plan to spend. In such patterns, time limits should be set. For example, a limit of twenty minutes is enforced if another person or group is signed up to follow.

Effectiveness

Computers are expensive if rarely used. But they can also be expensive even when used continuously. Stories abound of computers being used as time-killers in classrooms. Keeping your computer busy is one aspect, but making it contribute is another. You need to take steps to ensure that your computer

Who will use the computer, and when, and how, and for how long?

gets actively involved in the nitty-gritty business of the classroom—student learning.

In the business world, dollars and cents are the goal. In that world, a million dollar machine is not expensive if it generates in time savings or profits more than the million dollars that it costs. Computers become relatively inexpensive learning tools if they are employed all day long for worthwhile purposes. Even a fairly costly classroom computer is not expensive if it generates learning at a dollar cost that is lower than other possible methods.

Let us return to the idea of the computer as a teacher's aide. If one were to hire a human aide to do drill and practice type work with small groups of students, the cost would be a certain number of dollars per hour. If the computer can accomplish the same or similar tasks at a lower rate, it is more cost-effective. Despite a rather hefty initial cost, a computer can be made reasonably cost-effective in its first year if it is directed in appropriate ways during whatever time each day it is employed.

As the teacher, your primary charge is to produce student learning. If you plan your computer's tasks carefully, and match them to your students' learning needs, the machine can have a considerable impact in just a short time. Remember, too, that you can expect a computer to be around for several years. Where computers are wisely employed, they become inexpensive tools.

ENHANCING INSTRUCTIONAL SUCCESS

Employing a computer wisely means more than keeping it busy at valuable tasks. Thorough integration into the classroom goes beyond questions of how well it meshes with the physical environment and serves actively in classroom processes. For the teacher, it means weighing and acting on priorities. Computers are quite versatile and there are many options for how a computer can be used to enhance classroom instruction. How are you to decide among them?

In previous chapters we have surveyed different ways a computer could be used. A teacher might be using the computer to augment an existing teaching method—such as when an electronic blackboard is used to illustrate a math discussion. The computer may be a tool for the students, as when it assists them in creating written work. Or the computer may teach directly a new concept or problem-solving method, or provide drill and practice. Whatever the application, it is important that the computer help students to reach predesignated curriculum goals. We have seen far too many schools where computers were not properly linked to the curriculum being taught in the classrooms.

The Curriculum

A curriculum is generally composed of a set of goals and objectives that designates the needs of the school system for a given portion of its program. The curriculum typically has a broad set of goals for a unit of instruction, for example, science in the fourth grade. Table 7.1 lists a set of curriculum goals for such a unit.

Goals designate broad statements of educational intent. Although it may be possible to develop classroom materials around goal statements, it is helpful if goals are more fully explicated into curriculum objectives. These objectives are narrower statements of educational intent; in fact they are usually sufficiently narrow in scope that an instructional program can be planned to achieve them. For example, a school district has the following goal for a high school foreign language program: The student will develop listening and speaking skills in the given language. The school operationalizes this goal by formulating objectives. We have listed below the first eight of nineteen curriculum objectives from the school's curriculum guide.

1. Recognize and identify the sounds of the alphabet of a given language.
2. Imitate the above sounds using proper intonation.
3. Recognize and imitate sound combinations.
4. Recognize and imitate word order in sentences, with proper intonation, pitch, and stress.
5. Recall and reproduce orally frequently used sound structures.
6. Respond to directions to answer questions (presented in the foreign language).
7. Identify objects by means of audio and visual cues.
8. Identify an appropriate rejoinder to an utterance.

TABLE 7.1 Science Curriculum Goals

Five Developmental Goals for Fourth Grade Science

1. Develop *curiosity and interest* by exploring the real world of nature and of technology and by observing and understanding the significance of changes in living and nonliving things.
2. Develop *initiative and inventiveness* through investigation of problems using methods and tools of science. Children are encouraged to inquire and make discoveries and to pursue some of their own interests.
3. Develop skills of *observation and record keeping* necessary to communicate findings in a variety of ways. Children record observations in writing or represent them in posters, models, charts, or graphs.
4. Develop the *independent critical thinking* skills to test ideas before accepting or rejecting them. Children learn that there may be several ways to test an idea or make an observation.
5. Develop *persistence* to complete units or pursue other topics for investigation. Children learn to deal with distractions and relate observations that occur over a period of time.

Fairfax County Public Schools, Department of Instructional Services, Fairfax, Virginia, *Elementary Program of Studies, Science Curriculum K–6.*

The curriculum sets the overriding instructional intent for the period of instruction. The curriculum goal and corresponding objectives serve as the guiding framework as a teacher moves students through a school year or course of instruction. It is the task of the individual teacher to devise the day-by-day instruction that is required to reach the curriculum goals and objectives, and to develop or choose the evaluation methods to determine student achievement. Notice that, although the school level objectives are not written in performance terms, they are sufficiently narrow that a teacher with content expertise can easily develop performance objectives, unit and lesson plans, and the means to ascertain whether a given student has or has not achieved each instructional objective.

Figure 7.3 illustrates that curriculum goals lead to objectives, which lead to the development of the methods of teaching, which lead to instruction, which leads to evaluation, which leads to a reevaluation of whether the students achieved the goals and objectives.

A computer-using teacher can scrutinize a curriculum and determine whether or not to employ a computer as a means to achieve curricular goals.

Using a Computer to Reach Curriculum Objectives

As a general rule, you should start with the standard curriculum to see how to employ the computer. Initiate your analysis with the curriculum's listing of objectives for your course or level in hand. (If performance objectives are available, use them.) Then, examine each objective in turn, evaluating the feasibility of using a computer to reach it. Some objectives may invite computer assistance; others lend themselves to it; many will not. In some cases, computer enhancement of instruction would be feasible, but appropriate software is not

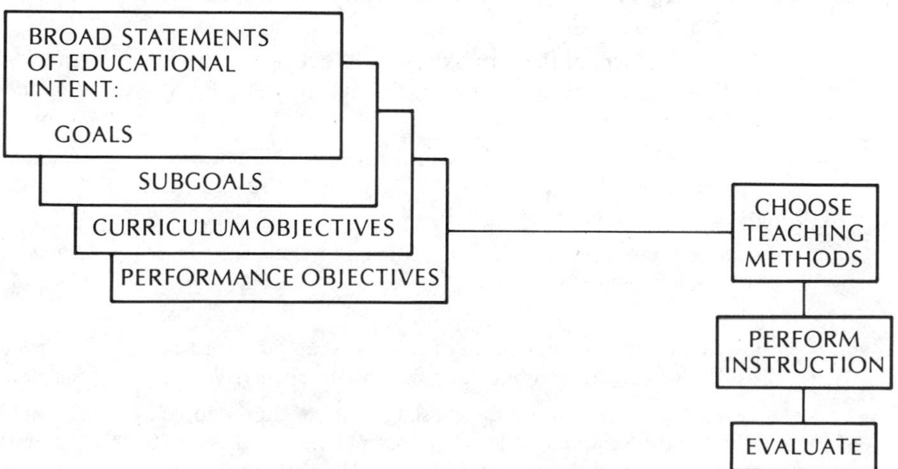

FIGURE 7.3 Flow from Goals through Evaluation

available yet. Many times, however, there are programs that seem designed for the job. For example, the curriculum objectives in Table 7.2 are ones that are easily reached using the computer programs listed.

Let's work through one complete example using the science goals previously illustrated in Table 7.1. One of the goals was:

2. Develop *initiative and inventiveness* through investigation of problems using methods and tools of science. Children are encouraged to inquire and make discoveries and to pursue some of their own interests.

A subgoal that could implement one aspect of this goal is:

2.1 The student will acquire skills in predicting and inferring.

Curriculum objectives to operationalize this subgoal are:

2.1.1 Construct one or more inferences from observations.
2.1.2 Identify those observations that support an inference.
2.1.3 Demonstrate that inferences may need to be revised on the basis of additional observations.
2.1.4 Construct predictions based on data represented by a table, graph, or model.

TABLE 7.2 Objectives by Computer Programs

Objective	*Exemplary Program*
Given a picture illustrating the relationship of moisture in the atmosphere and precipitation, the student will properly label the picture.	*Moisture in the Atmosphere* by IBM.
Given a problem of the form AX + B = CX + D, where A, B, C, and D are fractions or zero, the student will solve 85% of the equations.	*Solving Fractional Equations* by Mindscape.
Given a newsworthy school event, the student will take notes, provide a headline, and create a story for the school newspaper of not less than 300 words.	*Ace Reporter* by MindPlay
Given a theme, the student will create and write a song in 4/4 time of not less than 10 bars.	*Music Construction Set* by Electronic Arts
Given their own composition of not less than 500 words, the student will create a composition with no misspelled words.	*Sensible Speller* by Sensible Software
Given the assignment to make a school survey on the topic of whether the school should or should not have a dress code, the students will design, perform, tabulate, analyze, and develop tables and graphs to explain the results.	*Survey Taker* by Scholastic

Objectives 2.1.1 and 2.1.2 are curriculum objectives that can be taught by a computer program. The sample lesson plan for Objective 2.1.1, for example, uses a computer (see Figure 7.4) in two different situations.

In preparing the lesson to teach inference construction, the teacher has written a performance objective. When teaching the lesson, she uses the computer as an electronic blackboard to present to the class pictorial situations she has produced. One situation, for example, shows a pond with tracks leading into the pond but no tracks exiting. Early in the lesson the teacher guides the children in generating inferences to explain this observation.

Unit: Scientific Skills — Class: McKinley, 4th Grade

Lesson: Constructing Alternative Inferences
Curriculum Objective 2.1.1

Performance Objective

When presented with a simple situation and an accompanying observation, the student can produce alternative inferences to explain the observation.

Criteria: Students will produce at least two inferences per situation in three different situations

LESSON PLAN

Introduction (3 minutes)

Anticipatory Set: Show students an animal paw print; elicit possibilities about the size of the animal that produced it to stimulate some divergent thinking.

Purpose: Tell them today we are going to learn how to explain what we observe.

Lesson Development

1. Input (2 minutes)
   - set a tone—we're going to act like scientists
   - impress on them that our explanations must be sensible and realistic rather than fantasy
2. Strategy (20 minutes with teacher using the electronic blackboard—bringing up the pond and animal tracks, having them observe and then make inferences)

   Model with paw prints and the pond computer graphics (A)

   Model and guide with more pond graphics (B)

   Guide as necessary on other example computer situations:
   Pond (C); Balance; Balloons; Shadows; Mystery Box;
   - discuss the real situation the image represents
   - point out the observation
   - offer first alternative explanation:

     first time through, discuss inferences (may or may not be accurate; we can differ, etc.)

FIGURE 7.4 A Sample Lesson Plan that Makes Use of Classroom Computers

- discuss: emphasize feasibility, real nature, etc.
- present alternative explanation
- evaluate understanding and continue only as necessary

3. Transition to Practice (3 minutes)
   - give task directions (stations/time/team assignments)
   - check for understanding of rotation procedures
4. Practice Session (20 minutes)
   Station 1: Tire Tracks
   Station 2: Snow Tracks
   Station 3: Animal Tracks
   Station 4A: (computer) "Mysterious Events"
   Station 4B: (same as 4A, on teacher's computer)

Closure (while still in teams to avoid regroupings. 5 minutes)

Summary: Remind of lesson purpose; point out progress in their skill observed since lesson began

Informal Evaluation: (index card to each team)

Present them with "fingerprints on the ice box" picture. Challenge them to construct different explanations in three minutes; share orally

Resources

Instruction cards for Stations 1–3 (with corresponding scenes from the "Track Picture Book" and the "Mystery Tracks" set); six index cards; my computer file: "INFER.PIX"; software: "Detective Works" (program #3)

FIGURE 7.4 (continued)

When the teacher-directed portion of the lesson is completed, the teacher then forms "inference teams" and divides the class for practice sessions at previously-prepared classroom stations. At the two that are computer stations, a computer program provides additional pictorials of events to interpret. For each pictorial, the team types in as many inferences as the team can cooperatively produce. The team's work is saved on the computer in a file for the teacher to read.

Objective 2.1.3 is also a good candidate for teaching with a computer. After the students have been introduced to the concept of inferences, practice in identifying observations that support a given inference is done via *Discovery Lab* (MECC, 1984). This program has students design and conduct experiments to find the best environmental conditions for aliens. The students must make initial inferences about how much heat and light they can tolerate, and then make additional observations to determine if their inferences were substantiated or not.

Objective 2.1.4 could be handled as a combination laboratory and computer exercise. The teacher designs a lab sequence in which students place cups having punctured bottoms in water and measure the time to sink. Each day the students "sink" their cups in different ways, recording their data on a computer spreadsheet. Students investigate the effect of using different numbers of holes in the bottom, different size holes, different types of cups, and different weight in the cup. Using a spreadsheet after each lab, the class interprets the day's results, draws conclusions, plans the next experiment, and makes predictions.

The fourth grade science unit illustrates a valid approach to the selection of courseware. It focuses on the curriculum, not the computer courseware. The computer is used to support and enhance instruction. While it is best to design instruction by progressing through the sequence just presented (goals to objectives to instruction), the practicality of everyday teaching sometimes requires working backward. Given that you find a computer program you intuitively know would benefit your students, you may want to adjust your curriculum to include it.

COMMON PATTERNS OF CLASSROOM COMPUTER USE

Thus far this chapter has focused mostly on one computer in a classroom. This does not reflect the reality of many schools, where multiple computers are available. It is worthwhile to think a bit about the variety of patterns that are typical in schools.

One Classroom, Computer(s) from Elsewhere

Some teachers find themselves in the position of having no resident computer and they must borrow or check out computers when they need them. The situation is not conducive to frequent computer use, but it may adequately support a teacher who wishes to use one computer on occasions as an electronic blackboard. A teacher who wants to use a cluster of computers during a well-defined segment of instruction would also be adequately accommodated. Depending on the number of other computer-using teachers and the size of the computer pool, however, access to such computers may be very limited. In any case, in this situation one cannot expect to reach many curriculum goals with the help of computers.

One Classroom, One Computer

In many schools it is common to have one computer in a classroom. Problems associated with this situation include: (1) lack of computing power to accomplish desired tasks, and (2) isolation from other computer-using teachers. Advantages with this pattern are: (1) stability and flexibility of use, (2) ability to provide secure and organized software organization, and (3) class ownership of the computer.

One Classroom, Several Computers

There are a number of ways to get multiple computers into one classroom for teacher and student use. Some schools allot more than one computer to every classroom; others allot more to teachers who want them. Both situations ensure all the advantages just mentioned for a one-computer classroom. They also enhance the teacher's instructional options in proportion to the added number of machines. Disadvantages may also accrue, however, as machines increase in number: (1) reduced classroom space and flexibility of arrangement and (2) greater pressure on the teacher to maintain a high level of machine use. (This would probably be less likely in wealthier schools.)

In a resource-limited school setting, computer sharing among teachers may be the pattern. Machines are placed on carts, and for a segment of time dispersed in separate classrooms. At other times they are joined into a working unit, moving to one of the rooms to accomplish a specific task. This pattern has numerous disadvantages. Some of the problems that arise are: (1) lack of planning of who gets what when, (2) logistical problems of getting the computers from place to place, (3) software problems associated with diverse classroom needs, and (4) mechanical problems from the harsher treatment afforded carted computers.

Benefits of the pattern include: (1) more computers are available for specific tasks, (2) cooperative computing between teachers, (3) facilitation of legal software sharing (program travels with the computer), and (4) students can share experiences between classes as well as within their own classroom.

One Class, Available Computer Lab

The ability to have an entire class working on computers simultaneously, with only one or two students at a machine, is usually contingent on the school having some kind of specialized computing facility available. It generally involves a learning laboratory in the Learning Resource Center or an official computer lab, most often a room in which a computer-intensive curriculum (e.g., computer literacy, computer science) is customarily taught.

Classroom teachers can access the computing resources they need by moving their class to the computers. Time is scheduled well in advance of use, and the class is brought to the lab. Advantages of this pattern include: (1) maximum machines per student, (2) good control over what is taught since all students will be using the same program at the same time, (3) the possibility of having a resource person available who is responsible for the general care and handling of the machines, and (4) relatively high number of computing minutes per session.

Disadvantages of the lab can include: (1) a machine-dense atmosphere quite unlike a classroom, (2) disruption of normal class schedule by the need to be in the computer lab at a certain time, and (3) necessary adjustment to different computing rules (those of the lab).

Computer Sharing Considerations

Within an instructional setting, there are a number of patterns of computer sharing that may be developed, depending on needs and the number of computers that are present.

The first thing to realize is that computers used for delivery of instruction should not be allocated to students simply on an equal-time basis. There is no reason that each student in the classroom should be provided the same amount of learning time on a computer; individuals do not accomplish tasks at the same rate. One of the strongest features of the computer is its ability to match the way it teaches to the needs of the student. If a student is slow, the computer presents more instruction, until the student reaches the learning goals of the program. If a student learns quickly, the computer will certify lesson completion expeditiously.

If we use learning as the criterion for computer utilization rather than time spent, we can see other patterns than the customary one of allocating the computer on the basis that each student gets the same amount of time. See Table 7.3 for patterns of use and a brief discussion of each.

Patterns of use can be made clear to students, and procedures established for each pattern. All the patterns can operate within the same classroom at different times.

How Many Students Per Computer?

Whether you have one computer or multiple computers available, the question arises of how many students should use a computer station at the same time, and for what purposes. Table 7.4 lists some of the considerations regarding this question.

To reiterate one point made in the table, the number of users per computer should be dictated by the nature of the program being used rather than by the constraints of having too few computers. Computer programs designed to serve one student may also work well with more than one student at the station. On the other hand, some programs, such as one for keyboarding instruction, would be inappropriate for use with more than one learner at a time.

SUMMARY AND REVIEW CHECKLIST

Making curricular integration the central focus of your planning is the key to successful computer use. This is accomplished best if you start with your curriculum and integrate into it available courseware to support and enhance achievement of curricular goals.

Other planning aspects underlie the computer's successful integration

TABLE 7.3 Some Patterns of Computer Use

Name	*Pattern*	*Discussion*
Milestone	Distinct events or endpoints within the program are used as markers to determine how long a program session should be. The student works until reaching the milestone. Then the next student repeats the process.	This pattern is an appropriate one for learning programs, in which something new is being learned or something previously learned is being practiced. Best used with tutorials or drill and practice.
Timed	Each student (or team) is assigned a set amount of time to work on a specific task.	Use caution with this option. Although it appears to be the fairest method of dividing up the computer's time, it hides the fact that the quicker students will learn more than the slower.
Task-defined	The student (or team) is assigned a task to complete and given as much time as necessary to do the job. Generally applicable to projects, newsletters, and other "broad" tasks.	Differs from Milestone in that the criterion for how much time is spent on the computer is external to the computer program. What is learned is not the endpoint in this pattern; rather, what is accomplished is.
Open time	The students (or teams) are allowed to use the computer at their discretion (within some broad set of limits).	This pattern fits well for recreational or reward use of the classroom computer. It must be watched carefully, because the more aggressive and interested students will tend to monopolize the available time.

TABLE 7.4 Considerations Regarding the Number of Users per Station

Users Per Computer	*Advantages*	*Disadvantages*
One	The computer has the undivided attention of the student and can tailor tutorial lessons and drill and practice to the needs of the individual.	This is a rather expensive use of computer time. If each student spends ten minutes a day and there are thirty students, the computer will be in constant use for five hours, a rather unrealistic situation.
Two or three	This option has been given good reviews by the educational research literature. With many programs, two or three individuals	Not suitable for programs that are designed to address the specific needs of an individual user (typing, tutorials, etc.). May lead to

	can actually learn more than one at a time, due to interaction during the learning processes.	domination of the activity by one student.
Small groups	Four or five students can use the computer at one time. This is fine for simulation programs where a team can discuss and plot strategies and try out the results. Best used within some cooperative learning format with individuals being given specific responsibilities, and with a clear designation of one role as "computer operator."	Tasks and assignments must be very clear or valuable computer time will be spent in discussion and off-task behaviors. The decision to use small groups must be made on the basis of the type of program being used and not simply because computer power is scarce. Programs that enhance the concepts of small group learning are needed, along with adequate space near the computer to arrange for comfortable screen viewing by all participants.
Large groups, but less than the entire class	Project work can be employed nicely with groups of almost any size. Word processors, spreadsheets, data bases, and programs such as desktop publishers lend themselves to the delegation of such responsibilities to a subgroup within the large group.	In large group work the computer is a tool to augment the group's task accomplishment, so teams or individuals need to be assigned to do the computer portions of the broader task. Plans must be laid so that various groups are appropriately sharing the computer.
Whole class	An entire class can be engaged with one computer if only one or two members of the class are handling the operation aspect at any one time. The operator(s) could make project presentations, facilitate data analyses for the class, or use the computer to conduct some other class-based event.	Difficulties arise in seeing the screen, so such use requires either multiple screens, or a large and clear monitor, or a projection monitor (although it will probably be monochrome and not as interesting as a color monitor). Physical arrangement to permit keyboard operation and screen viewing by the operator and the simultaneous class-wide viewing of the entries is necessary.

into the classroom environment, such as looking ahead to issues of appropriate computer use and translating your expectations into supportive procedures.

Computers in the classroom can be used in many different patterns. Be careful not to fall into one pattern, such as scheduling one student on the computer for a set length of time. This pattern is one of weakest of all patterns for computer use, because it considers neither the software being used nor the student's needs. In computer-related planning, derive the patterns and procedures from your purposes, and you will be maximizing both computer integration in the classroom and its likely contribution to your teaching.

Checklist

[ ] I can identify three broad integration themes that encompass what teachers need to do when implementing a computer and software in a classroom.

[ ] I can describe environmental conditions and classroom practices that reduce the occurrence of problems with microcomputer hardware.

[ ] I can identify ways of storing and managing computer materials to minimize problems with classroom software.

[ ] I can identify some factors of physical placement and arrangement that impact whether computers appropriately support typical student and/or teacher activities.

[ ] I can state key equity and fair use issues in classroom microcomputer use, and guidelines for teachers to use in responding to these issues.

[ ] I can identify important variables to address to increase the cost-effectiveness of a classroom computer.

[ ] I can portray procedures to enhance the instructional success of a computer application and promote appropriate and effective curricular use of a classroom computer.

[ ] I can compare and contrast ways to arrange for students to interact with a single or classroom microcomputer, with multiple computers or with computers in lab settings.

[ ] I can outline various organizational patterns to facilitate student sharing of classroom microcomputer(s) while minimizing problems and optimizing use.

SUGGESTED ACTIVITIES

1. For a given classroom develop a sketch showing where computers should and should not be located, based on what is good and bad for their operating conditions.
2. Sketch in descriptions of the pattern of computer use for each of the following programs. Assume a class of thirty students each time. When you use the first chart assume you have one computer. For the second chart assume three. For the last, assume you have a computer lab with one student per machine.

CHART I One Computer in the Classroom

Software	*Description of Pattern You Would Use*
A tutorial program that tailors its presentation to the needs of the student. Three segments of learning, each takes about 25 minutes for the average student. Student can stop anywhere and the program will recommence at that point.	
A graphing program that requires keyboard entry of data. Students in groups of 4 are responsible for performing a chemistry experiment, recording a set of 50 observed data points, and then graphing the data.	
A desktop publishing program. The class is producing a social studies newspaper. They are developing a newspaper that corresponds to the same week of the year, but during the American Revolutionary War.	

CHART II Three Computers in the Classroom

Software	*Description of Pattern You Would Use*
A tutorial program that tailors its presentation to the needs of the student. Three segments of learning, each takes about 25 minutes for the average student. Student can stop anywhere and the program will recommence at that point.	
A graphing program that requires keyboard entry of data. Students in groups of 4 are responsible for performing a chemistry experiment, recording a set of 50 observed data points, and then graphing the data.	
The class is producing a social studies newspaper. They are developing a newspaper that corresponds to the same week of the year, but during the American Revolutionary War.	

CHART III A Computer Lab and One Classroom Computer

Software	*Description of Pattern You Would Use*
A tutorial program that tailors its presentation to the needs of the student. Three segments of learning, each takes about 25 minutes for the average student. Student can stop anywhere and the program will recommence at that point.	
A graphing program that requires keyboard entry of data. Students in groups of 4 are responsible for performing a chemistry experiment, recording a set of 50 observed data points, and then graphing the data.	
The class is producing a social studies newspaper. They are developing a newspaper that corresponds to the same week of the year, but during the American Revolutionary War.	

WORTH A LOOK: EDUCATION JOURNALS

Instead of software titles, this chapter lists the names of some education journals that often have articles regarding classroom management aspects of using the computer. A trip to the library or a note to the publisher should provide a sample copy of the journal for review.

Classroom Computer Learning. 5615 West Cermak Road, Cicero, IL 60065.

Computers in the Schools. The Haworth Press, 28 East 22nd Street, New York, NY 10010.

The Computing Teacher. International Council for Computers in Education, University of Oregon, 1787 Agate Street, Eugene, OR 97403.

Educational Technology. 140 Sylvan Avenue, Englewood Cliffs, NJ 07632.

Electronic Education. Electronic Communications, 1311 Executive Center Drive, Suite 220, Tallahassee, FL 32301.

Electronic Learning. Scholastic, 902 Sylvan Avenue, Box 2001, Englewood Cliffs, NJ 07632.

Journal of Computer-Based Instruction. Association for the Development of Computer-Based Instructional Systems, Computer Center, Western Washington University, Bellingham, WA 98225.

Media and Methods. 1511 Walnut Street, Philadelphia, PA 19102.

T.H.E. Journal (Technological Horizons in Education—free). Information Synergy, P.O. Box 992, Acton, MA 01720.

READINGS

Abruscato, J. *Children, Computers and Science Teaching.* Englewood Cliffs, NJ: Prentice-Hall, 1986.

Bitter, G. G., and Camuse, R. A. *Using a Microcomputer in the Classroom.* Reston, VA: Reston Publishing Co., 1984.

Caissey, G. A. *Microcomputers and the Classroom Teacher.* Bloomington, IN: Phi Delta Kappa Educational Foundation, 1987.

Culley, L. "Girls, Boys, and Computers." *Educational Studies,* 1988, 14(1):3–8.

Eckenrod, J. S., and Rockman, S. *Technology in a Curriculum for Citizenship.* Paper presented at the Annual Conference of the Social Science Education Consortium, June, 1986 (ERIC Document #273526).

Hattie, J., and Fitzgerald, D. "Sex Differences in Attitudes, Achievement, and Use of Computers." *Australian Journal of Education* 31(1):3–26 (April 1987).

Hawkins, J. "Computers and Girls: Rethinking the Issues." In *Mirrors of Minds,* edited by R. D. Pea and K. Sheingold. Norwood, NJ: Ablex Publishing Corporation, 1987.

Hawkins, J., and Kurtland, D. M. *The Beginning of a Story: Computers and the Organization of Learning in Classrooms* (Tech. Rep. No. 35). New York: Bank Street College of Education, Center for Children and Technology, 1985.

Lauterbach, R. G. "Computers in the Child's Home: Introducing Tomorrow's Crisis of Elementary Education?" *Education and Computing,* 1986, 2(1–2):39–46.

Lockheed, M. E. "Sex Equity in Classroom Organization and Climate." In *A Handbook for Achieving Sex Equity in Education,* edited by S. Klein. Baltimore: Johns Hopkins University Press, 1985.

Mawby, R., Clement, C. A., Pea, R. D., and Hawkins, J. *Structured Interviews on Children's Conceptions of Computers.* (Tech Report No. 19). New York: Bank Street College of Education, Center for Children and Technology, 1984.

Mehan, H. "Microcomputers and Classroom Organization: Some Mutual Influences." In *Computers in Classrooms: A Quasi-Experiment in Guided Change.* Final report to the National Institute of Education. La Jolla, CA: University of California, San Diego, Center for Human Information Processing, 1985.

Olson, J. *Computers in Canadian Elementary Schools: Curriculum Questions from Classroom Practice.* Paper presented at the Annual Meeting of the American Educational Research Association, April, 1986 (ERIC Document #271105).

Olson, J., and Eaton, S. *Case Studies of Microcomputers in the Classroom: Questions for Curriculum and Teacher Education.* Toronto: Ontario Institute for Studies in Education, 1986.

Parisi, L. *Sex Equity in Computer Education: Concerns for Social Studies.*

Boulder, CO: ERIC Clearinghouse for Social Studies/Social Science Education, 1984.

Sanders, J. S. *Reflections from the Computer Equity Training Project*. New York: Women's Action Alliance, 1985.

Sparks, J. A. *The Effect of Microcomputers in the Home on Computer Literacy Test Scores.* Research Thesis, Central Missouri State University, 1986 (ERIC Document #286491).

Sybouts, W., and Stevens, D. J. "A System Model to Introduce Computers into an Educational Program." *NASSP Bulletin* 70(489): 28–31 (April 1986).

Thompson, C. L., and Vaughan, L., eds. *Computers in the Classroom: Experiences Teaching with Flexible Tools.* Teachers Writing to Teachers Series. Chelmsford, MA: Northeast Regional Exchange, Inc., 1986.

West, C. E. "Microcomputers in the Classroom – Just What is the Cost?" *Educational Research Quarterly*, 1986, 10(1):46–56.

Wiske, M. S. et al. *How Technology Affects Teaching.* Newton, MA: Educational Development Center, Inc., 1988.

REFERENCES

Becker, H. J. *National Survey of School Uses of Microcomputers, Interim Reports 1–6.* Baltimore, MD: Johns Hopkins University, 1982.

Lockheed, M. E., and Frakt, S. B. "Sex Equity: Increasing Girls' Use of Computers." *The Computing Teacher*, April 1984.

MECC (Minnesota Educational Computing Corporation) *Discovery Lab*, St. Paul, MN: MECC, 1984.

Sanders, J. S. "The Computer: Male, Female, or Androgynous?" *The Computing Teacher*, April 1984.

8

Acquiring and Evaluating Microcomputer Courseware

OBJECTIVES

- Describe the range of sources of microcomputer courseware for use in the classroom.
- State procedures for acquiring information or programs from software sources, whether through electronic or regular channels.
- Identify the range of sources of information on quality of microcomputer courseware and state procedures for acquiring such information.
- Describe a procedure for requesting courseware for preview, identifying factors that tend to strengthen your request.
- State some guidelines for determining the extent of evaluation effort that any given software program should receive.
- Describe a procedure for conducting a review of the design of a program intended for instruction.
- Describe a procedure for conducting a tryout evaluation of an instructional program.
- Explain the value empirical evaluation data can have for teachers who want more cost-effective instructional software.

INTRODUCTION

There are over twenty thousand educationally oriented microcomputer programs available on today's market. However, it is common knowledge that teachers encounter many problems finding appropriate software for classroom use (Ahl, 1983; Cohen, 1983, Futrell and Geisert, 1986; Roth and Petty, 1988). The difficulty derives in part from the early history of the development of educational software.

When microcomputers first appeared, a burst of enthusiasm resulted that led to many programs being produced by teacher-programmers and hobbyists in their homes. This material was published, and some of it is still available commercially. Initially produced with good intentions, much of the early software that is around is of little value because of the faulty nature of the design. Some software publishers still rely on adopting materials produced by authors using unsophisticated means of design and development, so even today there are companies producing and selling second-rate new programs that have flashy graphics but little educational value.

Fortunately, educators have become more sophisticated as consumers, and it is becoming increasingly difficult to market inferior programs. Now, it seems, there is a blend of mediocre through marvelous programs reaching the market. More companies are pursuing sound developmental processes involving collaborations of content specialists, instructional designers, and expert programmers. This has led to some quite sophisticated learning programs becoming available.

In 1983, over 50% of the programs reviewed by the Educational Products Information Exchange (EPIE) were rated as "not recommended" (Komoski, 1984). Only 5% of the programs reviewed were judged "highly recommended." Despite progress in the quality arena, reviewers of educational software report the continuing availability of many inferior programs. Neill and Neill (1989) encountered an abundance of poor programs during the production of the 1990 edition of their software guide. Of the approximately 11,000 programs reviewed, only 766 (7%) met the criteria of being rated as "excellent" by at least two reviews, or excellent by one review and three more reviews of "good," and no negative reviews.

How should you proceed if you want to select good software to support your teaching? First, you should identify programs that have high potential for integration into your classroom curriculum. Then you should separate the good from the bad. This chapter provides the framework for you to do so.

Goals

- How can I find computer courseware which matches my curricular and classroom needs?
- How can I tell if a given piece of courseware is good, average, or bad, or whether it fits into my teaching?
- How can I select wisely from available commercial software, acquir-

ing for classroom use quality programs that will be cost-effective in supporting classroom instruction?

THE AVAILABILITY OF COMPUTER INSTRUCTIONAL MATERIALS

Before we address the procedures for acquiring courseware, let's take a look at some of the major resources you can use to learn what computer materials are available and how to obtain descriptive, cost, and acquisition information. You might use several or all of these resources as a part of any software search: (1) catalogs of publishers, dealers, and computer manufacturers, (2) professional journals, (3) popular journals, (4) professional meetings, (5) professional compilers of information, (6) demonstration centers, and (7) other teachers.

Catalogs

There are numerous companies that want to sell you instructional courseware. Most fall into one of these major categories: (1) publishers who produce a line of software, (2) companies and people who serve as clearinghouses or distributors, offering a variety of software published by different publishing companies, and (3) computer makers who provide information on how to obtain programs for their machines. Examples of the first category are Sunburst, the Minnesota Microcomputer Corporation (MECC), and Harcourt Brace Jovanovich. Examples of the second category include national dealerships such as ComputerWorld and Egghead Software, Inc. The Apple Corporation and the Tandy Corporation (Radio Shack) are representative of the third category.

These sources are generally easy to contact. Advertisements for their services will appear in the yellow pages, newspapers, and professional and popular journals. They also try to contact potential customers by direct mail, and through displays at professional meetings.

Almost every publisher and vendor except for some storefront dealers will have a catalog of products. Publishers will list only their own products while dealers will generally serve a broad range of publishers. With little effort you can quickly accumulate a file containing a large collection of the current offerings of courseware in your area of interest.

Professional Journals

Professional journals provide the best sources of ways to stay current with new courseware offerings. Many professional journals make an effort to continuously or periodically include computer-related information. There will be articles describing other teachers' experiences with microcomputers in the classroom, and there will be reviews of computer software and hardware as well. These publications often provide advertisements for various types of microcomputer programs to support instruction.

Popular Journals

Many popular periodicals devoted to computer materials are available on magazine stands. These popular magazines feature articles on the latest software and hardware. All have advertisements and list dealers of courseware. The advertisements are good sources for catalogs and can keep you current on new software offerings. These magazines also advertise national mail-order dealers selling software at large discounts. Such dealers are good sources of courseware and teacher tools whenever you know precisely what program(s) you want to purchase.

Of course this source of information will not be directly aimed at teachers, but since teachers are a large group, there will almost always be advertisements and some articles of interest included that are related to learning and teaching.

Professional Meetings

At local and national professional meetings you can usually meet representatives of some of the larger publishers of educational software and examine their product lines. Typically there will be one or more local area software dealers also attending to their display booths on the exhibit floor. You can get to know the local dealers, get a copy of their catalogs, and ask what types of services they can provide for you.

In addition, these meetings provide the setting for workshops and presentations on the classroom use of commercial microcomputer programs, often presented by classroom teachers who have used and know the good and bad aspects of a given program. Dealers also conduct commercial workshops at which they present talks and demonstrations of new products in the hope of sparking an interest in their materials.

Professional Compilers of Information

There are a number of groups that compile information on computer software. Some do this as a professional service and others offer the service for a yearly fee. Typically the compiler will gather together all the available information on programs of a given type, and all the publishers and companies that produce software. Some compile the names and a very brief description of everything known to have been published!

Compiled information can be found in book form, as periodicals, via special software evaluation newsletter subscriptions, and in electronic data banks that you can access directly by computer or through a library's electronic retrieval services.

The search for this type of material should start at the library. The librarian can lead you to the names of the books, journals, and newsletters, and may be able to help you to tap into the electronic data banks of information. College and university libraries are generally good sources of information on how to find and tap the information data bases. Popular magazines have the advertisements on the print sources that provide the listings and review services for current software.

Computer Materials Demonstration Centers

Some colleges and school districts have demonstration centers with a library of programs that have been used successfully by other teachers. These centers are often associated with courses, but they generally allow teachers and other professionals to examine and, in some cases, make limited use of their resources.

Other Teachers

Other teachers are fertile sources of information on programs that work for them. If you are a member of a large school district you may want to place a notice in your district newsletter asking for a meeting of people interested in talking over good software. Members of smaller districts may have to use the resources of local or national meetings to contact others of like interest. If you make sure that other computer-using teachers know you are interested in learning about what works for them in the area of microcomputers in the classroom, valuable information will be funneled in your direction.

It is also possible to use telecommunication to get in touch with other educators through national services such as Compuserve® and The Source®. These services will have electronic bulletin boards for questions and answers and the capability of putting you in direct touch with others whose computing interests match yours.

SEARCHING FOR SOFTWARE

All too often, teachers find classroom computer programs using a technique of browsing through a variety of computer programs, electing to purchase those that look good—leaving the task of finding where to use them in a curriculum until later. This method, in our view, is putting the cart before the horse. Much better, it seems to us, to target your software needs if you wish to end up with computer materials that genuinely contribute to your teaching and your students' learning.

The first step in the targeting approach to courseware acquisition is having a clear instructional goal that can be reached best, in your professional judgment, by using a computer program. In other words, we suggest that you identify the specific instructional area that you feel would be well served by computer, and then try to fill that need.

This approach to identifying microcomputer programs for a given instructional program will take time and patience since it requires your sorting through the courseware sources we have mentioned and coming up with what fits your particular needs. But ultimate success and long lasting use is more likely when you avoid the browsing approach, and use the targeting method. It's generally more economical in the long run since you will end up with much less unused or ornamental software in your classroom.

A Typical Identification Process

Here is the process Betty Cheung went through to find a program to teach graphing of equations in her tenth grade math classes.

First, after having taught students how to graph equations for five years, Betty realized that the computer could serve as an ideal teaching tool for this topic. The computer could present clear and colorful graphs and could save and store various sets of numbers that would generate the types of graphs she wished her students to learn. If a program were available to complement her approach, or perhaps even to assume aspects of the instruction directly, she would like to know of it. So Betty had a definite instructional goal before she set out to acquire a program.

Next Betty scanned the *The Mathematics Teacher* (a National Council of Teachers of Mathematics periodical) and found eight advertisements that offered catalogs of math-related programs. She sent letters (using her word processor, of course) asking for catalogs. She also went to her librarian and asked for an electronic search to be made of the BRS® information service. Her librarian jotted down the following information Betty supplied: computer type—Apple IIe, grade level—tenth, subject—math, topic—graphing equations. Betty also visited her local software store and asked the proprietor for the names of any good graphing programs appropriate for school use.

Two weeks later Betty Cheung had the names of several likely candidates. Her librarian had located four titles, Betty had found three in the catalogs, and one suggestion had come in from the software store. A total of six programs had been identified, spanning a wide range of prices. Betty realized she needed to know which of these six programs were good and which were bad, and which, if any, provided exactly the types of capabilities she was interested in and would complement her teaching style. She planned to make heavy use of the program, and she didn't want to take pot luck by purchasing something from the best-sounding paragraph description. Betty wished to determine the quality of the programs themselves before acquiring one.

DETERMINING COURSEWARE QUALITY

Written Reviews

A ready source of information about the quality of a given program is a printed review. Just as your daily newspaper reviews new books, movies, and TV shows, computer programs are also reviewed in a number of places. Sources of these reviews include popular and professional magazines, commercial reviewers who sell their review information, national educational organizations, state departments of education, local technical centers, media centers, and library associations. Almost all these sources provide similar review information. Besides publisher and price information, the review will describe what the program is intended to do and how well the reviewer feels the program has met its mark. A review can give you a general picture of a program and how it compares with other programs of the same type.

The weakness of the review as a source of purchase information is great, however. First, the review is generally an opinion article—it is one person's view of the product. (Any reader of film or book reviews will know that one critic can pan what another will hail.) Second, there is nothing that guarantees you that a reviewer has ever used the program with its targeted user group (e.g., students) or is even minimally informed about such use. More likely, the reviewer simply looked at the program. Third, reviewers often can get caught up in the "bells and whistles" of a program (for example, startling graphics presentation) and overlook the question of how well the program would be likely to work with students.

The collective opinion of the national educational review organizations generally can be deemed more authoritative than the opinion of a lone reviewer for a magazine. Still, for important acquisitions you should not purchase programs solely based on reviews. You will want to preview a program before buying it. The review information will be useful, however, for screening out programs that obviously lack features you require. It can alert you to programs that fail to meet general standards of quality. Multiple panning of a program provides a strong clue that purchasing it would be unwise.

A Typical Screening Process

Betty Cheung's school district has a media center that has reviews of computer-related educational materials on file. These reviews have been purchased from a national reviewing organization—the Educational Products Information Exchange (EPIE). Betty spent some time looking through those reviews and found that four of the six equation graphing programs she was interested in had been reviewed. She also asked her librarian to provide whatever review information on these six programs could be obtained from an electronic data base, asking for the data using the program titles.

By the week's end Betty had obtained from one to three quality reviews for each of the six graphing programs she was considering for purchase. Betty learned enough from the review information to screen out three of the programs. One, though well-reviewed, seemed designed for a very limited purpose, and two received sufficiently negative reviews that Betty was confident she no longer wished to consider these programs. The remaining three were still candidates for purchase.

Acquiring Courseware for Preview

Betty's next step is to try to get the three graphing programs for classroom preview. We say "try to get" since companies' policies vary regarding letting teachers preview materials before actual purchase. As a general policy, we take the position that a teacher should not buy a program that cannot either be examined before purchase or returned after purchase, if deemed unsatisfactory. This position is in accord with most publishers and dealers, but one should make sure of a company's policy before purchasing a program.

With most companies, a letter offers you the best likelihood of obtaining software for preview. When requesting that materials be sent for preview, make sure to include the following ideas and statements:

1. Write on school letterhead—make it official.
2. Ask to review only one or two titles—do not make a "shotgun" request to see a lot of their materials.
3. State specifically your reason for wanting to review the program(s)—tell them your instructional goal(s).
4. State that you will be personally responsible to see that the program(s) will not be duplicated. If your school has a specific written policy against the unauthorized copying of computer materials, enclose a copy.
5. Assure the return of the materials in a timely fashion—for example, within fifteen days of your receipt of them.
6. State that, if you decide not to buy the program(s), you will briefly tell the company your reasons for not purchasing.

This set of conditions should simplify your obtaining programs to preview, since it includes the main conditions that make a publisher or dealer happy. In some instances, a publisher may require you (or your school) to purchase a program before preview, with full return rights. This is a fair condition, as long as you don't have to justify your reasons for returning the material.

Some schools districts have buying and previewing policies, and teachers should be aware of and follow those procedures.

Previewing Courseware

Betty Cheung has now received the three graphing programs for her Apple IIe. How much time and effort should she spend evaluating them?

How Much Evaluation Is Enough?

Evaluation of instructional computer materials can be a time consuming task. There are a number of aspects you should consider: (1) the curricular importance of the program, (2) the number of students who will be involved with the program, (3) the cost of the program, and (4) the amount of money available compared to your time.

In your curriculum there are topics of more importance and those of lesser interest. It seems only reasonable for the evaluation emphasis you give to a piece of software to correspond to the curricular role you expect the material to play. A piece of software that deals with a large and important portion of your curriculum should receive considerably more evaluation than a program that supports only a minuscule or tangential curriculum topic.

If the program is being purchased only as a supplement or an adjunct to the regular curriculum, then the program warrants less review. Still, as we have emphasized previously, if you decide to turn a topic over to the computer to teach, then you want the computer to do a good job on the topic. Every program intended to directly promote learning at the keyboard needs enough scrutiny for a determination of adequacy in its teaching role.

The purchase price of a computer program must be balanced against the cost of the evaluation process. If a program only costs $15 and has received good reviews, it is obvious that you could very quickly invest $15 worth of time in the review. It seems more cost effective to simply purchase the program, discarding it later if it proves unsatisfactory. It's another story if the program costs $89 and you plan to buy five copies.

Adequate evaluation of software prior to its use informs the teacher about how well the computer will handle its task.

You must balance your software budget with your time. If you have more time than money, careful scrutiny of your purchases is in order. More money than time means less care may be in order before purchase. In general, however, we feel some review is warranted, regardless of how little a program costs. As long as teachers continue to purchase inexpensive programs casually, these low-cost but ineffective programs will continue to occupy a share of the educational software market.

Two Cautionary Notes

Perhaps at no other time will you be so vulnerable to making unwise decisions about commercial software as when you sit down to evaluate a program you have acquired on preview. We have included cautionary notes to alert you to the two main temptations. We hope that you will avoid them both and choose wisely.

FIRST IMPRESSIONS Beware of first impressions. The "bells and whistles" described previously as having lured software reviewers into overly positive reviews may also favorably impress you. It is reasonable, of course, to expect a good piece of courseware to make a good impression on you, but you must be wary of frills that will lead you away from the real question about instructional courseware, which is: Is the program well designed and does it work with students? An ineffective program often looks appealing initially. Quality programs, however, will withstand more serious scrutiny, and your students will benefit if you provide it.

COPYRIGHT After having acquired a program for preview and found it appealing, you might find yourself pondering the opportunity presented you to copy the program and return the original. We have found from experience that commitment to a strong policy of respecting publisher copyright brings with it many benefits, and we are pleased by the proportion of educators at all levels who take this position.

Taking Evaluation Seriously

In view of the importance Betty Cheung accords to the role of the topic of equation graphing in her curriculum, the number of students affected by her program choice, and the cost involved, Betty wants to take more than a cursory look at the three microcomputer instructional packages she has received on preview. She is ready to proceed with a formal evaluation of the three programs to decide which one is the best for her situation.

EVALUATION OF INSTRUCTIONAL SOFTWARE

Evaluation is the process of assigning value to a target. It is not an easy task, since rarely are computer programs produced that are all good or all bad.

Some aspects will tend to support the teacher's goals; others may work against them. To evaluate courseware, one needs to pursue a pattern of examination that develops facts about the program. Then these facts can be used to make a decision whether to buy the material or not.

The standards for good and bad courseware we will use throughout the remainder of this chapter derive directly from the framework of quality instruction presented in Chapter 6 and in Futrell and Geisert (1986). The framework is reiterated in Figure 8.1. It presupposes that the courseware being evaluated is *instructional* in nature.

Related to Figure 8.1 are three questions you will want to answer about an instructional computer program before purchasing it for integration into your classroom. All three necessitate that you have clarified the instructional reason behind obtaining the program. In other words, there are definite needs to be met through the program's use.

1. To what extent does the instructional intent of the program match and support the curricular goal(s) or objective(s) that have led you to consider the program? (The *purpose* corner of the triangle)
2. Does the program under consideration employ sound instructional techniques that should facilitate achievement of the instructional purpose? (The *processes* corner of the triangle)
3. Is there some way you can determine the actual effectiveness of the courseware before you purchase it? (The *measures* corner of the triangle)

As you preview a given item of instructional courseware, your evaluation procedure needs to continually highlight these three questions. By keeping them prominent in your mind, you will increase the probability that your final purchase decisions will be informed by relevant facts, and that the product chosen (if any) will be more readily and successfully integrated into your instructional program.

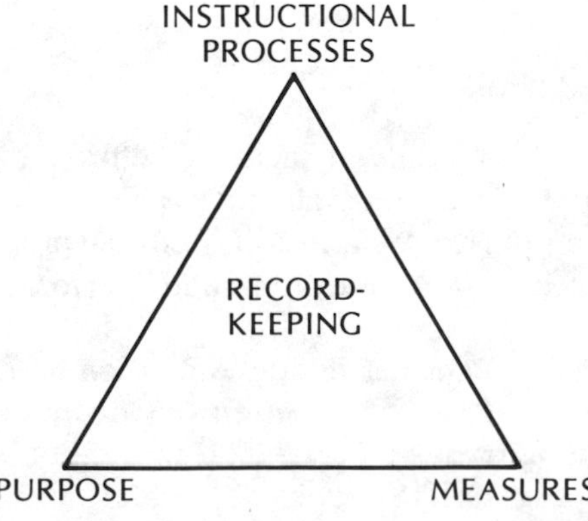

FIGURE 8.1 A Framework for the Selection of Instructional Courseware

Two Evaluation Targets

There are two major aspects of courseware that can be evaluated: (1) its design—how it looks and (2) its effectiveness—how well it works.

Design Evaluation

An evaluation of the design of courseware involves an assessment that asks questions such as: (1) Does the program state its goals and objectives? (2) Are the screen presentations clear and well organized? (3) Does the program include some measure of student performance if it claims to be teaching something? (4) Does the program provide examples and practice if it is teaching procedures? (5) Does the program keep records of student performance? and (6) Is the reading level correct for the population that will use the program? Answers to questions of this type provide clues to actual program effectiveness but do not ensure that the program will be effective with students in practice.

The evaluation of the design of courseware is akin to appraising the looks of a new car before buying it. Design evaluation looks at how well a given product appears to be put together. (It also may involve some judgments of general attractiveness to the potential buyer, such as does this car match your style? In the case of software the question becomes: Does the program seem to mesh with your philosophy and/or style of teaching?)

We all know of stupendous failures of designs followed by inadequate performance. The Edsel car comes to mind. All of us have bought products that looked like they would do well but that performed poorly. Still, design evaluations of software are very useful.

When you do a design evaluation you can get all the evidence you need for rejecting the software. Evidence of faulty workmanship surfaces, or your scrutiny may reveal the absence of important components. But, you may gain confidence as you examine the program's design, concluding: "It looks good." From a design evaluation, you may also say, "It looks like it will work." Remember, however, that a design evaluation can only provide indications of program effectiveness; it cannot say for sure.

Effectiveness Evaluation

The second type of evaluation that should be included before the purchase of important educational materials is a tryout evaluation. This type of evaluation pays attention to the question of "How well, in fact, does the program work?" It uses empirical measures of how well students actually perform when using the courseware.

In general, one should first consider design evaluation and then tryout evaluation, since a design analysis can often screen out badly designed programs from the time consuming tryout process. You would not want to provide unexamined software programs to students. Besides, you often learn much from a design analysis that is helpful to using the program with them.

A Complete Evaluation Process

A complete courseware evaluation will target both the design and effectiveness aspects, typically progressing through four basic stages, which are:

1. An evaluation of the design of the program.
2. A decision whether to continue the evaluation, or to reject it based on failure of its design.
3. An evaluation of the actual effectiveness of the program.
4. A decision whether to reject or to buy the program.

CONDUCTING A FORMAL DESIGN ANALYSIS

The major design categories that need to be evaluated for instructional software programs are: (1) statements of the purpose of the program, (2) tests and measures, (3) instructional presentation, (4) content, (5) record keeping, and (6) teacher/student documentation (written materials accompanying the program).

Selecting Design Criteria

For each design category, we have provided a table of questions focusing on some of the major criteria of importance to a sound analysis of that category. Though not intended to be exhaustive, the sets of questions provided in Tables 8.1 through 8.6 contain the major criteria you would want to consider. Commonly used criteria beyond the six categories appear in Table 8.7. When analyzing a microcomputer program, you could decide which of the questions in each listing to use, basing your selection of questions on their importance to you and their relevance to the type of program being evaluated.

TABLE 8.1 Design Evaluation for Purpose

Does the program documentation provide the teacher with statements of learning objectives?

Are the objectives presented to the students at the start of the computer program (written in such a manner that the target population will understand the program's intent)?

Do the objectives tell exactly what the learner must do in order to demonstrate that learning has taken place?

Are the conditions under which the learner's performance is to take place stated?

Do the objectives state the level of performance at which the learner is expected to perform? Example: the student will score 90% on a test.

Are the objectives arranged in order with prerequisites first, followed by enabling objectives, then terminal objectives?

TABLE 8.2 Design Evaluation for Measures

Are tests provided that measure whether or not a student has achieved the goals and objectives of the program?

Does the student have some degree of control over when to take and retake tests?

Are the test items written directly to the performance objectives?

Are there enough items to generate a pretest, posttest, and retests?

Are the test items valid?

Are the test items reliable?

TABLE 8.3 Design Evaluation for Lesson Presentation

Does the instruction motivate the student to learn, or provide some reason for learning the lesson?

Is the purpose of the lesson made clear?

Does the lesson provide a pretest to determine if a student needs the lesson?

Does the pretest generate a prescription for study?

Does the lesson review information or skills a student needs to be successful with the lesson, but which the lesson will not explicitly teach?

Are examples of student performance demonstrated?

Is the learner provided practice on the expected performance?

Do examples and practice have helps?

Is the prompting/cuing for practice items sufficient?

Is there feedback for correct answers?

Is there feedback for erroneous answers?

Does the student have control over the amount and type of feedback provided?

Is the feedback positive?

Is the feedback appropriate to the intended learners?

Is a posttest provided?

Does the lesson provide the learner help in retention of the material, rather than engaging only in short-term learning?

Does the lesson help the learner to generalize the learning to other situations?

Can the student exit the program at any time?

Is a learner who exits at a point in the program able to restart at the same location?

Can the student control the speed of the lesson?

Can the student change the sequencing of the lesson?

Can the student skip instruction?

Can the student ask for more help and not be presented with the same material again?

Does the computer employ active learning on the part of the learner, rather than being a page-turning device?

Does the lesson employ branching based on performance during the lesson?

Are the directions on how to do the lesson clear?

Are the directions on how to do the lesson sufficient?

Is the lesson structured around menus of lesson choices?

Are the lesson presentations clear?

Are the lesson presentations sufficient to accomplish the objectives?

Are the lesson procedures error free?

Is the reading level appropriate for the students involved?

Does the lesson have different difficulty levels for different students?

Does the lesson trap all keystroke errors, making it impossible for a student to abort the program by accident?

Is there appropriate "white space" allotment on the screen?

Are screens labeled so that a student can keep track of the lesson?

Is the use of graphics appropriate?

Is the use of color appropriate?

Is the use of sound appropriate?

Can the sound be turned off when it would interfere with other learners?

TABLE 8.4 Design Evaluation for Content

Does the lesson content focus precisely on teaching the objective?

Is the lesson content accurate?

Is there any racial stereotypes?

Are there any ethnic, religious, or cultural stereotyping?

Are there any sex stereotypes?

Is there any political bias?

Is the presentation objective?

Does the content have educational value?

Is the content appropriate for the learners involved?

Is the difficulty level of the grammar, vocabulary, and semantics appropriate to the learners involved?

Is there sufficient content in the lesson to teach the objective?

TABLE 8.5 Design Evaluation for Record Keeping

Are the program menus clear and easy to use?

Can the teacher have a password into the records?

Can the teacher change the password?

Can students have passwords to their records?

Can teacher opt to use or not use CMI during a given lesson?

Can records be easily backed up?

TABLE 8.5 (continued)

Are records private?
Are records secure?
Is it easy for the teacher to access records?
Is the capacity of the system sufficient for the number of students/classes?
Can student groups be created within classes?
Can subgroups be given names?
Can students/classes be added and deleted?
Can students/classes be modified with ease?
Can records be expanded?
Can records be expanded to include new objectives?
Can records be expanded to include new students?
Can records be expanded to include new test items?
Can the results of other forms of instruction be included in the records?
Is the availability of records flexible, allowing different types of reports?
Are records available for individual students?
Are records available by given class?
Are records available by subgroups?
Can records be cross-indexed to provide additional information?
Can one retrieve all the records a student has finished or is working on?
Can one retrieve an objective and all the students who have finished or are working on the objective?
Can one retrieve a class and the objectives accomplished or being worked on?
Can one retrieve attempts at a lesson by students or classes?
Can one retrieve attempts to pass a test by individuals or classes?
Can one retrieve the lessons completed by a student?
Can one retrieve the names of the students who have completed a given lesson?
Can one produce printed records?
Can one produce printed tests?
Can one print a list of lesson objectives?
Can one print student assignments based on work accomplished?
Can one produce reports (printed or otherwise)?
Can one produce reports of who is using system?
Can one produce reports of who is in which class?
Can one produce reports of attendance?
Can one produce reports of what work has been assigned?
Can one produce reports of tests?
Can one produce a report of who has completed given lessons?

TABLE 8.6 Design Evaluation of Program Documentation

Are operating instructions provided?

Are the operating instructions clear?

Are the operating instructions complete?

Are the operating instructions accurate?

Is a teachers' manual provided?

Is the manual clear?

Is the manual complete?

Is the manual accurate?

Are examples provided for how to introduce and use the program?

Are there suggestions on how to follow up the computer program with additional instruction?

Is other support material provided for the lesson? Example: homework problems for off-line time.

Are strategies provided on how to implement the program in a curriculum?

Are any additional resources provided to supplement the program's curricular implementation?

Are references provided for the program content?

Is there a field test report on the program's effectiveness?

TABLE 8.7 Miscellaneous Evaluation Questions

Are the requirements for the program specified?

Does the program require any special equipment needs?

Does the program tell the instructor how long it takes an average student to complete the objectives?

Is the program designed for independent study or teacher-directed study?

Is the program designed to be used by individuals, small groups, or large groups?

Does the company producing the program have a good reputation?

Does the producer support the program via telephone or other contacts?

You may not have to do all the selection of evaluation questions on your own. A number of national groups have developed courseware evaluation forms that are suitable for teacher use, including the National Science Teachers Association, the National Council of Teachers of Mathematics, and the Northwest Regional Laboratory's MicroSift Project. (See Figure 8.2.) They will be pleased to send you a copy of their evaluations to help you to decide which questions to ask. Many school districts have their own evaluation forms.

Software Evaluation Checklist

PROGRAM NAME: ________ SOURCE: ________ COST: ________
SUBJECT AREA: ________ REVIEWER'S NAME: ________ DATE: ________

1. INSTRUCTIONAL RANGE

________ grade level(s)
________ ability level(s)

2. INSTRUCTIONAL GROUPING FOR PROGRAM USE

___ individual
___ small group (size: ___)
___ large group (size: ___)

3. EXECUTION TIME

_____ minutes (estimated) for average use

4. PROGRAM USE(S)

___demonstration	___programming utility
___drill or practice	___simulation
___instructional gaming	___testing operations
___instructional management	___tutorial
___instructional support	___whistles and bells
___problem solving	___word processing
	___other (________)

5. USER ORIENTATION: INSTRUCTOR'S POINT OF VIEW

low				*high*	
•	•	•	•	•	flexibility
•	•	•	•	•	freedom from need to intervene or assist

6. USER ORIENTATION: STUDENT'S POINT OF VIEW

low				*high*	
•	•	•	•	•	quality of directions (clarity)
•	•	•	•	•	quality of output (content and tone)
•	•	•	•	•	quality of screen formatting
•	•	•	•	•	freedom from need for external information
•	•	•	•	•	freedom from disruption by system errors
•	•	•	•	•	simplicity of user input

7. CONTENT

low				*high*	
•	•	•	•	•	instructional focus
•	•	•	•	•	instructional significance
•	•	•	•	•	soundness or validity
•	•	•	•	•	compatibility with other materials used

8. MOTIVATION AND INSTRUCTIONAL STYLE

passive				*active*	
•	•	•	•	•	type of student involvement
low				*high*	
•	•	•	•	•	degree of student control

none	*poor*				*good*	
•	•	•	•	•	•	use of game format
•	•	•	•	•	•	use of still graphics
•	•	•	•	•	•	use of animation
•	•	•	•	•	•	use of color
•	•	•	•	•	•	use of voice input and output
•	•	•	•	•	•	use of nonvoice audio
•	•	•	•	•	•	use of light pen
•	•	•	•	•	•	use of ancillary materials
•	•	•	•	•	•	use of ________

9. SOCIAL CHARACTERISTICS

present and negative	*not present*	*present and positive*	
____	____	____	competition
____	____	____	cooperation
____	____	____	humanizing of computer
____	____	____	moral issues or value judgments
____	____	____	summary of student performance

Reproduced with permission from *Guidelines for Evaluating Computerized Instructional Materials*, copyright 1984 by the National Council of Teachers of Mathematics.

FIGURE 8.2 Evaluation Form

Analyzing the Courseware

The general flow of a formal design evaluation for a piece of instructional software proceeds in the steps illustrated in Figure 8.3. You evaluate one design category at a time, viewing and manipulating the program as necessary to obtain answers to the selected evaluation questions. Here are the steps.

1. Evaluate the design category, using a selection of evaluation questions in the relevant category to guide your thinking and answering them yes or no.

2. You then examine your set of answers to decide if the program's design (in this category) is acceptable.

3. If the program is acceptable thus far, you go on to evaluate the next design category (in other words, going back to Step 1 with the next set of questions).

4. If the program is not acceptable, you will need to decide whether to ignore its faults. (You can often compensate for faults by modifying how the program is used or supplementing it somehow.) If you choose to ignore faults, you move on to evaluate the next category (back to Step 1 again).

5. If you do not ignore the faults, you reject the program and return it to the supplier.

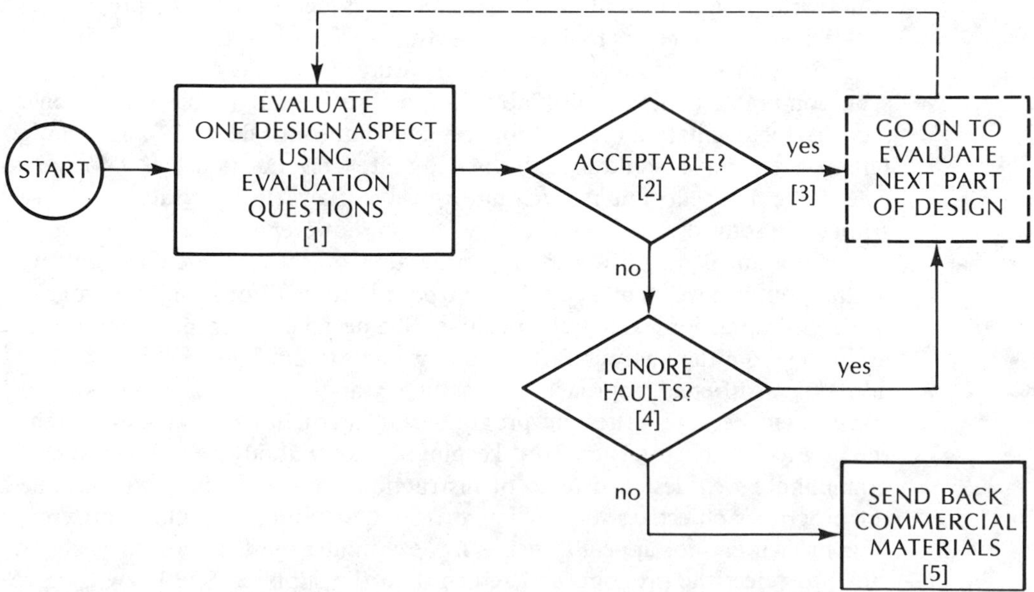

FIGURE 8.3 The Design Evaluation Process

The process of design evaluation is complete when you have used all the groups of questions in Tables 8.1 through 8.7. If the courseware being evaluated passes the design evaluation, proceed to the tryout evaluation.

Some Sample Evaluation Decisions

Betty Cheung's software budget was small, but she had plenty of time to spend in careful selection. So she planned an almost mathematical approach to her design analysis. She created a data base using her spreadsheet, with the rows being programs and the columns criteria. Cells became the location for Yes/No tallies, decisions, and comments about the performance of each program. She knew her principal would appreciate data to support her expenditure if she chose one of the two expensive programs.

Before Betty began to examine the three competing programs to teach graphing, she took a careful look at her photocopy of the sets of questions in Tables 8.1 through 8.7. She marked with an asterisk the ones she was most concerned about and jotted down two additional miscellaneous criteria from the NCTM's software evaluation form. Having decided the important criteria to examine, Betty then selected the first program to analyze.

Using the cycle in Figure 8.3, Betty proceeded to evaluate Program A on each of the criteria marked with an asterisk. She first examined the category of purpose (Table 8.1). There were some problems in this category, since the program did not have clear goal statements, but after deciphering the program purpose herself, she was pleased to note it matched her needs. She knew she could write objectives and hand them out to students using the program, so she decided to ignore this fault temporarily.

Betty then proceeded to evaluate measures (Table 8.2), instructional presentation (Table 8.3), content (Table 8.4), record keeping (Table 8.5), teacher/student documentation (Table 8.6), and miscellaneous (Table 8.7). The yes/no tallies were complete, and though she had quite a few nos (and a few not sures) listed, she had encountered no unforgivable flaws in Program A. It was stronger in some design categories than others, however.

Program B was different. The program's objectives were clear and well written, but not well matched to the purpose Betty had for using the program. Her first impressions were quite positive. She decided to accept it temporarily, and to explore the analysis further. She wanted to consider the possibility of adopting a different approach to teaching graphing. The program was well constructed because its testing program and instructional strategies matched the original purposes. The record keeping was very good. Betty knew she was examining a well designed piece of instructional software, however she knew the program's objectives were different from hers, and the resulting difference in approach did not appeal to her. After examining the fifth category, she decided to reject the program and return it to the supplier. She knew the program's design just wasn't for her.

Betty repeated the process with Program C. By this time she was comfortable with evaluating for design and needed much less time to complete the evaluation. Like Program A, this last program seemed to meet her needs. Program C survived the complete evaluation without rejection, and it displayed strengths and weaknesses across categories. Betty was unsure of the reason for the cost differences between the two programs. She planned to conduct a tryout evaluation of both of them, because they both passed all her main design criteria.

CONDUCTING A FORMAL TRYOUT EVALUATION

To be absolutely sure a program works, it must be tried out with students. This is not to imply tryout evaluation is a casual look at how students like the program. Rather, the tryout evaluation is a structured plan to make sure that a program performs as you want it to before buying it.

The purpose of a tryout evaluation is to compare actual student performance with desired student performance. In order to do this, you need to keep in mind why the program is being used with students. With instructional software, you should have clear teaching objective(s) for the program. In addition to knowing what the desired student performance is, you need some measure(s) to determine if students accomplish the goals and objectives through use of the program. You cannot determine what students have learned if you do not test them.

Some enrichment programs may not have any discernible goals and ob-

To see if a piece of courseware works, try it out with the students.

jectives and may be pursued out of interest alone. However, if you are evaluating a learning program, you need to determine whether students are learning or not while using the program.

A Procedure for Evaluating Effectiveness

Figure 8.4 presents the steps in a tryout evaluation.

1. State the program's intent in measurable terms (a performance objective). You must know what the program is supposed to do in order to decide whether it did it or not.

2. Select from one to four students from the population the program is intended to serve. It is very important that the tryout students be a typical sample of the students who will use the program. If you choose to conduct the tryout with above average students, you will know little about how it will work with students of lesser capabilities.

3. You use the program with the students in the same way you would use the program normally. You must not provide any more learning support than you intend to use with the class as a whole.

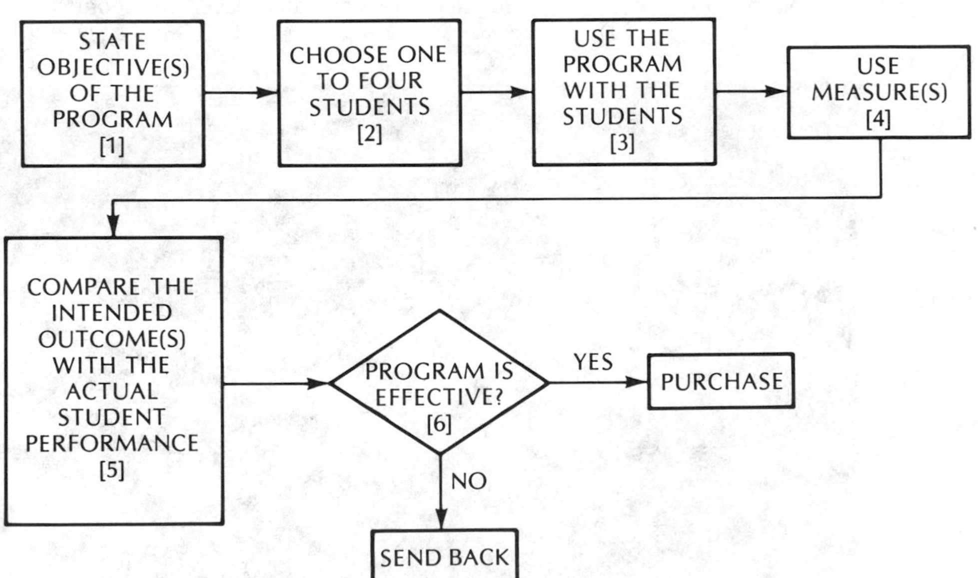

FIGURE 8.4 The Tryout Evaluation Process

4. Upon completion of the program by the students, you administer a test in order to determine whether the students reached the performance objective from Step 1.

5. Compare the students' actual performance to the desired performance to determine if the program worked or not. (If students also complete an attitude survey, you can determine what they thought of the program. Ask if they agree or disagree with such characteristics as these: interesting; clear; valuable; too many facts; easy to work with; well organized.)

6. If the program worked, it can be purchased. If not, return it to the publisher or dealer.

Some of the items you need to consider in advance of performing a tryout evaluation are presented in Table 8.8.

Empirical Evidence for Effectiveness

Betty Cheung learned a lot about the effectiveness of the two graphing programs from trying them with a small group of volunteer students from her ninth grade home room. (She would have these students in the tenth grade class in just a few months.) Though she was unable to test the entire package, she identified comparable portions and followed the exact procedure outlined in Figure 8.4, letting the students draw straws for the program they would use.

Because Betty had identified design flaws in both programs, she was pleasantly surprised by the results she obtained. She experienced few problems using either program, and students learned from both. She noted several differences between the two programs. Students using Program C asked fewer questions and seemed to experience less confusion than students using Pro-

TABLE 8.8 Tryout Evaluation Considerations

Are the goals clarified prior to the evaluation?
Are the objectives written prior to the evaluation?
Are the measures written prior to the evaluation?
Is the target audience carefully designated?
How many students should be used in the tryout?
Are the standards for the successful accomplishment established before the tryout is conducted?
Should student attitudes toward the program be evaluated using a survey?

gram A. Program C students seemed to require little of her time. Program C outperformed Program A on the performance measure for every portion. The results could not be explained by differences in student aptitude. Another unexplainable: Program C cost less, although it worked better. Students using Program C were able to complete their portions faster and still achieve a higher performance level. Clearly, Program C offered more cost-effective instruction.

Betty returned Program A to its publisher and purchased several copies of Program C. Betty had the evidence she needed for the purchase, and the confidence that this program would really support her instructional program.

ACQUIRING AND EVALUATING COURSEWARE: FACING REALITIES

Betty Cheung was able to pursue a relatively thorough search for courseware and to spend time to ensure that the computer program she purchased was the best of those available for her instructional program. Most classroom teachers find their situation to be far less conducive to the employment of such comprehensive and detailed procedures as Betty has used.

Adapting the Generalized Process

In your school, you may find that the available time, money, and support resources do not exist to permit you to pursue really systematic and thorough methods for getting courseware for your instructional program. You will need to take a somewhat more informal approach consistent with the realities that you face in your teaching situation.

Below is a brief summary of the steps in the acquisition and evaluation approach we have presented. You can use them as the basis for devising your own procedures for locating and evaluating microcomputer programs within your particular context, taking a more casual approach to some steps, a more thorough one to others, modifying the sequence, and perhaps even skipping a step (except for Step 1!) if necessary.

1. Identify a curriculum need that can be satisfied with a computer program (if a suitable piece of software can be found).

2. Review resource materials for possible programs.

3. Get specific review information.

4. Screen the programs.

5. Acquire the courseware for preview.

6. Decide on how much evaluation is needed.

7. Perform a design evaluation.

8. Perform a tryout evaluation.

9. Make final purchase (or not purchase) decision.

For the curriculum needs of your classroom, you want to make enlightened decisions on how to spend whatever money is allocated to you for computer resources. You will wish to avoid shortcuts and informality whenever possible. As a rule of thumb, the larger your curriculum need, the more you will want to pursue as thorough a process as available resources permit.

Building a Library of Educational Programs

Because the process of locating, securing, and evaluating instructional software can be a large task, it is one generally best done by groups of teachers rather than individuals. As we state in Chapter 9, schools and districts should set up procedures to facilitate and expedite the process. Teachers who wish to do so can become quite proficient in acquiring effective courseware for teaching.

In your own case, you will find that locating software for specific curricular needs becomes easier and easier to do. With experience, you will become aware of the many sources for programs. The securing of programs for the purposes of review will become routine as you find the letter (to publishers) that tends to work for you. The design evaluation process goes more smoothly as you learn more about what constitutes good instructional design for the computer and know how to look for it. The tryout assessment process will become familiar to your students and they will look forward to helping you to screen new computer programs.

Together these processes will allow you to gain a measure of control over the tens of thousands of computer programs that are available and your classroom library of programs will grow in a fashion that encourages the learning you intend to promote.

SUMMARY AND REVIEW CHECKLIST

In this chapter we have identified sources you can use to locate and acquire computer courseware for your classroom. By now you should have a clear idea of the challenge of identifying worthwhile programs from the large body of educational software and some strategies you can use to boost your chances of doing so.

We hope you recognize how valuable review information can be, both for eliminating dysfunctional programs from consideration and for informing your acquisition decisions. We also hope you see the value of previewing and evaluating courseware before purchase.

This chapter has emphasized instructional software design factors and systematic evaluation processes. In doing so, it has presented a broader spectrum of evaluation criteria and more rigorous strategies than most teachers would require, or use, for single software purchases. Within these, you can choose criteria and methods to suit your needs and preferences. The main intent is that you will be able to choose wisely from available commercial software and to acquire for classroom use a library of high quality programs that will be cost-effective in supporting your teaching.

Checklist

[ ] I can state a variety of sources of microcomputer courseware.

[ ] I can describe how to tap software information and acquire programs from sources through two channels.

[ ] I can identify the range of sources of information on quality of microcomputer courseware and describe how to acquire such information.

[ ] I can describe how to request courseware for preview and identify factors to include in a letter to strengthen the request.

[ ] I can state guidelines for making judgments regarding the extent of an evaluation effort that any given software program should receive.

[ ] I can describe how to conduct a complete review of the design of a program intended for instruction.

[ ] I can describe how to conduct a tryout evaluation of an instructional computer program.

[ ] I can distinguish between empirical evaluation data and intuitive judgment for evaluating courseware, and I could decide when to use one or the other.

[ ] I can outline elements of a realistic process for evaluating courseware for classroom use.

SUGGESTED ACTIVITIES

1. Develop a list of places (perhaps on an computer data base) to write to in order to acquire software; include publishers, dealers, and computer manufacturers.

2. Choose a specific content area. Using various approaches (catalogs, magazines, library sources, electronic information) obtain the names of up to ten programs that could be used to help teach the area. Make sure you survey the publications *(Worth a Look)* listed in the previous chapter.
3. Use reviews to screen the programs you have found for your content area.
4. Secure three courseware evaluation forms from national groups serving teachers and select the one you feel has the best set of evaluation items.
5. Using an available educational program, conduct a design evaluation to determine how well the program is made.
6. Using an available program, conduct a tryout evaluation using one student to determine if the program does what it claims to do.

WORTH A LOOK: SOFTWARE SOURCES

The listing of software publishers below is not intended to be comprehensive. Rather, it contains contact information for producers of the *Worth a Look* programs we have identified in other chapters of this book. You can contact the company and request further descriptive information on any program of interest to you. Since most of the listed companies produce numerous software titles, you can also request a general catalog of their current offerings.

Active Learning Systems
5365 Avenidas Encinas, Suite J
Carlsbad, CA 92008
800/423-0818
619/931-7784

Activision, Inc.
(see Mediagenic)

Addison-Wesley
2725 Sand Hill Road
Menlo Park, CA 94025
800/447-2226

Advanced Ideas
2901 San Pablo Avenue
Berkeley, CA 94702
415/526-9100

Apple Computer, Inc.
2525 Mariani
Cupertino, CA 95014
800/732-3131, ext. 254

Ashton-Tate
20101 Hamilton Avenue
Torrance, CA 90502-1319
213/329-8000

Baudville
5380 52nd Street, S.E.
Grand Rapids, MI 49508
616/698-0888

Borland International, Inc.
4585 Scotts Valley Drive
Scotts Valley, CA 95066
408/438-8400

Broderbund Software
P.O. Box 12947
San Rafael, CA 94913-2947
800/527-6263
415/492-3200 (CA)

Britannica Software
345 Fourth Street
San Francisco, CA 94107
800/572-2272
415/546-1866 (CA)

Broderbund Software
P.O. Box 12947
San Rafael, CA 94913-2947
800/527-6263
415/492-3200 (CA)

Bytes of Learning
150 Consumers Road, #202
Willowdale, Ontario
Canada M2J 1P9
416/495-9913

Claris Corporation
440 Clyde Avenue
Mountain View, CA 94043
800/334-3535
415/960-1500 (CA)

Collamore Educational Publishing
(see D.C. Heath / Collamore)

COMPress/Queue
562 Boston Avenue
Bridgeport, CT 06610
800/232-2224
203/335-0908

CONDUIT
University of Iowa
Oakdale Campus
Iowa City, IA 52242
319/335-4100

Davidson & Associates, Inc.
3135 Kashiwa Street
Torrance, CA 90505
800/556-6141
213/534-4070 (CA)

D.C. Heath/Collamore
P.O. Box 19309
2700 N. Richardt Avenue
Indianapolis, IN 46219
800/428-8071
317/359-5585 (AK, HI)

DesignWare, Inc.
185 Berry Street
San Francisco, CA 94107
415/546-1866

Didatech Software Ltd.
3812 William Street
Burnaby, B.C.
Canada V5C 3H9
604/299-4435

DLM Teaching Resources
P.O. Box 4000
One DLM Park
Allen, TX 75002
800/527-5030
800/442-4711 (TX)

Educational Activities
P.O. Box 392
Freeport, NY 11520
800/645-3739
516/223-4666 (NY, AK, HI)

Educational Materials and Equipment Corp.
P.O. Box 2805
Danbury, CT 06813-2805
800/848-2050
203/798-2050 (CT)

EduSOFT
P.O. Box 2560
Berkeley, CA 94702
800/EDU-SOFT

Electronic Arts
P.O. Box 7530
San Mateo, CA 94403
800/245-4525
415/571-7171 (CA)

EME (see Educational Materials and Equipment)

Encyclopedia Britannica
(see Britannica Software)

Focus Media
839 Stewart Avenue
P.O. Box 865
Garden City, NY 11530
800/645-8989
516/794-8900 (NY)

Gessler Publishing Co.
900 Broadway
New York, NY 10003
212/673-3113

Grade Busters
3610 Queen Anne Way
Colorado Springs, CO 80917
719/591-9815

Grolier Electronic Publishing, Inc.
95 Madison Avenue, Suite 1100
New York, NY 10016
212/696-9750

High Technology
Software Products
8200 N. Classen Boulevard, #101
Oklahoma City, OK 73114
405/848-0480

Holt, Rinehart & Winston
383 Madison Avenue
New York, NY 10017
212/872-2000

HRM/Queue
562 Boston Avenue
Bridgeport, CT 06610
800/232-2224
203/335-0908

IBM Direct Response Marketing
Dept. TR
101 Paragon Drive
Montvale, NJ 07645
800/IBM-2468, ext. 900/TR

The Learning Company
6493 Kaiser Drive
Fremont, CA 94555
800/852-2255

Logo Computer Systems
121 Mount Vernon Street
Boston, MA 02108
800/321-5646
617/742-2990 (MA)

Lotus Development Corporation
55 Cambridge Parkway
Cambridge, MA 02142
800/554-5501

MECC
3490 Lexington Avenue, No.
St. Paul, MN 55126
800/228-3504
800/782-0032 (in MN)

Mediagenic (Activision)
P.O. Box 7286
Mountain View, CA 94039
415/329-0500

MindPlay
100 Conifer Hill Drive
Building 3, Suite 301
Danvers, MA 01923
800/221-7911
508/774-1760 (MA)

Mindscape
3444 Dundee Road
Northbrook, IL 60062
800/221-9884
312/480-7667 (IL)

Odesta
4084 Commercial Avenue
Northbrook, IL 60062
800/323-5423

Savtek Corporation
P.O. Box 1077
Waltham, MA 02254
617/891-0638

Scholastic, Inc.
2931 E. McCarty Street
P.O. Box 7502
Jefferson City, MO 65102
800/541-5513
800/392-2179 (MO)

Science Research Associates
155 North Wacker Drive
Chicago, IL 60606
800/621-0476
312/984-7000 (IL, AK, HI)

Scott, Foresman
1900 E. Lake Avenue
Glenview, IL 60025
312/729-3000

Sensible Software
335 East Big Beaver, Suite 207
Troy, MI 48083
313/528-1950

Society for Visual Education
1345 Diversey Parkway
Chicago, IL 60614-1299
800/621-1900
312/525-1500 (IL)

Software Garden
Box 373
Newton Highlands, MA 02161
617/332-2240

Software Toolworks
One Toolworks Plaza
13557 Venture Boulevard
Sherman Oaks, CA 91423
818/907-6789

Sorcim/Computer Associates
2195 Fortune Drive
San Jose, CA 95131
408/942-1727

South-Western Publishing Co.
5101 Madison Road
Cincinnati, OH 45227
800/543-7007
800/543-7672 (OH)

Spinnaker Software Corporation
1 Kendall Square
Cambridge, MA 02139
800/826-0706
617/494-1200 (MA)

Springboard Software
7808 Creekridge Circle
Minneapolis, MN 55435
800/654-6301
612/944-3915 (MN)

Sunburst Communications
39 Washington Avenue
Pleasantville, NY 10570-9971
800/431-1934
800/247-6756 (Canada)
914/769-5030 collect

Techbyte Inc.
21 South Union Street
Burlington, VT 05401
800/361-4993

Tescor Inc.
461 Carlisle Drive
Herndon, VA 22070
703/435-9501

Timeworks
444 Lake Cook Road
Deerfield, IL 60015
312/948-9200

Tom Snyder Productions
90 Sherman Street
Cambridge, MA 02140
800/342-0236
617/876-4433 (MA)

Vernier Software
2920 S.W. 89th Street
Portland, OR 97225
502/297-5317

Wadsworth, Inc.
7625 Empire Drive
Florence, KY 41042
800/354-9706

Weekly Reader Software
Optimum Resource, Inc.
10 Station Place
Norfolk, CT 06058
800/327-1473
203/542-5553 (CT)

WordPerfect Corporation
329 N. State Street
Orem, UT 84057
800/321-4566
801/225-5000 (UT)

READINGS

Anderson, C.A. "Computer Literacy: Changes for Teacher Education." *Journal of Teacher Education* 34(5):6–9 (September/October 1983).

Bell, M. E. "The Role of Instructional Theories in the Evaluation of Microcomputer Courseware." *Educational Technology* 25(3):36–40 (March 1985).

Bork, A. "Education and Computers: The Situation Today and Some Possible Futures." *Technological Horizons in Education* 12(3):92–97 (October 1984).

Caffarella, E. P. "Evaluating the New Generation of Computer-Based Instructional Software." *Educational Technology* 27(4):19–24 (April 1987).

Collins, S., and Newman, J. *Computer Technology in Curriculum and Instructional Handbook: Courseware Evaluation*. Olympia, WA: Washington Office of the State Superintendent of Public Instruction, 1982.

Della-Piana, G., and Della-Piana, C. K. "Computer Software Information for Educators: A New Approach to Portrayal of Student Tryout Data." *Educational Technology* 24(10):19–25 (October 1984).

Gonce-Winder, C., and Walbesser, H. H. "Toward Quality Software." *Contemporary Educational Psychology* 12(3): 261–68 (July 1987).

Johnston, V. M. "The Evaluation of Microcomputer Programs: An Area of Debate." *Journal of Computer-Assisted Learning* 3(1):40–50 (March 1987).

Kruse, T. "Finding Helpful Software Reviews." *Classroom Computer Learning* 8(3):44–48 (November/December 1987).

Otte, R. B. "Courseware for the '80s." *Technological Horizons in Education* 12(3):89–91 (October 1984).

Riordon, T. "How to Select Software You Can Trust." *Classroom Computer News* 3(4):56–61 (March 1983).

Sanders, R. L., and Sanders, M. E. "Evaluating Microcomputer Software." *Computers, Reading and Language Arts* 1(1):21–25 (Summer 1983).

Savitsky, D. "A Publisher's Guidelines for Educational Software Development." *Educational Technology* 24(4):45 (April 1984).

Taylor, R. "Selecting Effective Courseware: Three Fundamental Instructional Factors." *Contemporary Educational Psychology,* 12(3):231–43 (July 1987).

Wujcik, A. *Educational Software Best-Sellers in the Home Market.* Washington, DC: National Institute of Education, 1984.

REFERENCES

Ahl, D. H. "Selecting and Buying Educational Software." *Creative Computing Software Buyer's Guide,* 1983:24, 26, 28.

Cohen, V. B. "Criteria for the Evaluation of Microcomputer Courseware." *Educational Technology* 23(1):9–14 (January 1983).

Futrell, M. F., and Geisert, P. G. *The Well-Trained Computer: Designing Instructional Materials for the Classroom Computer.* Englewood Cliffs, NJ: Educational Technology Publication, 1986.

Komoski, P. K. "Educational Computing: The Burden of Insuring Quality." *Phi Delta Kappan,* December 1984:244–248.

Neill, S. B., and Neill G. W. *Only the Best: The Annual Guide to Highest-Rated Educational Software for Preschool—Grade 12 (1990 Edition).* New York: R. R. Bowker, 1989.

Roth, S. K., and Petty, B. A. "Educational Software: Why Are Teachers Dissatisfied?" *Educational Considerations* 15(2):24–26 (Spring 1988).

9

School and District-wide Planning for Microcomputer Use

OBJECTIVES

- State some questions that should be tackled on a school-wide basis, rather than within a classroom.
- State some questions that should be tackled on a district-wide basis rather than in a school.
- Identify how schools and school districts are currently using microcomputers.
- Identify and describe some key influences operating to move schools to integrate microcomputers into their educational programs, including societal influences, local situations, and students' special needs.
- Explain factors that mitigate against the ability of schools to implement an innovation or technology despite good intentions.
- Outline some of the considerations to be used in decision making when integrating microcomputers school-wide, including hardware aspects, software factors, and teacher attitudes and skills.

- Describe a planning approach that leads to optimal microcomputer use that begins with establishing curricular need rather than with purchasing computers.
- Describe some issues relating to school-wide computer security.
- Identify some of the uses of the computer in special education.

INTRODUCTION

A number of forces are at work fueling the placement of computers in schools. Rising expectations for schools to use computers provide an impetus toward change.

Colleges and universities are establishing more rigorous criteria for incoming students and asking that they be able to demonstrate more sophisticated computer proficiency, especially in the areas of problem solving and thinking, and not just in the basic skills of keyboarding and using applications programs. K–12 programs are expected to prepare students adequately in computer use, and a school may feel pressure on the curricular front from the various post secondary level institutions toward which its students are bound.

The parents are concerned as well. The people of the local community look at the advances of computers in the business world and then wonder why the school is not making greater use of such a powerful tool. The changes that have occurred in other domains prompt questions about why technology has been so slow to create school-wide changes.

Such forces as these drive schools to try to develop their patterns of computer usage more fully. In this chapter we will examine how schools have proceeded in implementing technology thus far. Our interest is not only in *how* they do it, but also in how they might do it *differently.*

Goals

- What are the various factors that influence the way microcomputers are integrated into schools?
- What is the value of systematic, information-based planning over the more typical intuitive procedures for making microcomputers part of a school's instructional program?
- What role does district-wide decision making play in the integration of microcomputers into schools and classrooms.

GENERAL TRENDS IN SCHOOL COMPUTER USE

Although it is difficult to draw generalizations regarding the use of computers in education due to the great number and diversity of schools, it is interesting to look at some general trends.

How abundant are computers in schools? In late 1985 a report by Walcott (1985) documented that of the fifty states, Alaska led the nation with one computer for each 17 students (99,711 students and 5,779 computers). At the other end of the survey, Hawaii had 86 students to one computer. The average state was Wisconsin, with slightly under 50 students per computer.

The U.S. Office of Technology Assessment (1988) completed a study that shows that the average number of computers per 30 students has continually increased since 1983, but it stood in 1987 at slightly over one computer for every 30 students in high school (an unequal distribution leads to approximately 0.8 computer/30 students in elementary schools). This means that student wait time to use a computer might be long in a typical U.S. school.

How are schools using computers? Naron and Estes report several trends based on a national survey (1986). Although the sample was small, it showed a pattern of findings similar to other reports. Some of the things they found are:

- Public school districts have generally modified their instructional programs to incorporate the use of technology in three ways: (1) teaching with computers, (2) teaching about computers, and (3) using computers to record students' progress through the instructional program.
- The primary use of computers at the elementary level is for computer-assisted instruction in mathematics and reading.
- Computer literacy courses are generally introduced at the junior high level and continued at the senior high level.
- The impact of technology at the senior high school level is most evident in computer science courses and computer-related courses in mathematics, science, and vocational education.
- The most frequent use of computer instruction is for drill and practice, followed by enrichment and remedial purposes. Minimal use is reported for problem solving, simulations, or development of reasoning skills.
- The students with the greatest access to the computer are the gifted and talented and the slow, disadvantaged, and/or special education students.
- Few districts use CMI, but many districts keep track via computer of special education students' progress on the Individual Education Plans.
- Parents are overwhelmingly supportive of the instructional program. There is very little use of computers in home-based or distance learning.

- Overall, most elementary and secondary school districts are in the initial phase of planning and implementing the use of technology in the educational system.
- In general, the impact of technology on the instructional program is rather moderate. Most elementary curricula have remained unchanged, with teachers using the computer as another teaching tool to support or supplement the regular program of instruction.

Naron and Estes present a picture that has many interesting hues, but if we compare the potential of the computer with the reality of the information presented above, it does not seem to be a picture painted in very bright colors. What underlies the discrepancy? As we proceed, we will examine a few of the factors that tend to operate as schools respond to the arrival of computer technology on the educational scene.

TECHNOLOGY ENTERS THE PICTURE

In this chapter we will be examining the actions of a school as it responds to a strong impetus to develop computers as an integral part of its program. The school is somewhat illustrative of how many schools have proceeded. The developmental stages this school goes through and many of the development criteria that we describe were first explicated by Cory (1983). As we follow our school's path toward full-fledged computer integration, we will be on the lookout for lessons other schools can learn.

Robert T. Jones – Magnet School

The teacher's lounge was abuzz with rumors. The new school superintendent, known for his love of technology, was coming to Robert T. Jones High School to make an announcement. "Why would the Superintendent of Schools come here in the middle of the school year?" teacher's asked. Robert T. Jones High School was in a central city, and visits from high level administrators were rare.

The superintendent's speech that morning caused more excitement than the rumors themselves. Robert T. Jones High School was to become Robert T. Jones – Magnet School. It was to be a showcase for computer innovation! The faculty would have the remainder of the school year to think about the idea and prepare for it. The following year the school would accept all students who opted to go to a school heavily committed to the use of technology to further learning. The teachers who didn't wish to be a part of the magnet school had the option of transferring. Others from the city interested in the idea would then replace them.

A key figure in the planned change was to be Lucy Green, Principal. Lucy's leadership was valued highly by the Robert T. Jones staff and the superintendent wanted her to guide the transition to magnet school status. Lucy, as a principal who would go to the ends of the earth to get something better for her students, looked upon the superintendent's plan as a golden opportunity.

Although not technologically oriented or computer competent, the principal welcomed the idea of RTJHS becoming a magnet school for computing technology. Her comment in response to the new challenge was, "Why not, I doubt if the kids will get less than they are getting now, and they are very likely to get more! We can make this a success." She began an immediate campaign to see to it that all her students would be excited by the idea of their school's new program. The faculty was uncertain but hopeful. With Lucy's enthusiasm and industry, and with an influx of district funds for the purpose, essentially all of the RTJHS staff elected to stay for the school-wide change.

Getting on the Bandwagon

One of the first things Lucy Green decided was that everyone needed to know *all* the places in her school that might make use of computers. A small group of teachers (those with highest interest and most expertise) and a vice principal spent several weeks researching that information. They received helpful consultations from a professor at the city university. When they presented their report to the faculty, they used a diagram much like the one in Figure 9.1.

Awareness of all the potential uses a computer might have in their school provided incentive for RTJMS teachers to get on the bandwagon. Computers could be used almost everyplace in the school, so each department felt it had better join the program. At the same time, there was much ambivalence, uncertainty, and curiously, some mistrust, and even a bit of downright fear on the part of many teachers for whom computers were a brand new ball game. By the end of four months, however, the school had moved a long way.

The acquisition of hardware had become the primary focus. Every department wanted something, so the emphasis was on quantity rather than quality. As word of the new technology emphasis spread in the city, Robert T. Jones became known among computer vendors as a place to target for new products. Teachers saw demonstrations of all the wonderful things each type of computer could do. This orientation toward hardware capabilities meant that the school purchased a variety of hardware for a variety of purposes.

In the software area, very little was purchased initially. Several staff members admitted to being programming addicts, and they were given free time and directed to produce some programs to use in math and language arts.

No one had much time for staff development, because everyone was busy buying hardware, supervising the development of software, and planning for the coming year. A lot of teachers didn't know exactly what real usefulness the computers had for their teaching or how to put them to work. As vendors filled orders, computers began to show up in classrooms.

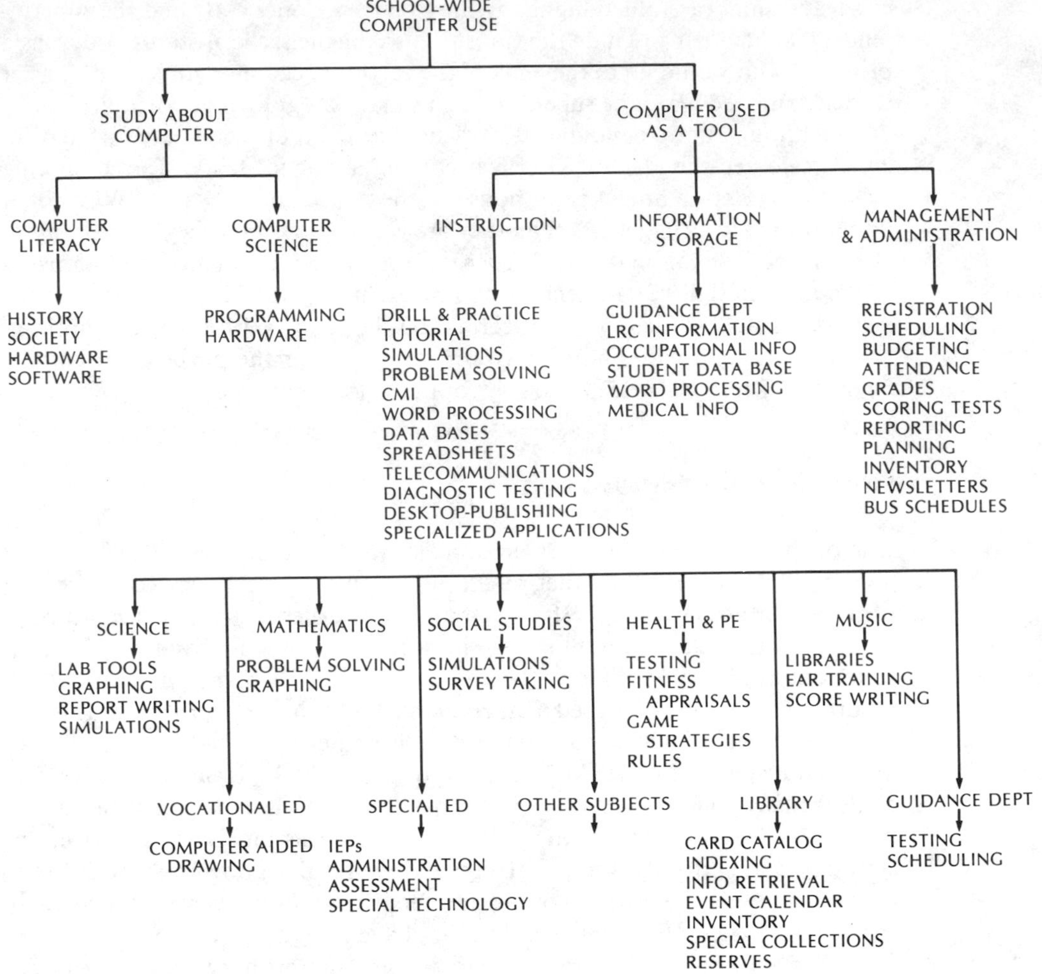

FIGURE 9.1 Overview of Planning Areas

Arcade game software appeared also. Without a clear understanding of the usefulness of the new hardware, many teachers saw them as good for "fun and games" during free time. Some teachers located software in their subject areas and purchased programs they located in catalogs if they sounded as if they might be useful.

A number of teachers suspected that computers would be transient and would pass away like other educational fads had done in the past. Despite the commotion and excitement, they envisioned a time when Robert T. Jones would settle back to normal.

The computer literacy aspects of the RTJM's original chart (Figure 9.1) got pushed aside as teachers tried out all the software they could get. A discovery was made by one of the teachers that there were a lot of free programs available called "public domain software," and these were duplicated en masse and a set given to all teachers.

Confusion began to set in.

The State of Confusion

The school had purchased a lot of hardware and still the topic of hardware acquisition continued to be the center of debate. A significant amount of the allotted monies had been spent, and yet systems were not up and running quite as smoothly as everyone had envisioned.

Many computers had been obtained before it was learned that special cards had to be added to make them more functional. Some funds previously designated for software were used for this purpose. The diversity of hardware purchased tended to present some initial compatibility problems to certain departments. Some funds had to be spent to ensure the features seen as critical were made functional. Each department was focusing on its own problem solving, so cross-departmental communication about technology stayed pretty low.

Another problem arose when the programs from the volunteer teacher-developers were delayed. Those that had been completed were found to be limited in usefulness. Some departments started using discretionary funds to purchase inexpensive software, having found much of the public domain software to be worth exactly what they had paid for it (nothing). School staff aired complaints about most computer programs being "full of bugs" and grumbled that computers "aren't worth the trouble."

To compensate for the paucity of software, the principal approved the purchase of the MECC library of programs in a few departments so that there would be something for the Apple computers to run. Some teachers spent their own money to buy a word processor or grade book program to use.

A number of teachers enrolled at a nearby college, taking a computer programming course in the evening. The instructor told them how important it was that all teachers learn programming, so they could understand computers and be able to make their new approach work. Some teachers pondered the potential value of teaching programming techniques to students, but others were turned off by the intricacy of programming technique and were glad to get the computing course behind them.

At one of the staff meetings, a consultant gave a one-time workshop on using drill and practice programs in instruction. Some teachers began to use some of these programs in their classrooms and were trying to match software to their curriculum. This process led them to a somewhat better understanding of the difference between using a program to teach, and teaching about using computers. The computer science teacher began to include in his program a special unit on how computers change the way society works.

As expectations for results began to increase (coming primarily from the district administration and the parents), available funds and staff morale seemed to diminish in turn. Some teachers were still excited and enthusiastic; others were nervous over their first exposure to a technology that didn't seem to do much, and there was uncertainty about where to go from here.

A HARD LOOK AT REALITIES

The Robert T. Jones school has arrived at a point that many schools before it have reached while attempting to incorporate a new technology into the instructional program.

James Rutherford, President of the American Association for the Advancement of Science, stated:

> There is no reason to believe that simply providing the schools with microcomputers will do much to improve education. Indeed, the thrust of our experience in the United States gives us every reason to believe that doing so will mostly be a waste. Time and time again we have flooded the schools with new instructional technologies . . . always to be disappointed in the end. (1984)

The prognosis for RTJMS and for the integration of computing technology into American education is not yet settled, but the path to failure is well-trodden. Perhaps history has something to teach. Let's examine two of the factors, with regard to an innovation or a new technology, that have led schools to failure in the past. For computers, these factors must be avoided or overcome if there is to be long-lasting integration and a profound effect on schools.

General Resistance to Change

Many teachers enjoy the thrill of change and welcome an innovation on its potential merits. But teacher resistance to change is a major variable in how the school-wide use of computers will proceed.

Teachers in general teach the way they were taught. The typical classroom is organized around the concept of one teacher and a group of students, with the teacher at the center of most, if not all, activities. If an innovation challenges this posture, its situation is quite precarious. For the innovation to succeed, its worth must become so clear that the teacher is willing to change some aspects of teaching. Time for the process of showing worth may be short.

If it is true that teachers teach as they were taught, then what will become of the computer? Although it has the power to work effectively with a student to help that student learn a series of concepts, will the teacher yield authority or time to the computer? This innovation, as others before it, can die not on its lack of merit, but rather because of its challenge to the status quo.

Initially, most of the teachers at Robert T. Jones seemed willing to give the computers a try, at least for a while. But, if the barriers are too high, or if computers do not fit in to a normal routine, or if computers cannot demonstrate effectiveness, or if the machines do not begin to contribute soon in some significant way, the technology's early welcome is very likely to wear thin. How can the computer hope to work its way, in any significant sense, into the RTJ curriculum within whatever grace period remains?

Technological Faddism

Schools are known for the fads that come and go. Gone are the teaching machines that were hailed as ". . . the new way to efficient, self-paced learning for every student." Gone, too, for most intents and purposes, are the open classrooms and the programmed instruction, both of which once had the educational world astir. Instructional TV was to revolutionize the classroom; so was mastery learning. Neither did. Pockets of usage remain for most of these innovations, but the overwhelming excitement and hope felt when each arrived on the scene has dissipated long since and classroom instruction today goes on much as it did before, class-based and teacher-directed.

Some innovations have proved more long lasting and consequential. In the 1960s, for example, outcome-based goals and objectives were new and innovative, and today this form of instructional technology is still much with us. The initial vision of how performance statements describing what students should learn would be employed in schools remains unrealized. Despite this fact, their use has become a part of the planning process of most American schools. The intended degree of contribution such objectives would make to children's learning has never been reached, but objectives have stuck around.

In retrospect, most educational innovations seem to have been initially oversold. Proclaimed as a panacea to solve teaching problems and change the face of American education, each in turn seemed to vanish from the educational scene almost as quickly as it arrived, or, as in the case of the mastery learning and objectives, to be so modified through the implementation process as to become almost unrecognizable to their creators and earliest proponents. Today's schools are into cooperative learning, VCRs, and, yes . . . computers. What will be their fate?

Will computer technology fail to live up to the promise? Is it destined to fade from the scene as have many innovations before it? As some senior faculty at RTJMS said when caught in the middle of their new whirlwind of change, "just wait around for a year or so, and it (the computer movement) will be gone." In the past, all too many such old timers were right. However, when educators are able to perceive the widespread usefulness of an innovation (such as the value of performance objectives as a means of describing instructional intent and focusing strategy), it has its best chance to succeed in the long run.

In this respect, computers do have something going for them. They are "working" in society at large. Computer technology will be around. It has already proven its worth to many areas of endeavor, so continuing development of the technology will proceed, irrespective of whether it becomes fully integrated into school-wide instruction. The extent to which computers will gain a place of influence in schools remains to be seen, but the option for full integration will remain.

FACING THE ISSUES OF COMPUTER INTEGRATION

All too often school microcomputer use is driven by the purchase of hardware. For one reason or another, computers appear in a school and the school is supposed to make appropriate use of them. This was the situation at Robert T. Jones. Its move to obtain computers was directed by the district administration. At other schools, it has been individual teachers or departments that have initiated the process. Unfortunately, regardless of where the impetus comes from, the "hardware first pathway" tends not to lead to successful school-wide computer use since it is seldom accompanied by adequate or appropriate planning.

The National School Boards Association reported (Pogrow, 1985) that 86% of the public school districts it surveyed in 1984 had no policies or guidelines about what they would do with the computers they were buying. Buying hardware was the major trend, as if some magical event would happen that would integrate that hardware into the school programs.

The Need for Planning

When schools give priority to acquiring hardware, the value of the new technology seldom becomes sufficiently obvious to the faculty at large and the reality tends to fall far short of the hoped-for results. For school-wide integration to take place, more attention must be given to the "peopleware" than to hardware or software. Resources directed toward *planning* can help the school to focus on those who are expected to carry out the change—primarily, the teachers—and to provide for their needs throughout the process.

All teachers require a clear understanding of where they are headed (the school's direction) and genuine confidence in their ability to proceed (their own efficacy) if their "status quo inertia" is to be overcome effectively and their valuable expertise brought to bear on the change situation.

Rather than focusing on hardware first, a school might pay particular attention to meeting the needs of those teachers not initially desirous of, or sufficiently (in their view) knowledgeable about, the new technology. Teachers could be asked to delineate what they felt their learning needs were and how they would like to proceed. Efforts could be directed toward ensuring that teachers who participated in in-servicing experiences would view them as positive, as genuinely meaningful, and as contributing to their own teaching. The focus could be less on what the hardware could do than what they, as teachers, might *want to do* with the computers, and then, how to go about it.

Without school-wide planning involving broad participation of teachers, schools have little reason to expect the magical event (school-wide computer use) to happen. With such planning, however, there is less chance that the enthusiasm for innovation among early proponents will slip away before full-scale integration becomes possible. Lack of immediate results and other frustrations may accompany the change process, and ongoing planning can sustain the momentum.

When hardware is center stage, curriculum issues and many other important factors critical to a successful integration process get pushed to the side. For example, without planning, there are no answers for such critical questions as these:

- What are the school's goals for computers and the priorities toward which efforts are to be directed?
- How will the school allocate and share available resources, and ensure equitable use of the technology among teachers and students?
- Where in the curriculum will keyboarding be taught?

When schools give priority to acquiring hardware, the reality tends to fall far short of the hoped-for results.

- How will the school secure its hardware and software, and what rules and policies will govern their use?

The Problems and Challenges of Planning

It takes time to plan, and time is a commodity that school staff do not have in rich abundance. It generally takes all the nonteaching time of the work day to get ready for the next day's lessons.

How can a busy teacher take time out for school-wide planning? The answer to this question lies not with the teacher, but with the school and district. School- and district-wide planning requires that a priority be given to the process and time devoted to its accomplishment. The planners must plan how the time to accomplish the task is to be taken from other endeavors.

Not only is time precious, but every school's curriculum is now full, and giving over any piece of the curricular domain to computers is difficult. How is an elementary teacher with a full teaching agenda to adjust the curriculum appropriately while the school is moving to integrate technology? How is an English teacher who wants to have students use computers for writing going to do it if students exhibit gross differences in entry skills in keyboarding and word processing?

Individual teachers cannot remediate such problems. Problems of these types need solving at a higher level, rather than at the classroom level. Decisions need to be made and plans laid down and executed on a district- or school-wide basis.

Different Approaches to Planning

If planning is viewed from a school-wide level rather than the classroom level, several weighty problems can be approached that a classroom teacher alone cannot solve. These problems include questions like:

- Given the limited computer availability in our school, will the teachers or the students be given the higher priority on using the machines?
- What will we do with students who are already doing their homework papers on home computers when we introduce the rest to what word processing means?

In many school districts, individual schools tend to answer such questions for themselves. They plan curriculum changes, resolve problems of resource sharing, and devise strategies for equitable use, primarily within the school. Schools who succeed when they take this approach often take the lead in their districts, becoming models of full-scale implementation for other schools. In other districts, however, schools become part of a district-level computer integration process. Questions and issues pertaining to the introduction of the technology are faced and resolved district-wide.

Just as there are individual teachers who succeed in integrating a computer into their classroom and those who fail, there are examples of successes and failures for both school-wide and district-wide approaches to integrating technology into schools. What aspects of planning for computer use should occur at the school level, and which at the district level?

Curriculum Planning at the District Level

Curriculum is such a major aspect of the computer integration process that the district itself should directly confront and resolve the main curriculum question: What set of computer competencies do we want all the students of this district to have upon graduation? This question is an ongoing one, subject to modification over time in response to outside priorities and changes (e.g., technological change, state curriculum mandates).

A district typically will have mechanisms for addressing curricular renewal issues. Some districts do it successfully, with adequate representation from within and without, and adequate input and information sharing. Other districts use inadequate procedures and thereby produce low faculty morale or inefficiency. Whatever the means employed to produce it, a district curriculum is what should guide the planning process. So, a set of goals for computer instruction is needed. Then decisions can be made about how to set up a curriculum in the schools to implement the curricular goals. Questions like the following will need to be confronted and answered:

- Where in the curriculum will keyboarding be taught?
- Should all students be taught to write using a word processor? If so, at what level? In what part of the curriculum?
- How should the use of word processors and spelling checkers tie in with the teaching of spelling at the elementary level?
- Will all students be taught some computer programming, and if so, what and when?
- Which portion and what proportion of the school population should study computer science?
- Should computer applications programs be taught in a special computer course, or should they be taught in courses that can apply the results directly, such as using spreadsheets in science and mathematics?

These questions are not easy ones to answer, and the answers will vary from district to district. Ideally, districts will want to employ what is known from research about these issues, and so will seek to garner information from and work with local colleges and universities. From such endeavors they could learn, for example, the negative effects of involving students in word processing instruction before providing adequate instruction in keyboarding, and how automatization of "hunt and peck" motor skills makes subsequent correction more difficult. Information on the experiences of other districts would also be of use.

Curriculum Planning at the School-wide Level

Depending on the district, an individual school may have a larger or smaller proportion of the total set of curricular decision making to do. Certainly many curricular and instructional questions will be left to be resolved at the school level, whether by intent or default.

At the elementary level, for example, these questions might still need to be answered:

- Will we teach our sequence of Logo competencies all together at one grade level, or teach them across grade levels?
- How will new transfer students learn the expected level of word processing to benefit from regular instruction?

At the secondary level, schools may still need to resolve:

- Will the school offer a separate computer course, mini-course, or unit, for example, or will the mandated skills be integrated into existing courses?
- How will the school confront the equity questions—with a unit, or by the efforts of every teacher who has computers in the classroom?
- If a high school student does not know keyboarding, how and when will it be taught?

Other Planning Challenges

Beyond curriculum, there are a number of other challenges to be faced at levels above that of the classroom. For example, resource issues must be faced. In the previous chapter we pointed out how involved the process of acquiring and evaluating software can be. Acquiring hardware to meet needs and ensuring computer compatibility are also issues that require planning and expertise on the part of school personnel. Policy on software duplication and sharing procedures requires explication. Equity issues need to be engaged and plans made toward ensuring appropriate and fair use. In-service training is a critical area to be addressed at some level.

In the interest of efficiency, it is best that issues be addressed at the highest level possible. It is helpful to all teachers when policies and procedures that save time or ensure quality (such as when procedures for software searches are standardized and made known) are established. Efficiency is not the only consideration, however. Diversity across schools means that flexibility must be preserved and idiosyncratic approaches pursued whenever appropriate.

Security: An Issue for School-wide Planning

At the school-wide level, plans must be made to keep computers secure, since electronic equipment has ready resale value after theft. These plans will depend on the conditions in a given school. In some schools, a locked classroom will be a sufficient deterrent. If this level of security is not sufficient, special computer cables can be purchased to lock the body and monitor of the computer to a table. A third level of security comes in the form of alarms with movement sensors attached to the body of the computers.

Although computers are fairly rugged, vandalism of the disk drives and of software is easily accomplished. Fortunately, occurrences are exceedingly rare. The same measures as taken for general security will apply to vandalism, but some degree of watching the computers during use may be required to reduce or eliminate the problem.

Computer hackers in a school can create havoc with software and computers. Hackers (computer-proficient enthusiasts "gone astray") can modify software, steal hardware and software, and can place various kinds of "viruses" into computers. A virus is an insidious computer program, which when placed inside a computer onto a hard disk, starts to duplicate itself or to imbed itself into other programs, causing more and more problems as it grows in size. Hackers can also use school computers to communicate with other computers in the school, especially where machine networks are present. That means they can possibly get into administrative records in order to view and perhaps change the contents.

Hackers are susceptible to identification within a school setting, because they generally have a reputation for their skill, and they are often around computers. Skilled students who do not and would not misapply their talents also spend a lot of time with computers, too. So, one must take care to avoid stereotyping students. Preventive planning is preferable to the need for responding to problem situations. School-wide consideration should be given to the questions of how to keep software, hardware, and school records secure from any computer-knowledgeable student.

Special Education: An Issue for District-wide Planning

There is a broad range of uses of the microcomputer with special students and students with disabilities, and a number of courseware programs have been identified as specifically recommended by educators for use in special education (Brown, 1985). These programs range across a variety of program types and subjects.

Though there are exceptions, usually the recommended software will not have been written originally for special education students. Instead, the programs are aimed at the regular student population, but have been identified as especially worthy of a special education teacher's consideration because they have proved themselves of demonstrable value when used in situations with special students.

The microcomputer has been used in a number of special circumstances for dealing with the needs of disabled students. In recent years there have been many reports of the uses of portable computers in the classroom and work place. More directly, the general purpose personal computer can be put to use as an assistive device for communication and learning.

Enlarged keyboards can be obtained for individuals who lack the dexterity to use a standard computer keyboard. As simple a device as enlarged keys or a simplified key arrangement can open the use of standard word processing programs and of special text programs to disabled students to print out products they write.

When the use of a modified keyboard is not sufficient, keyboard emulators may be employed for individuals who lack the needed hand and finger dexterity. Typically, emulators present choices of character sequences so that the user may select the whole phrase or sentence wanted with only one gross movement of a hand, arm, eyebrow, or leg. Emulators often feature the ability to elicit a sequence of keystrokes that can be recalled as a whole, such as words, phrases, or sentences.

However text is entered into the computer, the computer has the ability to output this text on the computer monitor, the printed page, or as a computer voice. A speech synthesis feature can accommodate most types of disabilities associated with vocalization.

Microcomputers offer a number of advantages to the visually impaired. The utilization of graphics allows text to be flexibly presented in very large sizes and colors that enhance the visually impaired individual's chances of decoding.

The hearing impaired can use a microcomputer in several ways. For example, certain programs can represent the spoken word in visual form on the screen. This type of capability is being used in combination with audio input technology to facilitate the efforts of speech teachers helping hearing impaired learners to improve their vocal production.

The use of a microcomputer with special populations has become a specialized application of the technology, and help is often needed in the augmentation of this use. Assistive device centers are available in some locations to provide this assistance. For example, the Assistive Device Center at the California State University in Sacramento is a joint endeavor of the School of Engineering and the Department of Computer Science. It provides services including direct client services, consultation to school districts, counselors, teachers, and therapists, through a center and through workshops (Cook and Coleman, 1987).

WHEN PLANNING ENTERS THE PICTURE

What would have happened if the faculty and staff of Robert T. Jones Magnet School had not taken the "hardware first" pathway? What if their early energies had gone toward more introspection and analysis of needs, including their own? Is the hop on the bandwagon inevitable? Is the state of confusion a must on the pathway toward full-fledged computer implementation?

Some educators seem to think so (Cory, 1983). It has been said that a school must purchase enough hardware and software and spend sufficient time learning to really understand what the possibilities for computers are. We are not so sure. The learning aspect does seem necessary, and experience *can* be a great teacher, but it seems there may be better ways to proceed.

When resources are a factor, as they typically are in a school, and when the technology is expensive, as it is with computer hardware, then more efficient and effective ways to learn seem called for. Still, as other schools have done, the faculty at Robert T. Jones learned through their experiences that school-wide planning would be necessary.

An Example of School-level Planning

For the faculty at RTJHS, the awareness that a real commitment of time for school-wide planning would be necessary came in the middle of all the confusion. At that point, Lucy Green was as uncertain and concerned as her teachers about the haphazard progress the school had experienced thus far in moving toward their goal of integrating computers into the instructional program.

The Revelation

In October, the principal decided to send out what she called "scouting parties" to see how some schools known for their computer-using programs were using the technology. One group of three teachers went downstate and came back with a slide presentation on Stanforth Junior High. It provided a snapshot of school-wide computer use that had impressed them. What a contrast to their situation!

When the Jones faculty viewed the presentation, here is what they saw. The computer-using school showed many definite *patterns* of use. Two computers were found in the administration office, dedicated to administrative work and serving to correct and score teachers' test papers. Individual classrooms had one or more computers at dedicated places in the room and additional computers on mobile carts for clustering when needed. The Stanforth library had its own computer and a cluster of computers for individual or small group student use. The mechanical drafting classroom had four computers networked to a teacher's computer. Finally, one room, primarily used for the teaching of computer programming, had enough computers to serve one class at a time.

The teachers from the scouting party described and showed slides of a variety of ways Stanforth teachers employed their computers, and how, through its guidelines and procedures, the school had ensured high machine use at all locations. For example, the computer programming classes were arranged so the lab was available for scheduling by other classes in the school on a regular basis.

The teachers of RTJMS knew that for them to turn their own situation into such a smooth operation, a lot of planning would have to be done. With the support of the principal, they resolved to form a school-wide committee to begin some kind of planning effort.

The Response: A Planning Process Begins

One of the committee members had recently attended a computer conference held at MECC in Minnesota. While there, this teacher had heard that the State of Minnesota provided a framework for schools regarding the planning processes that should occur. Minnesota school districts are encouraged to develop a written technology utilization plan. The plan must be written with the help of parents, community members, and the faculty.

The computer committee met and used many of the Minnesota criteria to produce a "white paper" for the RTJMS faculty calling for participation in school-wide planning to end the confusion. Some of the planning points they sought were:

- What are the school's goals for computers?
- What school and community needs will computers serve?
- How will the school guarantee equitable use of the technology?
- How will the school evaluate its efforts?
- How will the school involve the community in its efforts to use computers?
- How will the school review and revise the plan each year?
- How will the school involve the local college and tap the expertise of professors who have experience and information relevant to their problems?

The faculty saw the value of having these types of questions answered, and they began to gather the information. Steps were taken by RTJMS (see Table 9.1) to answer the questions in a structured way.

By involving the community in the planning process, the school both enriched its support and was better informed of expectations for the change process. By completing a survey of the community and of school personnel, the school guaranteed that all areas of need were covered.

RTJMS had a good statement of school philosophy, and a stated set of goals and objectives (the curriculum), so the needs assessment for them was an easy task. It consisted mainly of assessing which of the goals needed the most attention and setting priorities accordingly. From its survey of the community, the school found that the links between the world of work and the world of school were quite weak, so that was determined to be a high priority need for the school.

It is a general rule that the most effective planning proceeds from established needs. When Robert T. Jones school set its priorities, the school then

TABLE 9.1 Steps in a Community-wide Planning Effort to Put Computers into Schools

Step 1.	Form a community-wide committee of teachers, parents, administrators, and community members.
Step 2.	Do a survey (of community and school personnel) to determine the overall needs of the school.
Step 3.	Set priorities on the needs.
Step 4.	Determine how technology, including computers and software, might reduce the high priority needs.
Step 5.	Given computer technology can help, develop a plan on how to decide what software is needed.
Step 6.	Given you know the software that is needed, decide on what hardware is needed to run the software.
Step 7.	Make plans on how to train the school personnel on how to use the software and hardware to maximum advantage.
Step 8.	Set goals for the school year that clearly state the expected outcomes of getting computers and software.
Step 9.	Secure the software and hardware, and implement the plans formed in Step 7.
Step 10.	Evaluate the accomplishments before purchasing more technology.

could make clear decisions abòut which of its needs could be partially met through technology. In the priority example, for instance, it was decided that students were to be provided with computer-supported counseling services to tie together the things that were happening in school with the outside world's work situation.

Since there were clearly defined reasons for the use of computer technology, the school's acquisition of hardware and software tended to proceed quite readily. The committee used the resources of its Learning Resource Center to identify all the software related to the provision of computer-supported counseling. As a result of its study, a comprehensive work-guidance computer program was identified that seemed to accomplish just what the school needed. Once it was found, hardware decisions were clear, since the chosen software system was written for one specific computer, and it required a hard disk and printer to run.

The school ordered and subsequently acquired the hardware and software, and gave a computer-active counselor release time to study the documentation and set up the program, including the development of in-service for other counselors and teachers associated with this aspect. Goals were set for the school year that not fewer than fifty students would use the system each month, and that they would report (via an anonymous survey after using the computer system) that it was providing them valuable information.

Signs of Progress

With a school-wide focus on school and community goals and needs, and with a firm commitment to move ahead, the teachers and administrators at Robert T. Jones Magnet School started to put some things together.

Acquisition of hardware was no longer the primary focus. What purchases were being made were the result of need, and purchases were being coordinated across the school.

Teachers were no longer developing software. Instead they were purchasing more professionally produced and expensive materials. They were purchasing a wider variety of software, but the software was targeted to supporting specific curricular needs.

In the area of staff development, a vice principal was designated to coordinate the effort. Voluntary participation in a variety of courses was the norm, and the courses focused on computer-use in curriculum, not computer programming. Teachers were recognizing they didn't need to know any programming to be successful as computer-using teachers.

The faculty formed an acquisitions committee to screen and evaluate potential software for use by teachers. This committee had clear guidelines on the difference between computer literacy and computer-assisted instruction, and were setting good policies on how to use courseware to achieve both objectives. Software use was primarily for drill and practice, simulation, word processing, and tutorial instruction.

A second committee was formed to decide exactly what kinds of computer-focused studies would be included in the school's curriculum. Committee members also were trying to decide, from an appraisal of community needs, whether all students should receive some computer literacy instruction or whether it should be limited to special groups.

Some teachers had become radicalized to the point they felt the computer might be a panacea for all educational problems, while some others were increasing their resistance to the idea that computers might actually change the way they had to teach their classes. A broad spectrum of teachers were gaining interest and losing their fear. A visit by the superintendent buoyed their spirits as he told them they were on-track. He announced more financial support to push the magnet school to success.

Reaching Full Implementation

Acquisition of hardware continued, but down very different pathways than originally pursued. Now computers and other hardware were purchased for specific locations and applications, and teachers were purchasing the simplest and least expensive machine to do a given task. They purchased a variety of machines; one brand of computers for drafting, another for the Art Department, and two types for math.

All software purchases were based on plans, with priorities set on those that reached high priority goals and needs first. There was a small library of evaluated software in the LRC that teachers could review for use in their classrooms, and the librarian had established procedures for obtaining software for preview.

Staff development had differentiated. Different teachers found they had different computer learning needs, and classes were tied to broad system needs. Participation in one course a year was required (and rewarded), and the courses were often taught by in-house experts on the subject.

In the area of computer-assisted instruction there was a general recognition that learning via computer works better for some children than others (and that the same holds true for any type of teaching method). Research findings determined how and when to use the computer for learning. Teachers were looking at the curriculum and asking how it should be changed in order to make best use of the computer's powers.

Some aspects of computer literacy were taught throughout all grades in a sequenced fashion; it was taught in a spectrum of classes rather than in a self-contained course; and the computer literacy curriculum was defined to meet the needs of the community. There were computer-based minicourses for new students through the LRC.

The teachers and administration displayed an attitude of respect for the capabilities and limitations of the computers in their school setting. They also had a good general understanding of the role of computers in education.

Looking Ahead

Having arrived at full implementation of computers in the school, the Robert T. Jones Magnet School is ready to face one more point in its development. Up to this stage the faculty and administration has been trying to integrate the computer into RTJMS. They have allowed it into their school as America did its immigrants of the 19th century—expecting to integrate the new settlers into the existing ways and values. But the immigrants did not just integrate, they changed the face of America with their vitality, new ways of doing things, new values, and new approaches to old problems. A different America emerged. At Robert T. Jones a different school is ready to emerge, one that will showcase computer use for learning, as was the superintendent's original vision.

Computers in schools could very well change the ways in which schools operate. They could be used to remold curricula and teaching methods. The faculty and administration of Robert T. Jones Magnet School is ready to ask the final question:

> How can we change our school, our curriculum, our methods of teaching, and ourselves, in order to tap the true power of the computer to teach, to manage instruction, and to enable students to reach greater heights of learning?

SUMMARY AND REVIEW CHECKLIST

There are issues of computer use that cannot be resolved by an individual classroom teacher. The teacher is at the operational center of a number of levels of issues about using computers in the school (see Table 9.2 and Figure 9.2). Computer-using classroom teachers have responsibilities regarding the curriculum they teach but little control over broad issues such as at what level keyboarding should be formally initiated into the school curriculum. School-wide planning is the responsibility of the school faculty and administration, and it is they who need to initiate, plan, and implement the use of the computer as an integral part of the school.

TABLE 9.2 Some Issues Related to Computer Integration in Schools

Hardware Resources	Purchase of equipment (standards) Placement (who gets what) How to keep current with rapid changes Security at school level
Software Resources	Matching courseware to curriculum Evaluation, quality control Acquisition, setting priorities Security, placement Appropriate use
Teachers	Professional development goals Proficiency acquisition Changing teaching roles Professional needs, in-service training
Students	Types of students Proficiencies Interests Exit needs Special needs
District-wide	Broad goals Curriculum to implement goals Curriculum objectives related to computer use Instructional procedures using computers In-service for computer integration Teaching with computers Teaching about computers
Community	Expectations for general computer training (literacy) Expectations for computer training for vocational use Needs versus resources (willingness to pay to satisfy needs) Comparison of schools with businesses (efficiency)
Nation	International technological competition International commercial competition Need for computer literacy for voters to understand issues Military needs

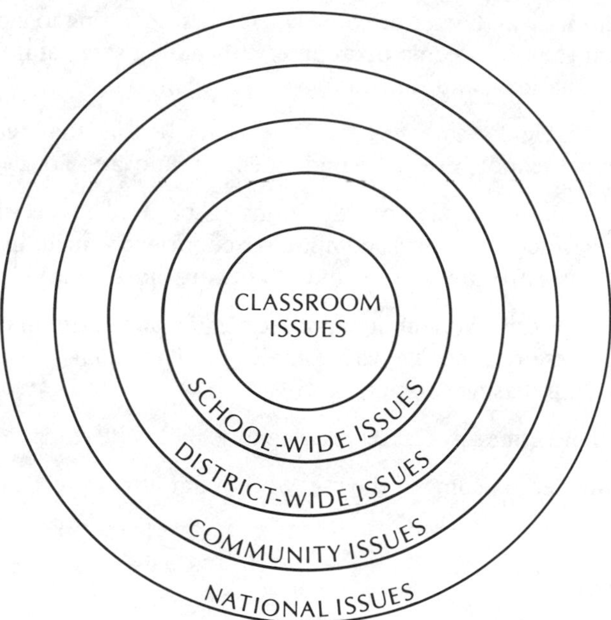

FIGURE 9.2 The Levels of Computer-use Issues

Planning for the use of technology is not a simple process. The technology is expensive and complex, and it is seldom easy to see how to integrate it into an existing program. As a school's experience with technology grows, its faculty and staff know better what computers can do for them and their students. Schools that succeed in integrating computers are those that tend to grow through their experiences with computers and better plan their patterns of computer use based on school-wide needs.

Although schools tend to respond initially to forces that encourage them to use computers, they may soon draw their impetus from within. When computer technology is employed successfully, it can lead a school to see new patterns for teaching and learning. Interestingly, the most powerful aspects of school computer use happen when schools are able to go beyond merely integrating computers into existing programs. Experience with the computer can point the way to new methods of teaching, and to new school-wide organizations for learning. Further movement toward more extensive computer use then continues, fueled this time by the technology itself.

Checklist

[ ] I can state and then categorize questions that should be solved: (1) in the classroom by a teacher, (2) on a school-wide basis, and (3) on a district-wide basis.

[ ] In general, I know how schools and school districts are using microcomputers currently.

[ ] I can state and describe some key factors operating to cause a movement to integrate microcomputers (including societal influences, local situations, and students' special needs).

[ ] I am able to state and describe some factors that tend to work against schools' efforts to implement an innovation or technology.

[ ] I can outline some considerations to be used in decision making when integrating microcomputers school-wide, including hardware aspects, software factors, and teacher attitudes and skills.

[ ] I can describe a planning approach that leads to optimal microcomputer use that begins with establishing curricular need rather than with purchasing computers.

[ ] I can describe some issues relating to school-wide computer security.

[ ] I can identify some of the uses of the computer in special education.

SUGGESTED ACTIVITIES

1. Visit a school that is using computers to find out how the school is using computers and how it deals with the issues presented in the chapter.
2. Interview the principal of a school that has successfully implemented computers to obtain words of wisdom and warning on planning for computer use.
3. Conduct a survey of teachers who use computers to learn about the problems they have faced, the ones they have resolved, and the challenges that remain.

WORTH A LOOK: THE OTA REPORT

The Office of Technology Assessment's report entitled, "Power ON! New Tools for Teaching and Learning," is available for $11 from the Superintendent of Documents, U.S. Government Printing Office, Washington, D.C. 20402-9325 (Stock #052-003-01125-5). A summary of the 250-page report is available at no charge from the Office of Technology Assessment, U.S. Congress, Washington, D.C. 20510-8025; (202) 224-8996.

The OTA report is worthwhile reading for anyone planning the implementation of computing technology in an educational program. Completed in 1988 for the U.S. Congress, "Power ON!" is an indepth report on the past, present, and future impact of technology on education. The mammoth study examines such issues as the cost-effectiveness of instructional technology, teacher training, the educational software market, and some of the newest technologies on the horizon.

Information for the OTA project came from a great many sources. In-depth case studies were commissioned. Existing data from current research were compiled. Formalized surveys and research studies were conducted. While the report was written to provide the Congress and other federal policymakers a base of information for making long-range decisions, the results are also worth the serious attention of state policymakers, school boards, administrators, and teachers alike.

A number of the most interesting findings of the OTA educational technology report were summarized for educators in the October and November/December 1988, and January 1989 issues of the journal, *Classroom Computer Learning.* In the words of the compiler and editor of the three articles for that journal, Len Scrogan, "Overall, if there is one theme to the OTA report, it is this: Technology *is* changing schools." To provide a sampling of the kind of information one can find in "Power ON!," we have excerpted a small portion from the journal's October issue.

What the OTA Report Reveals About Teachers and Teaching

The Bad News

- Despite the presence of computers in almost all American public schools, only half of the nation's teachers report ever using computers. The number of teachers who use computers regularly is much smaller.
- Very few teachers have adequate time for planning and preparing to use technology.
- The most recent data available indicate that only one-third of all K–12 teachers have had as much as ten hours of computer training. Also, much of this training has focused on learning how to use computers, not how to teach with computers.

The Good News

- New technologies are making possible imaginative approaches to teaching traditional subjects.
- One of the most significant impacts of computers has been on teaching style. Teachers can function as facilitators of student learning,

All material in this section is reprinted by permission of *Classroom Computer Learning.* ©1988 by Peter Li, Inc., 2169 Francisco Blvd. East, Suite A4, San Rafael, CA 94901

rather than in their traditional role as presenters of ready-made information.

And More News

- Educational technologies are not self-implementing, and they do not replace the teacher.
- The National Assessment of Educational Progress's report on computer competence found in its most recent (1985–86) survey of third-, seventh-, and eleventh-grade students that computers were seldom used in subject areas, but were used almost exclusively to teach about computers. This emphasis, however, is shifting toward content integration. Attaining more fully integrated use of technology across the curriculum is a desirable goal for teachers.
- Technologies can enhance and enrich teaching, but only when four interrelated conditions exist:

    adequate teacher training in the skills needed to operate the technology;
    a clear vision and understanding among educators of state-of-the-art developments and applications;
    support for experimentation and innovation;
    time for learning and practice.

- There is no one best way to teach with computers. Flexibility should therefore be encouraged, and teachers should be allowed to develop their own personal teaching approaches.
- The use of modems and electronic networks has the potential to help overcome one of the most basic problems of the classroom teacher—isolation.

What the OTA Report Reveals about Children and Computers

- New technologies are motivating children to try new ways of learning and of gathering information.
- Although new interactive technologies alone cannot solve the problems of American education, they have already contributed to important improvements in learning.
- Technologies can help children acquire basic skills as well as endow them with more sophisticated skills so they can acquire and apply knowledge over their lifetimes.
- At the current rate of allocation of resources, the nation can expect no more than spotty access to technology among children.

OTA Findings that Every School Board Member, Superintendent, and Principal Ought to Consider

- *Understand the potential.* The appropriate assignment of new technologies within an already effective school can make a big difference in academic performance, motivation, and dedication to learning.
- *Encourage flexibility.* The varied capabilities of the new technologies are the key to their power. Educators use interactive technologies for many purposes. Some of the most promising uses are these:

  drill and practice to master basic skills;
  development of writing skills;
  problem solving;
  understanding of abstract mathematics and science concepts;
  simulations in science, mathematics, and social studies;
  better understanding of concepts through manipulation of data bases;
  acquisition of skills for general purposes and for business and vocational training;
  access and communication for teachers and students in remote locations through telecommunications and distance learning;
  individualized learning;
  cooperative learning;
  management of classroom activities and record keeping.

- *Build in a budget line item.* Steady funding is vastly preferable to money that must be spent quickly.
- *Work toward developing a critical mass of machines.* Although access to computers has increased significantly, the vast majority of schools still do not have enough machines to make the computer a central element of instruction.
- *Provide adequate teacher training.* Teachers will need continuing in-service programs as technology changes, as more effective uses of technology are developed, and as research provides a better understanding of how children learn.
- *Pay special attention to the needs of special children.* Special needs populations have demonstrated some of the most impressive learning gains as a result of access to new technologies. Don't forget them in the rush.

READINGS

Ahl, D. H. "School Uses of Microcomputers." *Creative Computing* 9(10):185–86 (October 1983).

Andrews, J. F., Hass, D., and Waller, J. "How to Use the Microcomputer with Multi-Handicapped Hearing Impaired Students: Teaching Suggestions." *Perspectives for Teachers of the Hearing Impaired,* 1987, 5(3):1–34.

Ashcroft, S. C., ed. "Microcomputers for Visually Impaired." *Education of the Visually Handicapped*, 1984, 15(4):106–144.

Blohm, A. "Microcomputer Usage with Mildly Handicapped Special Education Students." *Catalyst for Change,* 1985, 14(3):18–19.

Blubaugh, W. L. *Choosing the Ethical Path to Excellence in Computer Education.* Paper presented at the Annual Conference on Microcomputers in Education, March, 1986 (ERIC Document #280456).

Cicchelli, T., and Baecher, R. E. "The Use of Concerns Theory in Inservice Training for Computer Education." *Computers and Education,* 1987, 11(2):85–93.

Cook, A. M., Leins, J. D., and Woodall, H. E. "Use of Microcomputers by Disabled Persons: A Rehabilitation Engineering Perspective." *Rehabilitation Counseling Bulletin,* June 1985, 283–292.

Kepner, H. S., Jr., ed. *Computers in the Classroom.* 2d ed. Washington, DC: National Education Association, 1986.

Khamis, M. *Having a Few Micros and a School Policy—Is It Enough?* Paper presented at the Annual Meeting of the Australian College of Education and the Australian Council for Educational Administration, September, 1987 (ERIC Document #291155).

King, R. A. *Computer Equity and the Role of District Level Computer Coordinators.* Paper presented at the Annual Meeting of the American Educational Research Association, April, 1987 (ERIC Document #285577).

Knupfer, N. N. *Change, Implementation, Equity: A Model Design for a Computer Education Plan.* Working paper, University of Wisconsin-Madison, 1986 (ERIC Document #273270).

Knupfer, N. N. *Implementation of Microcomputers into the Current K–12 Curriculum: A Critical Discussion of Issues.* Working paper, University of Wisconsin-Madison, 1986 (ERIC Document #275292).

Marshall, G. "Training Must Be Practical, Relevant." *Executive Educator* 10(3):26–27 (March 1988).

Martisko, L., and Ammentorp, W. "Take Five Strategic Planning Steps, and Turn School Goals into Realities." *American School Board Journal* 173(3):38–39 (March 1986).

Mathinos, D. A., and Woodward, A. "Instructional Computing in an Elementary School: The Rhetoric and Reality of an Innovation." *Journal of Curriculum Studies* 20(5):465–73 (September–October 1988).

Meister, G. R. *Successful Integration of Microcomputers in an Elementary School.* Stanford, CA: Institute for Research on Educational Finance and Governance, Stanford University, 1984.

Miller, H. *An Administrator's Manual for the Use of Microcomputers in the Schools.* Old Tappan, NJ: Prentice-Hall, 1988.

Office of Technology Assessment. *Summary Report of "Power ON! New Tools for Teaching and Learning.*" Washington, DC: Government Printing Office, 1988.

Olson, J. K. *The Cultural Context of Teacher Thinking and Its Significance for Innovation.* Paper presented at the Annual Meeting of the American Educational Research Association, April, 1988 (ERIC Document #293832).

Rettig, M., Shaklett, E., and Wyrsch, M. "Microcomputer Applications with Visually Impaired Preschool-Aged Children." *Journal of Visual Impairments and Blindness,* 1987, 81(3):120–122.

Rodgers, R. J., and Bonja, R. P. *Computer Utilization Training in Staff Development.* Paper presented at the National Council of States on Inservice Education, November, 1987 (ERIC Document #291374).

Stasz, C. et al. *Staff Development for Instructional Uses of Microcomputers: The Teachers' Perspective.* Santa Monica, CA: The Rand Corporation, 1984.

Stecher, B. M., and Solorzano, R. *Characteristics of Effective Computer In-Service Programs.* Research Report. Princeton, NJ: Educational Testing Service, 1987.

Strudler, N. B., and Gall, M. D. *Successful Change Agent Strategies for Overcoming Impediments to Microcomputer Implementation in the Classroom.* Paper presented at the Annual Meeting of the American Educational Research Association, 1988 (ERIC Document #298938).

Summers, E. G., and Gammon, G. H. "Creating the Least Restrictive Environment: A Case Study in Microcomputer Software Utilization." *B.C. Journal of Special Education,* 1987, 11(2):131–148.

Vockell, E., and Luncsford, D. "Managing Computer-Assisted Instruction in the Classroom." *Clearing House* 59(6):263–68 (February 1986).

Wagschal, P. H. "Computers in the Schools: Lessons from Television." *Curriculum Review* 25(3):32–34 (January/February 1986).

Wedman, J. F. *Educational Computing Inservice Design: Implications from Teachers' Concerns Research.* Paper presented at the Annual Meeting of the American Educational Research Association, 1986 (ERIC Document #267797).

Yin, R. K., and Moore, G. B. "The Use of Advanced Technologies in Special Education: Prospects for Robotics, Artificial Intelligence, and Computer Simulation." *Journal of Learning Disabilities,* 1987, 20(1):60–63.

REFERENCES

Brown, D. "Review: Computers and the Disabled." *American Rehabilitation,* 1985, 11(2):29–31.

Cook, A. M., and Coleman, C. L. "Selecting of Augmentative Communication Systems by Matching Client Skills and Needs to System Characteristics." Seminars in Speech and Language, May 1987, 8(2):153–167.

Cory, S. "A 4-Stage Model of Development for Full Implementation of Computers for Instruction in a School System." *The Computing Teacher,* November 1983, 11–16.

Naron, N. K., and Estes, N. "Technology in the Schools: Trends and Policies." *AEDS Journal,* Summer 1986, 19(4):31–43.

Office of Technology Assessment. *Summary Report of "Power ON! New Tools for Teaching and Learning."* Washington, DC: Government Printing Office, 1988.

Pogrow, S. *Computer Decisions for Board Members: Getting the Most from What Your District Selects.* Chicago: National School Boards Association/Teachum, Inc., 1985.

Rutherford, F. J. *Testimony of H.R. 3750 and H.R. 4628 before the (U.S.) Subcommittee on Science, Research, and Technology,* June 5, 1984 (mimeographed).

Walcott, P. "Funding Computer Technology." *Collective Bargaining Quarterly,* (December 1985) 8(3).

10

How Microcomputers Work

The Hardware Story Unfolds

OBJECTIVES

- State an analogy from everyday experience to illustrate how a machine can store information and make decisions.
- Explain how a string of 1s and 0s can have physical meaning to a microcomputer and also represent meaning to a human.
- Describe in general terms how a microcomputer processes what a human types in on the keyboard, and how it displays it on the monitor and prints it on the printer.
- Describe in a general way how a microcomputer stores a typed character on a disk and in its own memory circuits.
- State the major landmarks in the development of microprocessing technology.
- Discuss various factors that underlie a microcomputer's cost in terms of its physical or electronic attributes, and describe how to make wise hardware purchases.
- Outline important limitations on mixing and matching classroom hardware and how to avoid equipment incompatibility when selecting add-ons or when replacing such items.
- Identify maintenance and use factors important to decisions about microcomputer hardware.

INTRODUCTION

While most of this book has stressed how you can use a computer in the teaching and learning process, the next two chapters fill in the background on the mechanics of how the computer accomplishes its role in these processes. Such knowledge is valuable in providing a general understanding of computers, and in some situations may even help you to diagnose problems you encounter in computer operation. Still, you do not need to know much about how a computer accomplishes its tasks to be an effective computer-using teacher.

The concepts covered in this chapter relate to any brand or model of computer, since they all use the same basic electronic principles. It should be noted that, although this chapter may be conceptually accurate (with regard to how a computer operates), it is not necessarily technically accurate. Poetic license has been taken with regard to mechanical aspects of the computer, in order to keep the concepts of how a computer functions as clear and simple as possible.

Goals

- How do the major components of a microcomputer function?
- What are the key technological developments that led to the arrival of microcomputers in homes, offices, and classrooms?
- To what extent does a lack of knowledge of electronics interfere with adequate utilization of the computer in instruction?

ELECTRICITY TO ENGLISH

Suppose that five boxes have just been delivered to your classroom. They contain the computer system you ordered at the start of the school year. These components must be put together accurately and made to function as a unit. You need to know next to nothing about how a computer works in order to assemble the computer system and make it operate. But it is interesting to know some of the secrets of how the items in those boxes work, and to be able to explain, when you are asked by students, some of the things that happen inside of the computer.

The first box you open is the monitor, and its task is to turn an electric signal into words and pictures. The monitor has brightness and contrast knobs, an off/on switch, and a cable that links the monitor to the back of the computer. Information output from the computer will flow through this cable to the monitor in the form of electrical signals. There the electronic information is transformed into the words and pictures you see displayed on the screen. How does this happen?

The Monitor Screen

If you look at a computer monitor screen you will notice that an image, such as a letter, is made up of many little dots, similar to a picture in a newspaper (see Figure 10.1), that the human eye blends into a contiguous image. To produce English words on a monitor screen, the computer must have the power to place ordered dots of light onto a dark screen (or vice versa).

To accomplish this task, the screen of the monitor is coated with a phosphorescent material that lights up when struck by an electric charge. Inside the monitor there is an electron gun that shoots a stream of electrons toward the screen, starting at the upper left hand corner, across the top, down one row, and so forth, until the entire screen has been sprayed. An entire screen sweep is done very rapidly, many times each second.

For an analogy, just think of watering your lawn. The hose is the electron gun, the water is the stream of electrons, and the lawn is the monitor screen. You start at upper left hand corner, water to the right hand corner, move down a little bit, and repeat the motion in reverse. To keep our analogy appropriate, your timing with the hose must be accurate. You must proceed across the lawn in a dependable fashion, maintaining your progress at watering, and never pausing at any point for any reason.

If the monitor always acted in the manner just described, one sweep would have lighted all the screen's dots, and kept them lighted by the following sweeps of the electron gun. With complete sweeps occurring continuously, you would see only a brightly lit screen. Here the cable from the computer comes

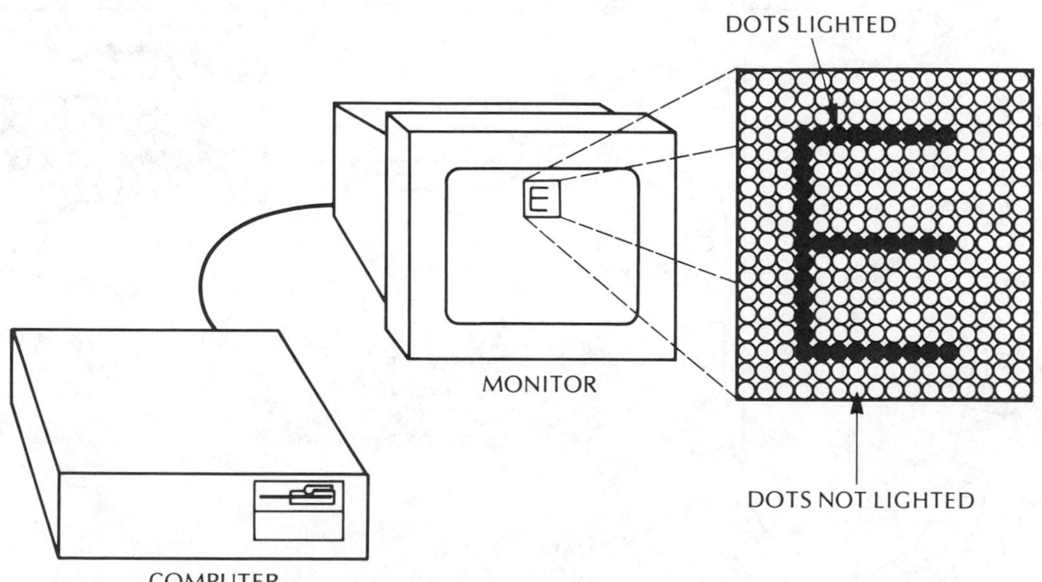

FIGURE 10.1 A Computer Monitor Image Is Made Up of Many Dots

into play. The computer can regulate the flow of electricity to the electron gun through the cable, much as someone with a hand on the faucet could regulate your lawn watering. A pulse of electricity tells the electron gun to shoot one "dot-worth of electrons" toward the screen. One pulse equals one lighted dot. If the electron gun does not receive a pulse, it does not send electrons and does not light up the screen. The dot remains dark.

Regardless of the signal sent by the computer, the electron gun keeps moving across the screen a row at a time, from top to bottom. As you can see, if the hand on the faucet turned off your water at a specified time every sweep of the hose, a spot on your lawn would stay dry indefinitely. Conversely, a watchful (or well-timed) faucet operator could keep designated portions of the lawn thoroughly soaked.

By regulating the faucet of electrons, the computer has just this type of power over each dot on the monitor screen. Since the electron gun is constantly scanning the total screen, and the computer is turning the electrons on and off by sending signals to the gun, images can be formed by turning on the gun the instant it passes designated dots on the screen. Figure 10.2 illustrates this total set of events.

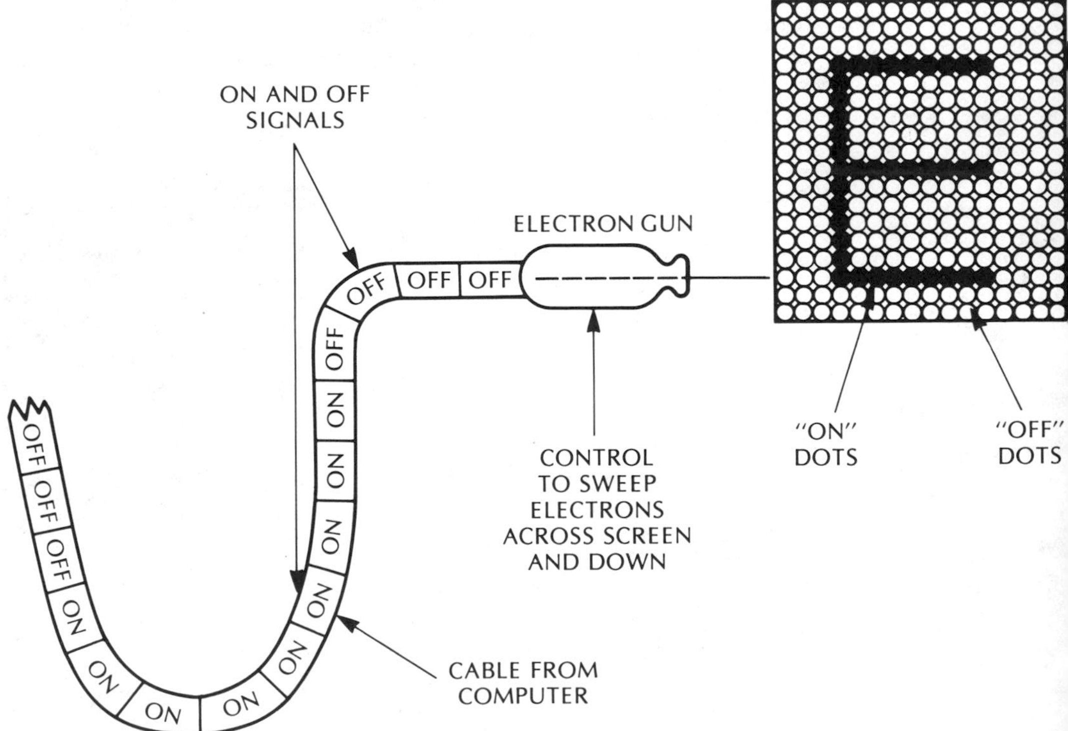

FIGURE 10.2 Events in the Formation of the Letter "E"

The Electronic Message

We introduce message making on a monitor as the first topic in this chapter because it so clearly and simply illustrates a major idea behind how a computer functions. The "message" coming from the computer to the screen, which produces a letter or any other figure, is the result of the intermittent flow of electricity to produce two conditions. These conditions are: (1) electricity is present at a point in space and time, and (2) electricity is not present.

If we could place a series of electrical volt meters at certain points above the cable leading to the monitor (see Figure 10.3), we would find that, at a given time, some would indicate a voltage of about five volts and others would indicate no voltage at all. If we observed any single meter over time, we would note the needle flopping back and forth. It would register five volts each time a pulse of electricity was passing through its spot in the cable, and it would indicate zero volts when none was passing through it.

Messages are sent from place to place in the computer via systematic regulation of the flow of electricity through the circuitry. Convention has it that a pulse of about five volts (the strength of about three flashlight batteries) is given the name "1" and a "no pulse" of zero volts is given the name "0." So computer literature often speaks in terms of sending 1s and 0s as a message string. To produce the letter "E" at a spot on the screen, the computer simply needs to regulate its electricity flow to the electron gun, sending the proper string of 1s and 0s to ensure it will fire at appropriate times and places.

Well, now that you have an idea of how the monitor works, let's open another carton!

Printing Messages

The second carton holds a dot matrix printer and its cable. The first thing that strikes us is that the printer cable is quite unlike the monitor cable. The moni-

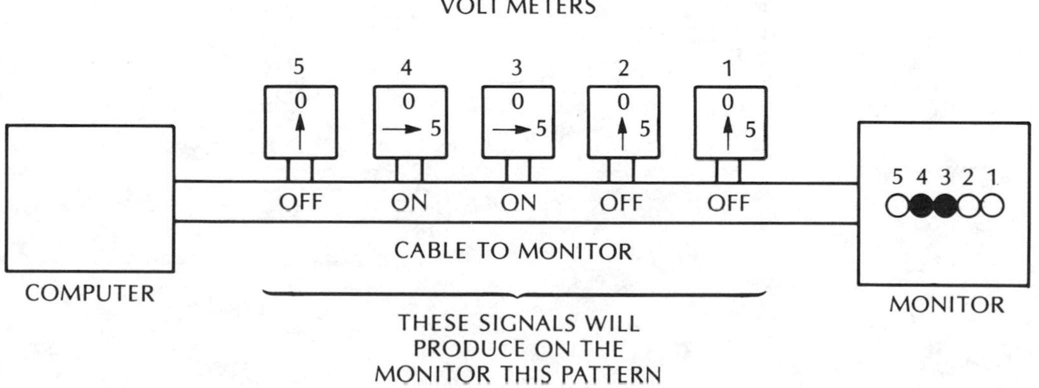

FIGURE 10.3 Signal Voltages along a Line

tor cable seemed to be one single wire but the printer cable seems to be a collection of many wires, each encased in a separate plastic channel (see Figure 10.4). The result is a thin flat object with unusual plugs at each end. There are several prongs where the printer cable plugs into the printer or into the computer.

Does it take more message wires to operate a printer than a monitor? The answer is no. The two types of wires represent two different ways of achieving the same end. Some wires send messages in a *series* down a single wire (Item a, Figure 10.5). Other wires send messages in *parallel* down a set of wires (Item b, Figure 10.5). Notice that the series wire and the parallel wires are sending the same message (sets of 1s and 0s) down the line from the computer.

A dot matrix printer produces a message in much the same fashion as a monitor. A print head moves across a line on the paper. Inside the print head

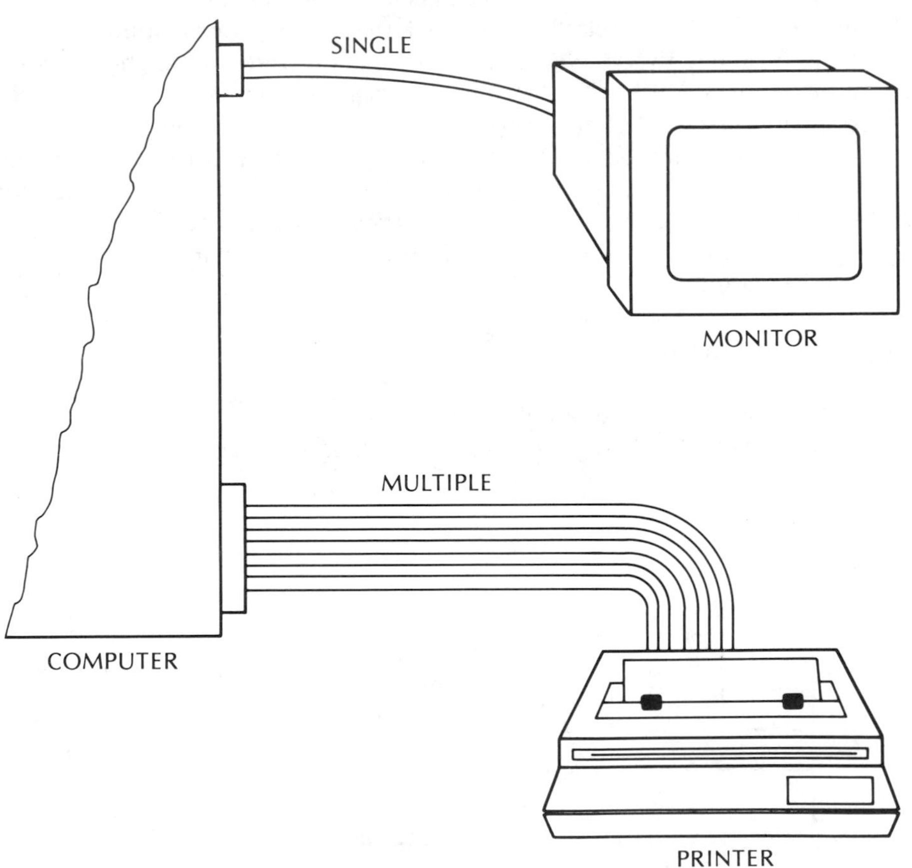

FIGURE 10.4 Printer and Monitor Cables

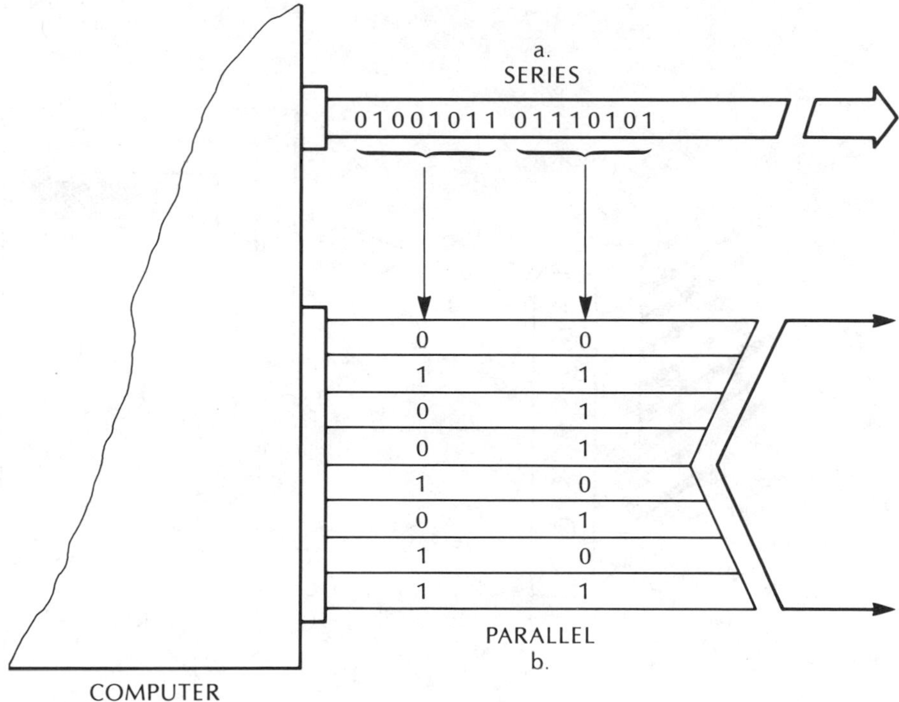

FIGURE 10.5 Parallel and Series Messages

are a series of pins, each of which can be projected toward the print ribbon and the paper by a magnet whenever the magnet is energized by a pulse of electricity (see Figure 10.6). Under direction from the computer, the printer can control when the pins are activated and thus it can place dots on the paper to form letters and graphics.

One major difference between the printer and the monitor lies in the message that is sent over the parallel wire. *Coded messages* for actual characters are sent to the printer, and the printer converts the codes it receives into appropriate pin strikes. In other words, the printer would receive a code for the letter "E" and then would energize ("fire") the appropriate pins as the print head was moving across the target position. Each letter, numeral, and punctuation mark has its own code, and there are codes for the printer's other typing functions, such as "line feeds" (paper moves), underlining, etc. The printer executes each function in turn as it receives the code through its printer cable.

How does the computer encode what it sends to the printer, and conversely, how does the printer interpret the codes that are sent to it by the computer?

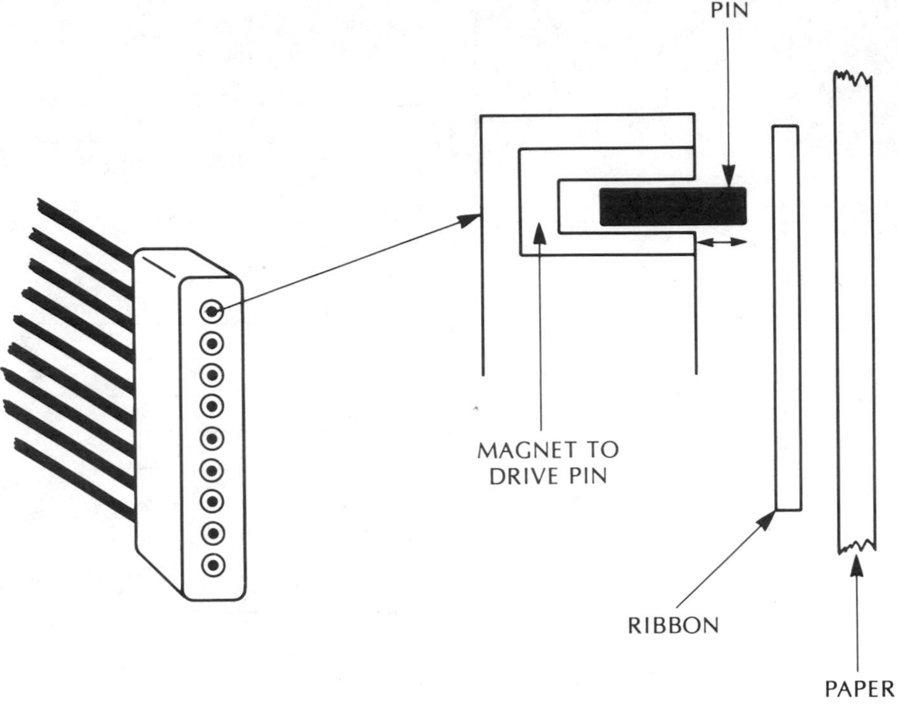

FIGURE 10.6 Print Head with Pins

Computer Code

Suppose we wished to devise our own code system for sending the letters of the alphabet to a printer, using a parallel eight-wire cable to do the job. Remember that all we have available for our coding are two conditions: the electric pulses (1s) and "no pulses" (0s).

What could we pick as code for the letter "A"? How about using the simplest possible configuration of the parallel cable, shown in Figure 10.7?

We will let (0 0 0 0 0 0 0 1) be the code for A. If the voltage on each of the first seven wires is zero and the last one is five volts, the printer will print the dots for the letter "A." Let's continue making up a simple but systematic code. We will code the letter "B" as (0 0 0 0 0 0 1 0) and "C" as (0 0 0 0 0 0 1 1) and "D" as (0 0 0 0 0 1 0 0). If we proceed in this fashion, we will be able to code all twenty-six letters of the alphabet well before using up the available wires. Figure 10.8 illustrates the word BAD in our code going down a parallel wire toward a printer.

The main concept behind our simplified coding effort is an important one at the heart of the real computer coding system. *All* the letters, numbers, and punctuation marks we use to write with can be assigned a code pattern consisting of nothing more than eight 1s and 0s.

If you had a magical eye that would allow you to look into any wire in a

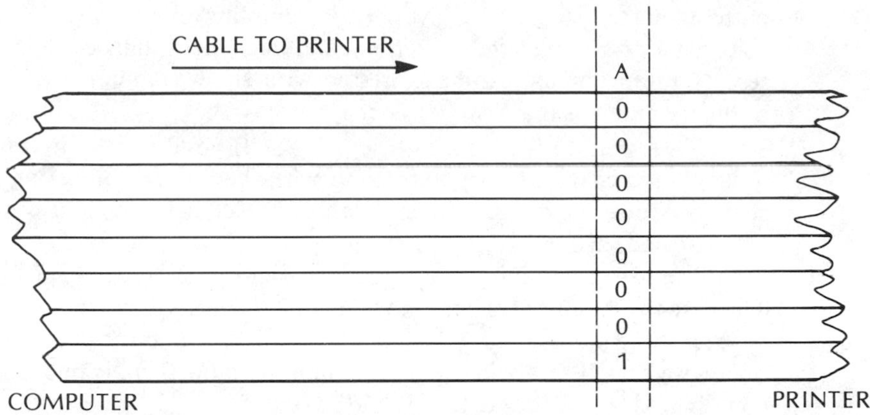

FIGURE 10.7 A Simplified Computer Code for the Letter "A"

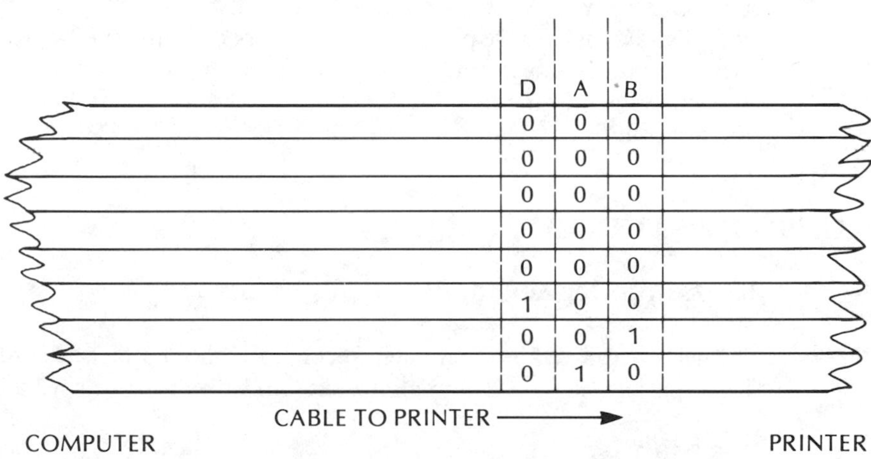

FIGURE 10.8 A Simplified Computer Code for "BAD" on a Parallel Line

computer, you would simply see a pattern of 1s and 0s flowing through the wires and physical components reacting to the coded patterns (as exemplified by the monitor and printer). The codes for the letters, numbers, and commonly used symbols in English (and similar languages) have been standardized. The early standardization of coding was largely responsible for the degree of electronic conversation across various computer systems that we have today.

ASCII Codes

Eight code positions produces 256 different patterns of 1s and 0s. The American Standard Code for Information Interchange (ASCII) assigned these 256 patterns names. Table 10.1 gives you a sampling of the ASCII standardized code names for some letters and numbers. Each eight-unit set of 1s and 0s represents a number that can be expressed with either standard Arabic numerals or binary numbers (base two number system).

If we were to list the entire set of ASCII code names, it would require quite a large chart. Persons unfamiliar with the binary numbering system are surprised to see how much information can be coded into eight positions with only two code symbols.

The base ten number system has ten digits: 0, 1, 2, 3, 4, 5, 6, 7, 8, and 9. The base two number system has two digits: 0 and 1. To count from zero in the base ten system, we count 0, 1, 2, 3, 4, 5, 6, 7, 8, 9, and then having run out of digits, we say: "Put a 1 in the tens column to show there is one ten, and keep counting." That is, 10, 11, 12, 13, and so on.

To count in the base two system we count: 0, 1, and then having run out of digits, we say: "Put a 1 in the twos column to show there is one 2, and keep counting." That is, 0, 1, 10. Look at Table 10.2 to see how to continue the count in base two. After counting 11 in base two (3 in base ten), there are no more digits to use, so we place a 1 in the fours column and 0s in the twos and ones columns. In this manner we can count upward in correspondence with the base ten system. Many math texts provide further information on the topic of a binary counting system.

ENGLISH TO ELECTRICITY

The Computer Keyboard

The next carton yields a computer keyboard with an attached cord. Is it a series or parallel cable? At first glimpse it looks like it is one cord and therefore

TABLE 10.1 ASCII Code Values for Selected Characters

Character	*ASCII Code in Arabic Numerals*	*ASCII Code in Binary*
A	65	01000001
B	66	01000010
C	67	01000011
D	68	01000100
E	69	01000101
a	97	01100001
b	98	01100010
c	99	01100011
d	100	01100100
e	101	01100101
1	49	00110001
2	50	00110010
+	13	00001101

TABLE 10.2 Counting in Bases Two and Ten

Base Ten, the Arabic Number System	*Base Two, the Binary Number System*
0	0
1	1
2	10
3	11
4	100
5	101
6	110
7	111
8	1000
9	1001
10	1010
11	1011
12	1100
↑↑ ones column; tens column	↑↑↑↑ ones column; twos column; fours column; eights column

probably a series cable. But by looking at the plug that fits into the computer body, we find that there are eight (or so) wires—hence the keyboard is sending parallel codes.

How does a key accomplish the trick of sending a specific code? Look at Figure 10.9. Think of a key as a device for turning selected switches off and on. If eight wires enter under a key, and there are eight switches, the key could be designed to press on the selected switches that correspond to its code name (number). The pulses going out of a key would correspond to whichever switches were closed. In Figure 10.9 the letter "Z" is sent down the line by turning on the switches corresponding to (0 1 0 1 1 0 1 0).

A keyboard has fifty keys or more and, together with shifts, control keys, function keys, and alt (alternate) keys, it can send a large proportion of the 256 possible code messages inherent in an eight-digit binary system.

Other Input Devices

There are many other devices that are used to send information into a computer. At the heart of the matter they all do the same thing—send strings of 1s and 0s in a coded pattern. But the physical layouts of the devices vary greatly.

For example, the Macintosh® computer makes central use of a mouse (please refer to Figure 10.10). This device translates directional moves of the mouse into corresponding moves on the screen. It is easiest to conceptualize

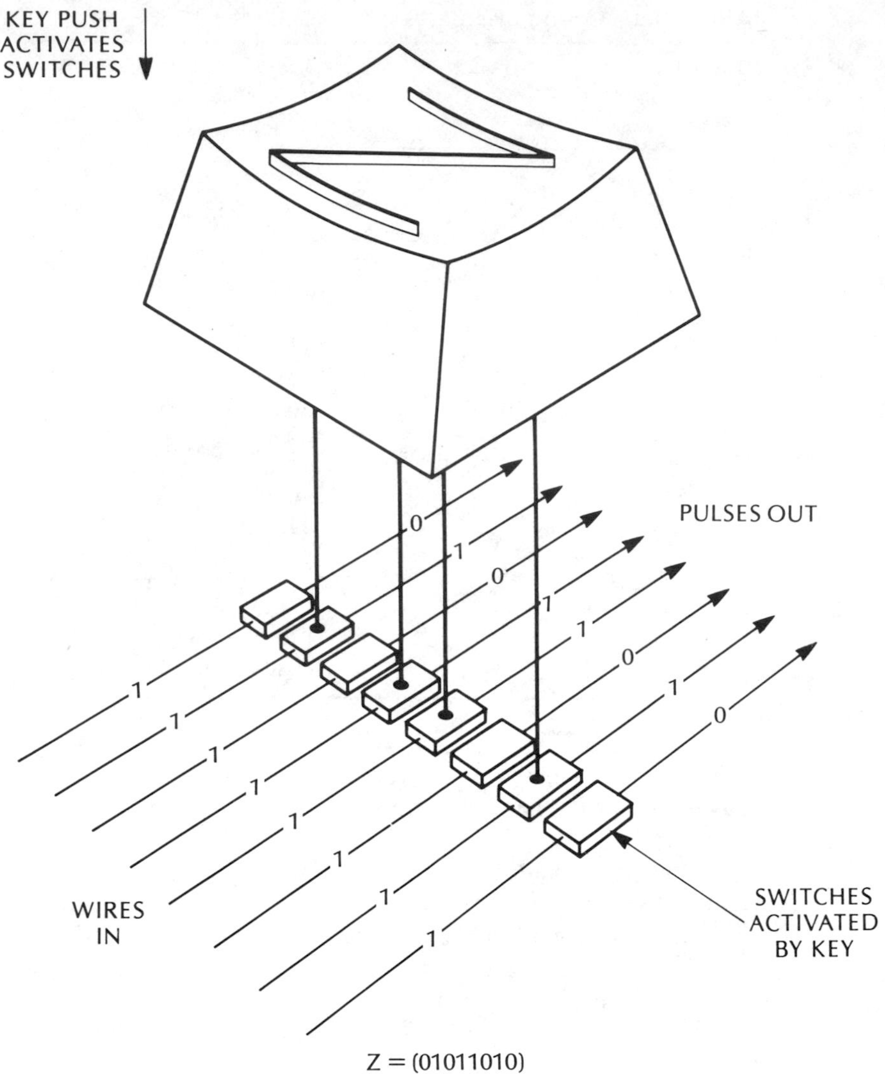

FIGURE 10.9 Keyboard Switches: Sending the Letter "Z"

the mouse as a means of automating the use of the arrow keys on a typical keyboard. Each time the mouse is moved, a roller ball in the bottom of the mouse turns. This generates a small current that is detected and a signal is sent to the computer regarding the direction and distance the ball was moved. The computer can then translate the movement into a corresponding move of a cursor or mark across the screen.

The joystick device translates physical movements of a "control arm" into computer code. It also serves as a way of automating cursor movement

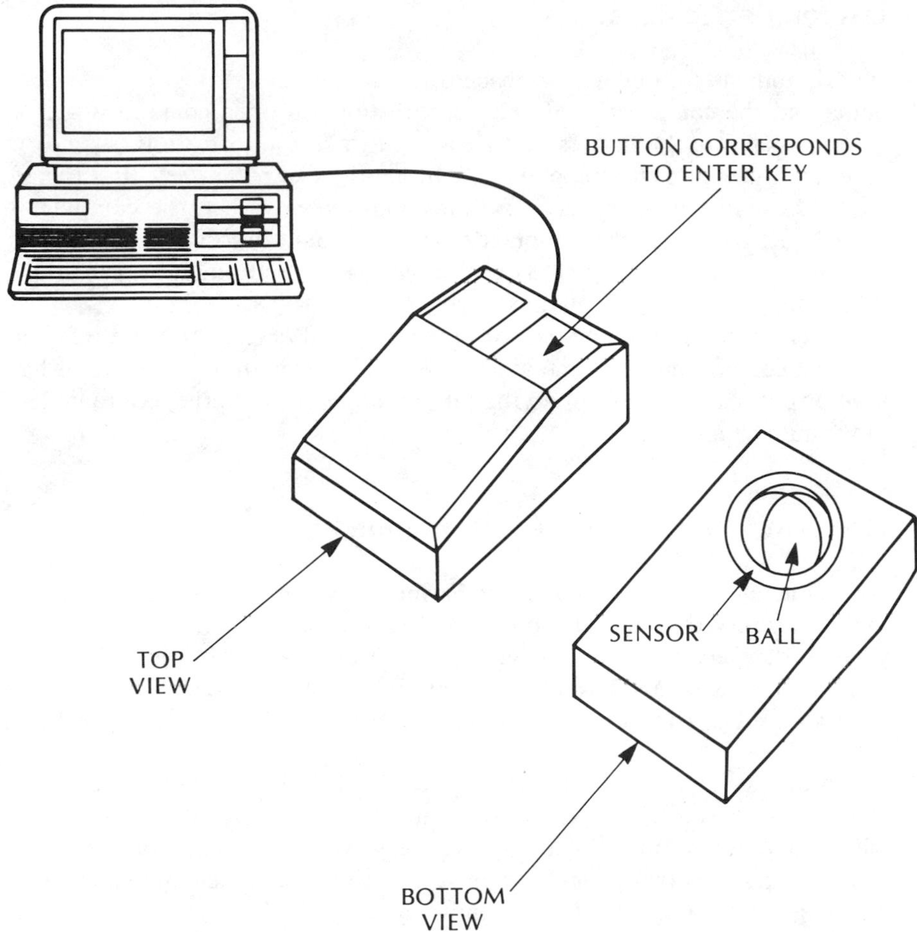

FIGURE 10.10 The Macintosh Mouse

but allows for much greater freedom of action, such as is useful in games where action takes place far faster than keyboard input via arrow keys, or even mouse input, would permit. The movement of the arm adjusts switches that regulate the amount of current flowing. A large move of the arm generates a large current, which is then translated into computer signals that determine the direction of the movement and its strength.

Other types of input devices (pads, touch screens, light pens, facsimile machines) work in a similar manner, each generating in its own way an electric current that can be interpreted by the computer to signal intensity and direction.

Before we move to the question of how all this incoming electronic information is processed, let's explore one more topic—how a computer stores information.

Information Storage

Two equipment cartons remain to be opened—the disk drives for your computer, and the computer itself. The first carton you open contains a pair of drives. These are the devices that allow you to save information beyond the time when you turn the computer off. Inside the computer itself (last carton) are RAM memory units that store information only when the computer is turned on. Also inside the computer case are the built-in ROM units that keep information the computer needs each time it is turned on. How can ROM, RAM, or a disk store information?

Let's consider the question of how a physical device can store information at a concrete and conceptual level. We will start with the question of how a set of pipes and valves can do the job, and then move to the electronic level of the microcomputer.

How a Machine Can Store Information

As a concrete example let's look at Farmer Jones' irrigation device. He has three fields served by one large pipe that fills when it rains and then carries rain water to the fields A, B, and C (see Figure 10.11). Each field is growing a different type of plant and has different watering requirements, so the water from the main feed pipe must be differentially controlled by Farmer Jones, using the valves.

Each feed valve has four settings: OFF, ON-low, ON-medium, and ON-full. Field A has a feed pipe with one valve (valve 1). Field B has a feed pipe with two valves arranged so that valve 2 *and* valve 3 must be on to provide water. Field C has two valves, and valve 4 *or* valve 5 must be on. The logic of watering Farmer Jones' fields is as follows:

If he wants water in field A then turn on valve 1.

If he wants water in field B then turn on valves 2 *and* 3.

If he wants water in field C then turn on valve 4 *or* 5.

These statements are tempered by the degree to which each valve is turned on—low, medium, or high. In anticipation of rain Farmer Jones will go to his fields, decide how much water each needs, and set the five valves.

The main conceptual point is: the pipe and valve settings are storing the information Farmer Jones has coded into them. By his action of setting the valves, he "programs" the irrigation system with his instructions. When the rain comes, the fields will be provided water in the correct amounts because the pipes and valves will "remember" how much water to distribute to each field.

The following may seem a rather shocking statement (we understand that we have laid little groundwork to support the idea). *All computer logic, hence any computer program, could be conceived and written around four simple switches* (valves in the example given): (1) the digital "yes/no" (off/on) switch, (2) an "and" combination switch, (3) an "or" combination switch, and (4) a

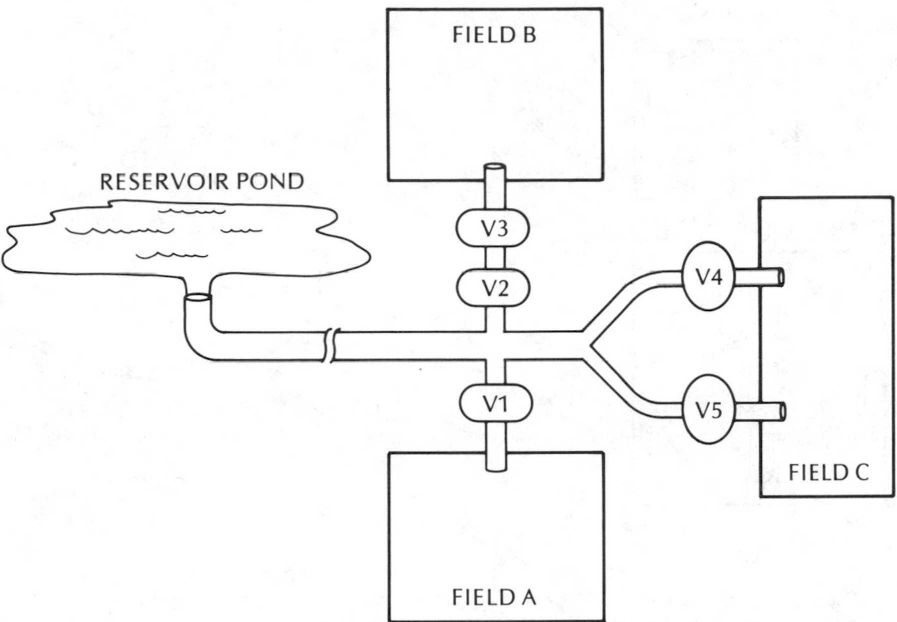

FIGURE 10.11 Farmer Jones' Fields

"not" combination switch (one switch we didn't introduce but which simply reverses the action of the other switches). If obtaining more detailed information on this aspect interests you, you will need to refer to a text on computer mechanics and logic.

How a Disk Stores Information

There are three main types of disks: the 5¼″ floppy disk found on a wide variety of computers, the 3½″ disk encased in a firm plastic cover, and a sealed unit—a fixed or hard disk. All three of these disk storage units store information in the same way. If we were to disassemble any one of these units we would find a disk that was capable of being spun, much like spinning a phonograph record. (See Figure 10.12.)

The architecture of all three disk drive units consists of a spinning disk of material with a surface that can be magnetized or demagnetized. Over the surface of the disk is an arm at the end of which is a small coil of wire that can either magnetize or demagnetize the disk's surface. As the disk spins and pulses of electricity arrive in the read/write coil, it can place magnetic spots on the surface of the disk in a circular track. (See Figure 10.13.)

You read earlier that information flowing through a computer consists of a linear series of timed pulses of electricity. In order to store a pattern of information on a disk surface, the disk drive unit makes use of an important

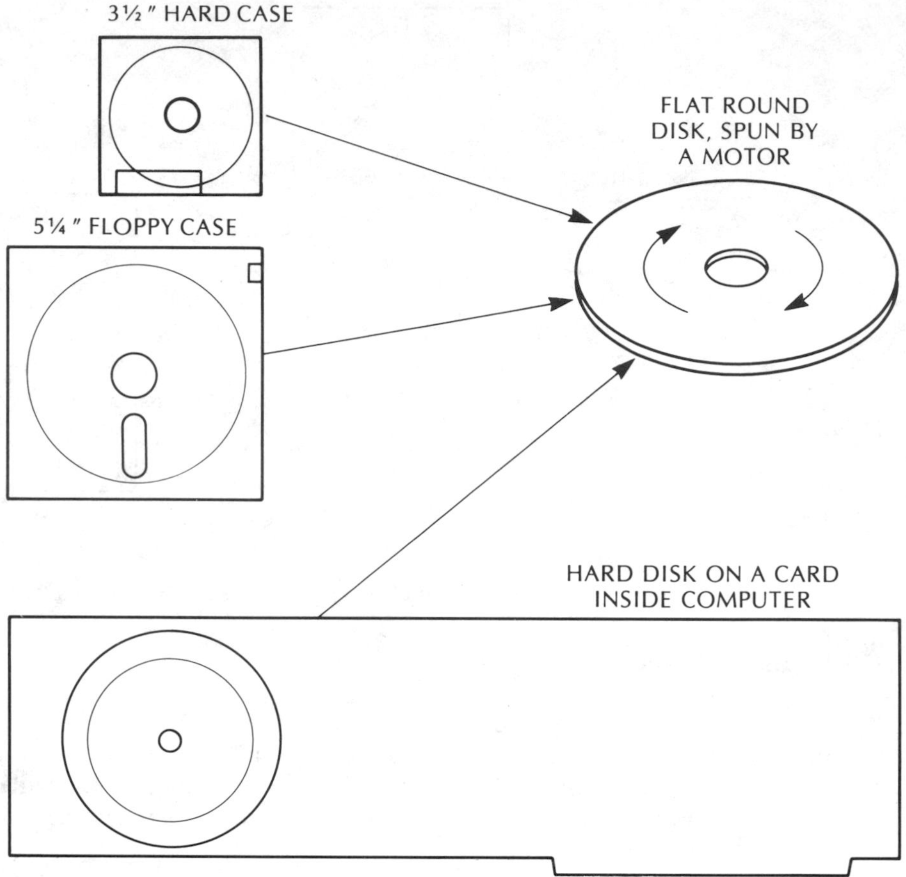

FIGURE 10.12 Disk Architecture

physical principle: Electricity flowing through a coil of wire produces a magnetic field.

The information flowing in a timed pattern through the computer is fed to the coil in the read/write head, so that when the spinning disk is properly timed to match the timing of the computer's pulses, a series of 1s and 0s is translated into a series of magnetic spots/no magnetic spots on the surface of the disk. Through this process, the electrical pattern flowing through the computer is captured on the disk as an exact magnetic image. (See Figure 10.14.)

There is more than one track per disk, so a mechanism is needed for moving the read/write head back and forth over the surface of the disk in a coordinated fashion. The number of tracks that can be placed on a given disk is a function of how accurately the disk is made, how much the surface varies, how fast the disk is spinning, and how sensitive the surface of the disk is to the magnetizing process. For these reasons, the smaller 3½″ diskettes hold more

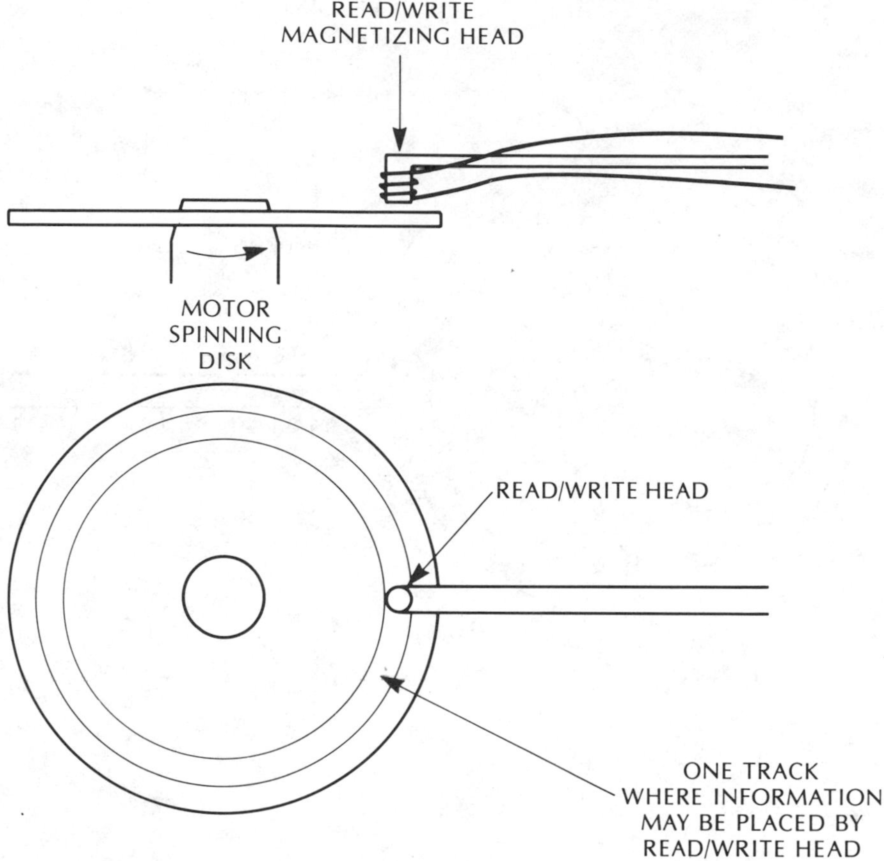

FIGURE 10.13 Magnetic Tracks of a Diskette

information than the 5¼″ versions, and the hard disk holds many times more information than either of its floppy counterparts.

Getting information off a disk is the opposite of putting it on and employs this physical principle: If a magnet moves past a coil of wire it will produce an electric current. So, if there is information on a track of a floppy disk, each time a magnetic spot moves under the head of the read/write arm, it can sense a small electric current. Simple electronic devices can amplify this current, and a string of 1s and 0s can be sent to the computer's network of wires for action (by the microprocessor) or storage (in memory).

ROM and RAM

As described in Chapter 2, a microcomputer can have information stored in RAM (read and write) and in ROM (read only). Both forms of memory are circuits printed on a chip cut from thin slices of large silicon crystals. A RAM

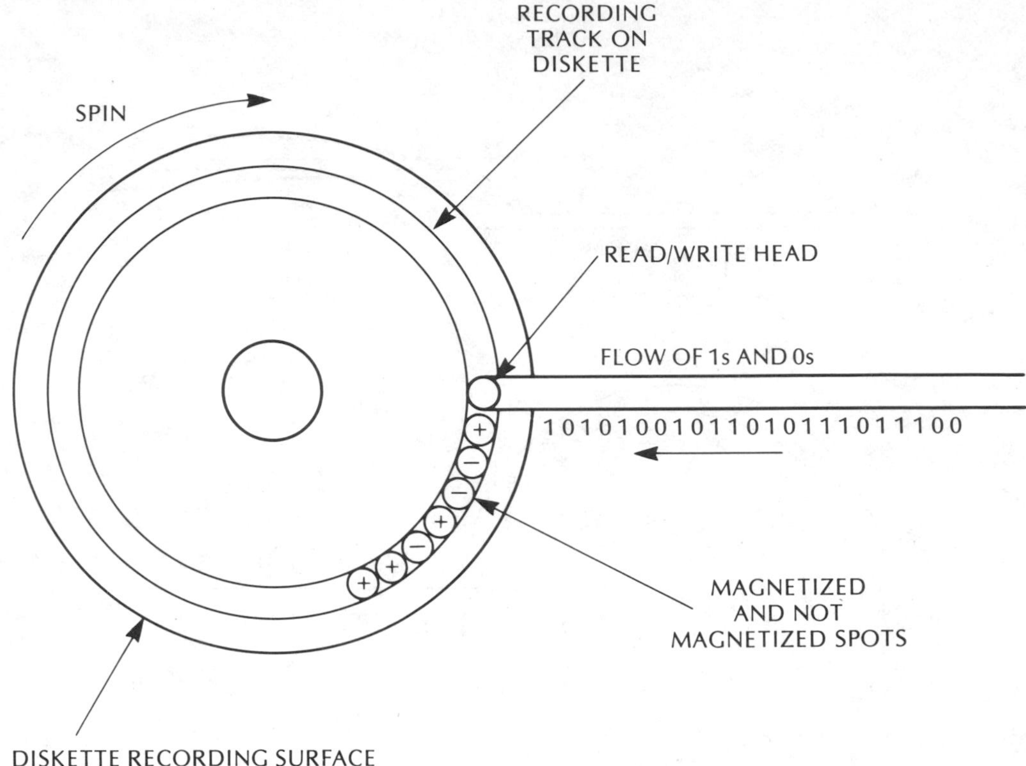

FIGURE 10.14 Magnetizing Head of a Disk Drive

or ROM unit can be thought of as a large matrix of cells in which each cell contains one unit of information (such as the letter "A," or the number "1," or a computer command code). One common analogy for computer memory is a broad expanse of tiny mailboxes, with each having room for just a set amount of information (mail), and each having a different address (mailbox number).

When the letter "A" is stored in a RAM unit, one very tiny piece of the chip's circuitry at a specific location (the address) is switched into the pattern, 01000001. Just as post offices vary in the number of mailboxes available, computer memory comes in different amounts. The standard measure for one unit of information is a *byte* (the letter "A" requires one byte), and one thousand bytes is known as a kilobyte (KB). Typical memory chips contain 16KB, 64KB, or 128KB of information, and a single computer may have several such chips—both RAM and ROM. A ROM chip is like a wall of mailboxes that comes already equipped—with an envelope of information for each box, whereas RAM chips are more flexible in terms of the information that comes and goes.

The amount of RAM memory capacity in a computer is important, because the microprocessor will use RAM memory locations when actively engaged in processing a program. Computers may have as little as 48KB of RAM to 1,000KB and up of accessible memory.

The Grand Coordinator

You have now unboxed all the components to make a working computer and given thought to the operation of each. By this time a question may have passed through your mind. With all these code messages flowing to the monitor, the printer, and from the keyboard, and with all the information available from disks and RAM and ROM, how does everything stay in order? For example, what happens if someone pushes down two or three keyboard keys at the same time? This question brings us to the heart of the computer, so let's plug all the cables into the body of the computer and talk about coordination.

If the wires of a computer are its nerves, then the microprocessor with its central processing unit (CPU) is its brain. One of the main functions of the microprocessor is to keep all the messages in a computer flowing and in appropriate order. It does this by producing a standard timing signal that controls every other component of the system. Every code flows in a stepwise fashion, one timed pulse at a time, in every part of the computer system.

As the central controlling element of the personal computer, the microprocessor uses the other components to accomplish its logical tasks. Although it's a sophisticated electronic device, the tasks the microprocessor carries out are simple functions: (1) it secures information from some other component, (2) it decides things based on simple logical functions, and (3) it takes actions (such as sending a message to a printer).

The microprocessor cannot think on its own, though it does carry out a certain number of functions automatically (such as the command to "add"). It needs to be told what to do and when to do it by a computer program, which must state, in linear fashion, the steps the microprocessor is to perform. For example, if the CPU is to add two numbers (typed in via the keyboard) and the total is to be displayed on the screen and also stored on diskette, the program must specify a set of commands to tell the CPU exactly how to accomplish each and every step of this task.

In the next section, we will place the development of the modern CPU into a historical context.

HOW IT ALL STARTED

Before we attach all the components together to create an operating computer, perhaps it would be interesting to move back in time and see what led up to the powerful microcomputer technology we have today. The history of computing is a fascinating aspect of the human endeavor.

Computing Engines and Decision-making Machines

In the early 1800s Charles Babbage had an idea that he could build a machine that would do many of the mathematical tasks commonly done by hand (such as addition, subtraction, multiplication, and division), and do them with complete accuracy. His plans for a "difference engine" resulted in a design for a system of thousands of gears and wheels, powered by a steam engine. After some initial work, it became clear that, although the theory behind the difference engine was sound, the technology was not sufficient to cope with the production of such a complicated machine. Still, Charles Babbage's active mind was hard at work, and he became interested in producing an even more complex type of machine, an "analytic engine."

An analytic engine would not simply add, subtract, and compute. It would employ well-known mathematical rules of logic to decide how to operate in various sets of circumstances. Babbage knew that statements such as "If X is true, and Y is true, then Z is true" could by modeled by a physical device. (We saw this exemplified by the water valves of the farmer's fields.)

As another example, many modern cars have electric fans on their radiators, rather than having the older type of fan that is constantly powered by a belt from the engine. When the car is first started, it is cold and there is no need for a fan. Therefore, somewhere in the car is a device that makes the following decision: If the engine is cold, then do not send electricity to the radiator fan; if the engine is hotter than 185 degrees Fahrenheit, then send electricity to the radiator fan. How can a car engine make a decision?

In this example, the logical device that controls the radiator fan is nothing more than a simple thermostat inside the radiator (see Figure 10.15). Inside the thermostat is a piece of metal that expands when heated. In the "cold" situation the metal is contracted and not making contact with the electrical wires, hence the fan is off. In the "hot" situation the metal has expanded and closed the circuit. In this manner, the thermostat is using environmental information and making a decision about when to turn the fan off and on.

If you think in terms of computer codes, when the engine is cold the thermostat is sending a 0 message, and when it is hot it sends a 1 message. Over the course of a day's driving, the sum total of the messages sent by a thermostat to a fan would be a series of 1s and 0s, analogous to the 1s and 0s found in a computer.

Although his analytic engine was never completed, Babbage's ideas did incorporate most of the ideas behind modern computers. For example, in his prototype analytic engines Babbage had punched cards (holes/no holes in positions) for information input. He also had a memory unit, a stored program (again on punched cards), a mechanical calculator, and an output device. The machine as designed could make decisions without human intervention.

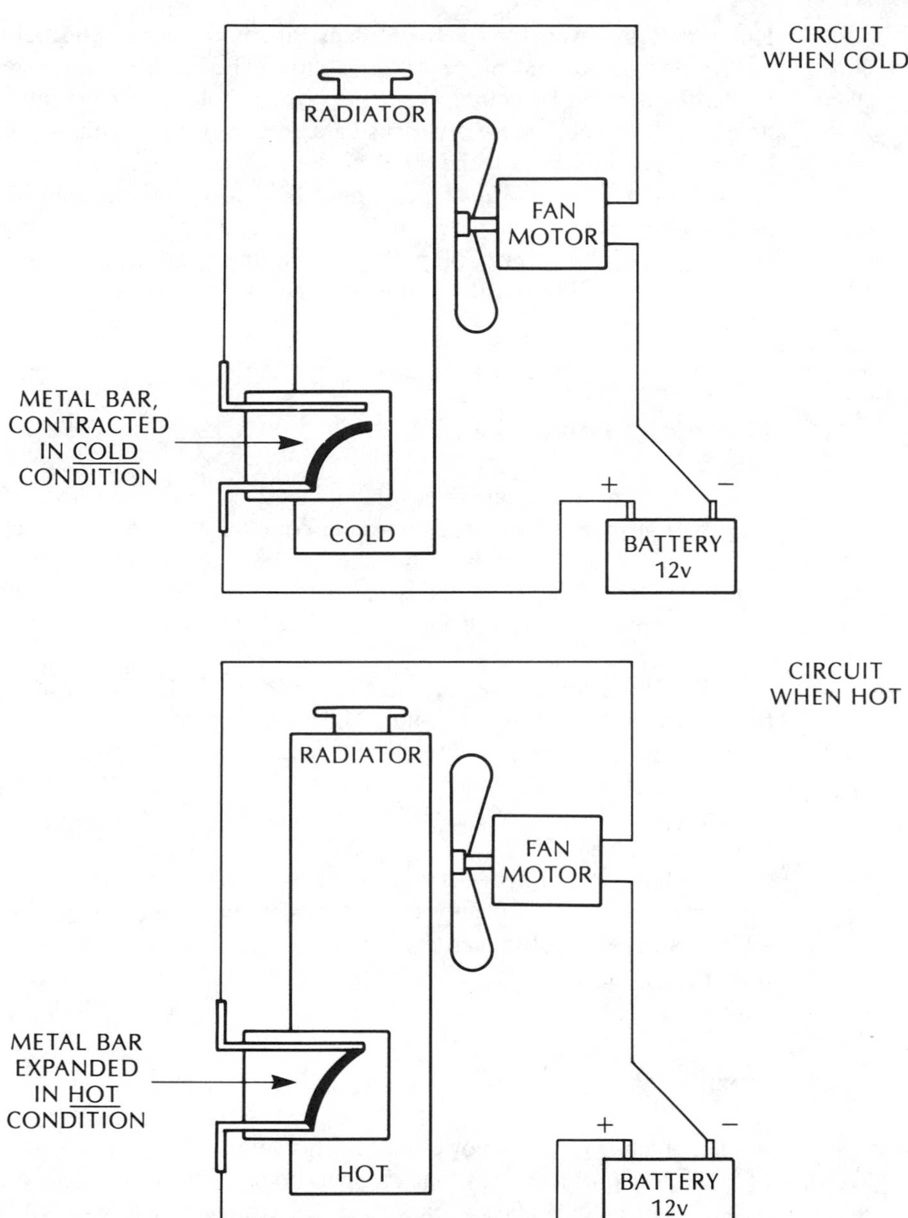

FIGURE 10.15 A Logical Mechanical Device

Mechanically Automated Data Processing

By the late 1800s the U.S. population had grown so large that it was taking the Census Bureau more than five years to complete each census count, and the requisite time was increasing each decade as the population increased. Herman

Hollerith, while working for the Census Bureau, designed and built machines to efficiently store and process information. The heart of the system was the Hollerith card, an 80-column card into which holes could be punched. Each hole coded a specific piece of census data, and various machines could identify holes and add and process the resulting data.

Using Hollerith's machines, the 1890 census tabulations were accomplished in fewer than two years. Hollerith formed his own tabulating company, which was sold to the Computing-Tabulating-Recording Company, which came to be the International Business Machines Corporation, the famous IBM.

Electronics Enters the Picture

It soon became clear that, since a machine able to process information can be created of gears and pulleys, a computer could also be designed using mechanical electric switches (like light switches) rather than gears. A visit today to an elementary school science fair is likely to reveal one or two science projects where the participants will have used light switches to illustrate computing principles.

The invention of the vacuum tube in the early 1900s provided the means to produce an electronic computer. The vacuum tube is nothing more than an electronic switch. The first operational vacuum tube computer is considered to be ENIAC (Electronic Numerical Integrator And Calculator), developed and used at the University of Pennsylvania from 1943 to 1946 to compute ballistic tables for artillery shells.

ENIAC was totally electronic and had 18,000 vacuum tubes, 70,000 resistors, weighed 30 tons, occupied a 20-by-40-foot room, and performed 5,000 additions or 300 multiplications per second. Today's desktop computer beats this much as an Olympic runner beats a one-year old in a foot race.

Flexibility

Although ENIAC was a powerhouse in its time, it had serious problems. One of its largest problems was that its operational pattern was determined by the physical setting of 6,000 switches, and the wiring of three walls of plug boards into which wires were plugged in a fashion that is similar to old telephone switch boards. Once all the switches were set (that is, the computer was programmed for a job), changing the program was not easy.

The first commercial computer, the UNIVAC (Universal Automatic Computer) solved this problem. John von Neumann at the Institute for Advanced Study at Princeton University is credited with developing the idea for a computer that would utilize a program stored in a memory bank. This concept, implemented in UNIVAC, allowed one to change the programs in the memory, thus allowing a computer to run an unlimited number of programs without having to physically move wires from place to place.

The Movement to the Modern Microcomputer

Sullivan et al. (1985) document the major steps in the movement from the vacuum tube computer to a fourth generation computer. Major aspects of change include the speed of the computers, their memory capacity, failure rate, method of data storage, and operating systems. It is clear from Table 10.3 that computers have made extraordinary advances in their capability of handling information.

Size changes were phenomenal, too. By the fourth generation, computers had shrunk to cabinet size. Integrated circuits handled information on a small silicon chip. There were thousands of microscopic transistors in a single microprocessor. These large-scale integrated circuits paved the way for the very small but very powerful desktop computers we now have.

A Change from the Mainframes

Mainframe computers are very large central computers that serve many terminals attached to the computer. Several hundred users may use the computer at the same time using time-sharing devices. Early computers were mainframe in

TABLE 10.3 History of Computer Improvements (Sullivan et al. 1985)

Feature	*First Generation of Vacuum Tubes*	*Second Generation of Transistors*	*Third Generation of Integrated Circuits*	*Fourth Generation of Large Scale Integration*
Speed (instructions per second)	up to 10,000	up to 1 million	up to 10 million	up to 1 billion
Memory capacity (in characters)	1,000 to 8,000	4,000 to 64,000	32,000 to 4 million	512,000 to 32 million
Failure rate	minutes	days	days to weeks	weeks
Relative cost (per operation)	$10.00	$1.00	$0.10	less than $0.01
External storage	cards	tape	disk	mass storage
Operating system	single user	single user	multiple user timesharing	multiple users and networks

concept, and mainframes are still used for large scale applications (telephone companies, the military, large businesses, research institutions). *Minicomputers* are smaller than the mainframe types, with from 40 to 50 simultaneous users and the same organizational principles as mainframes.

The *personal computer* revolution occurred with the development of a stand-alone desktop version of a computer that served one user at a time. In 1974 an Altair computer was advertised to be sold in kit form through the *Popular Electronics* magazine. It did not have a keyboard, monitor, disk, or printer, and it cost $395. The purchaser had to locate the other parts and get them to work. By wrapping up significant computer power in a small-scale package, Altair signaled the dawn of a new era for computers.

By 1975 an operating system named CP/M had been introduced and was soon being used on more than a million personal computer systems. Within a few years there were more than fifty brands of computers being sold in brand new computer stores that had just begun business operations. Computing clubs were formed, newsletters written, and magazines introduced.

During the period from 1977 to 1981 Steve Wozniack and Steve Jobs had developed and were marketing the Apple II computer, which was very successful because they sold it preassembled with a disk drive and programming system. Another company featured its computer, the Osborne 1, with software. The Radio Shack Corporation introduced its TRS-80 line, and the Commodore Business Machines its Commodore PET. New computer programs were developed, including the forerunner of all spreadsheets, VisiCalc. Word processing on the personal computer was initiated and AppleWriter and WordStar were introduced to a waiting public.

The very large computer manufacturers stayed solely with the production of mainframe and minicomputers until the early 1980s, when IBM and DEC entered the personal computer field. IBM's entry legitimized personal computers in the business world and set standards that could not be ignored. An entire population of IBM clones replicated the IBM machines and used the same operating system, MicroSoft Disk Operating System (MS-DOS).

By the mid-1980s two new ideas had been introduced, the integration of stand-alone computers via computer networks, and the integration of software in some lines of personal computers. Computers could communicate with other computers and share information, and various programs within one computer could do the same.

SOME PRACTICAL ASPECTS OF USING MICROCOMPUTERS

The history of computers is one in which computer power has grown, and computer costs have fallen. This seems to be the forecast for the future as well. There are several reasons for this phenomenon. First, major technical advances continue to be made, resulting in more computer power on smaller devices. Second, the growth of the computer industry has resulted in millions of these devices being sold each year, and although it costs a great deal to put a development (e.g., a new CPU) into action, the costs can be amortized over a large number of sales.

The electronics of a computer are similar to other electronic devices and, in general, there is a large worldwide demand for such products. The prices of CPUs and computers, along with other items, rise and fall as the competitive market reacts to consumer demands.

Compatibility

As with other electronic devices, different producers have come forth with a large number of types of computers. Whenever different versions of equipment exist, compatibility (or lack thereof) can be a problem. A teacher who shops for computer equipment needs to take steps to ensure that whatever hardware components are purchased will work with one another.

In many areas of commerce the trend has been in the direction of compatibility. For example, although there are hundreds of different brands of record players, you do not need to match player with record type because musical records were standardized. There is only one type of TV signal on the airways, so any brand of TV will bring it in. Computer technology presents a different story.

For computers, compatibility has been more the exception than the rule. For example, computer components from different manufacturers (Apple, IBM, Commodore, Tandy, Atari, the producers of IBM clones, and so forth) are, for the most part, incompatible. Even computers from the same manufacturers may vary a great deal (e.g., the Apple II series, the Apple Macintosh series), and their components are not compatible.

Still, there are some degrees of compatibility. For example, it is possible to purchase certain monitors that cross product lines. You may purchase disk drives from one manufacturer to use with a competitor's machine. Generally, however, each part of a given computer is specific to that line. The situation requires that you give careful consideration when purchasing components for a computer, because any crossovers must be checked out ahead. You cannot simply order randomly and expect all the parts to link together and work.

Although many computer users complain about this problem, incompatibility across brands is not unusual. In fact, we expect it with certain devices. If you own a Ford, you do not expect a Chevrolet dealer to have parts for your car. So it is with computers.

Cost

Computers range greatly in price, with the price being rather tightly linked to features. Thus, if you are interested in a computer that operates very quickly, you must expect to pay a premium for this feature. The same is true of the amount of storage space on a hard disk, the amount of RAM memory, and the resolution power of the monitor. In almost all cases, the price of the computer will correlate directly with the components chosen. Therefore, from a cost standpoint it is wise to know exactly how the computer will be used before any consideration is given to what computer to purchase. The key to a wise computer purchase lies in knowing exactly what type of computer power is required to do the job at hand. In the school setting this parameter is defined by the software. As previously stated in this book, you need to decide first on the types of software needed for the classroom, then purchase a computer to match the software needs.

Maintenance

In general, computers—as is true of most electronic equipment—are relatively reliable devices. The Oklahoma State Department of Education (1983) developed a good unit on caring for microcomputers. Important rules in this area are listed on Table 10.4.

With computers and peripherals, the number one bug is likely to be plugs and sockets and wires—lots of wires. All the computer peripherals attach to the body of the computer with wires, all plugging into ports and various sized jacks. When you have a problem with a printer that is printing strange characters, the first thing to check is the wires. Frequent plugging and unplugging of wires, such as happens when a computer is frequently moved, is a prime source of problems. Remember, computer information is a flow of rising and falling

TABLE 10.4 Maintaining Computers and Boosting Their Longevity (Oklahoma State Department of Education, 1983)

Hardware (General)

Do not expose system to extreme heat or cold.

Protect system from dust and any foreign materials (e.g. food and drink).

Install a line filter for the power cord to avoid power surges.

Minimize movement or vibration (hard on computers, especially those with a hard disk).

Ensure any equipment changes are made by someone familiar with system.

Follow recommended power-up/power-down sequences.

Type in the command to clear the screen in lieu of turning the power switch on and off between programs.

Watch for/minimize static electricity build-up/transfer (e.g. use grounding pad before touching computers in carpeted areas).

Disk Drives

Use a "head park" program if you have a hard drive.

Don't put a disk in or take a disk out of a drive when the "activated" light is on.

electric voltages, and any time that flow is hindered, computer information will be lost—and that will mean problems.

If problems arise and the computer does not work properly, Olivas (1985) has some good suggestions for trouble shooting and simple repairs. Some of his advice (together with ours) is listed in Table 10.5.

One problem that seems to arise in some school situations is the need for adjustment of the disk drives. The disk drive must spin the diskette at the correct speed, and the disk read/write arm must position itself correctly above each track. These two items may get out of synchronization and need to be adjusted.

There are programs that perform a check of the computer's parts and diagnose problems and potential problems, such as determining that the disk drive speed is slow and may cause disk-read errors.

SUMMARY AND REVIEW CHECKLIST

Computers have evolved from simple devices for adding and subtracting numbers into powerful machines that can perform logical analyses to rival, and in many areas exceed, human capabilities. They do their actions after being provided a set of instructions on what to do. Both instructions and actions involve the transfer of physical information in the form of patterns of electricity in precision-designed integrated circuits. For the information transfer processes to take place, all components must be compatible and proper connections between them are required.

TABLE 10.5 Trouble Shooting and Repair

Work your way from simple to complex in problem solving (look for simple solutions first).

Check software before hardware (substitute another program and see if problem persists).

Check all electrical connections and clean if necessary.

Substitute spare electrical cords, cables, and peripherals to narrow down where the problem is located.

Use a software diagnostic program to help identify problems with memory or disk drives.

Clean drive heads using a commercial cleaning kit.

Turn off all power before working on a computer, printer, etc.

Have a proper set of tools to work with; screwdrivers, longnose pliers, diagonal cutters, tweezers, etc.

Check all internal computer connections (cables, ribbon cables, cords, jacks, ports, etc.).

Clean all connectors with a pencil eraser.

Check all microchips.

We presented an example about how Farmer Jones opens various valves to provide the appropriate amount of water to three fields. He has a system of hardware designed and ready to conduct water as "instructed," just as a computer system, properly connected, is ready to transfer electronic messages. For all intents and purposes, Farmer Jones *programs* his valves to do the exact task he wants done. A computer's "valves" (electronic switches and circuits) must also be programmed to do certain tasks. In the next chapter, we will examine what one must do to "set the valves" on a computer to get the desired results. We will look at how a computer program works and some of the more common programming techniques used in the school setting.

Checklist

[ ] I can present an analogy from everyday experience to illustrate how a machine can store information and make decisions.

[ ] I can explain how a string of 1s and 0s can have physical meaning to a microcomputer and also represent meaning to a human.

[ ] I can state the general processes that a microcomputer uses to receive a typed message from the keyboard, display it on the monitor, and print it on the printer.

[ ] I can describe in a broad way how a microcomputer stores a typed character on a disk and puts it into the RAM memory.

[ ] I can state major landmarks in the development of microprocessing technology.

[ ] I can discuss various factors that underlie a microcomputer's cost, and state a guideline for making wise hardware purchases.

[ ] I can list important limitations on mixing and matching classroom hardware, and state a guideline for avoiding equipment incompatibility when selecting add-ons or when replacing such items.

[ ] I can identify maintenance and use factors important to decisions about microcomputer hardware.

SUGGESTED ACTIVITIES

1. With a colleague, devise a code that uses a flashlight to send information (off/on).
2. Using an available computer and its manuals, decide how much RAM memory the computer presently has. Using a sales catalog from a com-

puter company, determine the cost of adding more memory to this computer.

3. Take the cover off the body of a computer, and try to identify the major component parts.
4. Assemble the major components of a computer, attaching appropriate cables

WORTH A LOOK: SOFTWARE

Rocky's Boots. The Learning Company; Apple II family, Commodore, and IBM/MS-DOS computers. Teaches the logic of computer circuits in an outstanding fashion.

Robot Odyssey I. The Learning Company; Apple II family computers. Design robot to escape from a maze, uses wires, logic gates, and circuit chips.

Code Quest. Sunburst; Apple II family, Atari, Commodore, and IBM/MS-DOS computers. Decoding and coding explored.

High Wire Logic. Sunburst; Apple II family and IBM/MS-DOS computers. A language-based logic game for developing the Boolean logic skills that are the foundation for all computer logic.

Zandar III. Society for Visual Education; Apple II family computers. Students K–6 (or anyone) can learn an element of computer decision making (the "and" relationship) with a fun activity involving wizards, clues, and magic keys.

Simulated Computer. EduSOFT; Apple II family, Atari, and Commodore computers. A simulation of how a CPU operates. A simple set of commands directs a simulated computer to perform typical CPU actions.

READINGS

Freiberger, P., and Swaine, M. *Fire in the Valley: The Making of the Personal Computer.* New York: Osborne/McGraw-Hill, 1984.

Richman, E. *Spotlight on Computer Literacy.* New York: Random House, Inc., 1982.

Stern, N., and Stern, R. *Computers in Society.* Englewood Cliffs, NJ: Prentice-Hall, 1983.

REFERENCES

Oklahoma State Department of Education. *A Teacher's Guide to Classroom Computers.* Oklahoma City, OK: Department of Education, 1983.

Olivas, J. "Restoring Your Micro to Health." *Classroom Computer Learning,* September 1985:41–44.

Sullivan, D. R., Lewis, R. G., and Cook, C. R. *Computer Today: Microcomputer Concepts and Applications.* Boston: Houghton Mifflin Company, 1985.

11

The Software Side

An Introduction to Programming

OBJECTIVES

- State a skeptic's response to a recommendation that a particular computer language needs to be learned by every computer-using teacher.
- Describe the nature of an algorithm and how it relates to computer-style decision making and the writing of a computer program.
- Characterize (with an analogy) the challenge of learning a programming language, and explain why the task of writing a computer program is not uniformly appealing.
- Describe the boundaries of the spectrum of computer languages and the nature of some of the languages within those boundaries.
- Identify three programming languages that have found a place in school curricula, and describe their general applications.
- Describe key arguments related to the issue of teaching a programming language, such as Logo, within an instructional program.
- Compare and contrast the use of a specialized computer language like PILOT and an authoring system to prepare a computer lesson.

INTRODUCTION

With respect to programming, there are two basic questions to ask yourself as a teacher who makes use of computers.

- Should I learn how to program a computer?
- Should I teach my students how to program a computer?

In earlier chapters you learned that a computer program is a set of instructions the CPU carries out using other components of a computer. In this chapter we will explore more carefully the nature of a computer program and examine the spectrum of computer languages. We will survey the types of computer languages that are commonly found in the school setting and offer some perspectives to use when answering the two questions that we posed above.

Goals

- What is to be the role (if any) of programming languages and actions in your own classroom instruction and teaching activities?
- What is a computer language and what are the various types of computer languages?
- How does programming relate to school microcomputer use?
- How can a teacher decide whether to learn a given computer language?

To pursue these study questions, let's first look at computer languages and what they do, and then take a look at the classroom applications of the major computer languages used in schools.

THE NATURE OF A COMPUTER LANGUAGE

As you are aware by now, the CPU is the main "brain" of a microcomputer. Because of the speed with which a CPU can process information and produce computer actions, it can conduct a multitude of computer actions seemingly all at once. Of interest here is that the CPU can also "listen" and follow directions—directions given to it by a programmer.

Telling a Computer What to Do

You can program a computer yourself, causing the computer to do a task you want done, as long as the computer actions you request are among its built-in capabilities. To produce every action you desire, however, you must provide instructions to the CPU. Getting your message across requires that you speak a language a CPU can understand.

A *computer language* consists of a *set of commands* that govern the actions of a CPU. "Stop" is an example of one such command. If the CPU received this command, it would suspend action until it received another command. By carefully arranging some commands from the available set to be received by the CPU and "acted upon," you can direct the accomplishment of some desired computer actions.

For example, suppose you wanted the computer to add two numbers (typed in via the keyboard), display the total on the screen, and store the three on diskette. You, as programmer, would have to communicate instructions to the CPU to get these actions to take place. You would have to select and arrange commands to tell the CPU, step by step, just how to accomplish this task. In Table 11.1, we paraphrase (in English) some of the key steps of the command sequence for adding and saving numbers.

A successful arrangement of commands—in computer language rather than English—produces a *computer program* that works when it is run. Computer programs are typically stored on a floppy or hard disk under a given program name (such as "BOBSMATHGAME"). When the name of the program is entered from the keyboard, the CPU retrieves the program from the disk for running. Then, as it runs the program, the CPU processes the sequence of commands in the order received, resulting in a set of predetermined computer actions that accomplish the original goals of the programmer.

TABLE 11.1 Telling a CPU to Add and Store Two Numbers

Step	*Command (paraphrased in English)*
1	CPU, write on the screen: "Enter any number."
2	CPU, watch the keyboard for a number and a return keystroke.
3	CPU, if a number is typed and <enter> is pushed, store that number in RAM memory unit 1752.
4	CPU, write on the screen: "Enter a second number."
5	CPU, watch the keyboard for a number and return keystroke.
6	CPU, if a number is typed and <enter> is pushed, store the number in RAM memory unit 1753.
7	CPU, retrieve what is in memory unit 1752 and add it to what is in memory unit 1753 and then store the result in RAM memory unit 1784.
8	CPU, write on the screen: "The result of adding the two numbers is" and write what is in memory unit 1784 on the screen.
9	CPU, write on the floppy disk, track #17, the numbers in memory units 1752, 1753, and 1754.
10	CPU, clear the screen and write: "Do you want to add two more numbers?"

Computer actions resulting from a program reflect the intent of the person who wrote the program. Once a program has been written, it can be made available to others. Any user can run it then without knowing any computer language at all.

Why do people write computer programs? They want the computer to do some specific task or set of tasks. For example, a physicist might want to program a computer to do calculations with an equation that he or she believes simulates the universe at the instant of the Big Bang. The scientist might ask the computer to picture the conditions at one second, or some other specified time, after the event. A teacher might want to program a computer to present a simple drill and practice game on a particularly important topic for students to use in the classroom during their spare time.

In order for any computer program to operate correctly, the set of directions to the CPU must be written in such a fashion that the results are unequivocal. That is, no unexpected or erroneous computer actions or responses should pop up. If they do, then modifications in the command sequence must be performed. The problematic actions are called program "bugs," and the process of removing them is termed, "debugging." One can always count on spending time debugging a new computer program.

Communicating in a computer language requires exacting precision. The language "rules" are absolutely unyielding. Many persons find this frustrating and decide they are not cut out to program computers. Others take the challenges in stride and find great enjoyment in the programming and debugging processes. Anyone who spends much time in deciding upon tasks for computers to do, and then telling them how to go about it, should enjoy writing algorithms also.

Algorithms

"Think before you speak" is an old adage that contains wisdom for everybody. In the world of computer programming, we could rephrase the idea as: "plan an algorithm before you put it into computer language."

When a set of logical steps always leads to an unequivocal result, we call the arrangement of steps an *algorithm*. To a programmer, whose end goal is absolutely no bugs in the final program, an algorithm is an important tool. Through writing an algorithm, one can decide the general guidelines of what to say to the CPU to get the program to do the designated task *and* to work right.

To write an algorithm, one writes a set of statements (in English) describing the steps that must be taken to achieve a certain result. The following example presents an algorithm taken from science fiction.

You have just received a box with your new "robot chauffeur." The instructions say it understands English and has all the rules for "how to drive a car." But when you put it in the driver's position behind the wheel, you realize that apparently the manufacturer has forgotten to program the robot with the set of rules on "how to *start* a car." You need to tell the chauffeur how to do this task so that it will remember your rules and do those actions successfully each time it enters your car. In other words, you need to provide your robot with the algorithm for starting your car successfully.

There may be several different algorithms for accomplishing the car-starting task. Here is one way of getting the job done. "Robot, do the following things":

1. Check the automatic transmission lever to see if it is in the "Park" position.
2. If the lever is not in "Park," then move it to "Park."
3. Reach in your right pocket and retrieve your set of keys (robots are programmed to always carry their keys in the right pocket).
4. Find the key that has inscribed on it: ignition.
5. Find the keyhole, which is located on the left side of the steering wheel, about twelve inches below the wheel.
6. Place the key in the keyhole.
7. If it doesn't fit, rotate the key 180 degrees and try again.
8. Depress the gas pedal about one-half inch.
9. Turn the ignition key 90 degrees clockwise until you hear the starter.
10. If you do not hear a starter, call your owner and say, "The battery may be dead."
11. Listen for the engine running. (If this is your fourth time at this step, go to step 14.)
12. If the car has started, then turn the ignition key 90 degrees counter-clockwise and drive; else continue holding the key in position five seconds.
13. If the car has not started, turn the ignition key 90 degrees counter-clockwise, wait fifteen seconds, and repeat steps 9–11 (up to three times).
14. Check the gas gauge to see if it is empty.
15. If empty then call your owner and say, "The car is out of gas."
16. If the car has gas, then call your owner and say, "The car won't start, and I don't know why."

This sample algorithm is revealing, in that it shows the extent to which everyday human actions, like starting a car, really involve many decisions.

As a human, you have learned to do the steps and make the decisions surrounding such simple tasks seemingly without thinking and in a multitude of ways. To program a CPU, however, you have to think through the task and to be explicit if you wish the computer to do the job. Otherwise, there is no assurance that, once begun, the process will reach a satisfactory ending.

The following example is a somewhat shorter algorithm for a task that microcomputers are built to do well (unlike starting cars) and one that you, as a teacher, might direct a CPU to do. This algorithm has a computer solve the problem of how to average a set of class grades and assign a letter grade (given:

the computer has accessible a file of the students' names and scores on each of the five tests you have given).

1. Move to the record for the first student.
2. Count the number of tests taken by the student.
3. If less than five, then print "I (incomplete)" for the student in a box with the title "Final Grade," and go to step 7.
4. Add up all the scores for the student on all the tests.
5. Divide the total score by five and print this score in a box with the title "Average."
6. Compare the average for the student with the following statements, and print a letter grade for the student in a box with the title "Final Grade."
   If the average is at least 90 then print "A."
   If the average is less than 90 but at least 80 then print "B."
   If the average is less than 80 but at least 70 then print "C."
   If the average is less than 70 but at least 60 then print "D."
   If the average is less than 60 then print "F."
7. Move to the record for the next student. (If no further records, go to step 9.)
8. Go to step 2.
9. End of routine.

This algorithm has several "functions" that a computer can and routinely does use. The algorithm directs the computer to *find* a given piece of information on a disk or in memory, *add* numbers, *count* items, *divide* numbers, *compare* one number with another number, *use* logic in the form of "If X is true, then do Y," *move* from one record to another, and *jump* from one step in the algorithm to another.

Algorithms for computers are often represented in the form of a *flow diagram*, so termed since they are systematic and flow in a logical manner. Figure 11.1 shows the algorithm for the example of a robot that tries to start a car. It is pictured as a series of action boxes, with diamonds for major decisions and arrows to show how the flow returns to previous commands as a decision consequence. Figure 11.2 shows the "grade averaging" algorithm.

The two algorithms we present have been written in English. But, except for a few computers in university research labs, computers don't comprehend English (and even when they do it is more like a Pidgin English). An algorithm has to be translated into "computer language" in order for the CPU to "understand" the exact set of steps it is required to follow to accomplish the desired result.

Converting Algorithms to Code

Converting algorithms into computer code is the major task of a computer programmer. If you don't do any programming yet, you certainly could do so if you wanted to. It would simply require that you learn a new language, just as

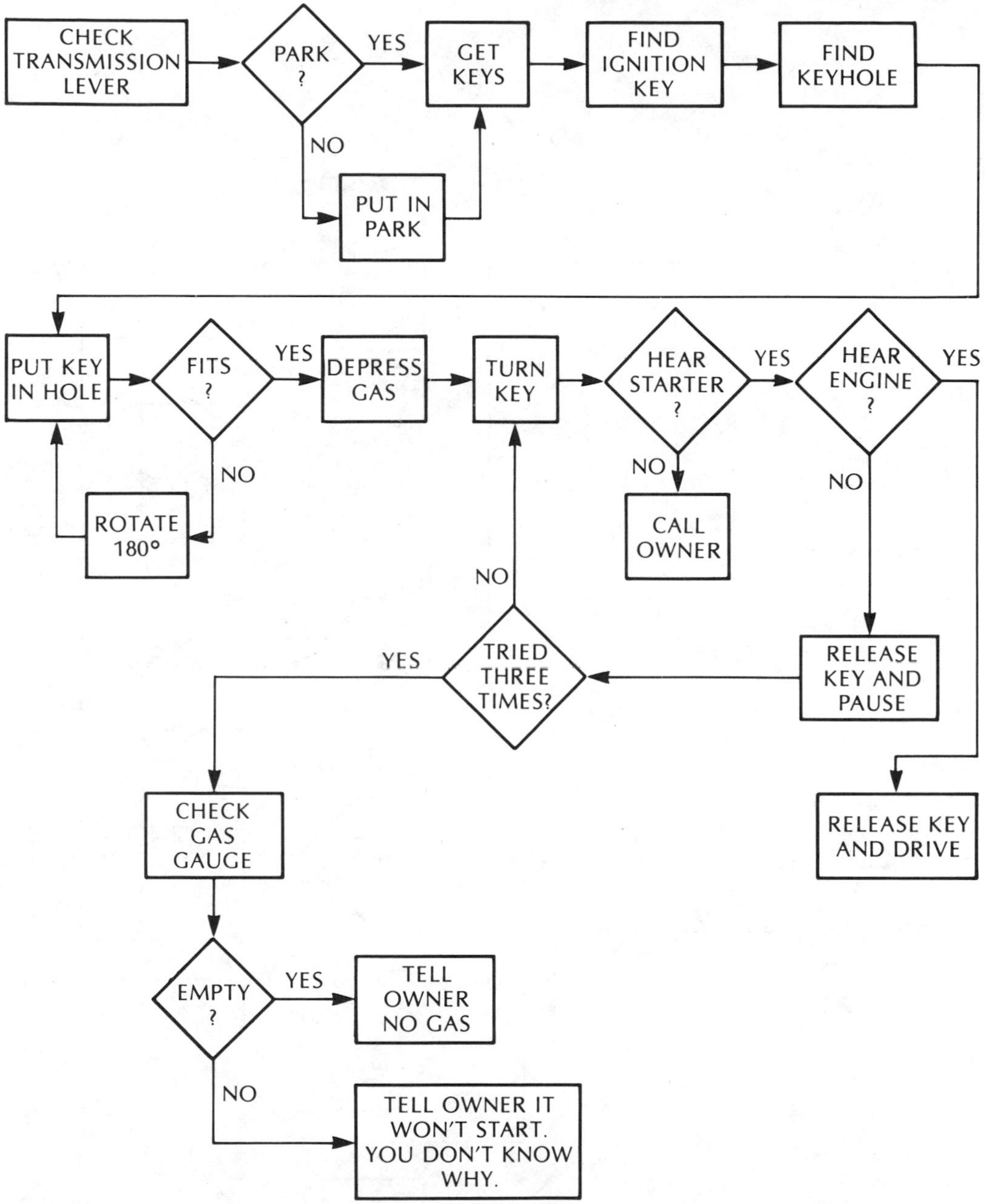

CHECK TRANSMISSION LEVER
PARK ?
YES
NO
PUT IN PARK
GET KEYS
FIND IGNITION KEY
FIND KEYHOLE
PUT KEY IN HOLE
FITS ?
YES
NO
ROTATE 180°
DEPRESS GAS
TURN KEY
HEAR STARTER ?
YES
NO
CALL OWNER
HEAR ENGINE ?
YES
NO
RELEASE KEY AND PAUSE
TRIED THREE TIMES?
NO
YES
RELEASE KEY AND DRIVE
CHECK GAS GAUGE
EMPTY ?
YES
TELL OWNER NO GAS
NO
TELL OWNER IT WON'T START. YOU DON'T KNOW WHY.

FIGURE 11.1 Flow Diagram for Starting a Car

you might have to learn some French or Spanish to write to someone in France or Argentina. But instead of coding what you wish to say in a natural human language, you would have to learn to code your meaning using the rules of a purposefully constructed (artificial) language. To tell a computer what to do

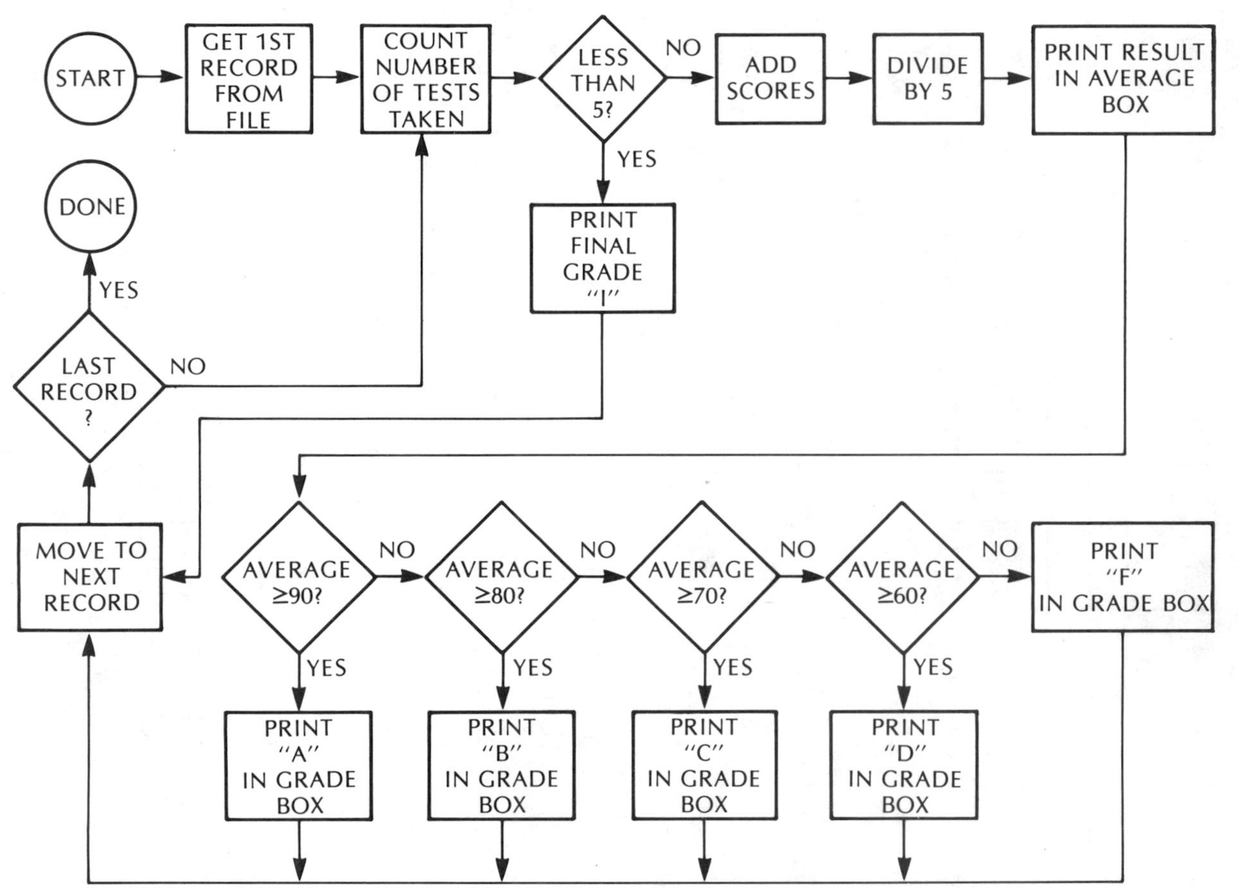

FIGURE 11.2 Flow Diagram for Grade Averaging Algorithm

means converting your algorithm for a task into comparable "lines of *computer code*" in some computer language.

Learning a computer language is akin to learning a foreign language, and efforts must be directed toward learning both commands ("words"), and the rules for their use. The endeavor should prove faster than learning a human language, however, because computer languages are logically constructed. Their rules can be counted on to a much greater degree than the grammar rules of spoken languages.

A SPECTRUM OF COMPUTER LANGUAGES

In the previous section we stated, "computers don't comprehend English," and yet, there are computers that *seem* to understand English (we have seen teachers using them in the classroom to teach spelling words). The user first says some English words, and the computer "memorizes" (stores) the speaker's speech patterns and can then respond to that speaker with words of its own. But such a computer is not programmed in English. It was programmed in a computer language and instructed in a detailed and sophisticated set of procedures for the handling of the sound information it receives. These procedures enable it, like the robot, to do what seems like an everyday thing—understanding and responding to spoken words.

As the computer program is constructed, the CPU accepts and processes the tidbits of physical information carried in the voice it "hears" so that it is able to handle the incoming sound and respond appropriately. Computers do not comprehend English at all. Computers are able to understand only computer language.

There are some devices that do communicate directly with a computer in the computer's own language (in electric voltages). For example, the tools for measuring temperature in science experiments "talk" to the computer by sending pulses of electricity from the sensor to the computer. People don't communicate with a computer in this fashion and need to use some other level of interaction.

Table 11.2 presents the spectrum of computer languages that have evolved, leading from pure English at one end (not yet a computer language) to pure computer talk at the other end (1s and 0s).

When one computer sends information to another computer, the message consists of a series of electrical pulses. Humans code those pulses (and lack thereof) as 1s and 0s. The resulting computer language is called *"machine language"* and is seldom used to program computers directly. One must be highly trained to deal with the blizzard of 1s and 0s that are required (and encountered).

At a slightly higher level (*assembly language*) mnemonics are used to represent clusters of 1s and 0s, making it easier for the programmer to write and read a program. At a much higher level (FORTH, FORTRAN, COBOL,

TABLE 11.2 A Spectrum of Computer Languages

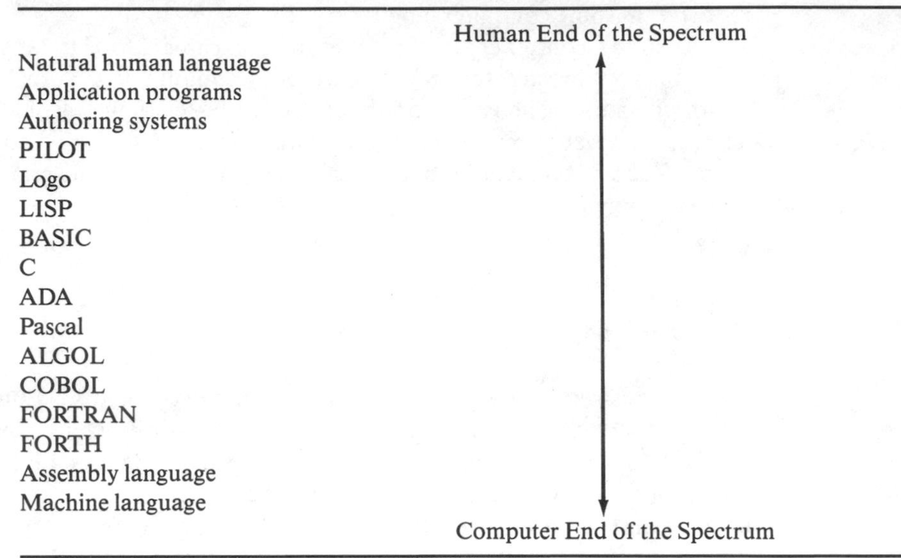

Language	
	Human End of the Spectrum ↑
Natural human language	
Application programs	
Authoring systems	
PILOT	
Logo	
LISP	
BASIC	
C	
ADA	
Pascal	
ALGOL	
COBOL	
FORTRAN	
FORTH	
Assembly language	
Machine language	
	↓ Computer End of the Spectrum

through PILOT) a combination of English and mathematical notation is used. The highest level programming language would be Natural Human Language (not yet available on any computer).

When assembly or higher level language is used by a programmer, a computer translation process takes place. Some of the effort of the computer is directed toward language translation. It follows a special program to process the commands of the assembly (or higher level) language and to produce the final machine language it uses.

Why does computing need so many different languages at so many levels? Each of the languages in Table 11.2 has been developed in response to special needs. For example, COBOL is a business-related language that simplifies using the computer with accounting and other similar financial functions. BASIC is a language that was developed for general purpose use by nonexperts, and Logo was initially designed to be used by children.

Just as there are a variety of vehicles such as vans, sedans, motorcycles, bicycles, and skateboards to get people around, there are a variety of computer languages, each having certain strengths and weaknesses.

The differences in computer languages are not reflected in the functions the languages accomplish. That is, all of them do essentially the same things. Computer languages do differ a great deal in the ease with which any given language can accomplish a given task. For example, it is much easier using Logo to make a colored spot scoot around on the monitor screen than it would be using APL (which is a powerful mathematical/scientific language).

With this idea in mind, let's explore the computer languages commonly found inside the school building in the classrooms (not inside business offices).

PROGRAMMING LANGUAGES IN SCHOOL CURRICULA

There are three major programming languages found in elementary, middle school, and high schools. These are: (1) Logo, (2) BASIC, and (3) Pascal.

Logo

Logo is a programming language commonly used in early and middle elementary school, but one not limited to the elementary environment. It is available for most types of computers, and there is a wealth of books and manuals to help teachers to implement the teaching of Logo in classrooms from the first grade through adult. It is widely used with children to introduce the basic ideas of programming a computer, and it has played a role as well in attempts to teach problem solving and creative thinking.

At its simplest level, Logo is easy to comprehend. For example, here is a small computer program using Logo. You may be able to see intuitively what the program will cause the computer to do.

```
TO DRAW
CLEARSCREEN
SHOW TURTLE          (a spot of light)
FORWARD 50                    (spaces)
RIGHT 90                     (degrees)
FORWARD 50
RIGHT 90
FORWARD 50
RIGHT 90
FORWARD 50
END
```

This is a program called "to draw." It clears the screen of anything displayed on it (clearscreen), then it shows a "turtle" (which can be displayed as a turtle figure or simply as a spot of light). The program moves the figure forward 50 units (leaving a trace behind it), it makes a right turn, and it repeats this action three times. The result is a box drawn on the screen when the program is run.

Does it seem rather silly having a high-powered and expensive computer involved in just drawing boxes? Well, it is not silly at all if your instructional intent is to teach elementary students how to program a computer (rather than to draw a box)!

Elementary students as low as the second grade can be taught to program a computer using Logo (an occasional child might be ready to begin even earlier). The commands in the Logo language are common English words, and the simplest Logo commands result in concrete representations on the computer screen—hence the student gets immediate feedback on the results of his or her programming efforts.

Logo is built around the idea of introducing programming via the use of geometric figures on the screen. The "turtle" on the screen can be manipulated and moved using appropriate computer commands. The turtle is able to leave a line behind it (or not) as it moves, and the student can see the explicit results of a given command. Hence, it can be used to create various shapes that will be produced as the program is run. As programming skills grow, the student learns how to store and repeat commands, and the complexity of the screen images increases.

Logo is not limited to drawing pictures. It has very powerful features such as recursion and structured programming. One of our colleagues used Logo to develop sophisticated on-line math lessons for his students.

To some teachers, Logo is an avenue toward the development of computer literacy in children. Others use it to foster development in the general area of cognitive strategies. Some of the projects teachers have accomplished using Logo include a function game for high school algebra, a supply and demand model for high school social studies, string art, a study of spirals for intermediate grades, a book report slide show, a musical scales from different cultures project, a pattern game with shapes and music for primary grades, and a multitude of problem-solving exercises (Maddux, 1985).

Because it has been so intertwined with various educational efforts, the "reality" of Logo is not easy to capture. This computer language has taken on meanings based on the contexts of its development and use. Logo is a philosophy, Logo is a pedagogy, Logo is a computer language for children, and Logo is a general purpose computer language.

Should you teach your students to program or not?

Why Teach Logo?

In the influential book *Mindstorms*, Seymour Papert (1980) established the educational theory behind Logo, building on the field of artificial intelligence and Jean Piaget's work on how children think. Papert suggested that the development of children's intellectual structures could be accelerated through educational intervention. Whether Logo can or cannot facilitate the development of mental processes has been the focus of much educational research in the 1980s.

Many claims have been established regarding benefits of learning programming, and especially for learning Logo. Feurzeig, Horwitz, and Nickerson (1981) provide an extensive set of cognitive outcomes expected from learning to program. They argue that learning to program is expected to bring about seven fundamental changes in thought:

1. Rigorous thinking, precise expression, recognized need to make assumptions explicit (because computers run specific algorithms);
2. understanding of general concepts such as formal procedure, variable, function, and transformation;
3. greater facility with the art of "heuristics," explicit approaches to problems useful for solving problems in any domain, such as planning, finding a related problem, solving the problem by decomposing it into parts, etc.;
4. the general idea that "debugging" of errors is a constructive and plannable activity applicable to any kind of problem solving;
5. the general idea that one can invent small procedures such as building blocks for gradually constructing solutions to large problems;
6. generally enhanced "self-consciousness and literacy about the process of solving problems";
7. enhanced recognition for domains beyond programming that there is rarely a single best way to do something, but different ways that have comparative costs and benefits with respect to specific goals.

Although specific teachers and projects at specific schools have reported great success in reaching many of the goals listed above, the more generalizable results of research on Logo are less optimistic about its benefits. In an article reviewing the cognitive effects of learning computer programming, Pea and Kurland (1987) point out the following findings: although children can learn to write lines of code (which is no small achievement), development of higher level programming skills appears to be lacking. A variety of reasons were discussed, including the relatively small amount of time spent on learning programming skills.

Those authors found, in sum, little evidence for the claims of broad cognitive impact from programming experience and claims of transfer of problem-solving skills from programming to other domains. At present there exist no substantial studies to support the claim that programming promotes mathematical rigor or that programming aids children's basic mathematical exploration. Finally, results thus far indicate that the Logo programming experiences have no significant effects on planning performances.

If the use of Logo in the classroom has not lived up to the expectations of the early 1980s, why then should one consider using it in the classroom?

First, it is very clear that many individual teachers can make Logo a significant learning event within the classroom. Just as one teacher may have success by using of a technique of producing class costume plays on historic events, another may employ the technique of using Logo to stimulate creativity and inventiveness.

Second, all the research is not in yet on the relationship of Logo and learning. Although the overly optimistic initial view of Logo has been eroded, this does not mean that the entire scheme of using Logo to reach specific educational goals should be discarded.

Third, as a teaching tool, Logo can be used to reach specific learning objectives, rather than the more global and diffuse concepts of "teaching thinking skills." Table 11.3 provides a list of some curriculum areas for which Logo might be an appropriate choice as a teaching tool.

TABLE 11.3 Some Curriculum Areas Suitable for Using Logo as a Teaching Tool

Computer Literacy
- keyboard skills
- using disks and disk drives
- using a keyboard
- assorted computer skills
- developing concept of what a program is
- programming skills: coding, etc.

Mathematics
- geometric figures, squares, triangles, rectangles, etc.
- measuring angles
- properties of lines: parallel, straight, curved, etc.
- measuring lengths
- using multiple strategies to complete a task
- algorithms
- combining figures

Art and Music
- concepts of similarity, size, shape
- color discriminations
- tone discriminations
- drawing of pictures
- looking for a pattern

Science
- developing a model
- looking for a pattern or sequence
- estimating
- predicting
- systematic organization of information

Given the current information, it appears that the key to using Logo is to implement it as a teaching tool to achieve specific and valued curricular objectives rather than adopting it as a general curriculum topic per se. One would not just "teach Logo for the sake of teaching it" or "put Logo into the curriculum" without considering the goals and objectives of a given program.

BASIC

John Kemeny and Thomas Kurtz developed BASIC (Beginners All-Purpose Symbolic Instruction Code) as a multipurpose computer language for students at Dartmouth College. They developed a language that can be used by an average individual who is not a professional computer programmer. Since its origination, a number of brands of BASIC have been developed.

BASIC has been used by more people worldwide than any other computer language, and it still is probably being used with more microcomputers than any other language. The reason for this is that BASIC commands are fairly literal, the structure of a program is linear, and it has a social history of being the first and easiest language to learn. BASIC is commonly the language included with the sale of a new personal computer. Table 11.4 lists some of the BASIC commands that control the computer's actions. There are of course many more commands in BASIC than are listed in Table 11.4.

Earlier in this chapter we presented a brief Logo program that draws a box. In BASIC this same program would require only three commands. The BASIC program to draw a box is:

```
RUN
BOX (50)
END
```

TABLE 11.4 Examples of Computer Commands

PRINT "x"	Place whatever is within quotes on the monitor.
LPRINT "x"	Send whatever is within quotes to a line printer (any type of printer).
INPUT	Store in memory what is typed into the computer from the keyboard.
END	End the program.
GOTO (x)	Go to a new position in the program.
IF (x) IS TRUE, THEN DO (y)	If a given statement is true, then perform some new action. If the given statement is not true, do not perform the new action.
BOX (x)	Draw a box having sides of dimension (x).
RUN	Run a program from start to END.

A program to add two numbers together is slightly more complex, but still within the intuitive grasp of a reader who knows no BASIC:

```
1   PRINT    "THIS IS A PROGRAM TO ADD TWO NUMBERS"
2   PRINT    "TYPE IN THE FIRST NUMBER"
3   INPUT    A$
4   PRINT    "TYPE IN THE SECOND NUMBER"
5   INPUT    B$
6   PRINT    "THE ANSWER TO YOUR PROBLEM IS"; A$;
             " + "; B$; " = "; A$ + B$
7   PRINT    "DO YOU WANT TO DO ANOTHER? TYPE Y OR
             N"
8   INPUT    C$
9   IF       (C$ = "Y") THEN GOTO LINE 1 ELSE END
```

If you know a few simple rules this program becomes clear. All items to be printed on the screen are preceded by the word "print." The item itself is in quotes. "Input" is a command to the computer to put a question mark on the screen and wait for a user to type something. Whatever is typed is assigned to the "A$," or the "B$," or the "C$." In line 6 the computer uses the ";" as a command to string together the words and values to produce the sentence: "THE ANSWER TO YOUR PROBLEM IS X + Y = Z," with the appropriate numbers for "X," "Y," and "Z." For example, a user would see "THE ANSWER TO YOUR PROBLEM IS 12 + 83 = 95" after typing in the numbers 12 and 83.

In schools, BASIC is often the language that follows Logo in the middle school or upper elementary grades. This is not to say that Logo is not used in high school classes, or that Logo needs to precede BASIC (or BASIC to follow Logo), or that BASIC is not used at the elementary level.

A few students will go on to study computer science in high school, and this generally means they will study in-depth either BASIC or Pascal. For many years BASIC was the language for the standardized evaluation of student programming proficiency, but it was superseded by Pascal when the Educational Testing Service adopted Pascal as its new standard for national level advanced placement testing.

Pascal

Perhaps the best way to understand the nature of Pascal is through the Educational Testing Service's own explanation of why it was chosen as the language for the national AP test. James Braswell of the ETS writes (1984):

> A primary objective of the AP computer science course is to teach students how to write logically structured, well-documented computer programs. Although good programmers can write such programs in almost any program-

> ming language, certain languages encourage good programming habits more than others; the AP course will require the use of such a language. The language must have certain technical characteristics that facilitate structured programming and a high degree of modularity. . . . (Note: several other requirements are specified here). . . . Recursion and dynamic allocation of storage are also necessary features.
>
> A consideration of the features of various programming languages, together with the support provided for these languages by existing textbooks and by computer systems commonly available at the secondary school level, led to the selection of Pascal as the sole language to be used in the AP Computer Science Examination at this time.

From this explanation we learn that Pascal has a structure that demands the use of good programming techniques. It is a structured language, but this does not result necessarily in a language that is easy to interpret intuitively. We've selected an example for you to try to decipher, however. The following is a Pascal program to find the areas of rectangles.

```
program areaofrectangle (input,output);
var length, width, area:real;
begin
   read(length,width);
   area: = length*width;
   write('Area = '',area)
end.
```

If one knows some Pascal rules, then interpretation of the program becomes simpler. For example the name of the program is "area of rectangle" and it will have both input and output. It needs any two numbers (the variables of length and width) to produce the variable called area. The program "begins," reads the length and width from the keyboard (or file), multiplies (*) the length times the width to produce the area, and writes the phrase "Area = X" (where "X" is the area value just calculated).

So far, we have presented three major programming languages a student might encounter in a school. The languages a student might learn are not necessarily the languages that would best serve teachers in their professional role.

COMPUTER LANGUAGES AND THE TEACHER

What computer languages does a teacher need to know? Possibly none! Whether you learn a computer language depends on your professional goals. Table 11.5 lists some professional goals that can be reached by learning one or more computer languages. Some of these goals can be reached in other ways. But if at this point in your career you do not have any of these professional goals, then you do not need to learn any computer language.

TABLE 11.5 Teaching Goals and Language Competencies

Goal (minimums)	*Suitable Language(s)*
Teach elementary students computer literacy	Logo
Teach special education students of any age computer literacy	Logo
Teach upper elementary students computer literacy	Logo and/or BASIC
Teach high school students computer literacy	Logo and/or BASIC
Teach high school students Computer Science	Pascal and BASIC
Develop your own computer literacy, including learning how to control a computer with a program	Logo or BASIC
Develop simple lessons on the computer for students to use	PILOT or an authoring system

There are advocates of the position that all teachers should learn at least one computer language in order to achieve real computer literacy. Bork (1987) has stated

> We need not make expert programmers out of teachers in a computer literacy program. But we should give them enough programming experience so that they can understand the *process* of programming and be able to *read* programs in an effective and powerful language (p. 35).

We do not advocate this position. We feel that a brief introduction to a given computer language would be sufficient for the average teacher (like that presented in this text). Once a teacher has the concept of how a computer program controls a computer, we feel the decision to continue in the study of a language should be based on the goals and interests of the teacher, rather than on some arbitrary rule that a teacher must be proficient to some level in a computer language to be called computer literate.

Teacher-Developed Software

In the early days of computer use, many teachers learned programming in order to develop simple programs for their own students. These programs were often unsophisticated but were of real value in the teacher's own classroom. Today, the era of teacher-developed software is gone (or in our opinion should be gone, because adequate quality is all too rare via this mode of software production).

The task of developing a new computer program for students should, in our view, be relegated to professional teams who can utilize a systematic approach and integrate into the development effort what is known from research on how people learn. Ideally, such a team would consist of instructional developers, content specialists, and professional computer programmers whose combined expertise would enable production of a product genuinely worthy of students' use.

Still, teachers have developed and will continue to develop small units of computer instruction that do work in their classrooms. There are many reasons for this among them pride in ownership, but probably the main rationale behind a teacher's programming efforts is that a lesson developed for personal use will fit perfectly into that teacher's lessons.

Having already stated that we do not advocate the teacher-developed software, we shall proceed now to discuss how any teacher who wishes to do so can develop his or her own computer program for classroom use! (We think it is important for teachers to know their options.)

One can employ a computer language like Logo or BASIC or Pascal to do the job. Any of the three languages could be used to develop complete lessons. But there are other programming tools to simplify your efforts. There are special *authoring languages* that have been developed specifically for the writing of lessons. The most prominent of these is PILOT.

PILOT

The PILOT authoring language has undergone many changes and enhancements since the original PILOT was developed by John Starkweather and his colleagues at the University of California at San Francisco. The developers' intent was to produce a simple language with powerful interactive capability, one that could be used as an authoring language by teachers for authoring software for computer-assisted instruction. Today there are many commercial versions of PILOT, all having common general features but different specifics.

The PILOT authoring language employs as computer commands sensible code that translates readily to the teachers' thinking while developing a lesson. For example, to place a word on the screen, the teacher issues the command <TYPE>. In PILOT, whatever follows the command will be placed on the screen. Other PILOT commands include <ACCEPT> to accept a student's response to a question, <MATCH> to match a student's response to correct and incorrect answers, <COMPUTE> to do math calculations, and <END> to end a program. In this manner a teacher can build a drill and practice, a test, or a tutorial lesson. Table 11.6 is an example of an annotated PILOT program that presents to a student a question and provides feedback on the student's answer.

PILOT is much more limited in scope than Logo or BASIC, but it is stronger in the area of writing lessons. PILOT is designed to do one task well—the interactive presentation of materials that a teacher would like to create. Interestingly enough, it can be argued that this very strength is also PILOT's real weakness! That is, some educators (ourselves included) feel that the computer materials developed using the PILOT language do not exploit properly the capability of the computer to present to students interesting and dynamic presentations—such as those that can be produced by professional programmers using a more versatile computer language.

TABLE 11.6 A Sample PILOT Program

T:	What is the capital of California? "T" is shorthand for the command to type. The sentence will appear on the screen for the student to read.
A:	(blank line) "A" is shorthand for the command to accept anything typed on the keyboard, until the time the student hits the return key.
M:	Sacramento "M" is shorthand for the command to match the student's answer with the teacher's correct answer.
TY:	Your answer is correct. "TY" is shorthand for TYPE if YES, that is, type the positive feedback when the student's answer is correct.
TN:	The correct answer is Sacramento. "TN" is shorthand for TYPE if NO, that is, the feedback that is provided if the student's answer does not match the teacher's answer.

(The program continues in this vein.)

One way a teacher can overcome many of the PILOT limitations is to move to a higher level language to produce instructional materials—the *authoring system*.

Authoring System

There are authoring systems that have the same end goal as the PILOT programming language—the development of a teaching program. The main differences between an authoring language and authoring system relate to the way commands are issued to the computer.

To produce an authoring system, a company develops a computer program that creates a "shell" around the operation of the computer. This shell serves as a bridge for the teacher between the English language and the capabilities provided by the actual computer language used to write the program that, though powerful and versatile, would be quite difficult to learn compared to the languages we have been describing.

An authoring system presents to the teacher English statements and menus from which the teacher may choose programming actions. For example, Figure 11.3 shows a menu of an authoring system. The teacher using the system needs to simply select the action desired for a given lesson.

As one makes a choice from the authoring system menu, one is led to another menu, and told in simple English how to proceed. In this manner, a teacher works through the development of the lesson and does not need to be

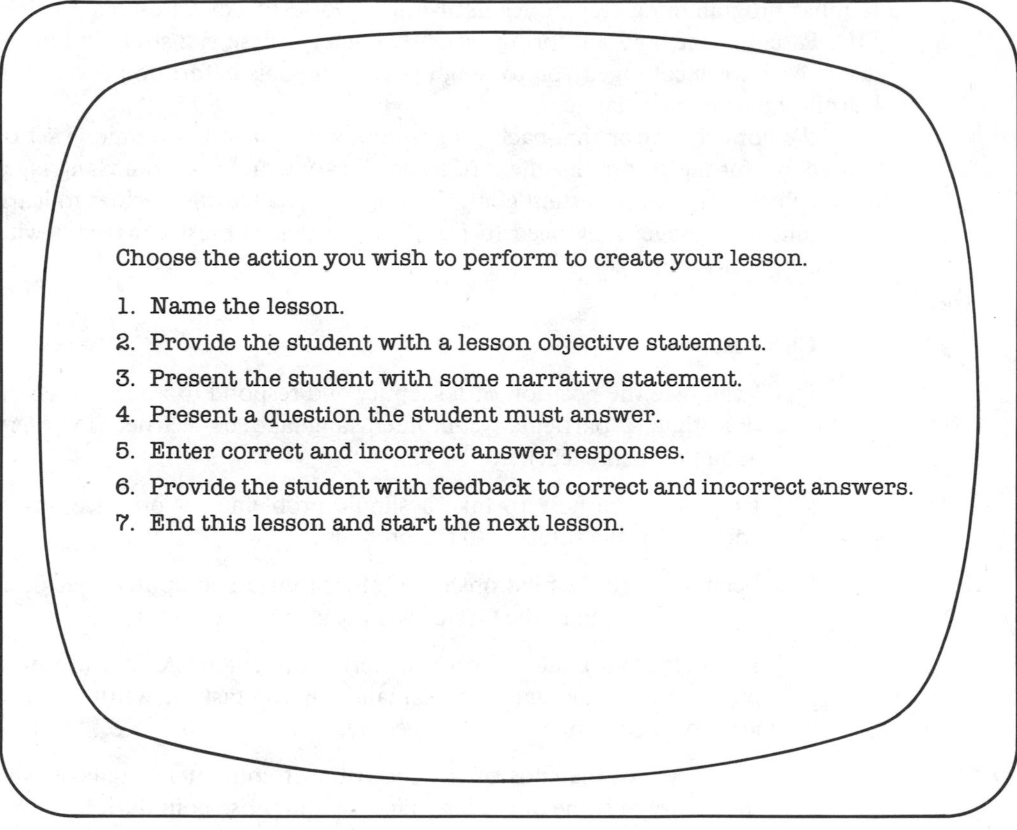

FIGURE 11.3 Authoring System Menu

concerned with exactly how to arrange the commands from the computer language to produce the lesson.

Many different authoring systems are available on the commercial market, some of which are very simple and even more limited than available versions of PILOT. Some are quite sophisticated, however, and provide for laser disk graphics and interactive instruction with spoken English responses. For any given classroom application, teachers will have to match their abilities and needs with the sophistication of the authoring systems available.

SUMMARY AND REVIEW CHECKLIST

This chapter has provided you with a conceptual foundation for programming languages and has offered just a brief acquaintance with some of the more familiar programming techniques used in the world of education: Logo, BASIC, Pascal, Pilot, and authoring systems. Each of these is a study in and of itself. We have encouraged you to weigh your own goals before you commit to learning any computer language.

We hope it is clear that each programming language has a unique set of procedures for the accomplishment of a specific goal, and that some languages are much more suited to certain goals than others. If a teacher decides to learn a computer language, they need to find the one that is most congruent with their own professional goals.

Checklist

[ ] I can take the position of a skeptic, and respond to a recommendation that a particular computer language be learned by every computer-using teacher.

[ ] I can describe how to take a simple problem and produce an algorithm for the solution to the problem.

[ ] I can describe the relationship of algorithms to computer-style decision making and to the task of writing a computer program.

[ ] I can state an analogy to characterize the challenge of learning a programming language and explain why the task of writing a program does not appeal to some people.

[ ] I can explain the ends of the spectrum of computer languages and the nature of some of the languages within those boundaries.

[ ] I can name three programming languages that have found a place in school curricula and describe their general applications.

[ ] I can speak to the issue of teaching Logo in schools, describing varied positions on its usefulness and its "proper" use.

[ ] I can compare and contrast the use of a computer language like PILOT and an authoring system to prepare a computer lesson.

SUGGESTED ACTIVITIES

1. Invent a brief algorithm for these simple everyday tasks: (1) getting out of bed, (2) feeding a pet, (3) cleaning out a fishbowl.

For the following activities you will need a computer and a program to allow you to use each of the following languages.

2. Use a simple elementary Logo exercise book to try some of the simpler procedures, such as making the Turtle move and making a box or a triangle.

3. Use a simple exercise book to try some of the simpler procedures of BASIC, such as printing on the screen.

4. Using a teacher's guide to PILOT, try developing a simple interactive computer learning program.

5. Secure from a publisher an examination version of an authoring system and follow the directions to review its features.

WORTH A LOOK: SOFTWARE

Algernon: An Introduction to Programming Logic. Sunburst: Apple II family, Commodore, and IBM/MS-DOS computers. By "programming" a mouse to find the way through mazes to cheese, children from grades 3 up get a feel for directing a computer. Useful as pre-Logo activity.

Discover Basic: Problem Solving. Collamore Educational Publishing; Apple II family computers. Provides an introductory course in BASIC programming and problem-solving thinking skills.

EZ Logo. MECC; Apple II family computers. A simple Logo version having a set of one-letter commands.

Turtle Tracks. Scholastic; Apple II family, Commodore, Atari, IBM/MS-DOS computers. Simple keyboard commands create colored shapes and music.

LogoWriter (see Chapter 5 software). A programmable word processor/graphics program that enables students to mix turtle graphics with text in the same document.

LEGO TC Logo. LEGO Systems; Apple II family and IBM/MS-DOS computers. Students from grades 4 and up can use Logo language to send signals to models and machines they have constructed out of LEGO bricks.

Turbo Pascal. Borland; Apple II family and IBM/MS-DOS computers. An inexpensive Pascal implementation that executes very rapidly.

Apple Super Pilot. Apple Computer, Inc.; Apple II family computers. Provides a programming language that lets teachers create and store text material, graphics, and music and construct student lessons.

Dan Bricklin's Demo II Program. Software Garden; IBM/MS-DOS computers. A professional programming tool for producing protypes, demonstrations, tutorials, and creating slides from scratch.

READINGS

Burger, M. L. "Authoring Languages/Systems Comparisons." *AEDS Journal* 19(2–3):190–209 (Winter-Spring 1986).

Collis, B., and Gore, M. "The Collaborative Model for Instructional Software Development." *Educational Technology* 27(2):40–44 (February 1987).

Flake, J. L., McClintock, C. E., et al. *Classroom Activities for Computer Education*. Belmont, CA: Wadsworth Publishing Company, 1986.

Nicholson, R. I., and Scott, P. J. "Computers and Education: The Software Production Problem." *British Journal of Educational Technology* 17(1):26–35 (January 1986).

Patterson, A. C., and Bloch, B. "Formative Evaluation: A Process Required in Computer-Assisted Instruction." *Educational Technology* 27(1):26–30 (November 1987).

Pea, R. D., and Sheingold, K. (eds). *Mirrors of Minds: Patterns of Experience in Educational Computing.* Norwood, NJ: Ablex Publishing, Corporation, 1987.

Sullivan, D. R., Lewis, T. G., and Cook, C. R. *Computing Today: Microcomputer Concepts and Applications*. Boston: Houghton Mifflin Co., 1985.

REFERENCES

Bork, A. M. *Learning with Personal Computers.* New York: Harper & Row, 1987.

Braswell, J. S. "Advanced Placement Computer Science." *The Mathematics Teacher* 77(5):372–79 (May 1984).

Feurzeig, W., Horwitz, P., and Nickerson, R. S. *Microcomputers in Education* (Report #4798). Prepared for: Department of Health, Education, and Welfare, National Institute of Education; and Ministry for the Development of Human Intelligence, Republic of Venezuela, Cambridge, MA: Bolt Beranek & Newman, October, 1981.

Maddux, C. D., ed. *Logo in the Schools.* New York: The Haworth Press, Inc., 1985.

Papert, S. *Mindstorms: Children, Computers and Powerful Ideas.* New York: Basic Books, 1980.

Pea, R. D., and Kurland, D. M. "On the Cognitive Effects of Learning Computer Programming." *Mirrors of Minds: Patterns of Experience in Educational Computing.* Norwood, NJ: Ablex Publishing Corporation, 1987.

12

Looking Ahead to a Microcomputer-Centered Classroom

OBJECTIVES

- Describe some reservations about how microcomputing technology is used in schools today.
- Describe the "personality" of today's microcomputer as perceived by users (teachers and students).
- State how capabilities of low-cost microcomputers are expected to evolve in the near future.
- Based on current developments, predict how teachers will be using computers five years from now.
- Describe how differences in students' interests, rates of learning, and academic achievement are handled in traditional classrooms and explain factors operating against further individualization of school instruction.
- Describe the phenomenon of artificial intelligence using current examples of today's research.
- Contrast the traditional classroom with an imaginary classroom in which microcomputers perform most tasks outlined in this text at optimal level.
- Describe how a school would be changed if such a

microcomputer-centered approach were generalized across a curriculum, and teachers got some help in implementing it from "intelligent" computers.

INTRODUCTION

Let us look ahead to the future of computer use in the classroom. Past history and present use provide a useful perspective from which to view the future. To better deal with the potentials and likely realities, we plan to do some recapping of the past and present.

In *A Christmas Carol* by Charles Dickens, Ebenezer Scrooge is visited by various ghosts of Christmas and is shown the past, present, and future. We will rearrange Dickens a bit. First we will ask the Ghost of Computers Present to summarize the current situation. The focus of our questions to this ghost will be on state-of-the-art technology and the current trends of technological development as they pertain to the teachers of today. Having heard this perspective, we will turn to the Ghost of Computers Future. We'll ask for a description of some of the exciting cutting-edge work being done that could have an impact on the future of education. Then, after meeting with the Ghost of Computers Past, we will give the Ghost of Computers Future the last word.

Goals

- What is the potential of effective microcomputer use for teacher role and pedagogy, for student learning experiences, and for the nature of the classroom environment?
- What are the current trends in the development of microcomputer technology and the projections for the future?
- What value to students might be occasioned by a microcomputer-centered classroom?

THE GHOST OF COMPUTERS PRESENT

We will only have one visit with this ghost, so we want to make the most of it. Our goal is to pick up from the present whatever clues we can about what the future may hold for computers in education. We want to ask the right questions! After some thinking, we have decided that what we need the most is an overview of current general trends in computer technology.

How Current Technology Is Evolving

Question to the Ghost of Computers Present: What are the evolutionary pathways by which microcomputers today are improving, and what is realistically available today for use by the teachers in their classrooms?

Response of the Ghost of Computers Present: Computers are (and have been) evolving down some pretty clear pathways. Some of these are of interest to the teacher and others are not. Let me try to summarize them.

The speed at which computers work is of great interest to the computer industry, which is always trying to get the CPU to work faster and more efficiently. Computer evolution is definitely toward faster machines. However, this is of little or no consequence to teachers. Many classroom programs don't require a fast computer to be effective, since other variables than CPU speed usually tend to be the limiting factors with classroom software.

A more important trend for educators is that computers of all kinds are getting cheaper. A tremendous consumer demand, coupled with improved manufacturing techniques and a competitive market, has established a clear and present reality of more and more power for less expense.

A third evolutionary pathway you should be aware of relates to the improvement of the storage of information. While the typical school computer still uses a floppy disk to store programs and data, the typical business computer uses an internal hard disk. Costs on hard disks have dropped precipitously and now are regarded in the business world as a standard computer feature.

The hard disk feature is one of real importance to teachers. It could mean the end to student use of floppy disks. If a teacher or a student wanted a program, it could be obtained from a hard disk inside the computer (which can store all the programs a class would be likely to use or produce). Along that same pathway (information storage), the CD-ROM offers great possibilities for classroom instruction.

A fourth evolutionary pathway is the integration of the computer with video images via a laser disk player. The capacity to recall selectively and view thousands of still and motion pictures is ready to serve teachers right now.

A fifth trend is producing networks of computers, rather than standalone configurations (see Figure 12.1). When computer technology was used first in education, a computer was a centralized machine having many terminals linking the one computer to the many users. The development of the personal computer really made a change. Users appreciated the freedom from a centralized machine and the necessity of sharing it with hundreds of other users. Today, even more options exist, now that computer networking has arrived on the scene.

Some school systems are moving to incorporate a network pattern, typically one central personal computer (ownership by the teacher) linked to simpler and less expensive personal student computers. The central computer has greater computing power and more features. Prominent among them is a hard

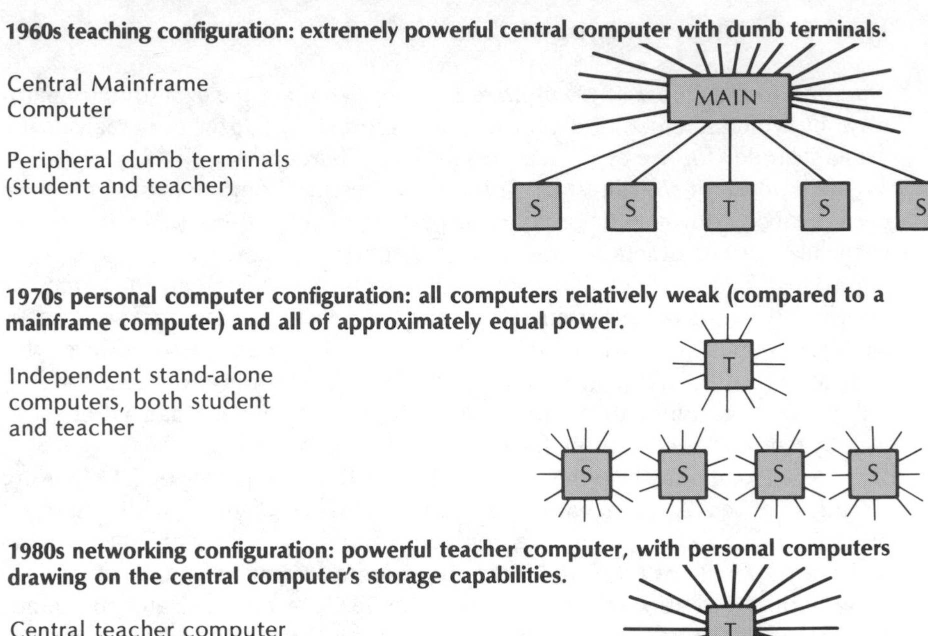

FIGURE 12.1 Computer Configurations in the 60s, 70s, and 80s

disk holding all the instructional programs and CMI information storage. Student computers tap the information from the central teacher computer, and then operate independently at the student station. For most intents and purposes, the student computers act as if they were totally independent of the central computer (the central computer is "transparent" to the students).

Advances in networking are leading to more extensive intercommunication among different brands of computers. For example, it has become possible for Apple computers to run IBM programs and vice versa. The trick is to install appropriate "cards" (circuit boards). And now there are computers that can run many different brands of software.

In another sense, the evolutionary pathway producing networks has implications of a broader nature. By using telecommunication between computers in different locations, one classroom can be networked with other classrooms, other schools, some state level repository of information, national data bases, and even foreign countries. When teachers decide to use this, the classroom computer will be a link to the world at large.

A sixth major evolutionary trend is in the area of the storage and utilization of graphic images and related aspects of desktop publishing. Facsimile machines, which allow a computer to import almost any type of picture or graphic image, have become everyday tools. ("Fax" service is now routinely available at nearby quick-copy shops.) Being able to receive and *publish* images right in the classroom is a present-day reality.

The seventh major trend is in the development of consumer software. The days of simple programs prepared by users for their own use in a classroom or business have passed. This function has been replaced by large companies dedicating resources to the development of effective and highly useful software. The result is more sophisticated but easy-to-use programs.

In the business world commercial companies forge ahead with innovative software packages. If the software allows people in business to do a job more effectively, it will be purchased and will be financially worth the development effort. A parallel course does not seem to be happening in the world of education, however, and can be explained.

To a large extent commercial publishers seem to be giving teachers and schools what they want in order to do business as usual, rather than providing innovative programs that do classroom tasks more efficiently, albeit perhaps quite differently than before. While some computers have made innovative changes in the way programs run (e.g., the Apple Macintosh), these machines cost more than schools are normally willing to pay. (See Table 12.1.)

TABLE 12.1 Present Computer Realities and Trends

Trend	*Relationship to Schools*
Faster computers	valuable in some programs (e.g. spreadsheets) and of less value in tutorials and drills
Lower cost	important aspect, although costs are still much larger for technology than the average school system is used to providing to teachers
Storage of data	important to teachers; such an improvement as a low-cost hard disk means the end to piles of floppy disks and to worries about how students are using them
Video integration	high potential for interactive video, but demand has not arisen to create a large body of software using the technology effectively
Networks	moving into some schools; the technology has the capability of lowering the cost of multiple machines, but software complexity continues to be a problem
Graphics	great potential for exploitation of the capability of duplicating, storing, manipulating, and sending pictures, charts, and so forth
Software	a critical area; the development of more user-friendly operating systems and software with useful features has been a welcome sign, although too few school computers can run the state-of-the-art programs

What Is Realistically Available at Present?

Though satisfied with our ghost's elucidation of general trends, we remain uncertain about just what specific technological features mentioned are presently available for purchase on the market. Our ghost touched on this aspect of our initial question, but let's try to nail him down with a further query.

Follow-up Question to Ghost of Computers Present: Of the items you have been describing to us, which could actually be obtained by schools, if or when the schools were to need them?

Our Ghost replies: Don't get me wrong. The trends I discussed in the last section are not flights of technological fancy. They represent the evolution trends of off-the-shelf products that can be purchased and put to use in classrooms.

As with the trends in software development, schools need to indicate clearly they really want to tap into the existing technology, or development will not proceed in their direction. Still, what I've described is not at all pie-in-the-sky. I'm not the "futures" ghost; my domain is the present. I can state firmly that, from a technological standpoint, everything I've been describing is well within immediate grasp, if schools were to but reach out to purchase it. For example, a very fast computer with a color monitor, hard disk, videodisc networking devices, you name it—all these items are available in the catalogs, and at a price far below the costs of five years ago (with user-friendly programs to make good use of them). If a school system were to seriously embrace such technology, I perceive its schools could be quite changed by it.

What If Current Technology Were Optimally Used?

Last Query to Ghost of Computers Present: If schools were really to put the computing technology that is available to good use, as you stated, what might classrooms be like?

The Ghost answers: I'll tell you straight out what I think. In many areas of schooling, teachers would be teaching less, and computers would be teaching more. The teacher would take on more learning management tasks and the computer would take on more direct instructional tasks. Learning would be more individualized and students would be working on their specific learning needs (e.g., mastering English as a second language) rather than on problems common to the whole class. There would be diagnosis of skills, knowledge, and attitudes, and clustering of students when they shared common learning needs rather than because there is just one teacher in charge.

Classes would be more directed toward problem solving and creative thinking, and less toward memorization of facts and drill and practice. Computer, together with videodiscs, CD-ROM, and data base programs, would be used to teach students how to organize and find great amounts of information, rather than memorize a small body of information.

Many school tasks, such as attendance, grade reporting and record keeping, and test generation would be done via cooperative teacher efforts, rather than being done by individual teachers in self-contained classrooms. Time spent in central whole-class "everyone-does-the-same-task-for-the-same-length-of-time" patterns would be drastically diminished. I'd see major organizational change so as to bring the available technology into the forefront and into a position where its contribution could be felt.

Where Education Stands with Present Technology

(Aha! When the Ghost of Computers Present starts reorganizing all of schooling just to show what technology might do, then he has departed from today's realities. If he even dreams of such an overhaul, he is hallucinating. We need to let him know that, though his ideas may seem feasible from a technological perspective, what he says is pie-in-the-sky from the other angle. He may see computers-present, but not schools-present.)

Mr. Ghost, we appreciate your thoughts, but from an educational point of view, we see some real world problems that work against your visions. Al-

If schools were to put to really good use the computing technology that is already available, what might classrooms be like?

though the technology of today is powerful and available, there are some serious factors limiting its use in schools, let alone leading to such changes as you have mentioned, which tread into areas of pedagogy and even philosophy that would touch many a raw nerve in the world of education. May we share with you a few notions of what tends to work against schools seriously embracing available computer technology?

He's interested.

The majority of school systems are not used to paying for expensive technology. The bulk of the average school budget is devoted to paying for administrators and teachers, and all too often little is left over for books and basics, let alone expensive technology. But even if resources were abundant, we'd be skeptical.

The "personality" of computers is not always viewed as pleasant. Computers have been perceived by the public as rather aversive creatures, the ones that send bills and then will not respond when queried on problems about the bill. Perhaps the public has come to understand that computers don't make the problems, but that the people who manage the computers do. This helps the computer's image to an appreciable degree, yet people aren't very comfortable with the idea of machines playing such a major direct role in the process of educating young people. Errors in this domain, regardless of how they come about, are more serious and longer lasting than billing errors.

All technology has image problems. It seems easier for people to label a problem as a technology problem rather than a people problem, and the technology is blamed. For example, when cities suffer air pollution, they point to too many cars rather than the fact that there are too many people driving, or just too many people, period. It's hard to imagine that your technology-centered school would be given much of a chance to prove itself because whatever problems might arise would be likely to be attributed to the technology itself. Sick days of the teachers might be taken in stride, but there would need to be lots of backups for any hardware failures.

We think a big factor working against modern computer technology is that it still is not simple (although it could and should be), and it takes time to learn how to use a computer, or a videodisc. Software programs of any complexity may take many hours to learn. Teachers generally don't have the luxury of time to learn difficult programs.

Perhaps a visit with the Ghost of Computers Future will give us some ideas about where the present technological trends will lead. It is possible that we are too limited in our own views of what computer technology is currently like to see it becoming as central to schools as your vision.

THE GHOST OF COMPUTERS FUTURE

Question to Ghost of Computers Future: What do you see on the horizon with respect to dramatic technological advances that might entice schools of the future toward substantive use of computers?

The Ghost answers: I see a day not too far in the future in which computers will become much faster and more powerful than they are today. They will integrate video fully. They will have essentially infinite information storage. What will make them even more appealing to educators is that they will be much more user-friendly and be directable via normal English (or other language) commands. Compared to computers today, they will be extremely communicative with one another, and vastly less expensive per unit of computer power.

So what else is new, you say? Let me tell you.

Artificial Intelligence (AI)

The pathway to the future having the most promise lies in the domain of artificial intelligence. Some research labs are teaching computers to think.

Do you doubt a computer can think? Consider this: If a computer is developed that acts like a human acts, shouldn't we credit it with equal thinking status? The British mathematician and philosopher, Alan Turing, proposed in 1950 a test to answer the questions, "Can a computer think?"

In "Turing's Test" a person is put in a room with two identical computer terminals. The subject is told that one of the terminals is connected to a computer and the other has a human at the other end. The person is to use the terminal, ask questions, analyze responses, and decide which is connected to the computer and which to another human. If the person cannot decide, or decides wrong, then the computer is communicating with as much capability as the human, and both should be labeled as thinking.

If you can't accept Turing's Test, mentally play with this little scenario. A spaceship arrives from outer space and lands near the White House in Washington, D.C. Upon inspection it is found to be sealed, but it has a port with directions on how to plug a terminal in to communicate with those inside. Communication is established and, over the next few months, we learn much new information about the universe that we didn't know before. We seem to be communicating with thinking beings. Or, are we just learning from a thinking computer? Does it matter?

Artificial intelligence research has several aspects. First, hardware is being developed to operate in new and different modes than our present computers. Our computers have a single CPU that processes a linear set of commands, one at a time in single file. A new line of computers is being developed with multiple CPUs, which all process information simultaneously in a parallel and nonlinear fashion. Each CPU can and does communicate with every other CPU simultaneously, and the action of one CPU is under the control of the others at the same time it is controlling all the other CPUs. This arrangement does not mean that this type of computer processes faster. It means it processes differently, more on the order of how the human brain processes information. This type of computer is on the market already for a few special applications.

Other research labs are working on the software aspects of developing artificial intelligence. The development of "expert programs" that mimic the actions of a human in problem solving are a reality. For example, there is a medical program used for the diagnosis of a specific class of blood diseases that is better at diagnosing than the average practicing doctor. That is, if you had a blood problem of the type at which this program is expert, you would be better off taking your problem to the computer than to your general practitioner. If this is so, which one is the better diagnostician, the computer or the GP?

Still other research labs are attempting to duplicate problem-solving thinking, and are teaching the computer how to program other computers. A computer is given a problem, it works out a solution, and then it writes the software to program another computer to solve the problem routinely.

In the area of problem solving, computers have already surpassed humans in the playing of chess, being able to beat all but the world masters. Because computers are being programmed to learn from their playing experiences (as contrasted to providing them with an algorithm to apply to every circumstance), the computers are getting smarter and smarter and will soon surpass all human chess players.

Educational Implications for AI

Follow-up Question to Ghost of Computers Future: What will children of the future find their schools to be like if we can bring into the educational process all the AI capabilities you foresee?

Response of the Ghost of Computers Future: Since you let me speak hypothetically with respect to what might be, I'll play the futurist and really put the artificial intelligence aspects of the technology to work.

In the future, I see that computers could take over many or most of the classroom tasks presently done by teachers. For example, I see new students to a school first interacting with a human who welcomes them, and second, interacting with a computer, which would talk to the students, gather their history and interests, do specific diagnostic tests based on the responses to the questions, and then assign appropriate study units. This would be done in the language of the students by simply talking to the computer in a warm, casual, and quite personal atmosphere vastly unlike the computer lab of today.

Much of the teaching of facts and concepts would be assumed by the computer, which would present instruction exactly at the students' level of competence, at the precise rate most conducive to the students' learning, and using the teaching methods that are most effective with each student. Periodic provision of drill and practice would be automatic, so as to make sure students retained appropriate information. All instruction would be via interactive video/computer images in which the students would be able to interact with the images being presented.

The teachers in this school will have stopped doing what teachers presently do, and instead will have new functions. The computer will do what it does best, and the teachers will do what they do best. That is, teaching will become much more humane, with teachers serving more in the role of helping students with personal development, with motivation to accomplish learning, and with thinking, problem solving, and creative endeavors. Routine tasks such as attendance, lesson-planning, testing, and teaching concepts and automating skills will have essentially no place in the teachers' work day.

Students will be interacting more with other students. Small teacher-led groups will be developing topics of study and using the computer as a source of stored information and as a production device for final video-supplemented reports on the groups' endeavors.

(We note that Ebenezer Scrooge feared most the Ghost of the Future, and what it might show, but we must confess a pretty positive feeling about what our own specter of the future has said was in the works in terms of computer technology, and what might come to pass if the technology were ensconced in education fruitfully. We venture a further question of this ghost, because we asked the previous one a bit too hypothetically. Let's be more blunt!)

Just One More Question, Please, Ghost of Computers Future: What is the chance that the new and innovative things you have described and the exciting ways that technology might be employed in the future will actually come to pass?

The Ghost's response is unexpected: Perhaps you have misphrased the question, but I am not really the one to whom you should pose this sort of query. Have you spoken yet with the Ghost of Computers Past? (No.) Well, then, it appears this question belongs more properly in his domain. He is the ghost who can tell you how well schools have, to the extent resources have permitted, made use of the technology already at their disposal. Perhaps from his answer, you can derive the probabilities you seek.

THE GHOST OF COMPUTERS PAST

We are uneasy at being directed to the past. For some strange reason we feel as Scrooge did when he awaited facing the Ghost of the Future. What is it about the proposition of facing the record of the past that is so unsettling? When probing this last ghost, we blurt out our question quickly and await the reply:

Question to Ghost of Computers Past: Looking back, how well would you say schools have made use of the technology that has evolved to date?

The Ghost Replies: Not well at all. The educational enterprise overall has not been enthralled at the idea of letting the microcomputer do those things at which it excels. In fact, a large portion of the educational world has seemed to view those functions an intrusive agent into the existing classroom patterns. Unlike the business world, where microcomputers were welcomed with open arms and put right to work, the machines were channeled to the sidelines of educational enterprise. I dare say they haven't made a dent in mainstream education.

Is it just a difference in finances? I don't think so. Teachers, in general, simply decided that they did not need a computer to do the things that they were doing, and they did not change the things they were doing to accommodate a machine. Perhaps I'm being too negative here, but it seems to me that American school systems have been especially adept at making sure that new and potentially subversive ideas have been submerged into the traditional pattern, thus rendering them harmless.

Follow-up Query to Ghost of Computers Past: We note your pessimism, but those things may not be true. What technological innovations were realistically available to teachers of the past that were not put into use in the classroom?

The Ghost summarizes: The technology of one computer with two disk drives and a color monitor attached to one printer was a powerful technology that could have made explosive changes in the classrooms of schools, but it did not. Instead, in selected classrooms the computer was fitted into already existing practices and modes of operation that were modified little, if at all. To have allowed the computer to do what it was quite capable of doing would have necessitated a different teaching style. Though computers arrived in the classroom, the classroom stayed basically the same.

There were several areas in which inexpensive computers and relatively good software went essentially unused. For example, computers are very good at computer-managed instruction, in which goals and objectives are assigned to students, instruction is provided either via computer or off-line, and the computer is used to test and manage assignments based on past performance. These programs were rarely employed because they demand a major change in the way classroom instruction is handled.

Drill and practice programs fell into disrepute due to the manner in which they were applied, that is, without due regard for a management plan that dictated exactly who needed to automate specific skills and when they should be reinforced. Drill became a time filler with little or no directed purpose.

After the advent of the word processor, experts all over the country assumed that the computer would explode in classrooms, due to the prominence there of the written word, but no real revolution occurred.

Research clearly demonstrated that computers could outperform teachers when compared on the same units of instruction (tutorials and drill and practice). But teachers did not rely on what their fellow researchers discovered and so did not employ computers in these roles.

To be fair, resource provisions have been slim. Teachers have been disappointed by underfunding. Even books were scarce in many portions of the country, so computers and expensive software were not a possibility at all. Much disappointment has surrounded the use of computers in schools.

I know your interest is in the future, and I shouldn't tread from my domain but I can't help offering my opinion. Based on what I see in the past, I am skeptical about the emergence of the computer to a role of prominence in schools in the near or even distant future. Perhaps you should return to speak with the Ghost of Computers Future, though. She has high hopes, and is much less a pessimist on this particular topic than I.

A NEW DAY?

We have called back the Ghost of Computers Future to answer one last question. We report the pessimistic picture of the previous ghost about the chance that computer technology will really become integral to the educational process.

Ghost of Computers Future, Our Last Question: Does the past dictate to us what will be, or can we change?

The specter replies: Schools will continue as in the past, with computers in a peripheral role, unless it is acknowledged that the present structure of schools is not the ideal or final one, and that change needs to occur in the basic pattern of school operations. If the future of computer technology is to get any brighter, you educators must look more seriously toward change in yourselves.

A computer's strength lies in its capability of producing, storing, and manipulating information. In order to tap this power, schools will need to direct their curriculum toward teaching students to be users of information, rather than being recipients of information. Were this more of a real goal for the school, the computer's role would be clearer.

And so would your own charge.

As you look to the future, perhaps the question is not so much one of how you are to make use of computers to help your students learn. Rather it is one of how you are to change your own ways to tap the computer's powers to do so. Perhaps readers of this book can respond to that challenge.

SUMMARY AND REVIEW CHECKLIST

The computer did not create a revolution in schools. The computer is not creating a revolution in schools. The computer may or may not create a revolution there in the future. Only teachers and administrators could do so, or will do so, and as yet, they have not.

Perhaps you, as the computer-using teacher of the future, will prove the skeptics wrong. It is clear that technology enters the classroom in significant ways when teachers (and administrators) decide that they need it to accomplish their job. One of the major goals of this book has been to show you how the curriculum can be served by the computer, and to inexorably link the two. Your challenge is to continue to ask two questions:

How can I accomplish the goals and objectives of our curriculum more effectively by employing a computer rather than using traditional teaching methods?

Given the emerging powers of the computer, what aspects of my teaching might I change in order to take fuller advantage of these capabilities?

Checklist

[ ] I can state some of the important limitations of how microcomputers are being used in schools today.

[ ] I can describe the "personality" of today's microcomputer as perceived by users (teachers and students).

[ ] I can describe how the capabilities of low-cost microcomputers are expected to evolve in the near future.

[ ] I can make my own prediction on how teachers five years from now will be using computers, based on current developments.

[ ] I can describe how differences in students' interests, rates of learning, and academic achievement are handled in traditional classrooms and explain factors operating against further individualization of school instruction.

[ ] I can contrast the traditional classroom with an imaginary classroom in which microcomputers perform most tasks outlined in this text at optimal level.

[ ] I can describe the phenomenon of artificial intelligence using a current example of today's research.

SUGGESTED ACTIVITIES

1. Describe in a brief scenario what the school of the future would look like if computers had the complete power to test, store records, and prescribe what the teachers should teach next.
2. Describe in a brief scenario what the school of the future would look like if computers had the complete power to test, store records, and prescribe what the teachers should teach next, and could do *all* drill and practice work (including seatwork now done using work sheets).
3. Describe in a brief scenario what the school of the future would look like if computers had the complete power to test, store records, and prescribe what each student should learn next, and could do *all* drill and practice

work (including seatwork now done using work sheets), and could do all routine teaching of facts and concepts (such as those in math, language arts, and social studies).

4. Describe in a brief scenario what the school of the future would look like if computers had the complete power to test, store records, and prescribe what each student should learn next, and could do *all* drill and practice work (including seatwork now done using work sheets), and could do all routine teaching of facts and concepts (such as those in math, language arts, and social studies), and could be accomplished by a student working at home (who would come to school for teacher-led sessions when assigned by the computer).

5. Consider the scenario you construct in Activity 1. How is the scenario different if computers fully incorporate artificial intelligence with the stated capabilities? (Note: If you already presumed AI in your scenario, consider the effects of subtracting it.)

6. Think about the scenario requested in Activity 4. How does it differ based on the presence (or absence) of extensive AI integration into teacher and student decision making?

7. Think about "Turing's Test" (page 315). Do you accept it as a valid way of deciding whether or not computers think? If not, decide what set of criteria would need to be applied before you would admit that a computer can think. (For example, would it be sufficient if the computer could talk directly to you in English and argue its case, making as good an argument as you present in countering it?)

8. If you have decided in Activity 5 that there is no set of criteria sufficient to make you say a computer can think, look at the following page, and decide why humans have taken the pathway shown in Table 12.2.

WORTH A LOOK: MICROCOMPUTER ZEITGEIST, 1989

Turbo Prolog, from Borland International, Inc. Turbo Prolog is a programming language using natural language. It is a fine introduction to the brave new world of artificial intelligence, and teaches you many things about this fascinating new man/machine relationship. Includes *GeoBase*, a natural language data base of geographic information.

HyperCard for the Macintosh computer, from Apple Computer Corporation. Hypercard is a data management tool and a programming environment. It lets one put information in stacks of index cards and then link elements of the data in incredibly varied and complex ways. Look for an assortment of programs designed to work with HyperCard.

CD-ROM for all types of computers. This medium includes *Bookshelf* by Mi-

TABLE 12.2 The Changing Criteria for Machine Thinking

Does a Machine Think?	
The left-hand column contains the criteria people have used in the past for the concept of "thinking." That is, *before the fact*, it was stated a machine could think if it could accomplish these criteria.	The "X" in the right-hand column indicates that the criterion was discarded *after* the computer was able to accomplish it. More stringent criteria were then applied.
Machine can add and subtract.	X
Machine can divide and multiply.	X
Machine can do logic, such as use "if. . . .then" statements.	X
Machine can combine logic and math to solve problems.	X
Machine can play chess.	X
Machine can play chess better than humans.	X
Machine can play chess better than most humans.	X
Machine can play chess better than all humans.	
Machine can talk (use natural language).	X
Machine can talk as well as average person.	
Machine can talk better than an average person.	
Machine can pass Turing's Test	

croSoft, *GEOdisk* from Geovisions, *Books in Print* from Bowker Electronic Publishing, *Apple Learning Disk* from Apple, and *Public Domain Software on File* by Apple.

Speech-based Software for many types of computers, including *Chatterbox* by Chatterbox Voice Learning Systems, LM Software for Basic Reading Instruction, *My Words* by MECC, *Talking Text Writer* by Scholastic Inc., and *Dr. Peet's Talk/Writer* by Hartley Courseware, Inc.

Eliza, public domain software that mimics a nondirective counselor. This primitive but historic program is an item of artificial intelligence software that could be used to initiate classroom discussions of what it means to "think." Interacting with Eliza can be insightful as well as lots of fun!

A.I.—An Experience with Artificial Intelligence. Scholastic; Apple II family and IBM/MS-DOS computers. Program introduces students from grade 6 to the "thought process" that computers use to develop decision-making capabilities. Students create games and watch as computer "learns" the rules.

Science Helper K–8, Version 2.0. PV-SIG, Inc. CD-ROM collection of nearly 1,000 teacher-prepared lesson plans in the areas of K–8 math and science. A complete retrieval system is built in.

AppleTalk Network, and numerous other networks. Networks link various types of computers and peripherals, and information and programs can be exchanged between machines. Companies that produce such networks include (but are not limited to) Apple Computer, Inc., which distributes the AppleTalk Network for its machines.

Scenario (Tools for the Mind). Techbyte, Inc. for IBM/MS-DOS computers. A complete set of tools to create powerful interactive software *with spoken text*, graphics, music, answer analysis, and interactive video capabilities.

First National Item Bank & Test Development System. TesCor, Inc. CD-ROM of test questions for elementary and secondary grade levels.

The Electronic Encyclopedia. CD-ROM by Grolier Electronic Publishing, having the entire *Academic American Encyclopedia* available for search and retrieval of information.

LaserDisk Players with Computer Control. Investigate the many types of laserdisk players that can be controlled with a microcomputer.

Portable and LapTop Computers. Having a small computer that can be taken to and from school presents many avenues of additional use.

Computer Projection Monitor. The many types of computer screen projectors that allow you to show a whole class what is on a computer monitor are certainly worth looking into.

Fax boards. Your computer may be able to send complete documents, such as tests, reports, and newsletters, to and from various schools in a district.

Scanner. With a scanner attached to a computer one can capture any image into a computer file. You might use this to create computer "transparencies," to capture student drawings for incorporation into a class newsletter, or to capture historic documents and pictures for use with a computer projection monitor.

READINGS

Bossone, R. M., and Polishook, I. H., eds. *New Frontiers in Educational Technology: Trends and Issues.* Proceedings of the Conference of the University/Urban Schools National Task Force, November, 1986 (ERIC Document #281524).

Colvin, L. B. "An Overview of U.S. Trends in Educational Software Design." *The Computing Teacher* 16(5):24–28 (February 1989).

Cook, J. E. "West Virginia Schools to Secure a State-wide Microcomputer Network." *Technological Horizons in Education Journal*, March 1984, 11(6).

Ediger, M. "Computers at the Crossroads." *Educational Technology* 28(5):7–10 (May 1988).

Educational Resources Information Commission. *Current Uses of Artificial Intelligence in Special Education.* Reston, VA: ERIC Clearinghouse on Handicapped and Gifted Children, 1987.

Feigenbaum, E. A., and McCorduck, P. *The Fifth Generation: Artificial Intelligence and Japan's Computer Challenge to the World.* Reading, MA: Addison-Wesley, 1983.

Flaherty, Douglas. *Humanizing the Computer: A Cure for the "Deadly Embrace."* Wadsworth Publishing Company; Belmont, CA, 1986.

Freiberger, P., and Swaine, M. *Fire in the Valley.* Berkeley, CA: Osborne/McGraw-Hill, 1984.

Gardner, D. P. "The Charge of the Byte Brigade: Educators Lead the Fourth Revolution." *Educational Record* 67(1):10–15 (Winter 1986).

Goodlad, J. I. *A Place Called School: Prospects for the Future.* New York: McGraw-Hill, 1984.

Gubser, L. National Task Force on Education Technology. "Transforming American Education: Reducing the Risk to the Nation." *TechTrends* 31(4):10–24 (May-June 1986).

Hawkins, J., and Sheingold, K. *The Beginning of a Story: Computers and the Organization of Learning in Classrooms* (Tech Rep. No. 35). New York: Bank Street College of Education, Center for Children and Technology, 1985.

Hebenstreit, J. *The Use of Informatics in Education: Present Situation, Trends and Perspectives.* Paris: UNESCO, 1986.

Hofmeister, A. M., and Ferrara, J. M. *Expert Systems and Special Education.* Logan, UT: Utah State University, 1984.

Hofstadter, D. *Godel, Escher, Bach.* New York: Vintage Books, 1980.

National Commission on Excellence in Education. *A Nation at Risk: The Imperative for Educational Reform.* Washington, D.C.: U.S. Department of Education, 1983.

National Science Board Commission on Precollege Education in Mathematics, Science, and Technology. *Educating Americans for the 21st Century: A Plan of Action for Improving Mathematics, Science, and Technology Education for All American Elementary and Secondary Students So That Their Achievement Is the Best in the World by 1995.* Washington, D.C.: National Science Foundation, 1983.

Olson, J. K. *Through the Looking Glass: Towards Thicker Description of Teaching.* Paper presented at the Annual Meeting of the American Educational Research Association, 1988 (ERIC Document #292799).

Papert, Seymour. *Mindstorms; Children, Computers, and Powerful Ideas.* New York: Basic Books, 1980.

Reigeluth, C. M. *The Search for Meaningful Reform: A Third-Wave Educational System.* Proceedings of Selected Research Papers presented at the Annual Meeting of the Association for Educational Communications and Technology, January 1988 (ERIC Document #295656).

Roth, G. L., and Tesolowski, D. G. "Technology Curricula and Instruction in the Information Age." *Technology Teacher* 46(1):27–33 (September-October 1986).

Seidel, R. J., Anderson, R. E., and Hunter, B., eds. *Computer Literacy: Issues and Directions for 1985.* New York: Academic Press, 1985.

Swadener, M., and Jarrett, K. "Computer Use in Content Areas in Secondary Schools." *Journal of Computers in Mathematics and Science Teaching* 6(2):12–14 (Winter 1987).

Sybouts, W. "Optical Disc Technology. Videodisc Technology: A National Plan for Its Use in Education." *Technological Horizons in Education* 14(8):47–48 (April 1987).

Taylor, R. P., ed. *The Computer in the School: Tutor, Tool, Tutee.* New York: Teachers College Press, 1981.

Tetenbaum, T. J., and Mulkeen, T. A. "Computers as an Agent for Educational Change." *Computers in the Schools* 2(4):91–103 (Winter 1986).

Waggoner, M. D., and Goldbert, A. L. "A Forecast for Technology and Education: The Report of a Computer Conferencing Delphi." *Educational Technology* 26(6):7–14 (June 1986).

Glossary

algorithm A finite set of steps that compose a well-defined mathematical or logical solution of a problem. Execution of the steps of a given algorithm will consistently result in achievement of defined goals.

application(s) program A computer program written with the needs of a user in mind, rather than being oriented toward computer operations. Increasingly, the term applies to programs that fill a broad category of user needs. Accounting programs, graphics programs, and word processing programs are examples of applications software.

archive copy A legal copy of a commercial program made to be used only in the event that the original fails to work.

arrow key A key that when pressed moves the cursor in a screen direction (left, right, up, down) indicated by an arrow on the keytop. Most keyboards have four such keys, also known as cursor-movement keys or cursor keys.

artificial intelligence (AI) Computer systems that behave in ways that are similar to or mimic the ways that humans think.

ASCII (*A*merican *S*tandard *C*ode for *I*nformation *I*nterchange, pronounced "AS-key") The standard code for communications between computers. Each individual letter, number, or other computer character or keystroke is represented in ASCII as a specific binary number.

assembly language A low-level programming language comprised of codes controlling the most primitive actions of a computer. It is similar in structure to the computer's native language, but it uses mnemonics and alphanumeric labels rather than 1s and 0s.

attitude learning Acquisition of a predisposition to react to certain ideas, situations, persons, or objects in a particular manner. Attitudes are not always consciously held (as are beliefs) or readily verbalized (as are opinions), but they are learned and do translate into human actions.

authoring language A high-level programming language designed for use in writing CAI materials.

authoring system A program that is structured to facilitate the creation of CAI materials. The instructional options available to the author and such other features as presentation format are preset, and the author produces and edits the product by menu selections and responses to prompts.

automatize To produce automaticity, the state at which a behavior can be performed without conscious thinking.

BASIC (*B*eginners' *A*ll-purpose *S*ymbolic *I*nstruction *C*ode) A high-level programming language that is fairly easy to learn and is widely used with microcomputers.

binary A number system whose base is 2 (therefore the only integers are 0 and 1).

bit (*b*inary dig*it*) Smallest unit of information recognized by a computer; represented as 0 or 1.

blocking A highly useful function in word processing that permits a user to mark a portion of a text file for subsequent action upon it. After blocking the text unit (e.g., a phrase or a cluster of paragraphs), the user can then perform an operation (e.g., copy, move, delete) on the entire segment.

boot To start a computer by providing operating system information, usually by inserting a system disk and turning on the computer.

bug A mistake in a computer program.

bulletin board A small information service, typically run by users, that permits electronic exchange of messages (usually across phone lines) and may be used as a forum for users with common interests.

byte A standard unit of computer information, composed of a sequence of binary units (usually eight).

calculation formula A mathematical expression that, when placed in a spreadsheet's cell, is used by the computer to produce a value for the cell.

card A circuit board that can be inserted into a slot (a type of plug) in a computer to add a feature, such as a graphics capability or expanded memory.

CD-ROM (*C*ompact *D*isk *R*ead *O*nly *M*emory) A technology that stores digital information on the surface of a plastic disk optically rather than magnetically. A CD-ROM device uses a laser beam to read the disk of stored information and provide data from it to the computer.

cell An area within a spreadsheet formed by the intersection of a row and a column and identified by their coordinates.

character Any symbol, digit, letter, or special mark that can be processed by a digital computer.

CMI system A type of computer program designed specifically to facilitate instructional management. CMI programs are typically used to test student performance, to provide information for a multitude of teacher decisions and, in many cases, to prescribe segments of study for individual students.

coding Writing instructions for a computer system in a programming language. (See also **programming**.)

cognitive strategies learning Acquisition of thinking patterns and approaches that govern subsequent learning and problem-solving behaviors.

command A signal or group of signals that cause a computer to perform an operation.

computer-assisted instruction (CAI) The use of computers to interact with students in the instructional process. Term also refers to software that is designed to promote student learning (e.g., a tutorial program or an instructional simulation).

computerese Terminology specifically tied to or derived from computers that, when used extensively, tends to limit understanding by persons not versed in the jargon.

computer language See **programming language.**

computer literacy General understanding of computers; an area of study that may or may not be formalized as a curriculum but that typically promotes a general ability to use computers, to understand their social impact, and to know the many ways in which they are used by others.

computer literate The state of having sufficient computer proficiency and knowledge to meet some expected standard.

computer-managed instruction (CMI) The use of computers to aid in managing the instructional sequence, but not necessarily in the instructional process itself. (See also **CMI system.**)

computer science An area of study that concentrates on computing concepts, computer programming, and computer operations.

computer-using teacher Descriptor for any teacher who employs a computer in some capacity as a part of the professional role.

control key A special key on the keyboard, usually labeled [CTRL]. This key, when held down, changes the actions of other character keys.

copy-protect To seek to prevent the copying of a program on a diskette through technical means. Some software manufacturers employ various schemes to make their programs exceedingly difficult to copy, and making a copy of such a program is illegal.

courseware Computer programs written especially for educational applications and usually accompanied by ancillary teaching materials.

CPU (*C*entral *P*rocessing *U*nit) The part of a general purpose computer that controls interpretation and execution of instructions, input, and output; this portion also provides timing signals for control of other units.

cursor An indicator symbol (typically flashing) on the display screen that lets the user know where the next typed character, or other action, will appear.

daisywheel printer A type of impact printer that uses a print wheel made of spokes radiating from its center. The wheel rotates to the appropriate character and strikes the ribbon, producing a high-quality image on the paper. However, this printer cannot do graphics and is slower than other printers.

data Coded information or information in text or numerical form; data are the elements of information that can be processed or produced by a computer.

data bank A collection of data organized for rapid search and retrieval. (See also **data base.**)

data base A logically connected collection of information, usually in a form that can be manipulated by a computer. It is commonly designed and organized in a consistent manner so as to be of value to a wide variety of users.

data base file A collection of related records treated as a unit, such as the collection of checks written in a year or the set of test papers for a class. (See also **file**.)

data base program An application program for setting up, searching, modifying, and maintaining electronic data bases. Programs are also called data base managers or data base management systems (DBMS).

data processing A systematic set of procedures for collecting, manipulating, and disseminating data to achieve specified ends; may be termed information processing.

debugging The process of detecting, locating, and removing mistakes from a computer program.

desktop publishing Using microcomputer software and a printer to lay out and produce pages of text and graphics.

disk A circular piece of material upon which computer information can be stored. (See also **magnetic disk** and **laser disk**.)

disk drive A mechanical device that holds and rotates a computer disk and enables transfer of information back and forth between the computer and the disk.

diskette A small platter-like magnetic disk unit made of vinyl plastic so thin and flexible as to give rise to an alternate name, **floppy disk.** Diskettes are inexpensive and very widely used as storage media for digital information.

display screen A unit for visual display of computer output, usually in a televisionlike or liquid crystal format. Almost every personal computer has some form of visual display unit. (See also **monitor**.)

DOS (*D*isk *O*perating *S*ystem) A computer program written to enable a computer to operate a disk drive and to store information on and retrieve information from a disk.

dot matrix printer A printer that uses pins in a print head to impact on a ribbon. The images it produces are patterns of dots. Relatively inexpensive and versatile (useful for graphics, as well as characters), this type of printer is commonplace in classrooms.

drill Exercise that involves a pattern of intensive practice and that, in CAI, is accompanied by computer feedback on responses. (See also **drill and practice program**.)

drill and practice program A type of CAI software in which the computer engages a learner in a sequence of exercises characterized by response elicitation and evaluation. (See also **drill**; see also **practice**.)

electronic blackboard A mode of computer use, usually for presentations with a class or audience, in which a single computer's display screen is integral to flow of discussion or presentation, as a blackboard often is to a teacher.

electronic grade book A type of teacher utility program for keeping student performance and/or progress records.

expert program (also **expert system**) A type of software that models the performance of human experts in a given field. The program contains both a base of knowledge in the field and procedural rules for making decisions, and it functions to make action recommendations equivalent to or better than those of human experts.

facsimile machine (fax) An electronic device that enables the transfer of printed text and graphic information from one location to another across telephone lines.

feedback Provision of information by an environment on the results of activity. In CAI, most feedback is output that informs students of the adequacy of their responses to the program.

field The part of a record or area of a screen reserved for a meaningful item of data, similar to the space on a form for a first name or the portion of an envelope for a return address.

file A cluster of information, whether consisting of data or program instructions, that is treated as a unit and named for storage. Computer programs and data are stored as files on disks. (See also **data base file.**)

file management system A type of data base program that is used primarily for file sorting and maintenance and for report production.

fixed disk See **hard disk.**

floppy disk See **diskette.**

flow diagram (also **flowchart**) A sketch made up of boxes of various shapes connected by arrows that portrays the structure and logic of a computer program.

formatting The process of arranging for placement of information. Most commonly: (1) placing and designating the appearance of text and graphics on a screen or a printed page, or (2) preparing a blank diskette for information storage.

function A built-in process in a program; in a spreadsheet program, a built-in procedure for accomplishing common mathematical operations, such as summing a row or a column, or finding an average.

function keys Keys on a computer keyboard that are programmed with commands instead of characters and are commonly labelled "F1," "F2," etc. The purpose of a given function key varies according to the program in use, but it typically enables a user to perform a common program function in one keystroke.

garbage Unwanted, meaningless, or unimportant information stored within a computer file. This concept gave rise to the phrase "garbage in, garbage out" (GIGO), which means that computer output is only as good as the program being used or information input.

graphics Visual material such as pictorial images, designs, or graphs displayed on a screen or as hard copy.

graphics pad (also **graphics tablet**) A peripheral input device that translates drawings on its flat surface into computer signals. When a stylus is moved over the boardlike tablet, the image transfers to the computer screen and may be stored.

hacker A person having computer expertise along with an obsession for probing the capabilities of computer systems. Some overenthusiastic hackers test and extend their skills in unacceptable and even illegal ways.

hard copy Computer output on paper or other durable surface (as distinguished from the temporary image presented on a computer's display screen).

hard disk A data storage device that uses a quickly spinning, rigid disk. Hard disks are of higher density than floppy disks and yield much greater storage capacity and faster access time. A **fixed disk,** permanently sealed inside its airtight drive unit at the factory, offers dependability too.

hardware The physical equipment in a computer system. One can touch or pick up computer hardware. (See also **software.**)

inkjet printer A type of printer that sprays tiny dots of liquid or powdered ink onto the surface of paper to create its images.

input Data communicated to the computer, usually by means of an input device such as a keyboard or optical scanner or disk drive.

instructional simulation program A type of CAI software in which computer simulation is incorporated as a major means of achieving the program's teaching intent. (See also **simulation.**)

integrated circuit A microscopic electronic circuit etched on a very tiny silicon chip.

integrated software Two or more application programs (such as a word processor and a spreadsheet) that work together, using a common group of commands whenever feasible and allowing data to move easily between applications.

intellectual skill learning Acquisition of the capability of performing intellectual operations or symbolic activities in a situation, remembering and applying pertinent information as necessary.

joystick A hand-operated input device that translates physical movement of a vertical lever mounted on a base into a computer signal. Joysticks are frequently used with games and graphics software to control the cursor on a display screen.

K (abbreviation for **kilobyte**) A unit of measure of the capacity of a computer's memory or of storage space on a disk (equivalent to 1024 characters).

keyboard A microcomputer input device that transfers information typed by a user to the computer.

keypad A specialized keyboard or portion of a keyboard in which keys are arranged to facilitate input of numerical information.

label Information, usually in the form of words, that labels or names a row or column in a spreadsheet.

laser disk A technology for storing large quantities of information in tracks on a plastic platter from which information can be read by a laser light source. (See also **videodisc.**)

laser printer A type of printer that uses a laser and photocopy principles to produce excellent print quality. The printer is currently acclaimed for its variety in character fonts and the very high quality of the graphics it produces.

learning A change in human disposition or capability that can be retained and that exhibits itself as a change in behavior not ascribable simply to the process of growth.

light pen A penlike input device typically used in conjunction with a specialized monitor. One can touch the pen to the screen to indicate responses rather than using a keyboard.

loading a file The action of placing a program or data into the memory of a computer.

local area network (LAN) A network of microcomputers linked into a system for sharing common information and hardware resources. A LAN typically operates within a limited geographic area and requires special software and a central hard disk.

Logo A powerful, but simple to use, programming language developed for the purpose of teaching young children how to program.

machine language A computer programming language, represented by code in binary digits. Unlike other types of code, machine code is executable directly by the CPU.

macro A single computer command that invokes a previously stored sequence of commands. Macros are typically used in applications programs to "automate" often-used sequences of keystrokes.

magnetic disk A disk having magnetic coating that can store digital information as magnetized spots in a manner somewhat similar to that by which musical information is stored on magnetic recording tape. The self-lubricating properties of the material permit physical contact between a disk drive's recording head and the disk surface.

mainframe Originally, the central processor of a computer system containing main storage as well as arithmetic unit and registers; more commonly now, a full-scale computer system capable of serving multiple peripheral devices and handling the computing needs of a large organization.

mark-sense reader A type of scanning device that reads pencil marks on answer forms.

MB (abbreviation for **megabyte**) A measure of information that is roughly equal to a million characters; called a **meg** in slang usage. Microcomputer users have found this unit to be handy for comparing the storage capacities of hard disks.

memory The portion of a computer where information and programs are stored; internal storage devices that store information and instructions on how the microprocessor is to work. (See also **RAM** and **ROM**.)

memory resident program A computer program that remains in the memory, ready to run or running, and that can be invoked when needed.

menu An on-screen display listing possible user actions.

microcomputer (also **personal computer**) A small, self-contained digital computer based on a microprocessor. Used in homes, schools, and businesses, it is powerful enough to perform many useful tasks and support some peripheral equipment. (See also **mainframe computer**.)

microprocessor An electronic logic device that can process information and make decisions. A programmable integrated circuit component, the microprocessor contains at least the logic of a complete central processing unit on a single chip.

minicomputer A computer offering power between that of a mainframe computer and that of a personal computer.

modem An electronic device that translates computer signals into signals appropriate for transmission via telephone wire or decodes a transmission into signals a computer can use. Two computers, each having a modem, can engage in data communications over telephone lines.

monitor A televisionlike device used to display output information for viewing while the computer is in use.

monochrome Descriptor for a monitor that displays only single-color images against a contrasting background. Monochrome is used primarily for display of text and is less expensive than color. Common colors are green on a black field, amber on black, black on gray, and white on black.

motor skill learning Acquisition of a behavioral pattern or capability involving muscles and movement, such as keyboarding.

mouse A hand-operated input device that translates movement into computer signals that have some meaning (e.g., moving the display cursor). A typical mouse is shaped like a small box and also has buttons that can be clicked to signal the computer (e.g., making a menu choice).

multiple-loading program Any commercial computer program that specifically permits a single purchased copy to simultaneously serve more than one microcomputer, as opposed to carrying the usual legal restriction on use that requires purchase of one program for every computer in use at a time.

network Several computers connected and able to share information with one another. (See also **local area network**.)

network/hierarchical data base management system A highly sophisticated data base program typically accessed via modem and telecommunication for the purpose of information retrieval from commercial providers.

networking Hooking together geographically separated computers over transmission lines, thus allowing them to communicate data and programs to each other.

on-line In direct communication with a computer. Term is commonly applied to describe such diverse circumstances as these: as a user gets connected to a remote data base; while a student takes a test at a keyboard; while a printer can receive output; whenever a user gets help or advice while in the midst of a program.

output Data presented from within the computer memory to the user, usually by way of an output device such as a printer or a screen.

parallel communications Sending information from a computer to a peripheral device, or from one computer to another, one byte (usually eight bits) at a time. The information moves through parallel wires. (See also **series communications.**)

Pascal A high-level programming language developed originally for the purpose of teaching programming concepts but now used for general programming as well.

performance measure An assessment tool or test for ascertaining the adequacy of a performance with respect to some standard performance level.

performance objective A statement of instructional intent that specifies clearly, in terms of behavioral performance, a desired learning outcome.

peripheral A device connected to a computer, typically located outside of the computer's housing and attached by a cable.

PILOT An authoring language employed in education by teachers to develop interactive learning materials.

pop-up program A computer program that can be instantaneously invoked at any time, even when the user is in the midst of another program.

practice Question exercises to test understanding and provide some refinement in knowledge, conceptual understanding, or skill. CAI practice exercises are accompanied by computer feedback on the quality of answers. (See also **drill and practice.**)

printer A peripheral device that makes permanent computer output, either mechanically or with some form of laser, heat, or chemical technology.

probe A peripheral sensing device used for testing or measuring. A probe transmits environmental data from its location to the computer.

problem-solving software A category label applied loosely to CAI programs that cause the students who use them to integrate skills in order to accomplish tasks or find solutions to puzzles.

process To transform data in a purposeful way (e.g., by arranging, classifying, summarizing), usually to make it more useful or meaningful.

program A set of instructions arranged for directing a computer to perform desired operations. The instructions on how to input, process, and move information in the computer must all be coded in a language that the computer can understand.

programming The process of writing a computer program. It involves creating a set of coded instructions to the computer that will cause it to perform a designated task.

programming language Any well-defined language used in preparing instructions for computer execution.

projection panel A device that enables the image that would be on a computer monitor to be projected onto a screen for large group viewing. Most versions work in conjunction with a common overhead projector.

RAM (*R*andom *A*ccess *M*emory) Internal memory, built from silicon chips and used to store data and programs temporarily while they are being processed. (See also **volatile memory**.)

ROM (*R*ead *O*nly *M*emory) A portion of computer hardware where information is stored as circuitry patterns at the time of manufacture. This "hard-wired" internal memory retains its contents irrespective of power supply. Information in ROM can be read but not changed.

record An integral collection of data items that is treated as a single unit, such as a given name and address, stored in a data base having thousands of names and addresses, or the information on a certain species, stored in a biological data base of species.

relational data base management system A type of data base program that has a common base of information accessible for different applications. An update of data in one application revises the data automatically for all others.

resolution A measure of the clarity and sharpness of an image on a display screen.

robotics An area of study dealing with the design, manufacture, capabilities, and uses of robots.

scanner A device that uses light to scan images (text, graphics, marks, bars, or characters) and send the information to a computer in a form it can use in a program. May be referred to as an optical recognition device, optical scanner, or optical character reader (OCR).

screen See **display screen**.

series communications Sending information from a computer to a peripheral device, or from one computer to another, where the information flows as a string of bits in sequence. (See also **parallel communications**.)

shareware Software that, though owned and usually copyrighted, is freely copyable for the purpose of acquisition and initial evaluation. Continued use of the software entails an obligation to pay for it (or pay a use fee).

simulation In software, using the computer to feign a real-world situation in which variables are changed. The computer program mathematically models a process or represents the behavior of a system as the user varies selected conditions. Such programs are of particular value in representing situations that are impractical or difficult to provide in actuality.

site license An arrangement in which an organization pays a set fee for the right to copy and run a program at a specific location.

software A program or programs that direct the computer in performing tasks or solving problems; of two types (see **system program** and **application program**).

spelling checker A program (or a feature of a word processing program) that checks the spelling of each word within a document and identifies a user's spelling errors.

split screen A circumstance in which two areas of the screen display different kinds of output, or output from two programs at once.

spreadsheet Originally a table or ledger generally used in a business environment for recording and/or performing calculations with financial data. A modern spreadsheet is typically electronic, and exhibits broad versatility of use (see **spreadsheet program**).

spreadsheet program A type of application program used for number processing. An electronic version of a spreadsheet, spreadsheet programs are designed primarily for displaying numerical data and solving problems involving computations.

system disk A disk containing programs for conducting certain computer actions, such as disk drive operation. Such a disk is often used when starting a microcomputer to provide requisite information not built into the computer or otherwise provided via a program.

system(s) program A computer program for coordinating the operation of computer circuitry and enabling the computer to work efficiently. A computer's DOS is an example of a system program.

teacher utility A computer program designed to enable teachers who use it to accomplish one or more teaching-related tasks more efficiently.

telecommunications The process of using telephone lines for communications between computers. For microcomputer users, it involves use of modems and special software.

terminal A device by which a person communicates with a mainframe; usually a keyboard and display screen.

test generator (also **test authoring program**) A type of teacher utility program that speeds test construction.

text analysis program (also **text analyzer**) A computer program that checks for selected features (e.g., reading level, grammatical structures) of a text sample.

tool program A frequently used computer program that provides a user with a convenient way of performing a task or some category of tasks. (See also **utility program**.)

touch screen A specialized display screen that can sense when and where a user points on the screen.

tutorial program A type of CAI software characterized by an attempt to teach a new concept or skill, or new information, and to assess the progress of the learner during instruction.

user A person who uses or interacts in some way with a computer or computer system.

user-friendly Descriptor applied to a computer program that can be utilized successfully by an individual having little or no computing experience, sometimes due to the program's inherent simplicity but in many cases because of structural clarity and excellent guidance; infrequently used to describe some hardware devices as well.

utility program A program designed for a practical purpose, such as for reorganizing files on a diskette. Originally associated with systems programs rather than applications, the term is now commonly applied to programs designed to save a user's time or achieve pragmatic ends efficiently. (See also **tool program** and **teacher utility**.)

verbal information learning Acquisition of capabilities of recalling and reproducing verbal sequences verbatim or of remembering information in a form that captures the gist of its meaning.

videodisc A laser-read disk of information, usually random access, that may incorporate moving as well as still images. A videodisc player is often used with microcomputers to produce interactive video displays or lessons. (See also **laser disk**.)

virus A renegade computer program that, subsequent to its introduction into a computer system, can cause havoc in the operation of other programs. A virus is generally placed on storage media in a subversive manner by a computer hacker, and then it duplicates and spreads to other disks.

volatile memory Internal computer memory that is dependent on sustained electrical power to the device. Information is lost when power to the computer is interrupted.

word processing The process of electronically producing, editing, storing, retrieving, and printing text. In more sophisticated forms this computer application may involve additional text manipulation and formatting capabilities and even the incorporation of graphics with text.

work sheet A spreadsheet program's column and row grid.

This page constitutes a continuation of the copyright page.

Trademarks

Apple, Apple II, and Apple GS are registered trademarks of Apple Computer, Inc.

AppleWorks™ is a trademark of Apple Computer, Inc., licensed to Claris Corporation.

AppleWriter is a trademark of Apple Computer, Inc.

Atari is a registered trademark of Atari Inc., a division of Warner Communications, Inc.

BRS is a trademark of BRS Information Technologies, a subsidiary of Maxwell On-Line, Inc.

Certificate Maker is a trademark of Springboard Software, Inc.

Commodore and PET are registered trademarks of Commodore Business Machines, Inc.

Compuserve is a registered trademark of Compuserve, Inc., a subsidiary of H & R Block.

CP/M is a trademark of Digital Research, Inc.

dBase IV is a registered trademark of Ashton-Tate.

IBM is a registered trademark of International Business Machines Corporation.

Lotus™ and 1-2-3™ are trademarks of Lotus Development Corporation.

Macintosh is a trademark licensed to Apple Computer, Inc.

MS-DOS is a registered trademark of Microsoft Corporation.

PRODIGY[SM] is a service mark and registered trademark of Prodigy Services Company, a partnership of IBM and Sears.

THE SOURCE is a registered trademark of The Source Telecomputing Corporation, a subsidiary of the Reader's Digest Association, Inc.

TRS-80 is a trademark of Tandy Corporation.

VisiCalc is a registered trademark of VisiCorp.

WordPerfect is a registered trademark of WordPerfect Corporation.

WordStar is a registered trademark of MicroPro International Corporation.

Index

405035

405